PEARSON EDEXCEL INTERNATIONAL GCSE (9–1)

ECONOMICS

Student Book

Rob Jones

Published by Pearson Education Limited, 80 Strand, London, WC2R 0RL.

www.pearsonglobalschools.com

Copies of official specifications for all Pearson qualifications may be found on the website: https://qualifications.pearson.com

Text © Pearson Education Limited 2017
Edited by Jeremy Toynbee
Designed by Cobalt id
Typeset by Tech-Set Ltd, Gateshead, UK
Original illustrations © Pearson Education Limited 2017
Illustrated by © Tech-Set Ltd, Gateshead, UK
Cover design by Pearson Education Limited
Picture research by: Sarah Hopper
Cover photo/illustration © alamy.com: David Noton Photography / Alamy Stock Photo
Inside front cover photo: Shutterstock, Dmitry Lobanov

The rights of Rob Jones to be identified as the author of this work have been asserted by him in accordance with the Copyright, Designs and Patents Act 1988.

First published 2017

20 19 18
10 9 8 7 6 5 4 3

British Library Cataloguing in Publication Data
A catalogue record for this book is available from the British Library

ISBN 978 0 435188 64 1

Printed by Neografia in Slovakia

Picture Credits
The author and publisher would like to thank the following individuals and organisations for permission to reproduce photographs:

(Key: b-bottom; c-centre; l-left; r-right; t-top)

123RF.com: dbvirago 56; **Alamy Stock Photo**: Pamela Au 48, B&JPhotos 88, Sanjay Borra 12bl, Kevin Britland 57, Cultura Creative (RF) 215, dbimages 202, Nigel Dickinson 4br, dpa picture alliance archive 107tr, Greg Balfour Evans vitl, 211t, Dominique Faget / AFP 120, Peter Erik Forsberg 98, S. Forster 316, Greatstock 5br, Mark Green 32b, Jan Halaska 318, Hemis 23, imageBROKER 135, 248, Pulsar Imagens 325, Islandstock 134, Norasit Kaewsai 333, Wing Lun Leung 63, Lou Linwei 96l, Jake Lyell 5bl, 112, David Lyons 29, Jenny Matthews 240, Remy Musser 81, Julian Nieman 231, Obstando Images 38, Pakistan Images 327, Chris Pearsall 342, The Picture Pantry 49, RaymondAsiaPhotography 100l, REUTERS 17, 20, Pep Roig 338, Leonid Serebrennikov 346, SPFH 233, Harry Stewart 4bl, Markus Thomenius 146b, Watchtheworld vibl, 211b, Wavebreak Media ltd 241, WENN Ltd 12tr, Kerry Whitworth 96r, Stanley Wilson 74; **Ferrari Media**: 225; **Getty Images**: lorenzodaveri 105l, yoh4nn 115, VCG 128; **Press Association Images**: 181 Chris Crewell / Zuma Press; **Shutterstock.com**: 1039759 268, Pierre-Yves Babelon 114, benjamas11 312b, Radu Bercan 70l, Max Blain 160, Byjeng 100r, Rob Byron 71r, chrisdorney 217, Kobby Dagan 107tl, Elena Elisseeva 164, EQRoy 16, Nataliya Hora 163, Alex Hubenov 12tl, jupeart 151, Vasileios Karafillidis 105r, Trevor Kittelty 4bc (right), Jon Le-Bon 4bc (left), Chad McDermott 53, Doug Meek 89, MehmetO 18, MNStudio 62, MoiraM 22, Monkey Business Images 108, Iaroslav Neliubov 343, Ociacia 166, Kharkhan Oleg 90, Palto 4tl, Alexey Y. Petrov 12br, Pixel1962 232b, Andrey Popov 174, Lee Prince 232t, Iryna Rasko 36, vibr, RossHelen 55, smereka 4tr, Sklep Spozywczy 33, vii, James Steidl 122, Stripped Pixel 60, Konstantin Sutyagin 67, svetlovskiy 32t, Valentyn Volkov 4tc (right), withGod 4tc (left); **The Bolt www.thebolt.club**:142.

All other images © Pearson Education

CONTENTS

ABOUT THIS BOOK

This book is written for students following the Pearson Edexcel International GCSE (9–1) Economics specification and covers both years of the course.

The course has been structured so that teaching and learning can take place in any order, both in the classroom and in any independent learning. The book contains four units that match the four areas of content in the specification: The Market System, Business Economics, Government and the Economy and The Global Economy.

Each unit is split into multiple chapters to break down content into manageable chunks and to ensure full coverage of the specification.

Each chapter features a mix of learning and activities. Global case studies are embedded throughout to show a range of situations and businesses within the context of the chapter. Summary questions at the end of each chapter help you to put learning into practice.

Paper 1 is Microeconomics and Business Economics and will test the information in the first two units. Paper 2 is Macroeconomics and the Global Economy and will test the information in the last two units. Knowing how to apply your learning will be critical for your success in the exam. To help with this, there are exam-style questions at the end of each unit and two full practice exam papers at the end of the book.

Learning objectives
Each chapter starts with a list of what you will learn from it. They are carefully tailored to address key assessment objectives central to the course.

Getting started
An introduction to the chapter, letting you think about the concepts you will be introduced to. Questions are designed to stimulate discussion and use of prior knowledge. These can be tackled as individuals, pairs, groups or the whole class.

Activity
Each chapter includes activities to embed understanding through case studies and questions.

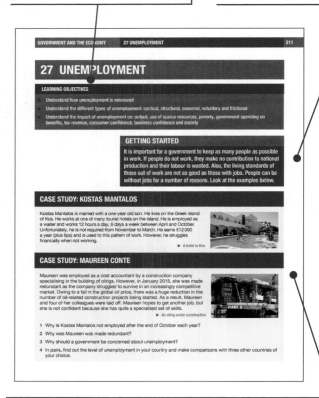

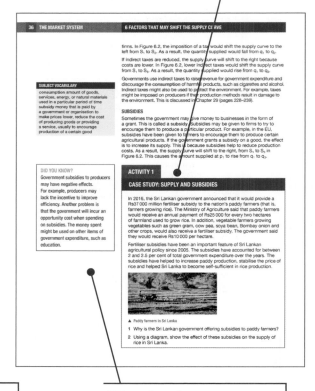

Case study
Getting started, Chapter review and Activities are all based around case studies. They are drawn from around the world and will help you see learning applied to real-world contexts.

Did you know?
Interesting facts to encourage wider thought and stimulate discussion.

Subject vocabulary and General vocabulary
Useful words and phrases are colour coded within the main text and picked out in the margin with concise and simple definitions. These help understanding of key subject terms and support students whose first language is not English.

Multiple-choice questions
Each chapter features multiple-choice questions to test your knowledge and prepare you for similar questions in the exam.

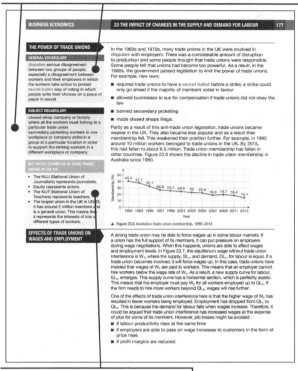

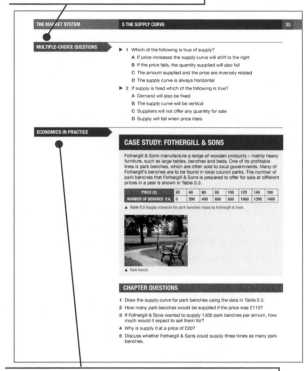

Key facts
Easy to understand, useful information to contextualise learning.

Economics in practice and Chapter questions
A summary case study and associated questions at the end of each chapter to consolidate your learning.

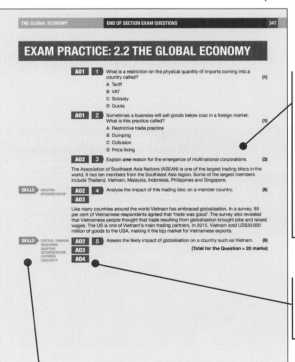

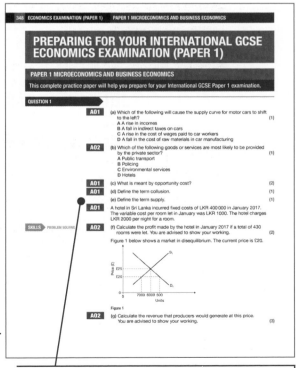

Exam practice
These exam-style questions are found at the end of each unit. They are tailored to the Pearson Edexcel specification to allow for practice and development of exam writing technique. They also allow for practice responding to the command words used in the exams.

Assessment objectives
Questions are tagged with the relevant assessment objectives that are being examined.

Skills
Relevant exam questions have been assigned the key skills that you will gain from undertaking them, allowing for a strong focus on particular academic qualities. These transferable skills are highly valued in further study and the workplace.

Preparing for your International GCSE Economics examination
A full practice exam for both Paper 1 and Paper 2 at the back of the book helps you prepare for the real thing.

ASSESSMENT OVERVIEW

The following tables give an overview of the assessment for this course. You should study this information closely to help ensure that you are fully prepared for this course and know exactly what to expect in each part of the assessment.

PAPER 1	PERCENTAGE	MARK	TIME	AVAILABILITY
MICROECONOMICS AND BUSINESS ECONOMICS Written exam paper Paper code 4EC1/01 Externally set and assessed by Pearson Edexcel Single tier of entry	50%	80	1 hour 30 minutes	January and June examination series First assessment June 2019

PAPER 2	PERCENTAGE	MARK	TIME	AVAILABILITY
MACROECONOMICS AND THE GLOBAL ECONOMY Written examination paper Paper code 4EC1/02 Externally set and assessed by Pearson Edexcel Single tier of entry	50%	80	1 hour 30 minutes	January and June examination series First assessment June 2019

ASSESSMENT OBJECTIVES AND WEIGHTINGS

ASSESSMENT OBJECTIVE	DESCRIPTION	% IN INTERNATIONAL GCSE
AO1	Recall, select and communicate knowledge of economic terms, concepts and issues	14–15%
AO2	Demonstrate understanding and apply economic knowledge using appropriate terms, concepts, theories and calculations effectively in specific contexts	48–49%
AO3	Select, organise and interpret information from sources to investigate and analyse economic issues	23–24%
AO4	Evaluate economic information to make reasoned judgements and draw conclusions	12–13%

RELATIONSHIP OF ASSESSMENT OBJECTIVES TO UNITS

UNIT NUMBER	ASSESSMENT OBJECTIVE			
	A01	A02	A03	A04
PAPER 1	7.5%	24.4%	11.8%	6.3%
PAPER 2	7.5%	24.4%	11.8%	6.3%
TOTAL FOR INTERNATIONAL GCSE	14–15%	48–49%	23–24%	12–13%

ASSESSMENT SUMMARY

PAPER 1	DESCRIPTION	MARKS	ASSESSMENT OBJECTIVES
MICROECONOMICS AND BUSINESS ECONOMICS **PAPER CODE 4EC1/01**	**Structure** Paper 1 assesses 50% of the total Economics qualification. There will be four questions on the paper, each worth 20 marks. Students must answer all questions. The sub-questions are a mixture of multiple-choice, short answer, data-response and open-ended questions. **Content summary** Each question will be based on a particular topic from the subject content related to microeconomics and business economics. Owing to the nature of economics, there is some interrelation between topics. **Assessment** This is a single-tier exam paper and all questions cover the full ranges of grades from 9–1. The assessment duration is 1 hour 30 minutes. Calculators may be used in the examination.	The total number of marks available is 80	Questions will test the following Assessment Objectives A01 – 7.5% A02 – 24.4% A03 – 11.8% A04 – 6.3%

PAPER 2	DESCRIPTION	MARKS	ASSESSMENT OBJECTIVES
MACROECONOMICS AND THE GLOBAL ECONOMY **PAPER CODE 4EC1/01**	**Structure** Paper 2 assesses 50% of the total Economics qualification. There will be four questions on the paper, each worth 20 marks. Students must answer all questions. The sub-questions are a mixture of multiple-choice, short answer, data-response and open-ended questions. **Content summary** Each question will be based on a particular topic from the subject content related to microeconomics and business economics. Owing to the nature of economics, there is some interrelation between topics. **Assessment** This is a single-tier exam paper and all questions cover the full ranges of grades from 9–1. The assessment duration is 1 hour 30 minutes. Calculators may be used in the examination.	The total number of marks available is 80	Questions will test the following Assessment Objectives A01 – 7.5% A02 – 24.4% A03 – 11.8% A04 – 6.3%

1.1
THE MARKET SYSTEM

This section looks at the basic economic problem, which is to do with the allocation of scarce resources. The section focuses on the way consumers, firms and the government make choices between different alternatives when faced with a limited budget. It also studies the underlying assumptions behind the behaviour of producers and consumers and the possible reasons why they may fail to maximise their profit or benefit, respectively.

Microeconomics is the study of individual markets. Therefore, this section looks at the way prices are determined in markets by the forces of supply and demand. It covers the factors that might influence supply and demand, and how supply and demand responds to changes in prices. Finally, the chapter addresses the ways in which market forces help to allocate resources in an economy, and what happens when markets fail.

1 THE ECONOMIC PROBLEM

LEARNING OBJECTIVES

- Understand the problem of scarcity
- Understand opportunity cost
- Understand production possibility curves
- Understand causes of positive and negative economic growth

GETTING STARTED

The planet we live on contains many resources that are used to produce **goods** we like to consume. However, there is a problem. Look at the images below.

SUBJECT VOCABULARY

goods things that are produced in order to be sold

CASE STUDY: RESOURCES AND NEEDS

▲ **Figure 1.1** Valuable resources

▲ **Figure 1.2** Needs

1 Describe the resources shown in Figure 1.1.

2 Are there enough of these resources in the world? Explain your answer with reference to the images in Figure 1.2.

3 In groups, discuss whether your country has enough resources. Draw up a list of measures that your government might take to increase the quantity of resources available. Present your ideas to the rest of the class.

THE PROBLEM OF SCARCITY

SUBJECT VOCABULARY

finite having an end or a limit

GENERAL VOCABULARY

fertile soil ground that is capable of producing crops

GENERAL VOCABULARY

health care activity of looking after people's health, considered to be an industry
needs basic requirements for human survival
wants people's desires for goods and services

SUBJECT VOCABULARY

infinite without limits

FINITE RESOURCES

All countries have resources, such as water, minerals, soil, plants, animals and people. However, in any country there is a **finite** quantity of these resources, which means that the quantity available is limited. As there is only a limited quantity, economists say that resources are scarce. These resources are often referred to as the four factors of production: land, labour, capital and enterprise (see Chapter 14).

Resources are scarcer in some countries than others. For example, in some African countries there are serious shortages of **fertile soil** and water. This means that food production is inadequate. Even where resources exist, a country may not be capable of exploiting them. For example, Ethiopia struggles to produce enough food for its population because only about 4 per cent of its fertile land is irrigated. The problem is not a shortage of water but the failure to exploit some of its huge rivers, such as the Awash and the Blue Nile. The country does not have the financial resources to invest in projects that would make use of the water for agriculture.

UNLIMITED WANTS

Economists distinguish between **needs** and **wants**. Needs are the basic requirements for human survival. Some of these needs are physical and include water, food, warmth, shelter and clothing. If these needs cannot be satisfied, eventually humans would cease to exist. In some countries in the world people do die because such needs cannot be met.

In addition to basic needs, humans also have other desires. These are called wants and may include more holidays abroad, a better house, more meals out, a bigger car, new golf clubs, a better education, improved **health care** and a cleaner environment. These wants are unlimited or **infinite**. People always want more whatever their current circumstances; it is human nature. The problem is made worse because many of the things that people want have to be replaced. Consumers regularly replace cars, computers, shoes, clothes and furniture, for example, either because they are no longer functional, or because better or more fashionable versions have become available.

ACTIVITY 1

CASE STUDY: NEED AND WANTS

▲ Figure 1.3 Different eating arrangements

1 How might the two images in Figure 1.3 illustrate the differences between needs and wants?

2 Why are resources finite?

THE ECONOMIC PROBLEM

SUBJECT VOCABULARY

basic economic problem allocation of a nation's scarce resources between competing uses that represent infinite wants

scarce resources amount of resources available when supply is limited

GENERAL VOCABULARY

allocate to decide officially that a particular amount of money, time, etc. should be used for a particular purpose

KEY FACTS

In China, many clothes manufacturers use large quantities of labour in production. However, in many Western countries the same goods may be produced using high-tech machinery.

GENERAL VOCABULARY

distribution act of sharing things among a large group of people in a planned way

OPPORTUNITY COST

GENERAL VOCABULARY

choices deciding between alternative uses of scare resources

All countries have to deal with what economists call the **basic economic problem**. The problem, summarised in Figure 1.4, occurs because the world's resources are scarce or finite and people's wants are infinite. Demand for resources is greater than their supply. As a result, decisions have to be made about how to **allocate** a nation's **scarce resources** between different uses. This is what the study of economics is all about.

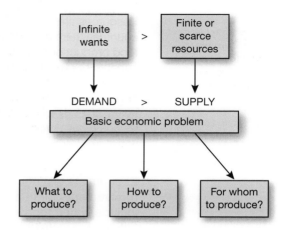

▲ **Figure 1.4** The basic economic problem

To overcome the basic economic problem, important decisions have to be made.

■ **What to produce?** Because it is impossible to produce all the goods that people want, a country must decide which goods will be produced. For example, should resources be used to provide more libraries, build more schools, expand the armed forces, make more cars, build more houses, construct more roads, make more toys, print more books, increase state pensions or train more doctors?

■ **How to produce?** Goods can be produced using a variety of different production methods. The four factors of production can be organised in different ways to produce the same goods.

■ **For whom to produce?** Once goods have been produced, there has to be a method of **distribution**. This means that the goods have to be shared in some way between members of the population. For example, should everyone get exactly the same quantities or should some receive more than others?

There are different solutions to the basic economic problem. This is because different courses of action can be taken when making the decisions outlined above. The way in which they are made depends on what sort of economic system a country has. This is explained in Chapter 11.

Whichever approach is used to solve the basic economic problem, all decision makers are faced with **choices**. Resources often have a number of alternative uses; as a result people have to make a choice about which way to use them. Individuals, producers and governments face this choice.

■ Individuals have to choose how to spend their limited budgets. For example, a university student, after all living costs have been met, may have £50 left at the end of the week. This student would like to buy some new books (£20), get the train home for the weekend (£30), go out for a meal with friends (£30), buy some new computer software (£20) or buy a new pair of designer jeans (£50). Clearly, a choice has to be made because all of these goods together would cost £150.

■ Producers may have to choose between spending £100 000 on advertising, training its workforce or buying a new machine.

■ A government may have to decide whether to spend £5000 million on increasing welfare benefits, building new hospitals, providing better care for the mentally ill or building a new motorway.

When making such choices, individuals, firms and governments will face a cost once their choice has been made. This is called the **opportunity cost**. This cost arises because a sacrifice has to be made when making a choice. If the government in the example above can place its spending desires in order of preference, the opportunity cost can be identified. Once the government has chosen the best alternative, the opportunity cost will be the benefit lost from the next best alternative. Assume that the government's spending desires are placed in order of preference as below:

1 new motorway

2 new hospital

3 increase welfare benefit

4 improve care for the mentally ill.

In this example, the new motorway is the government's preferred choice. Therefore, the £5000 million will be allocated to this project. The opportunity cost in this case is the benefit lost from not building the new hospital, that is, the benefit lost from the next best alternative.

ACTIVITY 2

CASE STUDY : OPPORTUNITY COST

In 2015, according to the Stockholm International Peace Research Institute (SIPRI), the value of global military spending was US$1 676 000 million. This was about 2.3 per cent of the world's gross domestic product (a measure of world income). This level of spending on military goods often attracts criticism about the possible opportunity costs it incurs. In some regions, more is spent on the military than on health care – Figure 1.5 identifies four of these regions. Figure 1.5 also shows that in western and central Europe spending on health care is far higher than that on military goods. Campaigners often say that government **expenditure** on the military is a waste of resources. They recommend spending at least some of this money on meeting human needs. For example, the Global Campaign on Military Spending called for a 10 per cent cut in worldwide military spending. It said the money saved should be used for development purposes. In support of this campaign, Kazakhstan's President Nursultan Nazarbayev said that all nations should give 1 per cent of their military spending to the United Nations Special Fund for Global Development. In 2015, the UN Food and Agriculture Organisation said that a redirection of just 13 per cent of the global military budget could **eliminate** extreme poverty and hunger.

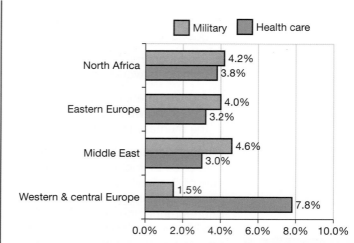

▲ **Figure 1.5** Spending on health care and military goods in a selection of regions (as a percentage of GDP)

1   Suggest one reason why spending on health care in western and central Europe is far higher than that on military goods, compared with the other regions shown.

2   What is meant by opportunity cost? Use this case as an example in your answer.

PRODUCTION POSSIBILITY CURVES (PPCs)

SUBJECT VOCABULARY

capital goods those purchased by firms and used to produce other goods such as factories machinery, tools and equipment

consumer goods those purchased by households such as food, confectionery, cars, tablets and furniture

production possibility curve (PPC) line that shows the different combinations of two goods an economy can produce if all resources are used up

Deciding which goods to produce and the concept of opportunity cost can be illustrated using **production possibility curves (PPCs)**. A PPC shows the different combinations of two goods that can be produced if all resources in a country are fully used. It shows the maximum quantities of goods that can be produced. A PPC for a country is shown in Figure 1.6. It is assumed that the country can produce **consumer goods** or **capital goods**. What does the PPC show?

■ At point A, 16 million units of consumer goods are produced and zero capital goods.

■ At point D, 8 million units of capital goods can be produced and zero consumer goods.

■ At point B, a combination of 14 million units of consumer goods and 4 million units of capital goods can be produced.

■ At point C, a combination of 8 million units of consumer goods and 7 million units of capital goods can be produced.

■ At point F, a combination of 8 million units of consumer goods and 4 million units of capital goods can be produced. At this point, not all resources in the country are being used – there are unemployed resources. This is because point F is inside the PPC. A country should aim to push production so that it is on the PPC. At points A, B, C and D resources are fully employed.

■ The combination of goods represented by point E is not possible. This is because it is outside the PPC. The country does not have the resources to produce 12 million units of consumer goods and 7 million units of capital goods.

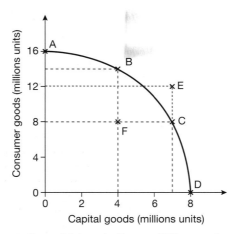

▲ **Figure 1.6** A production possibility curve for a country

WHAT HAPPENS WHEN AN ECONOMY MOVES FROM ONE POINT ON THE PPC TO ANOTHER?

For example, what happens if the economy in Figure 1.6 moves from B to C? By moving along the PPC, an opportunity cost is incurred. At point B, 14 million units of consumer goods are being produced and 4 million units of capital goods. By moving to C, the production of capital goods rises to 7 million units but production of consumer goods falls to 8 million units. To gain another 3 million units of capital goods, 6 million units of consumer goods are being sacrificed. The lost production of consumer goods (6 million units) is the opportunity cost.

The choice between different combinations of consumer goods and capital goods is an important one for a country. If a country produces more capital goods, it will probably be able to produce more consumer goods in the future. This is because capital goods are used to produce consumer goods. However, by doing so there will be fewer consumer goods today and some people will have less in the short term.

CAUSES OF POSITIVE AND NEGATIVE ECONOMIC GROWTH

At a particular point in time, a country cannot produce combinations of goods that lie to the right of the PPC. However, over a long period of time, an economy would expect to raise the production of all goods. This is called **economic growth**. There are several reasons for this.

■ **New technology**: As time passes, new technology is developed and this benefits businesses. For example, new machines such as robots, computers, telecommunications and the internet have been used by businesses to help increase productive potential. New technology is usually faster and more reliable in production and therefore more output can be produced.

■ **Improved efficiency**: Over time, resources are used more efficiently. New production methods, such as kaizen (continuous improvement) and lean production (using fewer resources in production), for example, have been developed and adopted. These more efficient methods replace the old ones and more output can be produced with fewer resources.

■ **Education and training**: An economy can boost the productive potential of a nation by educating and training the population. A country's economy becomes more productive as the proportion of educated workers increases. This is because educated workers can more efficiently carry out tasks that require reading and writing analysis, evaluation, communication and critical thinking. However, a country has to find the 'right' balance between academic and vocational education.

■ **New resources:** Some countries find new resources that enable them to produce more. For example, in recent years, the USA has raised its productive potential by producing more oil through fracking. Fracking involves shooting a mixture of mostly water and sand under high pressure against rock until it fractures or breaks. The sand fills the fracture, forcing oil out of the rock formation. Fracking now provides the USA with around 50 per cent of its oil needs. This is up from just 2 per cent in 2000.

If countries can produce more, the PPC will shift outwards. This is shown in Figure 1.7, PPC_1 represents an original PPC, while PPC_2 shows a new PPC resulting from improved efficiency, for example. Combinations of goods not previously possible can now be enjoyed. To generate economic growth in this way, a government needs to ensure that investment levels are adequate. Economic growth is discussed in more detail in Chapter 25.

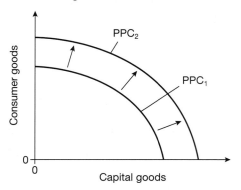

▲ **Figure 1.7** Effect of improved efficiency on the PPC

Finally, it is possible for the PPC to shift inwards. This would represent negative economic growth, that is, where a country's productive potential actually falls. It may be caused by resource depletion: where a country runs out of a natural resource, such as oil or coal. The productive potential of a country can also be reduced by weather patterns. For example, dry weather might prevent some nations from meeting their **agricultural** production targets. Economic growth in a particular country might also be negative if large numbers of highly qualified, skilled and experienced workers moved overseas. This might happen if these workers could earn more money employed in another country. Wars, conflict and natural disasters might also result in negative economic growth.

GENERAL VOCABULARY

agricultural practice or science of farming

MULTIPLE-CHOICE QUESTIONS

▶ 1 Which of the following questions is associated with the basic economic problem?

  A When to produce?

  B Who should produce?

  C What to produce?

  D Where should production be located?

▶ 2 Which of the following might be considered a need rather than a want?

  A Shelter

  B Holiday

  C Smartphone

  D Pet dog

CASE STUDY: PRODUCTION POSSIBILITY CURVES

A country is able to produce agricultural and non-agricultural goods. It is currently at point X on the production possibility curve, as shown in Figure 1.8.

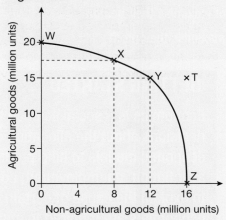

▲ **Figure 1.8** PPC of a country producing agricultural and non-agricultural goods

CHAPTER QUESTIONS

1 Describe what a production possibility curve is. Use this case as an example in your answer.

2 According to the PPC, the decision makers in this country must make what key choice?

3 Why is point T on the diagram currently unobtainable?

4 The country is considering a movement from X to Y. What will be the opportunity cost of such a movement?

5 Using a diagram, consider the effect that the discovery of fresh oil reserves might have on the PPC of this country.

2 ECONOMIC ASSUMPTIONS

LEARNING OBJECTIVES

☐ Understand the underlying assumptions in economics

☐ Understand why consumers might not maximise their benefit

☐ Understand why producers may not maximise their profit

SUBJECT VOCABULARY

variables something that affects a situation in a way that means you cannot be sure what will happen

GENERAL VOCABULARY

assumptions things that you think are true although you have no definite proof
irrational not based on clear thought or reason

GETTING STARTED

Economics is a social science that studies how individuals make decisions about the allocation of scarce resources. It often uses economic models to help predict the behaviour of **variables** (such as inflation, unemployment, consumer spending and wages) and to explain the cause of certain events. In using these models, economists are required to make some assumptions about the behaviour of individuals. Look at the example below.

CASE STUDY: MAKING CHOICES

In general, economists assume that an individual behaves rationally when making a choice. This means that an individual will make a thoughtful and logical decision when choosing between different courses of action. For example, a young student, Anita, is given Rs5000 to spend on anything she chooses up to that value. She draws up a list of the things she would like to buy and places them in order of preference. The items, each of which cost Rs5000, are shown in Figure 2.1. Option A is her most preferred option and option D is her least preferred.

 ◄ A Meal out to treat her friends

 ◄ B Ticket for India v England at Rajkot

 ◄ C A new outfit for a future wedding

 ◄ D Flight to Mumbai to visit her brother

▲ **Figure 2.1** Items that Anita would like to buy

1 Why it would be **irrational** for Anita to choose option C given the information above?

2 What is the opportunity cost of choosing option A?

UNDERLYING ASSUMPTIONS IN ECONOMICS

GENERAL VOCABULARY

rational based on clear thought or reason

When making economic decisions, individuals are usually faced with limitations. In 'Getting started' above, Anita could not buy all the things she wanted. She was limited by the amount of money she had available (Rs5000) and therefore had to choose one from four different options. However, to help her make the decision, she placed the four items of expenditure in order of preference. By doing this, she was able to select option A. This is **rational** because according to her list option A is the most preferred option, that is, the one that will give her the most satisfaction. Economists assume that individuals behave in a rational way. They make the following two assumptions in relation to rationality.

1 CONSUMERS AIM TO MAXIMISE BENEFIT

When making economic decisions, economists assume that consumers will always choose a course of action that gives them the greatest satisfaction. This will help them **maximise** benefit. In 'Getting started' above, Anita chose to spend her Rs5000 on the most preferred item in her list, that is, the meal out with her friends. This is a rational decision; economists assume that consumers will always do this. Two other examples of consumer rationality are outlined below.

SUBJECT VOCABULARY

maximise to increase something such as profit, satisfaction or income as much as possible

- If a consumer is faced with buying exactly the same product from three different suppliers, the consumer will always buy from the supplier that offers the cheapest price. To pay more for a product than is necessary is irrational. For example, why would a consumer pay €1.14 for a litre of petrol at a filling station, when less than 500 metres away another is selling the same petrol for €1.09 per litre?
- If a consumer is faced with buying a product from three different suppliers at the same price, the consumer will buy the best quality product. To buy a product of lower quality would be irrational.

2 BUSINESSES AIM TO MAXIMISE THEIR PROFIT

When business owners make decisions, they will always choose a course of action that has the best financial results. This is because economists assume that business owners will want to make as much profit as possible. Owners are assumed to be rational when making financial decisions about their businesses. Two examples are outlined below.

SUBJECT VOCABULARY

revenue money that a business receives over a period of time, especially from selling goods or services

- If a business owner can buy some raw materials from three different suppliers, the owner will always buy the cheapest available as long as the quality is the same. To pay more for raw materials than is necessary would be irrational.
- When setting a price for a product, a business owner will always choose the highest price that the market can stand. For example, if a business owner can sell a product for €5 in a market, that owner would not charge €4.50. This would be irrational. By charging the highest possible price, business owners will be maximising **revenue** and therefore maximising their profit. Economists assume that business owners will always do this.

REASONS WHY CONSUMERS MAY NOT ALWAYS MAXIMISE THEIR BENEFIT

In some circumstances, a consumer may fail to maximise their benefit when making a choice. There are three possible reasons that help to explain this.

- It is possible that some consumers have difficulty in calculating the benefits from consuming a product. This is because measuring the satisfaction gained from consuming a product is often very difficult. It is hard to quantify (express in numbers) the satisfaction gained from consumption. For example, in 'Getting started' above, how can Anita measure precisely the satisfaction gained from going out for a meal, going to the cricket match, buying a new outfit and visiting her brother? They are four very different acts of consumption. Anita has overcome the problem by placing the choices in order of preference. However, she may have overestimated or underestimated the possible satisfaction that any one of the four acts of consumption gives her. As a result, she may not have maximised her benefit when choosing the meal out.

■ Some consumers develop buying habits that may affect their ability to make rational choices. For example, over a period of time some consumers stay loyal to a particular brand. Once they become used to a brand, they continue to buy it habitually. Even when other brands on the market offer better value, they maintain their loyalty. This seems irrational but such behaviour can be observed. For example, many people buy the same newspaper all of their lives. They may start by choosing a particular title and then carry on purchasing this paper out of habit. They may ignore new publications and other options continually. This behaviour is not uncommon. Businesses are aware of this behaviour and many try to develop brand loyalty through their marketing activities. If businesses can establish a strong brand and build up a loyal customer base, they can often charge higher prices.

■ Another reason why some consumers do not maximise their benefit is because they are influenced by the behaviour of others. Young consumers may adopt some of the buying habits of their parents. For example, when young people leave home for the first time and make purchases that their parents once made, they may choose the same brands as their parents. This may be because they trust their parents or because they are familiar with the brands. It may not be because they prefer these brands to others. For example, it is reckoned that 59 per cent of people aged between 18 and 24 open their first bank accounts at the same bank as their parents. Also, some consumers are influenced by their friends or peers; they may copy their purchases in an effort to fit in or because they submit to pressure from their peers.

ACTIVITY 1

CASE STUDY: MAXIMISING CONSUMER BENEFIT

PandaCheck is a Chinese price comparison website. Like price comparison websites all over the world, they help consumers to find the cheapest deals when shopping online. The website is designed to help online shoppers find the best prices, search for current promotions, and learn some tips and tricks when ordering goods from China. For example, if you wanted to buy a battery for an ASUS laptop computer, you would type 'ASUS laptop battery' into the search engine and click on the search button. You would then see a list of the prices charged by all the Chinese online shops that stock the product. The user can change the order of the list but most people would probably want the list to show the cheapest suppliers at the top. Each listing gives a description of the product written by the supplier. This extra information may help consumers in their selection.

1 What is meant by a rational consumer?

2 How will PandaCheck help consumers to maximise their benefits?

3 Discuss one reason why a consumer may fail to maximise their benefits when making a purchase.

REASONS WHY PRODUCERS MAY NOT ALWAYS MAXIMISE THEIR PROFIT

It is possible that some business owners may not maximise their profits. Three key reasons may explain this.

- The performance of some businesses may be influenced by the behaviour of other people in the organisation. In some businesses, not all decisions are made directly by the owners. Business owners sometimes **delegate** decision making to others who may have different objectives to those of the owners. For example, managers in the sales department of a business may try to maximise sales revenue. They may do this because their salaries are linked to sales levels (the more they sell, the more **commission** they get). However, maximising sales may not result in the maximisation of profit. This is because to sell larger and larger quantities the price will eventually have to be lowered. When the price is lowered, the profit made on each extra unit sold will fall (and may become negative).

- Some producers have alternative business objectives. Although profit may be important to them, other issues may also be important. Consequently, by focusing on other objectives, it may not be possible for the producer to maximise profits. For example, some businesses focus on customer care; they may try to exceed customer expectations by providing high-quality customer service. This may mean that they spend more money on training their staff in giving good customer service. As a result, the extra costs incurred in training will reduce profitability.

- Some commercial **enterprises** operate as charities. They are sometimes called not-for-profit organisations. They aim to raise awareness and money for a particular cause. For example, UNICEF is an international charity that provides **humanitarian** and developmental help to children and their mothers. It collects money from donations and operates a number of commercial activities to generate revenue. This money is used to fund its humanitarian and developmental activities. Economists cannot assume that such organisations seek to maximise their profits, since they have other aims.

- Also, an increasing minority of businesses are being set up as social enterprises. These are organisations that operate commercially but aim to maximise improvements in human or environmental well-being. For example, MitiMeth is a Nigerian social enterprise that aims to find solutions to ecological problems. For example, many of Nigeria's waterways are 'clogged-up' with destructive water hyacinth plants. MitiMeth uses these nuisance plants (after they have been dried out in the sun) to make handcrafted products such as baskets, tableware and even jewellery. The sale of these products generates revenue but one of the key aims of the business is to solve an ecological problem.

Finally, consumers will be prevented from maximising their benefits, and producers from maximising their profits if they do not have access to all the information available. For example, if a consumer does not know that a particular product can be purchased at a lower price in another location, that consumer will not be able to maximise benefit due to a lack of information. However, in recent years, access to the internet and developments in social media, mean that the flow of information around the world has increased. This helps both consumers and producers to maximise their benefits and profits.

SUBJECT VOCABULARY

enterprises companies, organisations or businesses

GENERAL VOCABULARY

commission amount of money paid to someone according to the value of goods, shares or bonds they have sold

delegate to give part of your power or work to someone else, usually someone in a lower position than you

humanitarian concerned with improving bad living conditions and preventing unfair treatment of people

▶ 1 Which of the following would help consumers and producers to maximise their benefits and profits, respectively?

  A Lower prices

  B Access to more information

  C Improved transport networks

  D Better quality products

▶ 2 Which of the following is a reason why consumers may not maximise their benefits?

  A Some consumers are very poor

  B Opportunity costs may be too high

  C Some consumers may develop buying habits that are hard to give up

  D Some consumers save a high proportion of their income

retailer business that sells goods to members of the public, rather than to shops

CASE STUDY: MAXIMISING PROFIT?

ANNA'S SWIMWEAR

Anna Freeman runs a small company that manufactures swimwear. Most of her sales are made online to individual consumers. However, in 2015, she received an order for 3000 swimsuits from a **retailer** 100 kilometres away. She accepted the order and agreed to deliver the swimsuits herself. However, Anna needed to hire a van for 24 hours in order to make the delivery. She contacted three budget van hire companies and gathered the information shown in Table 2.1.

HIRE COMPANY	HIRE FEE (24 HOURS)	DISTANCE CHARGE	INSURANCE CHARGE	TOTAL
A	US$40	5 cents per km	US$12	
B	US$59	Zero	zero	
C	US$30	10 cents per km	US$15	

▲ **Table 2.1** Costs of hiring a van from three different van hire companies

▲ A self-drive hire van

MÉDECINS SANS FRONTIÈRES (MSF)

Médecins Sans Frontières (Doctors Without Borders) is an international not-for-profit medical humanitarian organisation. It employs 36 000 staff across 65 different countries. Its aim is to save lives and reduce the human suffering of people who are in danger by delivering medical care. MSF provides assistance to:

- victims of natural or man-made disasters
- victims of armed conflict
- other groups of people in distress.

MSF helps all people regardless of their gender, race, religion or political beliefs. In 2016, MSF helped refugees in Europe escaping from war, persecution and poverty. In Yemen, MSF provided lifesaving care to people affected by conflict. MSF also had units in Syria, South Sudan, Central African Republic and Iraq.

In 2015, MSF raised £42.7 million from donations. Eighty-six per cent of this money was spent on its medical operations, 12 per cent on fundraising and just 2 per cent on **administration**.

▲ MSF medical staff at work

CHAPTER QUESTIONS

1 Calculate the total cost to Anna of hiring a van for 24 hours from each van hire company shown in Table 2.1.

2 According to economists, which company would Anna select? Explain your answer.

3 Why might some of Anna's customers find it difficult to measure the benefit they get from buying a swimsuit?

4 Discuss why MSF does not aim to maximise profit. Give at least two reasons in your answer.

3 THE DEMAND CURVE

LEARNING OBJECTIVES

- Understand how demand is defined
- Understand how changes in price cause movements along the demand curve
- Understand what causes the demand curve to shift

GETTING STARTED

There is a strong link between the price charged for a good and the amount that people are willing to buy. Look at the example below.

CASE STUDY: CARPET STALL

Aziz Feddal makes carpets and sells them from his market stall inside the Henna Souk in Fez, Morocco. Table 3.1 shows the number of carpets that customers would buy per week at different prices.

PRICE (MAD)	60	80	100	120	140	160	180
WEEKLY PURCHASES	70	60	50	40	30	20	10

▲ Table 3.1 The number of carpets customers would buy at different prices

1 How many carpets would be bought at a price of MAD 100?

2 What happens to the number of carpets bought as the price increases?

3 What happens to the number of carpets bought when the price is lowered?

▲ Carpets on sale inside the Henna Souk, Fez, Morocco

EFFECTIVE DEMAND

Demand is the amount of a good that will be bought at given prices over a period of time. However, in economics it is **effective demand** that is really important. Effective demand shows how much *would* be bought (that is, how much people can afford to buy and would actually buy) at any given price. It does not mean how much people would like to buy if they had an endless amount of money.

THE DEMAND CURVE

Demand can be expressed graphically. This means that the relationship between price and demand can be shown on a graph. Consider the information in Table 3.2. This is a **demand schedule** and shows the demand for an electronic circuit board manufactured by a South Korean electronics company. The circuit boards are used in television production and sold worldwide.

SUBJECT VOCABULARY

demand curve line drawn on a graph that shows how much of a good will be bought at different prices
demand schedule table of the quantity demanded of a good at different price levels – can be used to calculate the expected quantity demanded
effective demand amount of a good people are willing to buy at given prices over a given period of time supported by the ability to pay
inverse relationship (between price and quantity demanded) when price goes up, the quantity demanded falls and when the price goes down the quantity demanded rises

PRICE (US$)	0.25	0.50	1.00	2.00
QUANTITY OF BOARDS PER ANNUM (MILLION)	140	70	40	20

▲ Table 3.2 The demand for an electronic circuit board

The information in this schedule can be presented on a graph. This is shown in Figure 3.1. Price is shown on the vertical axis and the quantity demanded is shown on the horizontal axis. The amount sold at each price in the schedule is also shown. If these points are joined up with a smooth line, a **demand curve** is formed. A demand curve shows the quantity demanded at any given price. For example, in this case, when the price is US$1 the quantity demanded is 40 million units.

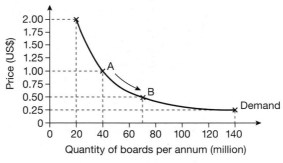

▲ Figure 3.1 Demand curve for circuit boards sold by a South Korean company

The demand curve slopes down from left to right; for most goods this is always the shape of the demand curve. This is important because it shows that price and the quantity demanded have an **inverse relationship**. This means:

■ when prices go up demand will fall

■ when prices go down demand will rise.

For example, when the price of circuit boards falls from US$1 to US$0.50, the demand for circuit boards rises from 40 million to 70 million units.

MOVEMENT ALONG THE DEMAND CURVE

When there is a price change, there is a movement along the demand curve. In Figure 3.1, when the price falls from US$1 to US$0.50, we move along the demand curve from A to B to identify the new level of demand. The movement along the demand curve in this case shows that the quantity demanded rises by 30 million units, from 40 million to 70 million units, when the price falls. This is important because other factors that influence demand, such as income, have a different effect on the demand curve. This is discussed below.

ACTIVITY 1

CASE STUDY: DEMAND FOR CRICKET TICKETS

An Indian cricket stadium has a capacity of 30 000. Figure 3.2 shows the demand curve for tickets to attend international cricket matches at the stadium.

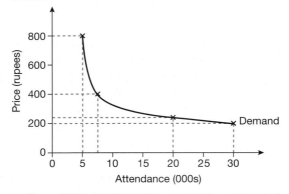

▲ **Figure 3.2** Demand for tickets at an Indian cricket stadium

▲ An Indian cricket stadium

1   What will the attendance be if Rs400 is charged to attend a match?

2   What price must be charged to fill the stadium?

STRAIGHT-LINE DEMAND CURVES

The demand curves shown in Figures 3.1 and 3.2 are both downward sloping curves. In economics, it is common to show demand using a straight-line demand curve. The reason for this is to simplify the drawing of demand curves and to make it easier to understand diagrams. Most demand curves are shown as straight lines, like the one in Figure 3.3. This demand curve shows the demand for car park spaces at a city-centre car park. It still shows the important inverse relationship that exists between price and the quantity demanded. For example, if the price to park for an hour rises from 60 pence to 80 pence, the number of cars parked falls from 300 to 150.

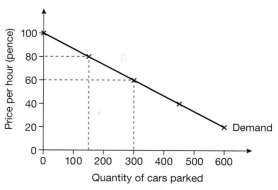

▲ **Figure 3.3** Straight-line demand curve showing the demand for spaces at a city-centre car park

A SHIFT IN THE DEMAND CURVE

If the price of a good changes, there is a movement along the demand curve. A change in any other factor, such as income for example, will be shown by a **shift in the demand curve**. The demand curve, D_1, shown in Figure 3.4, is for package holidays to the Maldives. At the price of p_1 consumers are currently buying q_1 holidays.

■ If there is an increase in incomes, the quantity demanded will rise at every given price. As a result, the demand curve will shift to the right, to D_2 shown in the diagram. At the price p_1, the number of holidays bought would rise from q_1 to q_2.

■ If there is a decrease in incomes, the quantity demanded will fall at every given price. This will cause the demand curve to shift to the left, to D_3 shown in the diagram. At the price p_1, the number of holidays bought would fall from q_1 to q_3.

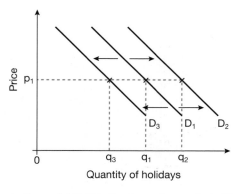

▲ **Figure 3.4** Shift in the demand curve for holidays to the Maldives

The factors that are likely to cause the demand curve to shift (as shown above) are discussed in detail in Chapter 4 (see pages 23–29).

MULTIPLE-CHOICE QUESTIONS

▶ 1 Which of the following statements is true about a demand curve?

    A When the price falls, the quantity demanded falls

    B There is a proportionate relationship between price and the quantity demanded

    C It slopes up from left to right

    D When there is a price change, there is a movement along the demand curve

▶ **2** Which of the following will cause a demand curve to shift to the left?

    A A fall in the price of a product

    B A rise in income (for example)

    C A rise in the price of a product

    D A fall in income (for example)

ECONOMICS IN PRACTICE

CASE STUDY: AL'S BIG BURGER

Alan Buschwacker makes a living by selling burgers from a van. He parks his van at busy locations in Seattle, Washington, USA, and sells 'gigantic' burgers, which have become his trade mark in the area. Most of the time his wife assists him. Details of weekly demand for Al's burgers are shown in Table 3.3.

PRICE (US$)	0.5	1	1.5	2	2.5	3	3.5	4
WEEKLY DEMAND	1600	1400	1200	1000	800	600	400	200

▲ **Table 3.3** The demand schedule for Al's Big Burgers

▲ Al's burger van

CHAPTER QUESTIONS

1 Describe what effective demand is.

2 Draw a demand curve using the information in Table 3.3.

3 Al currently charges US$3 for his giant burgers. How many burgers would he expect to sell at this price?

4 If Al wanted to sell 1400 burgers, what price would he have to charge?

5 Describe what the inverse relationship between the price and the quantity demanded for a product is. Use this case as an example in your answer.

4 FACTORS THAT MAY SHIFT THE DEMAND CURVE

LEARNING OBJECTIVE

☐ Understand the factors that cause a shift in the demand curve: advertising, income, fashion and tastes, price of substitutes, price of complements and demographic changes

GETTING STARTED

Chapter 3 showed that demand for a product is influenced by the price charged. Generally, if the price of a product is increased, the quantity demanded will fall. However, a number of other factors could affect the demand for goods. These can shift the demand curve. Look at the example below.

CASE STUDY: HOLIDAY TREAT

Jacob Atudo works for a big oil company in Kenya. In 2016, he was promoted and received a 20 per cent pay increase. He decided to spend some of his extra pay on a treat for him and his wife. He had seen a television advert recently placed by a travel company; the advert offered discounts on holidays to the Seychelles. He knew that his wife would enjoy a trip abroad so went ahead and booked the holiday.

▲ A luxury villa in the Seychelles

1 In addition to the price, what two factors might affect the quantity demanded for holidays in the Seychelles?

2 What would you expect to happen to the quantity demanded for holidays in the Seychelles during a recession? Explain your answer.

3 In pairs, choose any two products that you or your family regularly buy. Make a list of the things that might influence demand for these two products. Present your ideas to the rest of the class.

FACTORS THAT MAY SHIFT THE DEMAND CURVE

Price is the main factor that affects the quantity demanded. However, there are many other factors and each of them may actually shift the demand curve. Some of the most important factors are summarised in Figure 4.1.

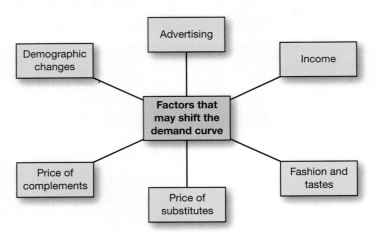

▲ **Figure 4.1** The main factors that may shift the demand curve

ADVERTISING

Businesses try to influence demand for their products through advertising and other forms of promotion. For example, in the highly competitive soft drinks industry, Coca-Cola spent US$3499 million on advertising in 2014. If goods are advertised more heavily, the quantity demanded is likely to increase. This helps to explain the huge amounts that some businesses, such as Coca-Cola, are prepared to spend on advertising. Although it might be difficult to measure the precise impact advertising expenditure has on the quantity demanded, most would agree that such spending will help to increase demand. An increase in advertising expenditure is likely to shift the demand curve to the right – from D_1 to D_2 in Figure 4.2.

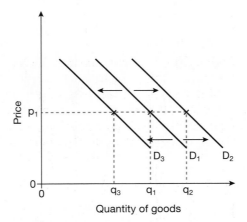

▲ **Figure 4.2** Shifts in the demand curve

ACTIVITY 1

CASE STUDY: DEMAND AND ADVERTISING

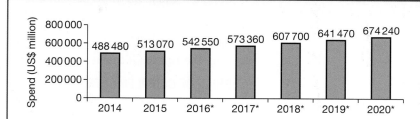

▲ **Figure 4.3** Global adspend, 2014–20 *Estimated

1   Calculate the percentage increase in predicted advertising expenditure between 2014 and 2020.

2   Why are some businesses prepared to spend so heavily on advertising?

SUBJECT VOCABULARY

disposable income income that is available to someone over a period of time to spend; it includes state benefits but excludes direct taxes

inferior goods goods for which demand will fall if income rises or rise if income falls

normal goods goods for which demand will increase if income increases or fall if income falls

INCOME

Generally, when **disposable income** rises, demand for goods will also rise. For example, if wages and salaries rise in the economy, people may decide to spend more money going out to restaurants. They may take an extra holiday or they may buy a new car. These are all **normal goods**. These are goods for which demand will rise when income rises. Most goods in the economy are normal goods. However, a minority of goods are **inferior goods**. This means that the quantity demanded will actually fall when incomes rise. Supermarket 'own label' brands or public transport may be examples of inferior goods. For example, consumers who generally buy a relatively cheap supermarket 'own label' brand of baked beans may switch to a more expensive brand when their incomes rise. Therefore, the quantity demanded for the supermarket 'own label' brand will fall. This would be shown by a shift in the demand curve to the left from D_1 to D_3 in Figure 4.2.

FASHION AND TASTES

Over a period of time, demand patterns change because there are changes in consumer tastes and fashion. For example, there has been a rise in demand for T20 cricket (cricket games that last for three hours) around the world in the last 10 years. This is reflected by the attendances at T20 fixtures in many different countries, such as India, Australia, Bangladesh and Sri Lanka. Stadiums are often full for international T20 fixtures. This compares with relatively smaller crowds at test match fixtures (cricket games that last for up to 5 days). T20 cricket has grown in popularity and increasing numbers of cricket fans find the style appealing.

The clothes industry is influenced strongly by changes in fashion. In many countries, there are a various buying seasons for clothes. Many of the clothes bought in one season would not be in demand in later seasons because they would no longer be in fashion.

Fashions and tastes may be influenced by social changes. For example, in recent years, millions of people have developed a keen interest in social media. Social media websites, such as Facebook, Twitter and Snapshot, have seen a huge increase in demand since their launch.

PRICE OF SUBSTITUTES

Many goods sold by businesses have substitute goods. For example, a consumer buying a can of Coca-Cola might have considered other brands, such as Pepsi, Virgin or supermarket 'own label'. Most consumers would consider these as good substitutes. The price of substitutes will affect demand. If the price of a substitute were lowered, demand for a product would fall. This would be shown by a shift to the left in the demand curve for that product from D_1 to D_3 in Figure 4.2. If a good has a lot of close substitutes, then the prices of these will affect demand significantly.

PRICE OF COMPLEMENTS

Some goods are purchased together by consumers. This is because the two goods are used together, for example, consumers of cornflakes will also buy milk, and people who buy cars will also buy car insurance. In these examples, milk and cornflakes and cars and car insurance are complementary goods. Demand for such products is likely to be affected by the price of a complementary good. For example, if the price of milk were to rise the demand for cornflakes may fall.

DEMOGRAPHIC CHANGES

Clearly, as the world's population grows, there will be an increase in demand for goods and services. However, demand will also be affected by the structure of the population as well as its size: demography affects demand.

■ The age distribution of a population is the number of people who fall into different age groups. For example, in many countries, there has been growth in the number of people aged over 60. This will have an effect on demand patterns. For example, as the population ages there will be more demand for goods such as retirement homes, specialist holidays for the elderly and health care.

■ In some countries, in the population overall there are more women than men. And there are many more women than men in older age groups. Consequently, the gender distribution of the population is likely to affect demand patterns. For example, there will be a greater demand for women's clothes than men's clothes, particularly in older age groups.

■ The geographical distribution may affect demand. Increasingly, in most developed and developing countries more and more people live in urban areas. As a result, demand for schools and hospitals in urban areas will be higher than in rural areas.

■ Many countries have ethnic groups in the population structure. If these ethnic groups grow in size, there is likely to be an increase in demand for products associated with their culture. In Australia, there is a large Southeast Asian population. This has resulted in the spread of restaurants offering Vietnamese, Malayan, Thai and Indonesian meals, for example.

ACTIVITY 2

CASE STUDY: DEMAND AND POPULATION

The population of the UAE has grown significantly since 2000. Between 2000 and 2010, it grew from 2.9 million to 8.3 million. The UAE has a very large immigrant population. It is estimated that around 90 per cent of the population were born overseas. As Figure 4.4 shows more than half of non-UAE nationals come from Southeast Asia.

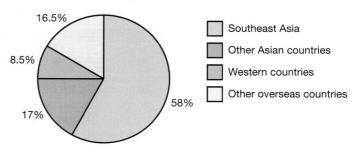

▲ **Figure 4.4** Origins of UAE's immigrant population

Most of the immigrants are attracted to the country by employment opportunities. There has been a huge boom in the construction industry, for example. The UAE government has invested revenues from the sale of oil and gas into **infrastructure** development, residential real estate and commercial properties.

The UAE has the largest difference in the male : female ratio in the world, with 2.2 men for every woman, or 2.75 men for every woman in the 15–65 age group. The graph in Figure 4.5 shows the growth in the population of UAE from 1980 to 2020.

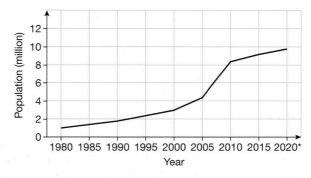

▲ **Figure 4.5** UAE population growth, 1980–2020 *Estimated

1 Why has the population of the UAE increased so sharply in recent years? Give one reason in your explanation.

2 How will the change in the size of the UAE's population affect demand?

3 A significant number of the people migrating to the UAE are Southeast Asian. How might this affect demand patterns in the UAE?

GENERAL VOCABULARY

infrastructure basic systems and structures that a country needs to make economic activity possible, for example, transport, communication and power supplies

MULTIPLE-CHOICE QUESTIONS

▶ 1 Cars and petrol are examples of which goods?

A Inferior goods

B Complementary goods

C Substitute goods

D Capital goods

▶ 2 A rise in the price of car insurance may have which effect?

A Increase the quantity demanded for cars

B Increase the quantity demanded for car insurance

C Shift the demand curve for cars to the left

D Shift the demand curve for cars to the right

ECONOMICS IN PRACTICE

CASE STUDY: GLOBAL DEMAND FOR CARS

Ever since cars became commercially available, demand for them has continued to increase. In 2016, it was predicted that 76.5 million new cars will be purchased worldwide. Rising demand is currently driven by rapid economic growth in countries such as India and China. Owning cars in such countries is a new experience for huge numbers of people. As people in developing countries become wealthier as a result of economic growth, more cars are purchased.

In recent years, the demand for electric vehicles (EVs) has increased. In 2015, total sales of EVs reached 1 million. It is estimated that by 2040 around 35 per cent of all cars purchased will be EVs. This growth in the demand for EVs is being driven by government investment in the public battery-charging infrastructure (with the rate of introduction of fast DC chargers growing by 350 per cent in China alone in 2015) and improvements in the driving range of EVs. Also, if oil prices recover to the pre-2014 levels (when oil was US$140 a barrel) the incentive to buy an EV will be even stronger.

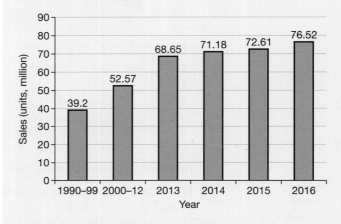

▲ **Figure 4.6** Global demand for cars, 1990–2016

CHAPTER QUESTIONS

1 Suggest one reason why the global demand for cars is rising.

2 Discuss the possible factors that might affect the demand for electric cars in the future. Give two factors in your analysis.

3 What effect will the following have on the global demand for cars: **(a)** an increase in global incomes; **(b)** a rise in the price of petrol. Use diagrams in your answer.

4 What is the difference between a movement along the demand curve and a shift in the demand curve? Use a diagram in your explanation.

5 THE SUPPLY CURVE

LEARNING OBJECTIVES

Understand how supply is defined

Understand how changes in price cause movements along the supply curve

Understand what causes the supply curve to shift

GETTING STARTED

Sellers or producers are responsible for meeting the needs of consumers. They provide goods and services that they hope people or other businesses will buy. There is a strong link between the price of a good and the quantity provided, for example, if prices are too low, sellers may not be interested in supplying the market because they may not be able to make enough profit.

CASE STUDY: CHICKEN FARMING

Tom Chang is a chicken farmer in rural China. He has reared chickens for 35 years and sells them to people in his local community. However, twice weekly, he takes chickens to a market about 15 kilometres away in order to boost sales. Table 5.1 shows the number of chickens he is prepared to offer for sale per week at different prices. For example, when the market price is CNY5, he is not prepared to sell any at all because he cannot make any profit at this price.

PRICE (CNY)	5	10	15	20	25	30	35	40
NUMBER OF CHICKENS	0	10	20	30	40	50	60	70

▲ Table 5.1 Number of chickens (per week) Tom Chang is prepared to offer for sale at different prices

▲ A chicken farm

1 How many chickens would Tom offer for sale if the price was CNY30?

2 In Table 5.1, what happens to the number of chickens offered for sale when prices rise?

3 Why do you think sellers, such as Tom, offer more for sale when prices are higher?

SUPPLY AND THE SUPPLY CURVE

Supply is the amount of a good that sellers are prepared to offer for sale at any given price over a period of time. For example, in 'Getting started' above, if the market price for chickens was CNY30, Tom Chang would sell 50 chickens during a week. This means that the supply of chickens by Tom Chang at CNY30 during a particular week was 50.

The supply of any product can be expressed graphically. This means that the relationship between price and the quantity supplied can be shown on a graph. Consider the information in Table 5.2. This is a schedule showing the supply of handmade golf shoes by M. Crammer and Son, a family business in Florida, USA.

PRICE (US$)	0	50	100	150	200	250	300	350
QUANTITY OF GOLF SHOES (PER ANNUM)	0	300	600	900	1200	1500	1800	2100

▲ **Table 5.2** Supply schedule for handmade golf shoes by M. Crammer and Son

The information in the schedule can be presented on a graph, as shown in Figure 5.1. Like the demand curve, price is shown on the vertical axis and quantity on the horizontal axis. The amount supplied by M. Crammer and Son at each price in the schedule is also shown. If these points are joined together, a **supply curve** is formed. This is a straight-line supply curve and shows the quantity supplied at any given price. For example, when the price of golf shoes is US$200, M. Crammer and Son will supply 1200 pairs **per annum**.

The supply curve slopes up from left to right, which means there is a **proportionate relationship** between price and the quantity supplied. This shows that:

■ when prices go up, supply will also go up
■ when prices go down, supply will also go down.

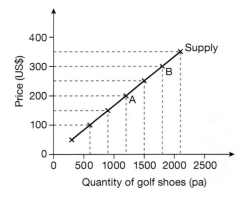

▲ **Figure 5.1** Supply curve for golf shoes made by M. Crammer and Son

For example, when the price of golf shoes rises from US$200 a pair to US$300 a pair, the quantity supplied will increase from 1200 pairs to 1800 pairs. This applies to the vast majority of goods. However, there are exceptions and one such exception is discussed later in this chapter (see page 32).

The reason for this relationship is mainly because businesses are motivated by profit. If prices are rising, existing businesses will be willing to supply increasing amounts of a good because they may make more profit. Or, more businesses will join the market in the belief that they can also make a profit. As a result supply in the market increases.

MOVEMENT ALONG THE SUPPLY CURVE

As with demand, when there is a price change, there is a movement along the supply curve. In Figure 5.1, when the price rises from US$200 to US$300, for example, we move along the supply curve from A to B to identify the new level of supply. The movement along the supply curve in this case shows that the quantity supplied is increased from 1200 pairs of golf shoes to 1800 pairs when the price rises. This only happens when there is a price change. If there are changes in any other factor influencing supply, the effect on the supply curve is different. This is discussed below.

A SHIFT IN THE SUPPLY CURVE

If the price of a good changes, there is a movement along the supply curve. A change in any other factor, such as production costs, will be shown by a **shift in the supply curve**. The supply curve, S_1, shown in Figure 5.2, is for any product. At the price of p_1, sellers are offering quantity q_1 for sale.

- If there is a rise in production costs, the quantity supplied will fall at every given price. This will cause the supply curve to shift to the left, to S_2 as shown in the Figure 5.2. At the price p_1, the quantity of goods offered for sale would fall from q_1 to q_2.

- If there is a fall in production cost, the quantity supplied will rise at every given price. As a result, the supply curve will shift to the right, to S_3 as shown in the diagram. At the price p_1, the quantity of goods offered for sale would rise from q_1 to q_3.

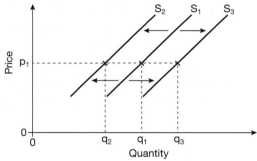

▲ **Figure 5.2** Shift in the supply curve for a product

The range of factors that are likely to cause the supply curve to shift (as shown above) is discussed in detail in Chapter 6 (pages 34–39).

ACTIVITY 1

CASE STUDY: STEEL SUPPLY IN A COUNTRY

The annual supply curve for steel in a country is shown in Figure 5.3.

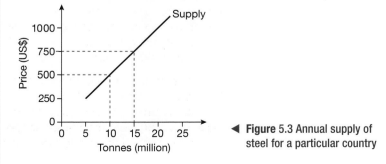

◀ **Figure** 5.3 Annual supply of steel for a particular country

▲ Steel production

1   What will happen to the supply of steel if the price rises from US$500 to US$750 per tonne?

2   Why are steel suppliers likely to offer more for sale at higher prices?

FIXED SUPPLY

In some circumstances, the supply of a product or service may be fixed. If this is the case, then the supply curve will be vertical. Supply will be fixed if it is impossible for sellers to increase supply even when prices rise. Supply at venues where sports matches and other events are held may be fixed. An example is shown in Figure 5.4. Centre Court at Wimbledon (the main stadium at the venue) has a capacity of 15 000. It is impossible to offer more than 15 000 seats for tennis matches at this venue. Even if the price of tickets were to rise, say, from £100 to £150 for a match, no more seats could be supplied.

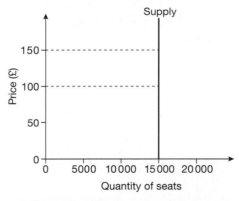

▲ Figure 5.4 Fixed supply – the capacity of Wimbledon's Centre Court

▲ Wimbledon's Centre Court

MULTIPLE-CHOICE QUESTIONS

▶ 1 Which of the following is true of supply?

    A If price increases the supply curve will shift to the right

    B If the price falls, the quantity supplied will also fall

    C The amount supplied and the price are inversely related

    D The supply curve is always horizontal

▶ 2 If supply is fixed which of the following is true?

    A Demand will also be fixed

    B The supply curve will be vertical

    C Suppliers will not offer any quantity for sale

    D Supply will fall when price rises

ECONOMICS IN PRACTICE

CASE STUDY: FOTHERGILL & SONS

Fothergill & Sons manufacture a range of wooden products – mainly heavy furniture, such as large tables, benches and beds. One of its profitable lines is park benches, which are often sold to local governments. Many of Fothergill's benches are to be found in local council parks. The number of park benches that Fothergill & Sons is prepared to offer for sale at different prices in a year is shown in Table 5.3.

PRICE (£)	20	40	60	80	100	120	140	160
NUMBER OF BENCHES P.A.	0	200	400	600	800	1000	1200	1400

▲ **Table 5.3** Supply schedule for park benches made by Fothergill & Sons

▲ Park bench

CHAPTER QUESTIONS

1 Draw the supply curve for park benches using the data in Table 5.3.

2 How many park benches would be supplied if the price was £110?

3 If Fothergill & Sons wanted to supply 1300 park benches per annum, how much would it expect to sell them for?

4 Why is supply 0 at a price of £20?

5 Discuss whether Fothergill & Sons could supply three times as many park benches.

6 FACTORS THAT MAY SHIFT THE SUPPLY CURVE

LEARNING OBJECTIVE

Understand the factors that may cause a shift in the supply curve: costs of production, changes in technology, indirect taxes, subsidies and natural factors, such as natural disasters and the weather

GENERAL VOCABULARY

volatile changing quickly and suddenly, for example, a volatile market rises and falls without much warning

SUBJECT VOCABULARY

ventures new business activities or projects that involve taking risks

GETTING STARTED

Chapter 5 established that the supply of a product is influenced by the price in the market and showed that as the price rises, sellers are willing to supply more. However, there are other factors that could affect the supply of goods. Look at the example below.

CASE STUDY: NIGERIAN FARMING

In 2016, growing numbers of Nigerian chicken and fish farmers were reducing production rates. Some were even abandoning their farms to pursue other business **ventures**. This was a response to **volatile** and rapidly rising feed costs. As a result, Nigerian politicians begged young people, and others who have left the countryside to seek a better life in the cities, to return to their family farms.

It is the rising costs of feed that has caused problems with supply. In Lagos state, fish farmers complained that feed prices had risen by as much as 80 to 100 per cent. Locally produced catfish feed has risen from NGN 6000 to NGN 9000, while imported feed has gone up from NGN 6000 to NGN 11 000 for a 15 kilogram bag.

1 Describe the main factor affecting supply in this case?

2 Calculate the percentage increase in the price of imported fish feed per 15 kilogram bag.

3 Why do you think the quantity supplied falls when production costs rise?

4 In pairs, choose any two products that you or your family regularly buy. Make a list of the things that might influence the supply of these two products. Present your ideas to the rest of the class.

FACTORS THAT MAY SHIFT THE SUPPLY CURVE

Price is the main factor that affects supply. However, a range of other factors may also have an impact. Unlike a change in price, which results in a movement along the supply curve, changes in these other factors can cause the supply curve to shift. These factors are summarised in Figure 6.1.

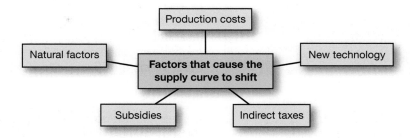

▲ **Figure 6.1** Factors that can shift the supply curve

COSTS OF PRODUCTION

The quantity supplied of any product is influenced by the costs of production, such as wages, raw materials, energy, rent and machinery. Assuming the price is fixed, if production costs rise, sellers are likely to reduce supply. This is because their profits will be reduced. This is what happened in the example in 'Getting started' above. The rising cost of fish feed resulted in some fish farmers leaving the industry, causing the quantity supplied to fall. A rise in costs will cause the supply curve to shift to the left. This is shown in Figure 6.2. When costs rise, the whole supply curve will shift to the left, from S_1 to S_2. At a price of p_1, the amount supplied in the market falls from q_1 to q_2.

If costs fall, the quantity supplied would increase because production becomes more profitable. As a result, the supply curve will shift to the right. This shows that more is supplied at every price. The new supply curve is S_3 and the amount supplied at p_1 will rise from q_1 to q_3.

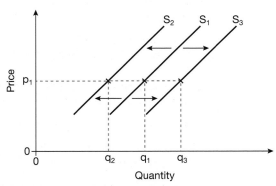

▲ **Figure 6.2** Shift in the supply curve

The availability of resources will also affect supply. If there is a shortage in some of the factors of production – for example, land, labour or capital – this will cause it to be difficult for producers to supply the market because their costs are likely to rise.

INDIRECT TAXES

Indirect taxes are taxes on spending. VAT (valued-added tax) and duties, such as those on petrol and cigarettes, are examples of indirect taxes. Such taxes have an effect on supply. When they are imposed or increased, the supply curve will shift to the left. This is because indirect taxes represent a cost to

KEY FACTS: PRODUCTIVITY

In recent years, the UK has tried to increase **productivity** in manufacturing. However, in a recent survey, 73 per cent of industry leaders said they had found it difficult to recruit skilled workers. Both the quantity and quality of candidates were lacking. Sixty-seven per cent of bosses said they were regularly forced to deal with a lack of technical skills, 64 per cent said there were too few people applying and 61 per cent said candidates lacked relevant experience.

SUBJECT VOCABULARY

indirect taxes taxes levied on spending, such as VAT
productivity rate at which goods are produced, and the amount produced in relation to the work, time, and money needed to produce them

firms. In Figure 6.2, the imposition of a tax would shift the supply curve to the left from S_1 to S_2. As a result, the quantity supplied would fall from q_1 to q_2.

If indirect taxes are reduced, the supply curve will shift to the right because costs are lower. In Figure 6.2, lower indirect taxes would shift the supply curve from S_1 to S_3. As a result, the quantity supplied would rise from q_1 to q_3.

Governments use indirect taxes to raise revenue for government expenditure and discourage the **consumption** of harmful products, such as cigarettes and alcohol. Indirect taxes might also be used to protect the environment. For example, taxes might be imposed on producers if their production methods result in damage to the environment. This is discussed in Chapter 29 (pages 228–239).

SUBSIDIES

Sometimes the government may give money to businesses in the form of a grant. This is called a **subsidy**. Subsidies may be given to firms to try to encourage them to produce a particular product. For example, in the EU, subsidies have been given to farmers to encourage them to produce certain agricultural products. If the government grants a subsidy on a good, the effect is to increase its supply. This is because subsidies help to reduce production costs. As a result, the supply curve will shift to the right, from S_1 to S_3 in Figure 6.2. This causes the amount supplied at p_1 to rise from q_1 to q_3.

SUBJECT VOCABULARY

consumption amount of goods, services, energy, or natural materials used in a particular period of time
subsidy money that is paid by a government or organisation to make prices lower, reduce the cost of producing goods or providing a service, usually to encourage production of a certain good

DID YOU KNOW?

Government subsidies to producers may have negative effects. For example, producers may lack the incentive to improve efficiency. Another problem is that the government will incur an opportunity cost when spending on subsidies. The money spent might be used on other items of government expenditure, such as education.

ACTIVITY 1

CASE STUDY: SUPPLY AND SUBSIDIES

In 2016, the Sri Lankan government announced that it would provide a Rs37 000 million fertiliser subsidy to the nation's paddy farmers (that is, farmers growing rice). The Ministry of Agriculture said that paddy farmers would receive an annual payment of Rs25 000 for every two hectares of farmland used to grow rice. In addition, vegetable farmers growing vegetables such as green gram, cow pea, soya bean, Bombay onion and other crops, would also receive a fertiliser subsidy. The government said they would receive Rs10 000 per hectare.

Fertiliser subsidies have been an important feature of Sri Lankan agricultural policy since 2005. The subsidies have accounted for between 2 and 2.5 per cent of total government expenditure over the years. The subsidies have helped to increase paddy production, stabilise the price of rice and helped Sri Lanka to become self-sufficient in rice production.

▲ Paddy farmers in Sri Lanka

1   Why is the Sri Lankan government offering subsidies to paddy farmers?

2   Using a diagram, show the effect of these subsidies on the supply of rice in Sri Lanka.

CHANGES IN TECHNOLOGY

Over a period of time, new technology becomes available that many businesses use in their production processes. New technology is more efficient and can therefore reduce the costs of production. For example, when the price of oil fell sharply in 2014, many oil companies began to use new technology to lower their costs. Some companies began to use lasers and other hi-tech data analysis equipment to help measure the potential yield from new oil wells. Others used new techniques to help them produce more oil from both old and new wells. Since the introduction of new technology will help to lower production costs, firms are likely to offer more for sale. As a result, there will be a shift in the supply curve to the right, from S_1 to S_3 in Figure 6.2.

NATURAL FACTORS

The production of some goods is influenced by natural factors, such as the weather, natural disasters, or the presence of pests (for example, rats or mice) or diseases. This is true of many agricultural products. For example, good growing conditions can help to improve crop yields, which will increase supply. This will shift the supply curve to the right – from S_1 to S_3 in Figure 6.2. In contrast, poor growing conditions can cause severe shortages and the quantity supplied may be cut. This will shift the supply curve to the left, from S_1 to S_2 in Figure 6.2.

In 2016, there was a shortage of squid due to the effect of El Niño. El Niño is a natural but irregular climatic event responsible for raising the temperature of the sea along the coast of Ecuador and Peru. It can have far reaching effects. For example, it reduces the amount of nutrients in the sea that are essential to support marine life. It can also cause a change in wind patterns across the Pacific Ocean, drought (long periods of unusually dry weather) in Australasia and heavy rain in South America. El Niño caused a shortfall in the supply of squid, which forced prices up from around US$1.80 to US$2.20 per prepared squid in the USA. Catch totals of squid for the 2015/16 season were 37 000 tonnes, only 35 per cent of the seasonal catch limit of 107 000 tonnes.

ACTIVITY 2

CASE STUDY: SUPPLY AND THE WEATHER

A number of countries in recent years have faced severe water shortages. For example, in 2015 people in São Paulo, Brazil, once known as the 'city of drizzle', started to dig through basement floors and car parks to gain access to underground water. In California, it was reported that the state was suffering its fourth year of drought in a row with January 2015 becoming the driest month ever recorded. In the Middle East, overconsumption and reduced rainfall have reduced large areas of the countryside to desert and devastated agricultural production.

Changing weather patterns and melting snow and ice caused by global warming is having a severe impact on the world's water systems. This means that around 1000 million people in the world do not have access to safe drinking water. The situation is also expected to get worse.

In the UAE, the government is taking measures to reduce the effects of drought. It is investing in desalination plants to convert seawater into drinking water and wastewater treatment units. It was reported that Crown Prince General Sheikh Mohammed bin Zayed al-Nahyan said, 'For us, water is [now] more important than oil.'

▲ Effects of drought

1 What are the causes of the water shortages outlined above? Give at least two reasons in your answer.

2 What measures are being taken by the UAE to increase the supply of water?

MULTIPLE-CHOICE QUESTIONS

▶ 1 Which of the following will shift a supply curve to the left?

　　A A decrease in indirect taxes

　　B Higher production costs

　　C The introduction of new technology in production

　　D A government subsidy

▶ 2 A bumper wheat harvest across the world resulting from favourable weather conditions will do what?

　　A Shift the supply curve for wheat to the right

　　B Reduce the quantity demanded for bread

　　C Increase the price of wheat

　　D Reduce the price of butter

ECONOMICS IN PRACTICE

CASE STUDY: HOUSING SUPPLY IN KENYA

Like many countries, Kenya suffers from a housing shortage. People moving into towns and cities from rural areas looking for a better life have created housing shortages in the cities of Nairobi, Mombasa, Kisumu and Eldoret. The high cost of traditional house-building methods has reduced the ability of the government and private constructors to build new houses. However, new technologies are now being used to help resolve the problem.

House builders are now using newly developed expanded polystyrene Styrofoam (EPS) panels and aluminium moulds in their construction plans. These building materials are superior to the use of traditional materials, such as concrete, stone and mortar. They are strong, lightweight, fireproof

GENERAL VOCABULARY

formwork temporary or permanent moulds into which concrete or similar materials are poured or injected

and long lasting. EPS also keeps properties warm effectively while aluminium **formwork** makes for better quality walls and can be painted easily. House builders also save money on other parts of the construction. This is because the lightweight technologies do not require builders to lay deep foundations. The amount of concrete used on walls and flooring is reduced. For example, EPS only requires a 5 cm layer of concrete on the walls and floors instead of the 20 cm needed when using conventional building methods.

Houses can also be constructed more quickly. This is because housing units are assembled from sections that are manufactured off-site. This reduces labour costs and improves business cash flow. Housing has also become more affordable. New housing units are now accessible to the lower middle-class and low-income earners.

CHAPTER QUESTIONS

1 How will the use of EPS panels and aluminium formwork improve the supply of housing in Kenya? Use a diagram in your explanation.

2 What are the benefits of the new technologies in house building to: **(a)** construction companies; and **(b)** Kenyan residents?

3 Describe one measure the Kenyan government could take to help increase the supply of houses in the country.

4 What is the possible effect on the supply of houses in Kenya if construction companies had to pay much higher wages to workers. Use a diagram in your explanation.

7 MARKET EQUILIBRIUM

LEARNING OBJECTIVES

- Understand how equilibrium price and quantity are determined
- Understand how shifts in the supply and demand curves affect equilibrium price
- Understand excess supply and excess demand
- Understand how market forces can remove excess supply and excess demand

GENERAL VOCABULARY

government intervention where the government becomes involved in a situation in order to help deal with a problem

GETTING STARTED

In any market (unless there is government intervention), the forces of supply and demand set the prices. The price consumers pay for goods and services is the price where supply and demand are exactly the same. Look at the example below.

CASE STUDY: PRICE, SUPPLY AND DEMAND

Table 7.1 shows the quantities of a product that will be offered for sale by producers, and purchased by consumers, at different prices (in a given year). For example, when the price is CNY 20, producers will offer 40 000 units for sale and consumers will want to buy 70 000 units. However, at this price demand is greater than supply. This is not the price that will be charged in the market.

PRICE (CNY)	5	10	15	20	25	30	35	40	45
QUANTITY SUPPLIED (1000S)	0	20	30	40	50	60	70	80	90
QUANTITY DEMANDED (1000S)	85	80	75	70	65	60	55	40	45

▲ **Table 7.1** The supply and demand schedule for a product

1 What price will be charged for the product in the above example?

2 How much is supplied and demanded when the price is CNY 40?

3 What will happen if producers set the price at CNY 40 for this product?

EQUILIBRIUM PRICE

SUBJECT VOCABULARY

equilibrium price price at which supply and demand are equal

The way in which the forces of supply and demand determine prices in a market can be shown on a graph. Figure 7.1 shows the supply and demand curves for a product. In any market, the price is set where the wishes of consumers are matched exactly with those of producers. This price, called the **equilibrium price**, is where supply and demand are equal. In Figure 7.1, the equilibrium price is £30. At this price, consumers want to buy 3000 units and producers want to sell 3000. The wishes of buyers and sellers are matched. There is no other price where this happens. For example, if the price were £40, sellers would want to supply 4000 units. However, at this price, buyers only demand 1500 units because the price is too high.

The equilibrium price is also known as the **market clearing price**. This is because the amount supplied in the market is completely bought up by consumers. There are no buyers left without goods and there are no sellers left with unsold stock. The market is cleared.

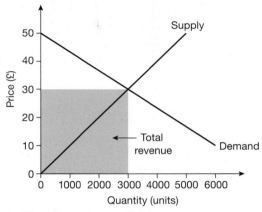

▲ **Figure 7.1** Market equilibrium

TOTAL REVENUE

Figure 7.1 also shows the **total revenue** or total expenditure at the equilibrium price. Total revenue is the amount of money generated from the sale of output. It is calculated by multiplying price and quantity.

Total revenue = Price × Quantity or TR = P × Q

In this example, the shaded area in the diagram shows the total revenue. It is:

TR = P × Q = £30 × 3000 = £90 000

ACTIVITY 1

CASE STUDY: EQULIBRIUM PRICE

The market for woollen hats in a country is represented by the supply and demand curves shown in Figure 7.2.

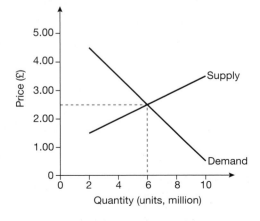

▲ **Figure 7.2** Market for woollen hats in a country

▲ A typical woollen hat

1   What is the equilibrium price and quantity?

2   What is meant by equilibrium price? Use this diagram in your explanation.

3   What is the value of total revenue at the equilibrium price?

SHIFTS IN DEMAND

The equilibrium price will change if there are changes in supply or demand. For example, if demand increases, price will rise. In Figure 7.3, an increase in demand for the product is shown by a shift in the demand curve to the right, from D_1 to D_2. This changes the equilibrium price because supply and demand are now equal at a different point. The price is forced up from p_1 to p_2 and the amount sold in the market has gone up from q_1 to q_2. If demand were to fall, the opposite would happen. The demand curve would shift to the left and the price would fall. (This is not shown in the diagram.)

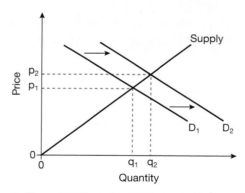

▲ Figure 7.3 Effect of a shift in demand for a product

SHIFTS IN SUPPLY

A change in supply will also affect equilibrium price. For example, if supply increases, the price will fall. In Figure 7.4, an increase in supply for the product is shown by a shift in the supply curve to the right, from S_1 to S_2. This changes the equilibrium price because supply and demand are now equal at a different point. The price is forced down from p_1 to p_2 and the amount sold on the market has gone up from q_1 to q_2. If supply were to fall, the opposite would happen. The supply curve would shift to the left and price would rise. (This is not shown in the diagram.)

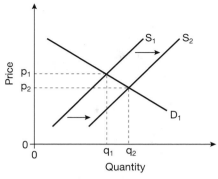

▲ **Figure 7.4** Effect of a shift in supply for a product

ACTIVITY 2

CASE STUDY: THE GLOBAL LITHIUM MARKET

In 2015, the global price of the metal lithium rose sharply, from US$6000 per tonne to about US$14 000 per tonne in just a few months. The quantity of lithium demanded has increased due to its growing use in car batteries for electric cars and devices such as smartphones, laptops and power tools.

At the moment, the main lithium-ion battery-makers are Samsung and LG of South Korea, Panasonic and Sony of Japan and ATL of Hong Kong. But China also has many battery-makers. The Chinese government is currently promoting the use of lithium-ion batteries and electric vehicles (EVs) – buses in particular. Sales of 'new energy' vehicles in China increased by almost three times in the first 10 months of 2015 compared with the same period in 2014. Tesla Motors, a US EV-maker, is starting large-scale battery production in Nevada. It hopes to supply lithium-ion batteries for 500 000 cars a year within five years. Much bigger carmakers are also increasing their demand for lithium. Toyota has begun using lithium-ion batteries instead of heavier nickel-metal hydride batteries in its Prius model.

Although the Earth contains plenty of lithium, extracting it can be expensive and time consuming. Consequently, the higher prices may not automatically increase the supply of lithium. Figure 7.5 shows the global lithium between 2008 and 2015.

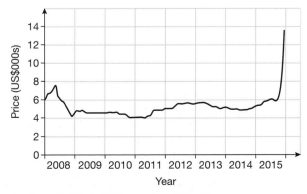

▲ **Figure 7.5** Global lithium price, 2008–15

1   Calculate the percentage increase in the price of lithium in 2015 (when it rose from US$6000 to US$14 000).

2   Why has the price of lithium increased? Use a supply and demand diagram in your explanation.

3   What impact will a government subsidy paid to lithium producers have in the market? Use a supply and demand diagram in your explanation.

SHIFTS IN SUPPLY AND DEMAND

It is possible for both supply and demand to change at the same time in a market. For example, demand might increase and supply decrease at the same time. This is shown in Figure 7.6. The original equilibrium price is p_1 where S_1 = D_1. The increase in demand is represented by a shift to the right from D_1 to D_2. The decrease in supply is represented by a shift to the left from S_1 to S_2. The new equilibrium price, where $D_2 = S_2$, is p_2. The price is higher and the amount sold in the market has fallen from q_1 to q_2.

It must be noted that it would be possible to redraw the diagram to show that, although the price will be higher, the quantity sold could also be higher. To do this, it would be necessary to make the increase in demand greater than the decrease in supply. In Figure 7.6, the increase in demand is smaller than the decrease in supply.

When there is a change in both supply and demand, it is not possible to show exactly what will happen to price and quantity unless it is known precisely by how much supply and demand shift.

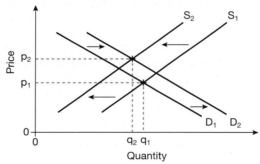

▲ **Figure 7.6** Shift in supply and demand for a product

EXCESS DEMAND

If the price charged in a market is below the equilibrium price, supply and demand will not be equal. In Figure 7.7, the equilibrium price is £60. At this price, the quantity supplied and the quantity demanded are both 6 million units. However, if the price is set lower, say at £40, the market is not in equilibrium. At this lower price, the quantity demanded is 9 million units and the quantity supplied is only 4 million units. There is **excess demand**, which means there is a shortage of goods in the market. In this case, there is a shortage of 5 million units (9 million – 4 million) at the price of £40.

EXCESS SUPPLY

If the price charged is set above the equilibrium price, again, supply and demand are not equal. In Figure 7.7, if the price is set higher, say at £80, the quantity demanded is only 3 million units while the quantity supplied is 8 million units. This time there is **excess supply**. This means that goods would remain unsold. In this case, the quantity of goods that would be unsold in the market if the price were set at £80 is 5 million units (8 million – 3 million).

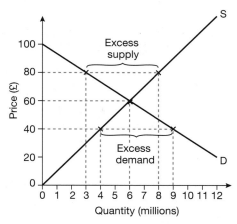

▲ **Figure 7.7** Excess demand and excess supply

REMOVING EXCESS SUPPLY AND EXCESS DEMAND

If there is disequilibrium in a market, producers can restore equilibrium by changing the price or adjusting supply. For example, if there is excess demand in the market, producers could raise the price. In Figure 7.7, excess demand existed when the price was £40. If producers raised the price to £60, the market would clear since both the quantity supplied and the quantity demanded would be 6 million units. Alternatively, producers could employ more resources and increase supply to 9 million units. If this action were taken, equilibrium would be restored at a price of £40.

If there is excess supply in the market, producers could lower their prices. In Figure 7.7, excess supply existed when the price was £80. At this price, producers wanted to sell 8 million units but consumers only wanted to buy 3 million units. If producers lowered their prices to £60, the excess supply would be removed since both the quantity supplied and the quantity demanded would be 6 million units at this price. Alternatively, producers could store the excess supply and release it onto the market at a later date. However, this might not be practical because storing goods costs money and some stocks, such as fresh food, need to be consumed quickly.

> **DID YOU KNOW?**
>
> The private taxi firm, Uber, uses something called 'surge pricing' to deal with excess demand. During very busy periods, such as New Year's Eve or at the end of a major event when thousands of people are looking for a cab home, the fares charged by Uber drivers can rise very sharply: perhaps by two or three times or even more. The purpose of this is to remove excess demand. The higher prices discourage some consumers from ordering a taxi, so demand falls. However, the higher fares also act as an incentive for dormant drivers (those who have gone home perhaps) to get back on the road, so supply increases. When the supply and demand for taxis is more evenly matched, the fares charged are restored to 'normal' levels.

▶ 1 Which of the following statements is true if the price is set below the equilibrium price in a market?

   A Supply and demand will be equal

   B There will be excess supply in the market

   C There will be excess demand in the market

   D Supply will be greater than demand in the market

▶ 2 If demand for a product falls and the supply increases which of the following will happen?

   A Price will rise

   B Price will fall

   C Total revenue will rise

   D There will be excess supply

DID YOU KNOW?

The 'black market' is an illegal market. The black market for FA Cup Final tickets means that 'touts' (illegal traders) sell tickets above their face value.

CASE STUDY: THE MARKET FOR FA CUP FINAL TICKETS AT WEMBLEY

Every year, the FA Cup Final is played at Wembley Stadium, London, the UK. Unfortunately, there are never enough tickets for all the supporters who would like to go. There is always a shortage. The English Football Association is aware of this but says it would prefer to keep the tickets 'reasonably priced' so that genuine football supporters can afford to go to the match, rather than only the wealthy or those using corporate hospitality. Evidence of ticket shortages is presented by the price of tickets on 'unofficial markets'. For example, sellers on the Edinburgh-based website FootballTicketPad were charging supporters up to £21 230 for a pair of £120 category 1 tickets, including a £1930 booking fee. This was for the final between Arsenal and Aston Villa in 2015. Figure 7.8 illustrates what is happening in the market. Note that the supply curve is vertical because supply is fixed: the capacity of Wembley Stadium is 90 000.

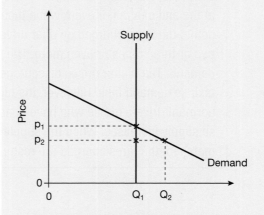

▲ **Figure 7.8** Market for FA Cup Final tickets at Wembley Stadium

▲ Aston Villa supporters at Wembley Stadium for the 2015 FA Cup Final

CHAPTER QUESTIONS

1 What is the equilibrium price of an FA Cup Final ticket according to the diagram in Figure 7.8?

2 Assuming that the FA charges p_2 for tickets, discuss why it does not charge the equilibrium price.

3 If the average price of a ticket were £60, what would be the value of total revenue?

4 If the FA could double the capacity of Wembley Stadium, what might be the effect on ticket prices?

5 To what extent is there excess demand in this market?

8 PRICE ELASTICITY OF DEMAND

LEARNING OBJECTIVES

- Understand how to define and calculate price elasticity of demand (PED)
- Understand how to use diagrams to show price elastic and price inelastic demand
- Understand how to interpret numerical values for PED
- Understand the factors that influence PED
- Understand the relationship between PED and total revenue following price changes

GETTING STARTED

Chapter 3 explained that a price change will result in a movement along the demand curve. For example, if a price falls, there will be an increase in the quantity demanded. However, price changes can bring about different responses in the quantity demanded. The demand for some goods changes more than others when prices change. Look at the examples below.

CASE STUDY: ELECTRICITY

In August 2016, the Patel family received their electricity bill for the previous 3 months. It had increased by 13 per cent to US$164. The reason for the increase was a price rise by the supplier, not because they used more electricity. Mr Patel mentioned the 'bill' to the rest of the family and suggested that everyone should try to 'economise' when using electrical appliances. Everyone agreed, but Mr Patel knew that asking his family to reduce their electricity use was probably not going to make much difference to the size of the next bill. Indeed, when the next bill arrived in November, he was proved right. The bill had gone down but only slightly to US$159.

▲ An electricity bill

CASE STUDY: CHINESE TAKE AWAY

Bob and Anne Jones enjoy Chinese food very much. Every Saturday night, they order a large Chinese meal from the China Garden, their regular supplier. However, one day in September 2016, they received a leaflet advertising a new take away service by China Dragon. It was offering a 20 per cent discount on take away orders. Bob said it was an attractive offer and suggested that they try the new supplier that coming weekend. Anne agreed saying that 'The food can't be that different can it?' When the food arrived, Anne was proved right and they saved over US$10.

▲ A Chinese meal

1 What happened to the Patel's demand for electricity after the 13 per cent price increase?

2 Describe one possible reason for your answer to (1).

3 Do you think demand for Chinese take away food is sensitive to price changes?

WHAT IS PRICE ELASTICITY OF DEMAND?

For some goods, a price change will result in a large change in the quantity demanded and for others a smaller change. It all depends on the type of good. Figure 8.1 helps to illustrate this. Two demand curves are shown with different slopes representing two different products: A and B. The demand curve for product A is steep and the demand curve for product B is flatter. At a price of £10, the quantity demanded for both products is 100 units. However, when the price falls to £8, the quantity demanded increases by different amounts for each product. Demand for product A only increases slightly to 110 units. But for product B, demand increases a lot more, to 150 units. Demand for product B is more responsive to the price change. This relationship that exists between the responsiveness of demand to a change in price is called price elasticity of demand.

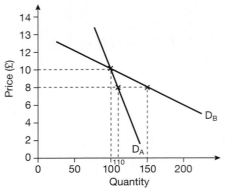

▲ **Figure 8.1** Effect of a price change on the demand for two different products: A and B

PRICE INELASTIC DEMAND

SUBJECT VOCABULARY

inelastic demand change in price results in a proportionately smaller change in the quantity demanded (alternative term: price inelastic)

In Figure 8.1, for product A, the price change resulted in a small change in demand. The change in demand was not as big as the change in price. The price fell by 20 per cent but demand only increased by 10 per cent (from 100 units to 110 units). When this happens, economists say that the good has **inelastic demand** or that demand is price inelastic. A minority of goods have inelastic demand. Electricity is one, used in 'Getting started' above.

PRICE ELASTIC DEMAND

SUBJECT VOCABULARY

elastic demand change in price results in a greater change in the quantity demanded (alternative term: price elastic)

In Figure 8.1, for product B, the price change resulted in a *significant* change in the quantity demanded. This means the change in demand was greater than the change in price. The price fell by 20 per cent (from £10 to £8) while the quantity demanded increased by 50 per cent (from 100 units to 150 units). When this happens, economists say that the good has **elastic demand** or that demand is price elastic. Goods with elastic demand are more *responsive* to price changes.

ACTIVITY 1

CASE STUDY: ELASTIC DEMAND

Figure 8.2 shows a demand curve for a product. The price currently charged is US$5. At this price, 3000 units are purchased.

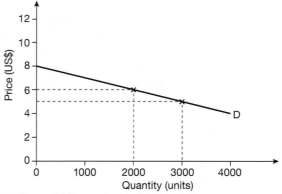

▲ **Figure 8.2** Demand curve for a product

1 If the price increases from US$5 to US$6, what happens to the amount demanded?

2 What is meant by elastic demand? Use this case as an example in your explanation.

CALCULATING PRICE ELASTICITY OF DEMAND

It is possible to calculate the price elasticity of demand (PED) of a good using the formula shown below.

$$\text{Price elasticity of demand} = \frac{\text{Percentage change in quantity demanded}}{\text{Percentage change in price}}$$

For product A in Figure 8.1 when price falls from £10 to £8, the PED would be:

$$= \frac{10\%}{-20\%} = -0.5$$

For product B in Figure 8.1, when the price falls from £10 to £8, the PED would be:

$$= \frac{50\%}{-20\%} = -2.5$$

There is a minus number in the calculation because the price fell by 20 per cent (from £10 to £8). Since the price change was negative, a minus sign must be shown. Whenever price or quantity demanded falls in the calculation, it is proper, and may be helpful, to show the minus sign.

GENERAL VOCABULARY

fraction part of a whole number in mathematics, such as ½ or ¾.
decimal fraction (= a number less than 1) that is shown as a full stop followed by the number of tenths, hundredths etc. – the numbers 0.5, 0.175 and 0.661 are decimals
infinity abstract concept describing something without any bound or larger than any number

INTERPRETING THE NUMERICAL VALUE OF ELASTICITY

The values calculated above show whether demand is price elastic or price inelastic.

- If the value of PED is less than 1 (that is, a **fraction** or a **decimal**), demand is said to be inelastic. Demand for product A in Figure 8.1 is price inelastic because price elasticity is –0.5.

- If the value of PED is greater than 1, demand is said to be elastic. Demand for product B in Figure 8.1 is price elastic because price elasticity is –2.5.

- If the value of PED is *zero*, demand is said to be **perfectly inelastic**.

- If PED is equal to **infinity** (∞), demand is said to be **perfectly elastic**.

- If PED is exactly -1, demand is said to have **unitary elasticity**.

SUBJECT VOCABULARY

perfectly elastic demand where PED = ∞ (an increase in price will result in zero demand)
perfectly inelastic demand where PED = 0 (a change in price will result in no change in the quantity demanded)
unitary elasticity where PED = –1 (the responsiveness of demand is proportionately equal to the change in price)

PRICE ELASTICITY AND THE SLOPE OF THE DEMAND CURVE

The demand curves for the two products in Figure 8.1 have different slopes. For product A, the demand curve is steep. This is common for goods that have inelastic demand like product A. For product B, the demand curve is much flatter. Goods that have elastic demand, like product B, tend to have relatively flatter demand curves. There are also some *special cases where PED is either 0, infinite or equal to –1*. These are shown and explained briefly below.

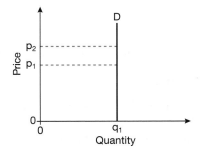

▲ **Figure 8.3** Perfectly inelastic demand where PED = 0

The vertical demand curve in Figure 8.3 shows the demand curve for a good that has perfectly inelastic demand. This means that a price change will not affect the quantity demanded. For example, if the price increases from p_1 to p_2, there is no change in the quantity demanded, it remains at q_1. The value of price elasticity in this case is zero.

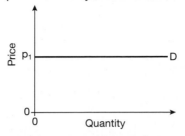

▲ **Figure 8.4** Perfectly elastic demand where PED = ∞

The horizontal demand curve in Figure 8.4 shows a demand curve for a good that has perfectly elastic demand. This means that buyers purchase as much as they possibly can at price p_1. However, if the price rises above p_1, the quantity demanded will fall to zero. The value of price elasticity in this case is infinite.

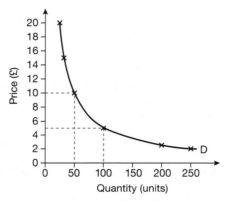

▲ **Figure 8.5** Demand curve with unitary elasticity

The demand curve in Figure 8.5 shows the shape of a demand curve where PED = −1. This is a special case in economics and when there is a price change the effect on total revenue is unique. The demand curve for a product that has unitary elasticity is called a rectangular hyperbola (a mathematical term). When the price is £10, the quantity demanded is 50 units and total revenue is £500 (£10 × 50). Alternatively, when the price is £5, the quantity demanded is 100 units and total revenue is still £500 (5 × 100). When demand has unitary elasticity the total revenue will be exactly the same at every price. Therefore, a price change will result in no change in total revenue. The relationship between PED and total revenue following a price change is discussed in detail below.

In Figure 8.1 the demand curve labeled D_A shows a relatively inelastic demand curve. In contrast, the demand curve D_B is a relatively elastic.

ACTIVITY 2

CASE STUDY: THE HEPTON TENNIS CLUB

The Hepton Tennis Club appeared likely to close in 2015 due to a decline in membership. After an emergency committee meeting in January 2016, it was decided to slash the membership fees from US$500 p.a. to US$300 p.a. for 2016. As a result, membership grew from 400 to 600.

▲ Hepton Tennis Club

1 Calculate the PED for Hepton Tennis Club membership.

2 What evidence is there in the case to suggest that demand is elastic in this example?

FACTORS AFFECTING PRICE ELASTICITY OF DEMAND

The value of PED for a good depends on a number of factors.

AVAILABILITY OF SUBSTITUTES

Goods that have lots of close substitutes will tend to have elastic demand. This is because consumers can switch easily from one product to another. For example, if the price of strawberry jam rises, consumers can switch to other types of jam such as raspberry, blackcurrant, plum, apricot or loganberry. Consequently, the demand for strawberry jam is likely to be elastic. In contrast, if there are few or no real substitutes for a product, demand will be inelastic.

DEGREE OF NECESSITY

Goods considered 'essential' by consumers will have inelastic demand. This is because if the prices of essentials, such as food and fuel rise, consumers cannot reduce the amounts they purchase significantly – they are necessities. In contrast, goods that are not essential – for example, luxury products, such as boats, sports cars and holidays – will have more elastic demand. If a product is habit forming, it may become a necessity and therefore it will have inelastic demand.

PROPORTION OF INCOME SPENT ON A PRODUCT

It may be argued that if consumers spend a large proportion of their income on a product, demand will be more elastic. For example, most consumers buying a flat screen television for £400 will be using up a significant proportion of their monthly income. Such items are one-off or infrequent purchases and so consumers may be prepared to wait a few months to see if the price drops.

Consequently, price changes in such high value items result in significant changes in the quantity demanded. In contrast, demand for products that cost very little in relation to income – for example, stamps or pencils – are more price inelastic. Often these lower price items are more of a necessity, a consumer cannot post a letter without buying a stamp.

TIME

In the short term, goods have inelastic demand because it can often take time for consumers to find substitutes when the price rises, for example. In the long term, demand is more elastic because consumers can search for alternatives and are more prepared to switch.

THE RELATIONSHIP BETWEEN PED AND TOTAL REVENUE

When there is a price change, there will be a change in the quantity demanded and therefore a change in total revenue. The value of price elasticity shows whether revenue will rise or fall following a price change. Consider the example shown in Figure 8.1. The demand for product A is price inelastic and the demand for product B is price elastic.

At the price of £10, the quantity demanded for both products is 100 units. However, when the price falls, the quantity demanded for product A rises to 110 units while the quantity demanded for B rises to 150 units. The different effects on total revenue for each product are outlined below.

For product A, when the price falls from £10 to £8 there is an increase in the quantity demanded from 100 units to 110 units. This means that total revenue will change. This is shown by the following calculations.

When P = £10 TR = £10 × 100 = £1000

When P = £8 TR = £8 × 110 = £880

The price reduction from £10 to £8 has resulted in a £120 fall in total revenue (£1000 – £880). This shows that when demand is inelastic, a price cut will cause total revenue to fall. The opposite will happen if the price is increased. If demand is inelastic, a price increase will cause total revenue to rise.

For product B, when the price falls from £10 to £8, the quantity demanded rises from 100 units to 150 units. The effect on total revenue is calculated below.

When P = £10 TR = £10 × 100 = £1000

When P = £8 TR = £8 × 150 = £1200

This time, for product B, the price reduction has resulted in a £200 increase in revenue from £1000 to £1200. This shows that when demand is elastic, a price cut will result in an increase in total revenue. The opposite will happen if the price is increased. If demand is elastic, a price increase will cause total revenue to fall. The effect of price changes on total revenue for different price elasticities is summarised in Table 8.1.

PRICE ELASTICITY	VALUE OF ELASTICITY	PRICE CHANGE	EFFECT ON TR
Inelastic	< 1	Decrease	Fall
Inelastic	< 1	Increase	Rise
Elastic	> 1	Decrease	Rise
Elastic	> 1	Increase	Fall

▲ Table 8.1 The effect of price changes on total revenue when demand is elastic and inelastic

Finally, the importance of elasticity to businesses and the government is discussed in more detail at the end of Chapter 10 (pages 63–69).

MULTIPLE-CHOICE QUESTIONS

► 1 What is the PED for a perfectly inelastic demand curve?

A −1

B 0

C −0.1

D Infinity

► 2 If the value of PED for a product is −0.87, an increase in price will result in which of the following?

A An increase in demand for that product

B A decrease in demand for a substitute product

C A rise in total revenue

D A fall in total revenue

ECONOMICS IN PRACTICE

CASE STUDY: NG CHOCOLATES

The market for chocolate in China has seen some significant growth in recent years. Hershey, the US confectionery company, said that Chinese chocolate sales in 2014 were worth US$2700 million and were expected to grow to US$4300 million by 2019. This represents a growth of about 60 per cent. However, it is reckoned that European suppliers dominate 70 per cent of China's chocolate

▲ Handmade chocolates

market. Chinese brands have struggled to make a big impact in the market. This is because many Chinese consumers have worries about the safety of some Chinese food products. However, one small producer, Ng Chocolates, is determined to benefit from growth in the market.

Ng Chocolates produces handmade chocolates that are sold in decorative boxes to retailers in Shanghai. Ng currently charges retailers CNY 20 per box and in 2015 sold 12 000 boxes. However, many of their customers reckoned that if Ng reduced the price to CNY 16, demand would probably rise significantly. Ng carried out some research and estimated that demand would rise to 16 000 boxes p.a. if they lowered the price to CNY 16.

CHAPTER QUESTIONS

1 Describe what PED is.

2 Calculate the PED for Ng Chocolates and state whether demand for Ng Chocolates is elastic or inelastic.

3 Calculate the change in total revenue for Ng Chocolates if Ng lowers the price to CNY 16.

4 Should Ng lower the price of their chocolates to CNY 16? Explain your answer.

5 Discuss the main factor in this case that influences the value of PED.

9 PRICE ELASTICITY OF SUPPLY

LEARNING OBJECTIVES

■ Understand how to define and calculate price elasticity of supply (PES)

■ Understand how to use diagrams to show price elastic and price inelastic supply

■ Understand how to interpret numerical values for PES

■ Understand the factors that influence PES

■ Understand how the PES for manufactured and primary products are likely to be different

GETTING STARTED

Chapter 8 showed that after a price change, the change in quantity demanded will vary in quantity depending on the type of good. The same can also be said of supply. When the price rises, for example, the quantity supplied will increase sharply for some goods but hardly at all for others.

CASE STUDY: HOUSING

Many countries around the world have housing shortages. Growing populations may cause housing shortages, particularly in areas where immigration is high (internally from rural areas and externally from other countries). However, it is not just rising demand that causes problems. The supply of new houses is often slow to increase, particularly affordable houses. For example, in the UK the National Housing Federation estimated 974 000 homes were needed between 2011 and 2014. However, information provided by 326 regional councils showed that only 457 490 were built. One report suggested that there were ten buyers for every house on the market in parts of the UK. One of the problems with the supply of new houses is that houses take several months to construct. Finding suitable land and obtaining planning permission for house building can take significantly longer and cause long delays in the UK. The average house price rose from £154 452 in March 2009 to £218 255 in January 2017.

▲ Construction of new houses can be slow

SUBJECT VOCABULARY

fast-moving consumer good (FMCG) goods, especially food, that sell very quickly and in large amounts

CASE STUDY: POTATO CRISPS

Potato crisps are a **fast-moving consumer good (FMCG)**. They are marketed in many countries in the world and produced in huge quantities. For example, Lays, one of the biggest crisp manufacturers worldwide, produces and sells millions of packets every year. They are mass produced in a number of factories around the world.

▲ Potato crisps, a FMCG

1 Why is the supply of houses slow to increase in the UK?

2 Describe the problems caused by a lack of supply in the UK housing market.

3 Do you think potato crisp producers could increase output at short notice? Explain your answer.

4 How would holding large stocks of potato crisps affect producers' ability to increase supply at short notice?

WHAT IS PRICE ELASTICITY OF SUPPLY?

When the price of a good changes, the amount supplied will also change. However, the size of the change in supply is not likely to be the same for all products. For example, Figure 9.1 shows the supply curves for two different products: A and B. At a price of £4 the quantity supplied for both products is 20 000 units. When the price increases by 25 per cent to £5, the quantity of product A supplied rises by 12.5 per cent from 20 000 units to 22 500 units. The percentage increase in quantity supplied is not as great as the percentage increase in price. However, for product B, the 25 per cent price increase results in a 100 per cent increase in the quantity supplied, from 20 000 units to 40 000 units. The supply of product B is much more responsive to the price increase than product A. This relationship between the responsiveness of supply and a change in price is called **price elasticity of supply** (PES).

SUBJECT VOCABULARY

price elasticity of supply responsiveness of supply to a change in price

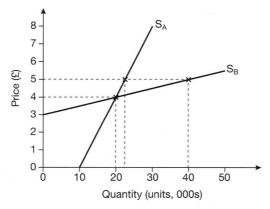

▲ **Figure 9.1** Effect of a price change in the supply of two different products: A and B

INELASTIC SUPPLY

SUBJECT VOCABULARY

inelastic supply change in price results in a proportionately smaller change in the quantity supplied (alternative term: price inelastic)

ELASTIC SUPPLY

SUBJECT VOCABULARY

elastic supply change in price results in a proportionately greater change in the quantity supplied (alternative term: price elastic)

In Figure 9.1, for product A, the change in price resulted in a smaller percentage change in quantity supplied. The 25 per cent price increase resulted in a smaller percentage increase in the quantity supplied of just 12.5 per cent. When this happens, economists say that product A has **inelastic supply**. The supply of houses in 'Getting started' is very price inelastic. Also, many agricultural goods have price inelastic supply because farmers cannot increase supply at short notice. It takes time to grow farm produce.

In Figure 9.1, for product B, the change in price resulted in a larger percentage change in quantity supplied. The 25 per cent price increase resulted in a 100 per cent increase in quantity supplied. When this happens, economists say that product B has **elastic supply**. Provided firms have spare capacity, the supply of many manufactured goods, like crisps in 'Getting started', tends to be elastic.

ACTIVITY 1

CASE STUDY: INELASTIC SUPPLY

Figure 9.2 shows the supply curve for a product. The current price is £20 and the amount supplied is 5000 units.

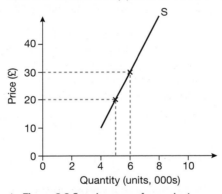

▲ **Figure 9.2** Supply curve of a product

1   What happens to the quantity supplied when the price increases from £20 to £30?

2   What is meant by inelastic supply? Use this case as an example in your explanation.

CALCULATING THE VALUE OF PRICE ELASTICITY OF SUPPLY

Like price elasticity of demand, PES can be presented numerically. The formula for calculating PES is given below.

$$\text{Price elasticity of supply} = \frac{\text{Percentage change in quantity supplied}}{\text{Percentage change in price}}$$

For product A in Figure 9.1 PES would be:

$$= \frac{12.5\%}{25\%} = 0.5$$

For product B in Figure 9.1 PES would be:

$$= \frac{100\%}{25\%} = 4$$

INTERPRETING THE VALUE OF PRICE ELASTICITY OF SUPPLY

SUBJECT VOCABULARY

perfectly elastic (supply) where PES = ∞. (producers will supply an infinite amount at the given price)
perfectly inelastic (supply) where PES = 0 (the quantity supplied is fixed and cannot be adjusted whatever the price)
unitary elasticity (with regard to supply) where PES = 1 (a change in price will be matched by an identical change in the quantity supplied)

The values calculated above show whether supply is price elastic or price inelastic.

■ If the value of PES is less than 1 (that is, a fraction or a decimal), supply is said to be *inelastic*. Product A in Figure 9.1 has inelastic supply because price elasticity is 0.5.

■ If the value of PES is greater than 1, supply is said to be *elastic*. The supply of product B in Figure 9.1 is price elastic because price elasticity is 4.

■ If PES = 0, supply is said to be **perfectly inelastic**.

■ If PES = ∞, supply is **perfectly elastic**.

■ If PES = 1, supply has **unitary elasticity**.

PRICE ELASTICITY AND THE SLOPE OF THE SUPPLY CURVE

The supply curves in Figure 9.1 have different slopes. For product A, the slope is steep and, generally, this shows that supply is price inelastic. In contrast, the supply curve for product B is flatter. This generally shows that supply is price elastic. However, whether or not supply is elastic or inelastic really depends on whether the supply curve cuts the price axis or the quantity axis. Straight-line supply curves that cut the price axis are elastic and those that cut the quantity axis are inelastic.

There are also some *special cases.* They are shown Figure 9.3.

■ A perfectly inelastic supply curve, S_1 in Figure 9.3, is vertical. This means that a price change will not affect the quantity supplied at all. The quantity supplied is fixed and the value of PES in this case is zero. An example of fixed supply was shown in Chapter 5. Here the supply of tickets to a tennis match was fixed at 15 000 because the capacity of the stadium was fixed.

■ A perfectly elastic supply curve, S_2 in Figure 9.3, is horizontal. This means that producers are prepared to supply any amount at a given price. The value of price elasticity in this case is infinite.

■ Any straight-line supply curve that passes through the origin, S_3 in Figure 9.3, has a price elasticity equal to 1. This means that the percentage change in price is always the same as the percentage change in the quantity supplied.

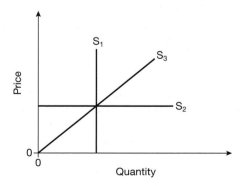

▲ **Figure 9.3** Supply curves – special cases

In Figure 9.1 the supply curve labeled S_A shows a relatively inelastic supply curve. In contrast, the supply curve S_B is relatively elastic.

ACTIVITY 2

CASE STUDY: AMPAT HOLDINGS

Ampat Holdings manufactures a range of replica sports shirts. They are produced in a large factory in Chittagong, Bangladesh. The shirts are sold to retailers and **wholesalers** all over the sub-continent. In 2016, the price of these shirts fell from BDT 800 to BDT 640. As a result, Ampat Holdings reduced supply from 1.6 million to 1.2 million shirts.

▲ Replica sports shirts are very big business in many parts of the world

1   Calculate the PES for the replica shirts in this case.

2   What is meant by elastic supply? Use this case as an example in your explanation.

FACTORS INFLUENCING PES

The supply of some goods is not very responsive to price changes, whereas the supply of others is. Generally, PES is influenced by whether producers can increase supply easily, or not. If producers can increase the quantity supplied easily, supply will tend to be elastic. However, if there are barriers that prevent producers from increasing the quantity supplied, then supply will be more inelastic.

FACTORS OF PRODUCTION

If producers have easy access to the factors of production such as labour, **raw materials**, energy, tools and machinery, they will be able to boost production if necessary. This means that supply will be elastic. For example, if there is an increase in the price of training shoes, producers should be able boost production and increase the quantity supplied fairly easily. This is because there is no reason why the resources needed to produce training shoes should not be available. Consequently, the supply of training shoes should be elastic.

Supply will also be more elastic if production factors are mobile. If production factors such as labour and materials can be switched to other uses easily, supply will be elastic. However, if specialised resources are needed for production, such as skilled labour, such resources are less mobile (it may take time to train workers in new skills) and supply will be more inelastic.

AVAILABILITY OF STOCKS

Producers that can hold stocks of goods can respond quickly to price changes so supply will be elastic. However, where it is impossible or expensive to hold stocks, supply will be inelastic. The supply of some perishable goods, such as fruit and vegetables, will be inelastic because they cannot be stored for very long.

SPARE CAPACITY

Supply will be more elastic if producers have spare capacity. With spare capacity, producers have the ability to produce more with their resources. In contrast, if firms are running at full capacity supply will be inelastic. This is because output cannot be increased at short notice. Given more time, though, even firms running at full capacity can increase supply. This is because they can build a bigger factory or buy more machinery, for example.

TIME

The speed with which producers can react to price changes in the market can affect PES. Generally, all producers can adjust output if they are given time. As a result, the more time producers have to react to price changes, the more elastic supply will be. Where it is not possible to increase supply quickly, due to production limitations, supply will be inelastic. For example, it will take nearly a year to increase the supply of many agricultural products in many countries because growing seasons are so long. This is discussed in more detail below.

PES FOR MANUFACTURED AND PRIMARY PRODUCTS

A number of factors can influence the speed at which producers can react. Goods that can be produced quickly are likely to have elastic supply. Modern manufacturers can be quite flexible and can adjust production levels at short notice. For example, a car engine manufacturer could increase production quickly by stepping up the rate of output in the factory. This might involve asking employees to work overtime and keeping the factory open for longer. More raw materials and components will be required but this should not be a problem. Whereas, the producers of many primary products, such as agricultural goods, are not able to react quickly to price changes. For example, a strawberry producer cannot increase supply until more strawberries can be grown. This might not be possible until next year. As a result supply is inelastic.

The supply of other primary goods, such as gold and diamonds, is likely to be inelastic. This is because there are few sources around the world. The production of such goods is also expensive and time consuming. As a result, supply is not very responsive to price changes. It is likely to be very inelastic.

MULTIPLE-CHOICE QUESTIONS

▶ 1 What is the value of price elasticity of supply for a straight-line supply curve that passes through the origin?

A 1

B −1

C 0

D Infinite

▶ 2 The price of a product rises by 12 per cent. As a result, producers increase the amount supplied by 18 per cent. What is PES?

A 12

B 0

C 1.5

D 0.67

ECONOMICS IN PRACTICE

CASE STUDY: THE GLOBAL SUPPLY OF COCONUTS

There has been a sharp increase in the global demand for coconuts (and products made from coconuts) in recent years. For example, in supermarkets, coconut milk is being sold with ring pull opening devices that allow it to be drunk like a soft drink. Also, reports have suggested that coconut sugar is a much healthier alternative to traditional sugar and celebrities have been observed consuming coconut products. For example, actress Gwyneth Paltrow claimed that she uses coconut oil as a mouthwash for oral health and whitening her teeth. The rising demand has resulted in higher prices for coconuts. Figure 9.4 shows the price of coconut oil between 2015 and 2016.

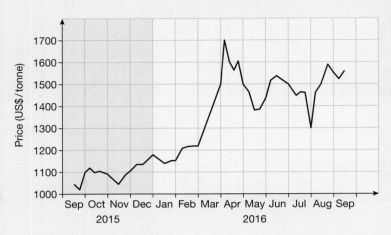

▲ **Figure 9.4** Price of coconut oil, September 2015–September 2016

Unfortunately, suppliers have not been able to react to the rising prices by increasing the quantity supplied. Globally, the supply of coconuts is falling. One reason for this is linked to the age of the industry. Most coconut trees are grown in India and Southeast Asia and their trees are simply past their best. Today's coconut trees were planted more than 50 years ago, according to Hiroyuki Konoma, a representative for a United Nations Food and Argriculture Organization. That puts them more than 20 years past their peak production time. Also, the Philippines is still recovering from the damage caused by typhoon Haiyan, which wiped out about 15 per cent of its trees in 2013. It will take at least another year for new trees to bear fruit. Finally, Indonesia, the world's top producer of coconuts, has failed to replace old low-yielding coconut trees. This means that estates are less productive. The government is also encouraging more production of corn and soya. It is reckoned that production growth is currently 8 per cent behind demand growth.

▲ Many of the world's coconut trees are past their best

CHAPTER QUESTIONS

1 Describe what price elasticity of supply is.

2 Why is the supply of coconuts likely to be inelastic?

3 Describe why the price of coconuts has risen sharply recently.

4 How might the ability to store coconuts for long periods of time affect PES?

10 INCOME ELASTICITY

LEARNING OBJECTIVES

- Understand how to define and calculate income elasticity of demand
- Understand how to interpret numerical values of income elasticity of demand
- Understand the significance of price and income elasticities of demand to businesses and the government with regard to the imposition of taxes and subsidies and changes in income

GETTING STARTED

After price, income is one of the most important factors that can affect the demand for products. For most products, a change in income will result in a change in the quantity demanded. However, the change in demand may vary according to the nature of the product.

CASE STUDY: NEW CARS

In September 2016, Marion Wright was promoted at the market research agency for which she worked. The promotion came with an attractive increase in salary. It rose from £49 000 to £63 000 p.a. As a result, she planned to pay off some debt and buy a new car. She bought a new VW Golf GTI.

▲ VW Golf GTI

CASE STUDY: MILK

The Spencer family consumes 9 litres of milk per week. In 2016, Charlie Spencer was made redundant from his £65 000 p.a. sales job at an insurance company. Charlie quickly found employment as a driving instructor but only earned £31 000 p.a. However, the family's consumption of milk remained much the same at around 9 litres per week.

1 Which is most responsive to changes in income: demand for cars or demand for milk?

2 What reason can you give for your answer to **(1)**?

3 In pairs, draw up a list of products that might respond in the same way as the demand for new cars to changes in income. Present your findings to the rest of the class outlining the reasons for your choice.

WHAT IS INCOME ELASTICITY OF DEMAND?

SUBJECT VOCABULARY

income elasticity of demand responsiveness of demand to a change in income

Income elasticity of demand measures the responsiveness of demand to a change in income. Consider two products: A and B. If incomes rise by 10 per cent and the quantity demanded for product A rises by 25 per cent, demand for product A is very responsive to the change in income. Economists would say that demand for product A is income elastic. In contrast, if the quantity demanded for product B only rose by 5 per cent, economists would say that demand for product B is income inelastic. This is because the percentage increase in quantity demanded is less than the percentage increase in income.

CALCULATING INCOME ELASTICITY OF DEMAND

It is possible to calculate the income elasticity of demand for a good using the formula below:

$$\text{Income elasticity of demand} = \frac{\text{Percentage change in quantity demanded}}{\text{Percentage change in income}}$$

For product A in the example above, income elasticity of demand would be:

$$= \frac{25\%}{10\%} = 2.5$$

For product B in the example above, income elasticity of demand would be:

$$= \frac{5\%}{10\%} = 0.5$$

INTERPRETING THE VALUE OF INCOME ELASTICITY OF DEMAND

The values calculated above show whether demand is income elastic or income inelastic. They also show something about the nature of the goods in relation to how demand changes in response to changes in income.

NECESSITIES

Necessities are 'basic goods' that consumers need to buy. Examples include food in general, electricity and water. Demand for these types of goods will be income inelastic. Another example of a good that is income inelastic is petrol. If the value of income elasticity of demand is between +1 and −1, demand is said to be income inelastic. Demand for product B is income elastic because income elasticity is 0.5.

LUXURY GOODS

Luxuries are goods that consumers like to buy if they can afford them. Spending on these types of goods is called **discretionary expenditure** – this means that it is optional. Demand for these goods is income elastic. Examples include air travel, satellite television, designer clothing, and many goods and services in the leisure and tourism industry. It is also argued that the demand for imported goods is income elastic. If the value of income elasticity is greater than 1 or less than −1, demand is said to be income elastic. Demand for product A is income elastic because income elasticity is 2.5.

NORMAL GOODS

The value of income elasticity can also show whether goods are normal or inferior (see Chapter 4, pages 23–28). For normal goods, where, for example, an increase in income results in an increase in the quantity demanded, the value of income elasticity will be positive. Products A and B above are both normal goods because income elasticity is positive in both cases.

INFERIOR GOODS

For inferior goods, where, for example, an increase in income results in a decrease in the quantity demanded, the value of income elasticity will be *negative*. This shows that the quantity demanded and income have an inverse relationship. Examples of inferior goods might include those bought at 'Pound' or 'Dollar' shops, where everything sold is either £1 or US$1.

ACTIVITY 1

CASE STUDY: CALCULATING INCOME ELASTICITY OF DEMAND

In 2016, average incomes in a country rose from €30 000 to €32 400. This caused a change in the quantity demanded for two particular products: X and Y. Total annual quantity demanded for product X rose from 24 million units to 30 million units. However, the quantity demanded for product Y fell from 10 million units to 9 million units.

1 Calculate the income elasticity of demand for products X and Y.

2 Are the two products (X and Y) income elastic or income inelastic?

3 Are the two products X and Y normal or inferior? Give an explanation in your answer.

DID YOU KNOW?

As developing nations become better off, their demand for imports rises significantly.

PRICE ELASTICITY AND BUSINESSES

Price elasticity can provide useful information for businesses. For example, it can help firms predict the effect of a price change on total revenue. When a firm changes its price, there will be a change in the quantity demanded and therefore a change in total revenue. It would be useful for the firm to know what effect a particular price change might have on total revenue. The value of price elasticity can help here. Look at the example in the box.

EFFECT ON TOTAL REVENUE OF A PRICE INCREASE WHEN DEMAND IS INELASTIC

If a business has inelastic demand for one of its products, it knows that a price increase will increase revenue. For example, if price elasticity of demand (PED) = –0.8 and current demand is 2 million units, a 5% price increase from US$20 to US$21 will increase revenue. The following calculations prove this.

The change in demand is give in by:

$$PED = \frac{\% \text{ change in demand}}{\% \text{ change in price}}$$

Therefore:

$$-0.8 = \frac{\% \text{ change in demand}}{5\%}$$

–0.8 × 5% = % change in demand

–4% = change in demand

Therefore the new level of demand following the price increase will be:

= Previous demand –4%

= 2 million – (4% × 2 million)

= 2 million – 80 000

= 1 920 000

The change in total revenue is given by:

When price is US$20 TR = US$20 × 2 million = US$40 million

When price is US$21 TR = US$21 × 1.92 million = US$40.32 million

Therefore the price increase has resulted in a rise in total revenue of US$320 000.

The relationship between price elasticity and the effect of price changes on total revenue is fully summarised in Chapter 8 (pages 48–55).

To conclude, if firms know the value of price elasticity for their products, they can predict the effect on total revenue of any price changes they make. They will know, for example, that if demand for their product is elastic, a price reduction will increase total revenue. This might help to explain why many rail companies charge much-reduced prices for 'off-peak' rail travel. By lowering the price, more travellers are attracted and revenue rises. Demand during the 'off-peak' period must be price elastic.

INCOME ELASTICITY AND BUSINESSES

Many firms will be interested in income elasticity of demand. This is because changes in income in the economy may affect demand for their products. If firms know the income elasticity of demand for their products, they can respond to predicted changes in incomes.

Some manufacturers have flexible resources and can switch from the production of one good to another. For example, a manufacturer of plastic products may be able to switch from the production of plastic buckets to plastic toys. A predicted rise in incomes may encourage such a firm to make more plastic toys if demand for them was income elastic.

Also, firms that produce goods that are income elastic will expect changes in income to affect demand. So, if incomes are expected to rise in the future they can plan ahead, making sure they have enough capacity, for example. In contrast, if a recession were expected, such firms would plan to cut output. This is because incomes are likely to fall during a recession. In 2008, as a result of the global recession, car manufacturers started to cut their output. However, producers of inferior goods might start to build capacity if they believed a recession was coming. When incomes fall, the quantity demanded for inferior goods, such as those sold by low cost supermarkets, starts to rise.

PRICE ELASTICITY AND THE GOVERNMENT

SUBJECT VOCABULARY

excise duty government tax on certain goods, such as cigarettes, alcoholic drinks and petrol that are sold in the country

valued-added tax (VAT) tax on some goods and services – businesses pay value-added tax on most goods and services they buy and if they are VAT registered, charge value-added tax on the goods and services they sell

INDIRECT TAXES

Governments often raise revenue by imposing indirect taxes such as **value-added tax (VAT)** and **excise duty** on products. It is important for governments to select products that have inelastic demand. This is because consumers will avoid heavily taxed products if demand for them is elastic. Therefore, governments target goods that are either necessities or have few substitutes. However, most governments do not target goods, such as food and water, which are essential to human survival. Popular targets for governments when imposing taxes are cigarettes, alcohol and petrol. Demand for these products is very price inelastic. Look at the example in Activity 2.

SUBSIDIES

Governments might also consider PED when granting a subsidy to producers. The effect of a subsidy is to move the supply curve to the right (that is, to increase supply). If the subsidy is designed to help the poor by making the good cheaper, it is important that demand is price inelastic. If demand is not price inelastic, an increase in supply will only reduce the price slightly. This might explain why subsidies are often given to farmers. Since demand for many food products is inelastic, a subsidy to farmers will help to keep food prices lower.

ACTIVITY 2

CASE STUDY: PETROL TAX AND PED

One of the products chosen by many governments for indirect taxes is petrol. In December 2016, the average price of a litre of petrol in the UK was around £1.13. However, 57.95 pence of this is fuel duty that goes to the government. In addition, VAT is charged on petrol at 20 per cent. UK drivers pay some of the highest prices for petrol in the world due to taxation.

▲ Petrol filling station

1 How much fuel duty will the government collect from a driver who buys 50 litres of petrol per week?

2 If it costs a driver a total of £60 to fill up a car with petrol, how much of this is paid in VAT?

3 Comment on the amount of tax taken by the government from the sale of petrol.

4 Why do governments choose products like petrol to impose heavy duties on?

▶ 1 Which of the following shows the income elasticity of demand for an inferior good?

A –1.2

B 1.7

C 1.9

D 0.7

▶ 2 The PED for a product is –2.4. What will happen if the price of this product is increased by 10 per cent?

A Demand will fall by 10 per cent

B Total revenue will rise

C Total revenue will fall

D Demand will rise by 24 per cent

ECONOMICS IN PRACTICE

CASE STUDY: INCOME ELASTICITY FOR RED MEAT IN A DEVELOPING COUNTRY

The income per capita (per head) for a developing country between 2001 and 2017 is shown in Figure 10.1. The consumption of red meats, such as beef or lamb, in the same developing country between 2001 and 2017 is shown in Figure 10.2.

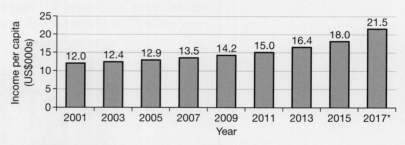

▲ Figure 10.1 Income per capita for a developing country

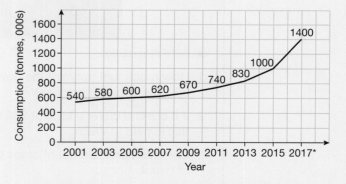

▲ Figure 10.2 Annual red meat consumption for a developing country *Prediction

CHAPTER QUESTIONS

1 Calculate the percentage change in average income between 2001 and 2015 for the developing country in Figure 10.1.

2 Calculate the percentage change in the quantity demanded for red meat between 2001 and 2015 for the developing country in Figure 10.2.

3 Calculate the income elasticity of demand for red meat in the developing country.

4 Is demand for red meat in the developing country income elastic or income inelastic?

5 What evidence is there to suggest that red meat in this developing country is a luxury good?

6 How might income elasticity be of use to businesses in this developing country? Give two reasons in your analysis.

11 THE MIXED ECONOMY

LEARNING OBJECTIVES

- Understand the difference between the public and private sectors
- Understand how the ownership, control and aims of private and public sector organisations differ
- Understand what is meant by a mixed economy and how the problems of what to produce, how to produce and for whom to produce are resolved
- Understand market failure and why government intervention may be needed
- Understand the role played by the private and public sectors in the production of goods and services including public goods
- Understand the relative importance of the public and private sectors in different economies

GETTING STARTED

Goods and services are produced to meet the needs and wants of consumers. However, the way in which different countries organise the choice, production and distribution of goods will vary. For example, in some countries most goods and services are produced by privately owned businesses. In others, the state might take more responsibility. In most countries it is common for both the state and private businesses to provide goods and services. Look at the two sets of images below.

CASE STUDY: PRIVATE AND PUBLIC GOODS

▲ **Figure 11.1** Groceries and consumer durables

▲ **Figure 11.2** Water and policing

1 Who provides the goods and services shown in Figures 11.1 and 11.2?

2 Why do you think there are two sets of providers? Explain your answer.

3 In groups, discuss who provides most of the goods and services in your country.

THE PUBLIC AND PRIVATE SECTORS

SUBJECT VOCABULARY

economy system that attempts to solve the basic economic problem
private sector provision of goods and services by businesses that are owned by individuals or groups of individuals
public sector government organisations that provide goods and services in the economy

An **economy** is a system that attempts to solve the basic economic problem: decision makers in an economy have to decide what to produce, how to produce and for whom to produce. In any economy, goods and services may be provided by the **public sector** or the **private sector**. In the private sector, individuals or groups of individuals are free to set up businesses and supply goods and services to anyone who wants to buy them. In the public sector, a range of organisations, such as government departments, public corporations and other agencies, provide services that are often supplied inefficiently by the private sector. Examples include health care, education and defence. Most public sector services are provided free by the state and are paid for from tax revenue or borrowing.

PRIVATE SECTOR ORGANISATIONS

GENERAL VOCABULARY

durables products that are intended to have a life of more than 3 years from when they are made or bought
groceries food and other goods that are sold by a grocer or a supermarket
professions careers that need a high level of education and training in order to work in them, traditionally including medicine, law, teaching

SUBJECT VOCABULARY

shareholders people or organisations that owns shares in a company

OWNERSHIP AND CONTROL

Goods and services in this sector are provided by businesses that are owned and controlled by individuals or groups of individuals. In many countries, most consumer goods, such as **groceries** and consumer **durables** like those shown in 'Getting started', are provided by the private sector. Private sector enterprises can vary in size and type of ownership. They may be:

■ **sole traders**: where the business is owned and controlled by one person (these are often retailers, and tradesmen such as plumbers, electricians or taxi drivers)

■ **partnerships**: where the business is owned and controlled by two or more people working together. They are often found in the **professions** and may operate as accountants, solicitors, estate agents and architects, for example

■ **companies**: where **shareholders** own the business. They elect a board of directors to run the business on their behalf. These vary in size and can be found in a number of different business sectors, such as manufacturing, construction, public transport, media, financial services, oil and gas, pharmaceuticals and engineering.

In most countries, private sector businesses are relatively small and include only sole traders, partnerships and small companies. A minority of businesses are large but contribute enormously to the provision of goods and services. Some are multinationals, which means they have factories and other operations all over the world.

AIMS

In the private sector, the aims of firms are likely to be determined by their owners. The main aim of most owners is to make a profit. However, a number of other aims need to be considered.

- **Survival:** When a firm is first set up, many owners will not expect to make a profit immediately. It takes time to establish a business and new business owners often encounter unexpected difficulties. As a result, the initial aim of a firm might be simply to survive. Survival is also important when trading conditions are difficult. In 2008 and 2009, because of global financial difficulties and recession, many firms began to struggle due to falling sales and difficulties in raising finance. During this time, many of them were happy just to survive.

- **Profit maximisation:** The owners of most firms are in business to make a profit. Economic theory assumes that firms will aim to maximise profits (see Chapter 2, pages 12–17). This is where a firm will make as much profit as it possibly can in a period of time. Companies pay their shareholders a share of the profit through a **dividend**. Many of these shareholders want dividends to be as high as possible and therefore profit maximisation is an important objective. However, some firms are content to make just enough profit to keep the owners satisfied. In a small firm, this might mean that an owner does not want to take on the extra responsibility of growth and is content to make a satisfactory profit. In a large company, it might mean that the managers who run the firm make enough profit to satisfy shareholders.

- **Growth:** Many firms aim to grow because bigger businesses enjoy a number of advantages. For example, large firms can reduce average costs by exploiting economies of scale (see Chapter 17, pages 124–131). Growth also means that profits will be higher in the future. Growth will also benefit other stakeholders such as workers, managers and directors. For example, their jobs will be more secure. However, one of the problems with growth is that profit is often used to finance it. Shareholders may not like this because dividends may be lower.

- **Social responsibility:** An increasing number of firms aim to be good corporate citizens. This means they aim to please a wider range of stakeholders. Owing to pressure from the government, the media, environmentalists, local residents, consumers, workers and other interested parties, some firms are aiming to become more socially responsible.

PUBLIC SECTOR ORGANISATIONS

OWNERSHIP AND CONTROL

Public sector organisations are owned and controlled by local or central government. Some of the main examples are outlined below.

- **Central government departments**, such as, in the UK, the Ministry of Defence, which is responsible for the armed forces, the Department of Health, which is responsible for the National Health Service, and the Department for Transport, which aims to manage the provision of a reliable and safe transport system, play a significant role. These departments are usually controlled by teams or boards led by a government minister.

DID YOU KNOW?
Some large, public corporations are part owned by the private sector. For example, the 'Indian' government owns about 60 per cent of the State Bank of India and private individuals, financial institutions, foreign institutions and other private owners own the rest.

- **Public corporations or state-owned enterprises (SOEs)** are owned by the government. This means that the government selects the people who run the organisation, often a board of directors. The government is also responsible for its key policies. Public corporations are usually incorporated businesses, which means they have a separate legal identity. They can sue, be sued and enter into contracts under their own name. Public corporations are state-funded, which means that the government provides their capital. The money comes mainly from taxation. All the **assets** and **liabilities** of public corporations belong to the state. However, they can also borrow money and are free to re-use revenue from the sale of any goods or services. The nature and number of public corporations around the world can vary in each country. For example, although a great number of public corporations around the world exist to provide a public service, there are many that operate commercially with the aim of making a profit – in the Middle East, Russia and India, for example.

- **Local authority services**, delivered by local councils, include recreation, such as libraries, sports halls and swimming pools; emergency services, such as the provision of fire and police services; and housing, which includes the provision of council housing and facilities for the homeless. Councillors who are elected by residents in the local community run local authorities.

- **Other public sector organisations**, such as the BBC, the Post Office, the Bank of England and Network Rail (all in the UK) are run by a trust or a board led by an experienced expert selected by a government body, or the Queen, following government advice.

AIMS

Public sector organisations have different aims from those in the private sector. Without aims, they are likely to deliver poor-quality services and waste resources. Each organisation in the public sector will have its own specific aims depending on the services they provide. However, there will be some common themes.

- **Improving the quality of services:** Public sector organisations generally aim to improve the standard of their services. Performance indicators may be used to monitor quality. For example, in the railway industry, targets might be set for reliability and punctuality. In the education system, league tables may be published to show student success rates in exams at individual schools. In general, performance indicators might focus on reliability, professionalism, levels of customer service and speed of service.

- **Minimising costs:** Government resources are scarce and it is important that waste is minimised. In the past, public sector organisations have been criticised for being inefficient. As a result, the government is regularly looking for ways to cut costs in all areas.

- **Allow for social costs and benefits:** Since their aim is not to make a profit, public sector organisations are better placed to take into account the needs of a wide range of **stakeholders**. As a result, when making decisions they can take into account externalities (see Chapter 13, pages 89–96).

- **Profit: in some countries, the government owns a number of large businesses that aim to make a profit.** In the UAE, Emirates Airline and Dubai World, an investment company that manages and supervises a range of businesses and projects for the Government of Dubai, are examples.

ACTIVITY 1

CASE STUDY: UGANDAN WATER SUPPLY

Water and sewerage services in Uganda, like many other countries in the world, are supplied by a government-owned organisation. The Ugandan government owns 100 per cent of The Ugandan National and Water Sewerage Corporation (NWSC). Its mission is: 'To sustainably and equitably provide cost effective quality water and sewerage services to the delight of all stakeholders while conserving the environment.' A board of directors, which is accountable to a government minister, runs the organisation.

NWSC has enjoyed much success in recent years. Its revenue increased from UGX 21 000 million to UGX 220 000 million between 1998 and 2016. NWSC is active in 162 towns, an increase from 27 towns in 2013. NWSC increased its number of account holders from 58 260 in 1998 to 450 000 in 2016. NWSC employs over 2800 people and has also enjoyed improvements in productivity. For example, in 1998, it took 36 staff to make 1000 connections; in 2016, this was reduced to six staff per 1000 connections.

NWSC is aiming to supply everyone with clean safe water within a 200 metre distance of all towns and urban centres (supply in these areas is currently 78 per cent). It links up with customers and local communities through NWSC Water Communication Clubs. On the NWSC website, it states that 'The customer is the reason we exist. We do everything to the delight of our customer.' According to annual surveys carried out by NWSC, 90 per cent of its customers are satisfied with the service provided.

▲ Bringing water to the people

1 Who owns and runs the Ugandan National and Water Sewerage Corporation (NWSC)?

2 What are the aims of NWSC?

3 Why do you think the government gets involved in business ownership?

TYPES OF ECONOMY

Different economies have different approaches to providing goods and services. The type of economy used to choose, produce and distribute goods varies according to the role played by the public sector. There are three types of economy. Historically, a country's type of economy was shaped by its political ideology: capitalist countries adopting a market economy and communist countries a command economy.

- **A market or free enterprise economy** relies least on the public sector for the provision of goods and services. The vast majority are provided by private businesses. Market forces, that is, supply and demand, determine the allocation of resources. The role of the public sector is limited to providing a legal system, a **monetary** system, key state services like defence and policing and ensuring that competition exists between businesses. The most economically free countries in the world are often considered to be Singapore, Australia and the USA.

- A **command** or **planned economy** relies entirely on the public sector to choose, produce and distribute goods. All resources in planned economies belong to the government and the state is responsible for planning, organising and coordinating the whole production process. Goods are distributed from state-owned shops where they are sold to consumers at prices set by the state. There are few, if any, examples of planned economies in the world today. Cuba, Myanmar and North Korea are the closest examples.

- **A mixed economy** (see below) relies on *both* the public sector and the private sector to provide goods and services. Currently, the majority of countries have mixed economies.

THE MIXED ECONOMY

In reality, no economy is entirely planned or free market. Most countries in the world have a **mixed economy** and the decisions what to produce, how to produce and for whom to produce are made by both consumers and the state.

WHAT TO PRODUCE?

A mixed economy recognises that some goods, such as consumer goods, are best provided by the private sector. Goods such as food, clothes, leisure and entertainment, and household services are best chosen by consumers. The market system ensures that businesses produce the consumer goods that people want. Other goods, such as education, street lighting, roads and protection, are more likely to be provided by the state. The public sector tends to provide goods that the private sector might fail to provide in sufficient quantities. This is often caused by **market failure**.

HOW TO PRODUCE?

In the private sector, individuals or groups of individuals who set up businesses with the aim of making a profit provide goods. Competition exists between these firms and this provides choice and variety for consumers. To meet consumers' needs, firms will use production methods that help them to maximise quality and minimise costs. Public sector services will be provided by the government organisations outlined above. They will decide how these services should be provided and attempt to supply them efficiently. However, some public sector goods are produced by the private sector. For example, governments are usually responsible for the provision of roads and motorways, however, they may pay private sector businesses to carry out the actual work of construction and maintenance.

FOR WHOM TO PRODUCE?

The goods produced in the private sector are sold to anyone who can afford them. The market system is responsible for their allocation. In contrast, most public sector goods are provided free to everyone and paid for from taxes. In some mixed economies, the state also makes provision for people who cannot work due to illness or disability, for example. A system of financial benefits exists to make sure that people have enough money to survive.

Finally, different governments around the world will decide on the 'degree of mixing' in this type of economy. Some countries, like France, allow the government to play a greater role in the economy. For example, government expenditure in France is around 57 per cent of its national income. In such countries, social provision is greater but taxes are higher. Figure 11.3 shows the proportion of national income spent by the government in three different countries – Singapore, Ireland and France.

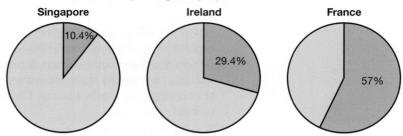

Government spending as a proportion of national income

Singapore   Ireland   France

10.4%   29.4%   57%

▲ **Figure 11.3** General government spending as a proportion of national income in Singapore, Ireland and France

MARKET FAILURE AND THE NEED FOR GOVERNMENT INTERVENTION

Although markets may have a reputation for using resources efficiently, because of market failure, resources are sometimes wasted. Market failure is where markets lead to inefficiency. It can occur for a number of reasons.

EXTERNALITIES

Sometimes firms do not take into account all the costs of production. For example, a firm producing chemicals may pollute the atmosphere because it has not taken measures to clean its waste. This imposes a cost on society, such as poor air quality. Any damage done to people or things outside the business such as ill health, as a result of this activity is called an external cost (see Chapter 13, pages 89–96). The market system has resulted in the chemical firm failing to meet any cost imposed on those affected by the pollution.

LACK OF COMPETITION

A market may fail if there is no competition and it becomes dominated by one or a small number of firms. When this happens, the **dominant** firm(s) may exploit consumers, by charging higher prices and limiting choice, for example.

MISSING MARKETS

Some goods and services, called **public goods**, are not provided by the private sector. Examples include national defence, policing and street lighting. The nature of public goods is discussed below (see pages 78–79). Other goods, called **merit goods**, such as education and health care are underprovided by the private sector. This is because they are so expensive that many people would not be able to afford them.

LACK OF INFORMATION

Markets will only be efficient if there is a free flow of information to all buyers and sellers. Consumers need to know everything about the nature, price and quality of all products. Businesses also need information about the resources and production techniques used to make a product, for example. However, this is not always possible. A lack of information may result in the wrong goods being purchased or produced, or the wrong prices being paid.

FACTOR IMMOBILITY

For markets to work efficiently, factors of production need to be *mobile.* This means that factors, such as labour and capital, must be able to move freely from one use to another. In practice, though, factors can be quite immobile. For example, a specialised laser machine designed specifically to cut sheet glass may not have any further use if the glass-making factory has to close down. As a result, the machine may have to be destroyed, which is wasteful.

Owing to the threat of market failure, the government often has to intervene in markets. Some examples are given below.

- Businesses that impose externalities may be heavily **regulated** or fined for polluting the atmosphere, for example.

- The government can use **legislation** to prevent businesses from dominating markets. For example, it can investigate whether a **merger** is in the interests of consumers and block them if they are not.

- State money can be used to provide public goods and merit goods. Since these goods and services are important to the well-being of everyone, the public sector can provide them free of charge.

- To overcome the problem of poor information, the government can help by passing legislation forcing firms to provide more information about products. However, in recent years the internet has improved the flow of information about products.

- The government may be able to help to make some factors more mobile, such as retraining workers when their previous jobs become redundant. But it can do little to avoid the waste of the machine in the above example.

GENERAL VOCABULARY

legislation law or set of laws
merger occasion when two or more companies or organisations join together to form a larger company
regulated industry that is closely controlled by the government

KEY FACTS: LACK OF COMPETITION

- In many countries, most people have to buy their water supply from one provider. They have no choice and have to pay the prices charged by the water company.
- The role of the government in this case is to monitor and control the prices charged by dominant firms or pass legislation to ensure that competition exists.

ROLE OF THE PRIVATE AND PUBLIC SECTORS IN THE PRODUCTION OF GOODS AND SERVICES

In most countries, the private sector is responsible for providing the everyday goods and services bought by people. This would include food, clothes, consumer durables, such as electrical goods and cars, personal and household services, financial services, entertainment and holidays. It would also include raw materials, components, machinery and commercial services, such as cleaning maintenance, IT and insurance, which businesses buy. Very few governments would get involved in the provision of these goods and services.

However, the public sector tends to provide public services. In particular, it focuses on the provision of public and merit goods. Such goods would not be provided in sufficient quantities by the private sector. For example, public goods would not be provided at all. This is because it is virtually impossible for private firms to charge users for their consumption. The reason for this is because public goods have two particular characteristics.

- **Non-excludability:** This means that once a public good is provided in the market, any individual consumer cannot be prevented or excluded from its consumption. Also, an individual consumer cannot refuse consumption of the good even if they wanted to. For example, it is argued that the protection given by the police service is a public good. An individual cannot be excluded from the protection provided in a community by the police force. Neither can an individual living in that community refuse to benefit from that protection.

- **Non-rivalry:** This means that consumption of a public good by one individual cannot reduce the amount available to others. For example, someone benefitting from the protection provided by the police does not prevent others benefitting from the same protection.

Governments have to provide public goods because of market failure. If the private sector were to provide public goods there would be a **free rider** problem. Since it is impossible to exclude the consumption of a public good by an individual consumer, there is little reason for people to pay for it. A free rider is someone who enjoys the benefit of a good but allows others to pay for it. Public goods like defence, policing, the judiciary system, prisons and street lighting will significantly increase the standard of living in a country. Consequently, the government takes responsibility for their provision – assuming there is enough money to pay for them.

ACTIVITY 2

CASE STUDY: PUBLIC GOODS IN BANGLADESH

Bangladesh has serious annual flooding problems. The country lies in the Ganges Delta where many tributaries flow into the River Ganges on its route to the Bay of Bengal. Flooding usually occurs during the monsoon season between June and September. To help protect large numbers of the population, flood defences are built in the country.

▲ An example of a flood defence in Bangladesh

1 Why are flood defence systems classified as a public good?

2 Why do governments need to intervene when there is market failure?

THE PUBLIC SECTOR AND PRIVATE SECTOR IN DIFFERENT ECONOMIES

The balance between public sector activity and private sector activity will vary in different countries. In some countries, governments play a key role in the provision of key public services, such as education, health care, security services and infrastructure. However, at the same time, they also own significant stakes in large commercial organisations, such as banks, airlines, water companies, energy provision and transport. Some examples of countries where the public sector plays a dominant role are China, Hungary, Russia, Sweden and the UAE.

In contrast, some governments believe that a greater quantity of goods and services should be provided by the private sector. In countries such as the USA, Singapore and Australia, the state has much less involvement in the provision of goods and services. Figure 11.3 shows that different countries vary their commitment to government involvement in the provision of public services. For example, France plays a much bigger role in the provision of goods and services than Singapore.

2 PRIVATISATION

RNING OBJECTIVES

- derstand how privatisation is defined
- derstand the effects of privatisation on consumers, workers, businesses and the government

VOCABULARY

olies situation where a business is controlled by only one ny or by the government, and companies do not compete with it **sation** act of selling a ny or activity controlled by the ment to private investors

VOCABULARY

pt not having enough money to your debts

GETTING STARTED

Since the 1980s, some governments around the world have transferred public sector resources to the private sector. This process is called **privatisation.** In Europe, some large industrial **monopolies** were privatised to improve competitiveness and efficiency. In Eastern Europe, privatisation was a result of the political and economic changes that took place after the break-up of the Soviet Union. Look at the example below.

SE STUDY: GREEK AIRPORT PRIVATISATION

r the financial crisis in 2008, it was discovered the Greek government had acquired extremely debts. To help deal with these debts, Greece to borrow large amounts of money from the EU event the country from going **bankrupt**. In order ceive a package of loans worth €86 000 million, d to promise international lenders that it would t selling some state assets. One significant deal made in 2015 when the Frankfurt airport operator, ort, obtained a 40-year agreement to upgrade operate some Greek airports, including those on tourist islands of Corfu, Mykonos, Rhodes and torini. The deal raised €1230 million for the Greek ernment. Fraport will also pay Greece an annual rating fee of €22.9 million and invest €330 million rport facilities. The investment was expected prove the quality and efficiency of airport tions.

▲ Fraport began operating Corfu airport in 2015

e future, Greece is expected to sell other assets such as the railways, the national lottery, utilities, ports and aps some of its islands.

hy were the Greek airports privatised?

escribe the possible benefits of the privatisation to consumers.

n pairs, carry out some research to see if any state organisations have been privatised in your country. Try to identify the reasons why they have been transferred to the private sector and how much money the government raised. Present your results in a report.

WHAT IS PRIVATISATION?

Privatisation involves transferring public sector resources to the private sector. During the 1980s and 1990s in the UK, the government sold off a large number of state assets to the private sector. For example, in 1987, British Airways, Rolls-Royce, Leyland Bus, Leyland Truck and the British Airport Authority were all privatised. It was argued that these organisations would be more efficient if they were operated without government interference. Privatisation has taken a number of forms in the UK.

- **Sale of nationalised industries: Nationalised industries** such as British Rail, British Airways and British Telecom were once private sector business organisations. However, for a number of reasons they were taken into public ownership. For example, it was felt that they should supply services that were unprofitable, such as railways in remote areas. Many were **natural monopolies** and would serve consumers more effectively under state control. However, after years under state control, they were sold off. They became private sector businesses, owned by private shareholders.

- **Contracting out:** Many government and local authority services have been 'contracted out' to private sector businesses. This is where contractors are given a chance to bid for services previously supplied by the public sector. Examples include the provision of school meals, hospital cleaning and refuse collection.

- **The sale of land and property:** During the 1980s, people renting local, council-owned properties were given the right to buy their own homes. They were given generous discounts to persuade them to buy. As a result, about 1.5 million council-owned houses were sold to private individuals in the UK.

WHY DOES PRIVATISATION TAKE PLACE?

Different reasons have been put forward for privatisation.

- **To generate income:** The sale of state assets generates income for the government. Figure 12.1 shows the revenue raised globally by privatisation between 2000 and 2015. The graph suggests that governments around the world are still keen to sell off state assets for money. As outlined in 'Getting started', Greece has been under pressure in recent years to raise money from the sale of state assets in order to meet the demands of international lenders.

- **Public sector organisations were inefficient:** Some nationalised industries lacked the **incentive** to make a profit and often made losses. It was argued that in the private sector they would have to cut costs, improve services and return profits for shareholders. They would also be more **accountable**. For example, in the private sector, if customer needs were not met, a company may lose customers and struggle to generate enough revenue and profit to survive (assuming there was competition in the market).

- **To reduce political interference:** In the private sector, the government could not use these organisations for political aims. They would be free to choose their own investment levels, prices, product ranges and growth rates, for example. In the past, some nationalised industries have been unstable due to constant government interference. This has often held back their performance.

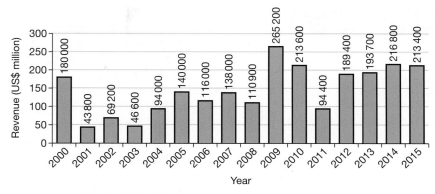

▲ Figure 12.1 Global revenue from privatisation, 2000–15

In recent years, a number of countries around the world have adopted privatisation programmes. For example, because of the economic crisis, and pressure from the World Bank and the International Monetary Fund, in 1991, India began privatising state assets. It began by selling the Bharat Aluminium Company and a few airports such as Bangalore, Delhi, Hyderabad and Mumbai. More recently, in 2016, India has said it will sell off controlling stakes (ownership of more than 50 per cent of shares in a company) in 22 companies. This includes some large state-run companies such as Container Corporation of India, Bharat Earthmovers, three steel plants and the Cement Corporation of India.

There have also been huge privatisation programmes in many Eastern European countries. Before the break-up of the Soviet Union, public sector groups conducted nearly all production. Afterwards, governments decided to develop mixed economies (see Chapter 11, pages 70–80) and began privatising vast quantities of public sector resources.

ACTIVITY 1

CASE STUDY: PRIVATISATION MOTIVES

Below is an extract from a government White Paper 'Working Together'.

'Just as a strong government is required to steer the economy through a recession, it is also the case that a responsive state should withdraw from areas in which it is no longer required. Now more than ever government must prioritise its interventions and secure the greatest possible efficiency for every pound of taxpayers' money it spends. As we redouble our efforts to reform and renew our public services, it is vital we are bolder in our efforts to strip out waste, improve productivity and sell off public assets that the state no longer needs to own. The government will set out proposals on these issues at the budget.'

1 To what extent does this extract suggest that the government is committed to more privatisation in the future?

2 According to this extract, what are the motives for future possible privatisation?

3 Suggest two other possible reasons for privatisation.

Privatisation has had a big impact in some nations. The effects have been felt in a number of areas and some evidence suggests that there have been both advantages and disadvantages resulting from privatisation.

CONSUMERS

It is hoped that consumers will benefit from privatisation. Once in the private sector, businesses are under pressure to meet customer needs and return a profit for the owners. This should mean that businesses will be efficient, try to provide good quality products, charge a reasonable price and grow. However, consumers have seen both improvements and a decline in price and service. F example, in the UK, according to the water and sewerage regulator Ofwat, sinc the privatisation of ten water providers in 1989, the number of customers at risk of low water pressure has fallen by 99 per cent. In telecommunications, the waiting time for a new BT line has fallen from around 6 months to just 15 days. contrast, though, since the privatisation of the rail industry in the UK, the amou of government subsidies given to the rail industry rose from just over £1000 million in the late 1980s to more than £6000 million in 2006/07. Even in 2014/1! the subsidy was still £4000 million. Taxpayers feel this increased financial responsibility. Rail fares to consumers have also risen sharply. Rail users in the UK now pay some of the highest fares in the world. For example, tickets similar to the £357.90 monthly season pass from Chelmsford to London would cost just £37 in Italy, £56 in Spain and £95 in Germany. There have been suggestions in recent years from some UK politicians that the country's railways could be renationalised in future to improve service to customers.

WORKERS

Quite often in the run up to privatisation, and after an organisation has moved into the private sector, quite large numbers of people are made redundant. Although this may reduce costs, many see this as a negative effect Evidence of this is provided by what happened in the UK after a number of privatisations. For example:

- when the coal industry was privatised, more than 200 000 jobs were lost
- British Telecom shed more than 100 000 jobs when it was sold to the private sector
- the Rail, Maritime and Transport Union suggested that there were 20 000 to 30 000 job losses as a result, of rail privatisation
- British Energy shed one-quarter of its workforce just before privatisation
- British Steel shed 20 000 jobs before it was privatised.

Mass redundancies often weaken companies through the loss of experienced staff and make it more difficult and more expensive to scale up in future. In addition to job losses, in an effort to improve efficiency, many workers may have been pressed into raising their productivity. They might have been forced to adopt more flexible working practices, for example. Those who support the process of privatisation would suggest that these measures were necessary in order compete in global markets. However, the impact on many communities of mass unemployment within the UK is still felt today.

BUSINESSES

Once in the private sector, firms are left without government interference and have to face competition. They have been affected in a number of ways in the UK.

- Their objectives have changed. For most firms, profit has become an important objective. For example, the profits of British Telecom increased from around £1000 million in 1984, when the company was first privatised, to nearly £3170 million in 2016.

- Many firms have increased investment following privatisation. For example, many of the water companies raised investment levels to fund new sewerage systems and water treatment plants. Immediately after privatisation, investment rose by about £1000 million in the water industry. However, more recently, some figures suggest that investment levels are falling.

- There have been a number of mergers and **takeovers** involving newly privatised firms. For example, Hanson bought Eastern Electricity and an American railway company bought the British Rail freight service. North West Water and Norweb joined together to form United Utilities and Scottish Power bought Manweb.

- Many privatised businesses have **diversified** into new areas. For example, British Telecom now provides television programmes and has invested heavily in broadcasting Premier League and Champions League football in the UK.

GOVERNMENT

One way in which governments have benefited from privatisation is the huge amount of revenue that has been generated. However, privatisation has been expensive. In particular, the amount of money spent advertising each sale has been criticised. The money spent on television advertising was at the taxpayer's expense. It has also been suggested that some state assets were sold off too cheaply. As a result, governments failed to maximise the revenue from sales. Governments are no longer responsible for running the newly privatised companies. As a result, it can focus more sharply on the business of government.

The Polish government has almost completely stopped the privatisation process. In 2016, a minister said that the privatisation policies of previous governments were wrong and would be ended. Only companies in trouble, or those 'without importance to the national economy', would be sold off in future. One reason for the change in policy was that too many state-owned companies were the subject of a **hostile takeover** after privatisation. Furthermore, the government also said that it might try to renationalise some of the companies that had been privatised. One target would be energy, it was claimed.

ACTIVITY 2

CASE STUDY: PRIVATISATION IN CHINA

In recent years, China has begun to sell off state-owned assets. However, in 2014, the government made a statement saying that it planned to accelerate the process in order to 'clean up and integrate some of China's state-owned enterprises (SOEs)'. Little detail was given in the announcement but it was clear that the government wanted make its SOEs more innovative and internationally competitive. SOEs have underperformed in recent years and it is felt that private sector involvement will help to increase investment and improve efficiency. The announcement also made it clear that mixed ownership was preferred.

Over 100 companies were under central government ownership in China in 2014 with local governments also owning and managing around 25 000 SOEs. This sector employs nearly 7.5 million people. The privatisation process will allow state firms to attract investors to help spread share ownership. In addition, many state firms will be encouraged to reorganise so that they are eventually suitable for a stock market listing. Some felt that the slowing of growth in the Chinese economy caused the acceleration of privatisation. The government said growth in China's investment and factory output had missed forecasts. As a result, it was felt that Chinese economic growth might dip below 7 per cent for the first time since the global financial crisis.

Finally, it has been suggested that there may be some opposition to the acceleration in privatisation. For example, many local governments may not be happy about sharing ownership of SOEs with private investors. This is because their ties with SOEs are very strong. Another problem might be attracting interest from the private sector. There was a stock market crash in China in 2016 and many private investors will be wary of buying shares again.

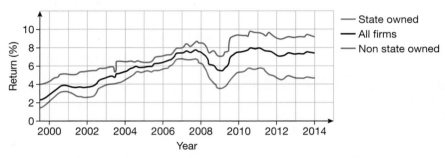

▲ **Figure 12.2** Performance of state-owned enterprises compared to private sector organisations

1 What is meant by mixed ownership in this case?

2 Discuss why the government wants to accelerate the privatisation process in China. Include two reasons in your answer.

3 Assess one possible difficulty that might be encountered when encouraging the private sector to get involved in the running of SOEs in China.

MULTIPLE-CHOICE QUESTIONS

▶ 1 Which of the following is a motive for privatisation?

   A Improve the welfare of shareholders

   B Generate money for the government

   C Increase growth in the public sector

   D Reduce externalities

▶ 2 Many workers suffer as a result, of privatisation because of which of the following reasons?

   A They are often relocated

   B They are not allowed to belong to a **trade union**

   C Their jobs are at risk

   D They have to pay more tax

GENERAL VOCABULARY

trade union organisation representing people working in a particular industry or profession that protects their rights

CASE STUDY: WATER PRIVATISATION

The World Bank has predicted that by 2025 two-thirds of the world's population will not have enough water. In addition, 2400 million people will face serious water shortages. After many years of privatisation, the water supply in many countries has been placed in the hands of private sector businesses. Many argue that the privatisation of water is not in the interests of consumers. However, supporters of water privatisation disagree. It is not easy to settle the argument. In some cities, like Guayaquil in Ecuador, Bucharest in Romania and in Colombia, Morocco and Senegal, it has been claimed that water privatisation has been successful. However, in Bolivia, Tanzania, Indonesia, and in parts of Europe, water privatisation is said to have failed. In one example, in Manila, the Philippines, a 25-year, US$2700 million project, using both private and public sector ownership, took control of the water supply. This was claimed to be a success because the project provided an extra 1.7 million people with clean water, reduced cases of illness such as diarrhoea by 51 per cent, and offered customers significant savings, charging 20 times less than previous water vendors. However, opponents claimed that Manila's water privatisation led to continual price increases, legal challenges, investigations, failures to provide certain districts with water, and has given the companies unfair returns for their work.

Generally, one of the main criticisms of water privatisation is that prices rise. Once water supply is taken into private ownership, there is very little, if any, competition. As a result, water companies can raise prices with very little opposition. Table 12.1 shows the prices charged by a selection of water companies in the UK.

	2003/04	2013/14
Northumbrian	£207	£359
Southern	£252	£449
Wessex	£263	£478
Thames	£203	£354

Note: Inflation between 2003 and 2012 was 36.1 per cent

▲ **Table 12.1** Annual prices charged by a selection of UK water companies in 2003/04 and 2013/14

Another reason why water privatisation is opposed is because water quality is not always maintained. This is because water companies, by seeking to maximise profit, can sometimes minimise costs and overlook the environmental impact of their activities. In the USA, the National Association of Water Companies (NAWC), which represents the US private water industry, has put pressure on the Environmental Protection Agency not to adopt higher water quality standards.

Opponents also say that private water providers, as a result of the 25–30-year deals done with governments, become monopolies and are accountable only to shareholders. This means that profits become the main focus of the companies and the interests of consumers are ignored. For example, Northumbrian Water's operating profit jumped from £165.3 million in 2001/02 to £338.8 million in 2011/12 (more than double), while

South West Water's operating profit increased dramatically from £107 million to £204.7 million over the same time period.

Water privatisation also results in job losses as companies minimise costs. The privatisation is also difficult to reverse. This is because once water companies have been sold to the private sector, the cost of buying them back is too high. Plus, many of the water companies are (or are part of) giant multinationals, which have a great deal of power.

Those in favour water privatisation argue that efficiency and the quality of service will improve. This is because businesses in the private sector have to perform well or they will not survive. They also say that the private sector will provide far more investment in water infrastructure than the public sector. For example, since privatisation, UK water companies have invested nearly £120 000 million in water infrastructure, such as new pipes, treatment plants and sewers. Private companies are more capable than governments of raising funds to finance investment. This is because private companies specialise in one area whereas governments have many different areas of investment to consider.

Finally, another benefit of water privatisation is the money generated for the government. Not only does the government get the money from the sale of water companies, but it also receives taxes every year on the profits made by the water companies once they start operating in the private sector.

▲ A water treatment plant

CHAPTER QUESTIONS

1 Calculate the percentage increase in water charges for the four water companies shown in Table 12.1.

2 Describe one reason why a government might benefit from the privatisation of water supplies.

3 Why might privatisation result in better efficiency?

4 What impact might privatisation have on businesses? Give two impacts in your analysis.

5 Consider the impact of water privatisation on consumers.

13 EXTERNALITIES

LEARNING OBJECTIVES

- Understand how external costs are defined with examples
- Understand how external benefits are defined with examples
- Understand the definitions and formulae for social costs and social benefits
- Understand the government policies used to deal with externalities

SUBJECT VOCABULARY

spillover effects effect that one situation or problem has on another situation

GENERAL VOCABULARY

emissions gas or other substance that is discharged into the air.

GETTING STARTED

Economic activity, such as building a new factory or transporting a ship full of oil from Qatar to Japan, will affect those inside the business. However, economic activity can also have an impact on those outside. There are **spillover effects**, which can result from both production and consumption. Look at the examples below.

CASE STUDY: PRODUCTION

In 2016, a European waste management company was fined €1.4 million for breaking emissions limits in an urban area. For 2 years, residents had complained to the local authorities about the 'dreadful smell' coming from the waste disposal plant located near to the area. The plant was using an industrial incinerator to burn refuse that it collected from households. A local television broadcaster interviewed one resident. She said, 'The situation has become intolerable. There are times when the smell penetrates through the structure of the house. If you go outside into the garden sometimes your eyes sting from the fumes.' A spokesman from the company said that measures would now be taken to reduce emissions to comply with EU standards.

CASE STUDY: CONSUMPTION

Every year from 1 December, children and many adults, look forward to passing the house belonging to Mr and Mrs Salomonsson. This is the day that the couple turn on their Christmas lights. They spend 2 weeks decorating their house in Gothenburg, Sweden, with around SEK 5000 of new lights. People from many miles away make a special journey to ensure that they pass the attractive display of lights.

▲ Christmas lights

1 Describe one possible reason why a business might continue to impact negatively on those outside the business as a result of its production activities.

2 How might the consumption of a good by one person bring benefits to third parties? Use this case as an example in your explanation.

3 In pairs, make a list of examples of business activity that has an impact on third parties. Present your ideas to the rest of the class, explaining the various impacts.

EXTERNAL COSTS OF PRODUCTION

GENERAL VOCABULARY

third parties someone who is not one of the two main people or organisations involved in an agreement or legal case

SUBJECT VOCABULARY

external costs negative spillover effects of consumption or production – they affect third parties in a negative way

Some production activity results in costs that are incurred by **third parties**. Third parties are people outside the business. They are neither owners nor employees – they may be individuals, such as local residents, organisations and property owners, or a resource, such as a river. These **external costs** are the spillover effects of production. In 'Getting started', the effect of the emissions discharged by the waste management company was an example of an external cost. Residents living close to the waste disposal plant felt this cost. Some other examples of external costs are shown in Figure 13.1.

▲ **Figure 13.1** Examples of external costs

ACTIVITY 1

CASE STUDY: EXTERNALITIES IN FACTORY FARMING

Factory farming involves raising a large number of farm animals in a restricted space. The farm operates as a factory attempting to produce the highest output at the lowest cost by relying on economies of scale, modern machinery and biotechnology. However, this approach requires medicines and chemicals, such as antibiotics and pesticides, to control the spread of disease caused by crowded living conditions. Factory farming has resulted in farms that are easier to run with lower labour costs and more output. However, it has also resulted in:

■ serious animal welfare problems

■ an increased number of antibiotic-resistant bacteria due to the excessive use of antibiotics

■ air quality problems

■ the pollution of rivers, streams, and coastal waters with animal waste.

▲ An example of factory farming

1 What is meant by external costs? Use the example in this case in your explanation.

2 Discuss how the growth in the popularity of free-range chickens might affect the size of the external costs in this case.

EXTERNAL BENEFITS OF CONSUMPTION

The consumption of certain goods can have positive spillover effects. These are called **external benefits** and might be enjoyed by third parties such as individuals, organisations and communities. Some examples of external benefits are outlined below.

EDUCATION

Education will clearly benefit those who attend schools, universities and colleges. They are likely to get better jobs, earn more money and enjoy a better quality of life. However, education can also benefit the wider society. This is because if people are well educated they may do highly skilled and socially useful jobs, such as doctors, teachers, pilots, senior administrators or research scientists. As a result, productivity will be higher and the standard of living for society as a whole will rise. It could also be argued that higher levels of individual education will lower unemployment, improve household mobility and raise rates of political participation – all of which will benefit the wider society.

HEALTH CARE

Individuals that consume health care will benefit if their own personal health improves. They will feel less pain, can return to work and enjoy life more. However, the consumption of health care by an individual can also benefit third parties. For example, if people are healthier they are able to work more effectively making contributions to economic output and paying taxes. This will benefit the wider society.

VACCINATIONS

If an individual receives an injection to protect against an infectious disease, he or she benefits directly. This is obviously beneficial to the individual but third parties will also benefit. This is because if more individuals are given vaccinations to prevent infection, the likeliness of others (who do not get vaccinated) contracting disease is lower. This is because the number of people who might pass on the disease is reduced because they have been vaccinated.

SOCIAL COST

The production or consumption of a good will have costs that can be divided into **private costs** and external costs. Those who consume or produce a good meet private costs. For example, the private cost to a smoker might be the US$100 per month that is spent on cigarettes. The external cost will be the discomfort and health risk that a third party might be exposed to as a result of inhaling cigarette smoke.

In production, the private cost to a property developer of building a retail centre might be the US$220 million financial cost of the project. The external costs might include the:

- noise generated from the development site during construction
- congestion caused in the local area by construction vehicles and workers arriving and leaving the site each day.

The costs to society as a whole of an economic activity, the **social cost**, are made up of private costs and external costs.

Social cost = Private costs + External costs (negative externalities)

SOCIAL BENEFIT

The production or consumption of a good will also have benefits that can be divided into **private benefits** and external benefits. Those who produce or consume a good enjoy private benefits. In 'Getting started', the private benefits to Mr and Mrs Salomonsson of spending SEK 5000 on their Christmas lights is the satisfaction and pleasure they receive from designing their display and seeing the lights when they are switched on. They might also get pleasure from the fact that others come to see the lights. The external benefit in this example is the enjoyment third parties get from seeing the displays. These are the people who did not pay for the Christmas lights but nevertheless are able to enjoy the display as they pass the house.

In production, the private benefits to the property developer of building the retail centre described above are the financial returns it makes from the investment. This might include the rents received from those who rent the retail units. The external benefits are the benefits enjoyed by third parties such as the creation of employment and the provision of a brand new shopping facility in the area.

The benefits to society as a whole of an economic activity, the **social benefits**, are made up of private benefits and external benefits.

Social benefits = Private benefits + External benefits (positive externalities)

ACTIVITY 2

CASE STUDY: COSTS AND BENEFITS OF CAR OWNERSHIP

After starting a new job for a global software developer, Sally Wright took out a US$12 000 loan to buy a new car. However, she was a little shocked when she had to pay US$3300 for a year's insurance. She decided to pay this in 12 monthly instalments to spread the cost over the year. She had been looking forward to the convenience and flexibility that car-ownership provides for many months. She was also looking forward to taking her mum shopping each week.

1   What are the possible private **(a)** costs and **(b)** benefits to Sally of buying the car?

2   What are some of the possible external costs resulting from Sally's purchase?

3   What is meant by social cost? Use an example from this case in your explanation.

GOVERNMENT POLICIES TO DEAL WITH EXTERNALITIES

A government will want to discourage economic activities that result in negative externalities and encourage those that result in positive externalities. How can this be done?

TAXATION

Taxation can be used to reduce external costs of production. For example, if a tax is imposed on a chemical firm that produces damaging emissions, production costs will increase and the prices charged by the firm will rise. This should result in a fall in demand for the firm's product and therefore a reduction in pollution.

Taxes can also be used to reduce the external costs of consumption. For example, high taxes on cigarettes should reduce supply, which will raise the price. As a result the demand for cigarettes should fall and fewer third parties will be affected by smoke. However, cigarettes are addictive and when prices rise as a result of the tax, demand may not fall by very much.

SUBSIDIES

The government can offer money, such as subsidies and other financial rewards, to firms as an incentive to reduce external costs. For example, a firm might receive a subsidy if it builds a plastics recycling plant. This might encourage households and firms to recycle their plastic waste instead of dumping it. The government can also give subsidies to firms that generate external benefits. For example, some governments around the world have given subsidies to the producers of solar energy. This results in an increase in the supply of solar energy, which should stimulate more demand. If more solar energy is used to generate power, then less 'dirty' energy will be produced, which will benefit the environment. Subsidies to university students, in the form of grants, should encourage more people into higher education. As a result, the wider society will benefit from a better-educated population.

One of the problems with government subsidies is the opportunity cost. The money spent by governments on subsidies to reduce external costs or raise external benefits might be spent more effectively on other government projects.

FINES

In some countries, a system of fines is used to reduce external costs. For example, fines may be imposed on those who damage the environment. In 2016, a court in China ordered six unnamed companies to pay a total of US$26 million for polluting the environment discharging waste chemicals into rivers. Also, in Kenya, Mombasa County Government said in 2016 that it would introduce fines to reduce pollution in the nation's main tourist spots. For example, vehicle owners found dumping litter in the streets would be fined KSH 250 000 and motorists or matatu (mini-bus) owners whose vehicles emit smoke would be fined KSH 200 000. Also, drivers who play loud music would be charged a similar amount.

GOVERNMENT REGULATION

Pressure has grown on governments in recent years to pass more legislation to protect the environment. Much of the pressure has emerged because of growing concerns about global warming. Many countries around the world have laws that are designed to protect the environment. Most of these laws are directed at businesses and aim to reduce the external costs of production. For example, in the UK, the Environment Act 1995 was set up to monitor and control pollution. It also laid down regulations relating to polluted land, abandoned mines, national parks, air quality and waste. One of the problems

DID YOU KNOW?

One reason why rail companies are subsidised in many countries is because they take traffic off the road and therefore help to reduce congestion and carbon emissions. Subsidies also reduce demand for new roads and the expense of repairing and maintaining existing roads.

with government regulation in some countries is that even though laws exist, it is not easy to make companies and people obey them. Governments may lack the commitment to enforce laws or they may not have enough resources for enforcement. Also, some of the companies responsible for pollution are powerful, well-resourced multinationals and are prepared to stand firmly against governments in legal disagreements.

POLLUTION PERMITS

Governments can issue a **pollution permit** to a company. These documents give businesses the right to discharge a certain amount of polluting material – say 1 tonne per year. These permits are 'tradable'. This means that a business can sell its pollution permit to another business if it has found a way of reducing its own level of pollution. Therefore, a business that is struggling to control levels of pollution can buy a permit and discharge more polluting material legally. This further creates an incentive in the market for companies to introduce new technology that reduces pollution because they can then sell their pollution permits for cash. This can help to raise profits.

One problem of using pollution permits is that a government has to decide how many of these permits to issue. It will be affected by carbon dioxide reduction deals that each country has signed up to. However, pollution is difficult to measure and a government might end up giving out too few or too many permits. Also, the costs of permit administration are quite high and businesses may disguise their levels of pollution if it is difficult to measure.

GENERAL VOCABULARY

pollution permit government issued document that gives a business the right to discharge a certain quantity of a polluting material into the environment

MULTIPLE-CHOICE QUESTIONS

▶ 1 Which of the following is an example of an external cost resulting from production?

  A Smoke fumes from cigarettes

  B Loud music from a noisy neighbour

  C Noise pollution from an aircraft

  D Job creation resulting from the development of a brownfield site

▶ 2 Which of the following represents social cost?

  A Private costs + Private benefits

  B Private benefits + External benefits

  C Private costs + External costs

  D Private costs – Private benefits

CASE STUDY: POLLUTION IN CHINA

AIR POLLUTION

In recent years, rapid economic growth in China has resulted in some serious pollution problems. For example, in 2010 a report said that in about one-third of the 113 Chinese cities surveyed air quality was below national 'safe' standards. According to the World Bank, 16 of the world's 20 most polluted cities were in China and even the Chinese government admits that about one-fifth of city dwellers breathe badly polluted air. A World Health Organisation (WHO) study said that the amount of airborne suspended particulates in northern China is about 20 times higher than 'safe levels'.

Much of the pollution comes from heavy industry. Many cities are spoiled by the smell of high-sulphur coal and cheap petrol. In Shanghai and Beijing, the pollution is so bad that airports have to be closed because of poor visibility. It has been said that people living above the fifth floor in some city tower blocks cannot see the ground beneath them and the sight of blue sky is rare. At the end of 2015, Beijing authorities finally issued a 'red alert' for air pollution.

WATER POLLUTION

Another problem in China is water pollution. For example, around 60 per cent of China's underground water supplies are polluted. In addition, much of the drinking water in rural areas is unfit for human consumption because of pollution from fertilisers, pesticides and industrial activity. A report in a UK newspaper said that Chinese water authorities admitted in 2012 that up to 40 per cent of the country's rivers are 'seriously polluted'. Also, a report in 2012 found that up to 200 million rural Chinese have no access to clean drinking water. Pollution-induced algae blooms, causing the surface of the water to turn a bright green, often affect China's lakes. In many rural areas there are no systems to treat wastewater.

GOVERNMENT INTERVENTION

In 2016, the Chinese government planned to ban industrial plants, paper mills and refineries that pollute the country's water supplies. This was part of a wider plan to improve water quality. The government wanted to increase the proportion of good quality water to more than 70 per cent by 2020 in seven major river basins. Already the government has blocked some industrial projects, such as coal gasification plants, because they use up too much water or pollute water systems. The plan will focus on small-scale paper factories, leather, printing and dying, oil refineries, electronic plating and pharmaceutical factories. One of the benefits of this plan was expected to be a CN¥ 1.9 trillion boost in China's environmental protection industries.

In addition to higher water and wastewater prices, the wastewater discharge permits and new stricter industrial standards should help to reduce pollution. The price of water discharge permits traded has already risen sharply, as will fines. The new environmental laws will mean tough penalties for polluters with threats of jail for parties responsible for pollution. Recently, the China National Petroleum Corporation agreed to pay CN¥ 100 million following claims it allowed benzene to leak into waterways in Lanzhou, north-east China. The government also plans to target corrupt officials who have encouraged polluting industries in the past.

The government is also targeting air pollution. Companies polluting the atmosphere will also face heavy fines. Non-government organisations will also be encouraged to sue offenders and local governments will be held accountable for introducing environmental policies. New laws give rights to newly established Environmental Protection Bureaux (EPBs) to fine polluting companies. It has been reported that during the first 8 months of the new law's introduction in 2015, there were 405 cases of groups fined for these separate offences, with fines worth a total of CNY 330 million.

▲ Air and water pollution in China

CHAPTER QUESTIONS

The number of cars in China is expected to grow from 90 million to 400 million by 2030.

1 Calculate the percentage increase in the number of cars in China between now and 2030.

2 Comment on the size of the external costs identified in this case.

3 Discuss the methods used by the Chinese government to reduce external costs.

4 Discuss one possible problem of using legislation to reduce external costs.

EXAM PRACTICE: 1.1 THE MARKET SYSTEM

A01 **1** Following a price reduction, the demand for a product remains unchanged. This suggests that demand for the product is: **(1)**

A Inelastic

B Elastic

C Perfectly inelastic

D Perfectly elastic

A02 **2** Which of the following is an example of an external cost? **(1)**

A An increase in job opportunities

B Higher levels of inflation

C Pollution

D Low economic growth

A01 **3** What is meant by a mixed economy? **(2)**

A01 **4** Define the term normal good. **(1)**

A01 **5** Define the term public good. **(1)**

A firm is considering a price increase for one of its products from US$50 to US$55. The quantity demanded at the existing price and the predicted demand at the higher price are shown in Table 1.

	QUANTITY DEMANDED
When price = US$50	4 000 000
When price = US$55	3 200 000

▲ Table 1

SKILLS PROBLEM SOLVING **A02** **6** Using the data in Table 1, calculate the price elasticity of demand for this product. You are advised to show your working. **(2)**

A02 **7** Using Figure 2, show the effects of rising production costs on the equilibrium price and quantity. Label the new curve, the new equilibrium price and quantity. **(3)**

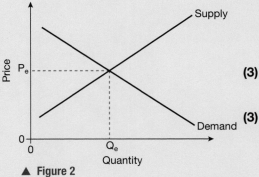

▲ Figure 2

SKILLS CRITICAL THINKING **A02** **8** Explain how excess demand might exist in a market. **(3)**

In 2016, the Iranian government announced that it wanted to privatise its motor vehicle industry. The industry expects to produce 1.6 million cars by 2018 and 2 million by 2020. The sale of the motor car industry is hoped to attract foreign investors. The industry currently operates with outdated technology and needs modernisation to help take advantage of the large export market in the Middle East.

SKILLS CRITICAL THINKING ANALYSIS **A02** **A03** **9** With reference to the data above and your knowledge of economics, analyse the impact of the proposed privatisation on the government of Iran. **(6)**

(Total = 20 marks)

1.2
BUSINESS ECONOMICS

Assessment Objective AO1

Recall, select and communicate knowledge of economic terms, concepts and issues

Assessment Objective AO2

Demonstrate understanding and apply economic knowledge using appropriate terms, concepts, theories and calculations effectively in specific contexts

Assessment Objective AO3

Select, organise and interpret information from sources to investigate and analyse economic issues

Assessment Objective AO4

Evaluate economic information to make reasoned judgements and draw conclusions

Businesses play a huge role in resource use. This section explores the nature of the resources used by businesses, how they organise production, their efficiency in production and how their costs behave in relation to output. The calculation of different costs, revenue and profit will also be discussed. This section also looks at the degree of competition in different markets or industries and the advantages and disadvantages of different market structures.

Specific attention is paid to the role of labour in production. Factors affecting the supply and demand for labour, wage determination, the importance of labour to businesses and the role played by trade unions are all covered. Finally, it is possible for business activity to have a negative impact on people, the environment and the economy. Therefore, the ways in which governments can intervene and deal with such problems is also discussed.

14 THE FACTORS OF PRODUCTION AND SECTORS OF THE ECONOMY

LEARNING OBJECTIVE

Understand the four factors of production: land, labour, capital and enterprise

Understand the different sectors of the economy: primary, secondary and tertiary

Understand the changes in the importance of these sectors in terms of employment and output over time in developing and developed economies

GETTING STARTED

Businesses use a range of resources to make goods or deliver services. Examples include raw materials, components, buildings, energy, tools, equipment, machinery and people. Businesses will try to make the best use of these resources to help keep costs down and become more efficient. Look at the example below.

CASE STUDY: LG ELECTRONICS

LG Electronics is a large South Korean electronics company. It employs over 80 000 people in operations in over 100 different countries. The company is divided into four key divisions:

- home entertainment
- mobile communications
- home appliances, such as televisions and refrigerators
- vehicle components.

In 2015, the company enjoyed revenue of US$48 800 million – slightly lower than the previous year.

▲ Resources used by LG Electronics

1 What resources does LG Electronics use in its production activities?

2 What is the size of LG's workforce?

3 What might be the impact on LG Electronics if resources become more expensive?

WHAT IS PRODUCTION?

SUBJECT VOCABULARY

factors of production resources used to produce goods and services, which include land, labour, capital and enterprise
production process that involves converting resources into goods or services

Production is a process that involves converting resources into goods or services. These goods and services are provided to satisfy the needs and wants of people. Some examples of production include:

■ a baker using flour, yeast, salt and water to make bread

■ a large computer manufacturer using people to assemble components in a factory to make laptop computers

■ a dentist using surgical instruments to extract a diseased tooth

■ a taxi driver using a car to transport a family from their home to an airport.

All of these examples involve using a range of resources to produce goods or provide services. Economists put these resources into different categories called the four **factors of production**. These are summarised in Figure 14.1.

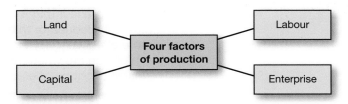

▲ **Figure 14.1** Four factors of production

LAND

Businesses often require a plot of land on which to locate or operate their premises. For example, a large supermarket may require one or more hectares of land on the outskirts of a town to locate a large store with car parking facilities. However, land also includes natural resources, such as coal, oil, iron ore, rainwater, forests, rivers, and fertile soil.

■ Some of the land resources used by businesses are *non-renewable*. This means that once they have been used they cannot be replaced. Examples include mineral deposits like coal, oil, diamonds and limestone. It is likely that one day these resources will completely run out.

■ *Renewable* land resources are those like fish, forests and water, which are replaced by nature. These resources should not run out but there is a risk that if some of them are not protected or over exploited they could disappear.

DID YOU KNOW?

Less than 7 per cent remains of Brazil's Atlantic Forest, which once covered 130 million hectares. Expanding urban areas, increased agricultural and industrial development threaten this rich, endangered forest.

SUBJECT VOCABULARY

human capital value of the workforce or an individual worker
labour people used on production
working capital or circulating capital resources used up in production such as raw materials and components

LABOUR

Labour is the workforce in the economy. Manual workers, skilled workers and managers are all members of a nation's workforce. The quality of individual workers will vary considerably. Each worker is unique, possessing a different set of abilities, characteristics, skills, knowledge, intelligence and emotions. The value of an individual worker to a business is their **human capital**. It is possible to increase the value of human capital through training and education. This will help to make workers more productive.

CAPITAL

Capital is often said to be an artificial resource because it is made by labour. There are two types of capital.

■ **Working capital or circulating capital**, which refers to stocks of raw materials and components that will be used up in production. It also includes stocks of finished goods that are waiting to be sold. Retailers such as supermarkets and chain stores often hold large quantities of stocks because they specialise in selling finished goods.

■ **Fixed capital,** which refers to the factories, offices, shops, machines, tools, equipment and furniture used in production. It is fixed because it will not be converted into a final product. Fixed capital is used in production to convert working capital into goods and services. A company like Honda would have very large stocks of fixed capital because their production methods involve using large amounts of hi-tech machinery.

ENTERPRISE

Entrepreneurs play a special role in the economy. They are responsible for setting up and running businesses. Without them production would not take place. But what exactly do entrepreneurs do?

■ **They come up with a business idea**: This might involve the production of a completely new product. However, this is unusual. Most new businesses supply goods or services that are currently produced by others. That said, an entrepreneur might feel that there is a gap in the market for a slightly different product, or that it is possible to supply exactly the same product more effectively. For example, an entrepreneur might open a new restaurant in a city centre when there are dozens already trading. However, a different cuisine might be offered, such as Lebanese or Malaysian.

■ **They are business owners**: They usually provide some money to help set up a business and are responsible for its direction. For example, a business owner might decide to expand the business in the future or extend the range of products.

■ **Entrepreneurs are risk-takers**: For example, they are likely to risk their own money in the venture. If the business collapses, they may lose some or all of their money. However, if the business is successful they may make a lot of profit. But when they start up, they do not know what will happen – they are taking a risk.

■ **Entrepreneurs are responsible for organising the other three factors of production**: They have to buy and hire other resources such as raw materials, tools, equipment and labour. Entrepreneurs need to use a range of skills such as decision making, people management, time management and financial judgement to organise production factors effectively.

LABOUR- AND CAPITAL-INTENSIVE PRODUCTION

Some firms use relatively more labour than capital when producing goods and services. Therefore, production is said to be labour intensive. For example, in China, labour is very cheap and many firms choose **labour-intensive** production methods. The provision of services is also generally labour intensive. In contrast, if relatively more capital is used than labour, production is said to be **capital intensive**. Firms in Western economies often favour capital-intensive production methods because labour is more difficult to manage. The production of FMCGs often relies on heavily automated plants.

DID YOU KNOW?

Some economies rely heavily on migrants when increasing production. For example, during the 2000s, large numbers of Eastern Europeans moved to Germany looking for work. Many of them were employed in the service industries to help increase production.

ACTIVITY 1

CASE STUDY: ALONSO CORTEZ

Alonso Cortez set up a small bus company to provide an express passenger transport service from Madrid city centre to Madrid Barajas International Airport, Spain. He invested €20 000 in the venture and employed two drivers to work for him. He spent €10 000 on a 50-seater coach and rented a small office in the bus station. He also purchased a computer, mobile phones for his drivers and some office furniture.

▲ An airport bus service

1 Suggest **two** examples of capital that Alonso will use.

2 Why is Alonso Cortez is an entrepreneur? Use evidence in this case to support your answer.

PRIMARY SECTOR

SUBJECT VOCABULARY

primary sector/industry production involving the extraction of raw materials from the earth

The economy is divided into different sectors. In developed countries, such as the USA and Germany, most businesses provide services. They may be fitness centres, insurance brokers, retailers or provide services for businesses, such as market research or IT support. In some countries, such as China, there are large numbers of manufacturers. Finally, in less developed countries, many businesses concentrate on producing agricultural goods. Economic activity is classified into three sectors. In the **primary sector**, business activity involves extracting raw materials from the earth. Here are some examples.

■ **Agriculture** involves a range of farming activities. It is probably the most important primary sector activity for most countries. Most agriculture is concerned with food production. However, other examples include decorative or exotic products, such as cut flowers, nursery plants and tropical fish.

■ **Fishing** involves netting, trapping, angling and trawling fish. It also includes catching or gathering other types of seafood, such as mussels, prawns, lobsters, crabs, scallops and oysters. China is the world's largest fish producer.

■ **Forestry** involves managing forests to provide timber for wood products. Modern forestry also involves protecting the natural environment, providing access and facilities to the public and managing areas for wildlife.

■ **Mining and quarrying** involves the extraction of raw materials such as coal, iron ore, copper, tin, salt and limestone from the ground. This sector also includes the extraction of oil and gas. Saudi Aramco, the largest oil producer in the world, is an example of a primary sector business, as it extracts oil.

SECONDARY SECTOR

SUBJECT VOCABULARY

assembly plants factory where parts are put together to make a final product
secondary sector/industry production involving the processing of raw materials into finished and semi-finished goods

In the **secondary sector**, business activity involves converting raw materials into finished or semi-finished goods. All of manufacturing, processing and construction lie within this sector. Secondary sector business activities include metalworking, car production, textile production, chemical and engineering industries, aerospace manufacturing, energy utilities, engineering, food processing, construction and shipbuilding.

Some businesses focus on the production of semi-finished goods (sometimes called intermediate goods or producer goods). These goods are sold to other businesses and used as inputs for the production of final goods, which are then sold to consumers. Examples of semi-finished goods might include the parts used in **assembly plants** to make motor cars such as steering wheels, car seats, brakes, light fittings, engines, electric cables, switching mechanisms and exhaust systems. A single car may use around 30 000 different parts in assembly.

In many developed countries, the secondary sector has declined in recent years. This is discussed in more detail below.

TERTIARY SECTOR

SUBJECT VOCABULARY

tertiary sector/industry production of services in the economy

The **tertiary sector** involves the provision of a wide variety of services. Some examples are given below:

■ **commercial services**: freight delivery, debt collection, printing and employment agencies

■ **financial services**: banking, insurance, investment advice and pensions

■ **household services**: plumbing, decorating, gardening and house maintenance

■ **leisure services**: television, tourism, hotels and libraries

■ **professional services**: accountancy, legal advice and medical care

■ **transport**: train, taxi, bus and air services.

CHANGES IN THE IMPORTANCE OF DIFFERENT SECTORS

SUBJECT VOCABULARY

de-industrialisation decline in manufacturing

The number of people employed in each sector does not stay constant over time. Different sectors grow and decline according to economic and social changes. In the UK, before the Industrial Revolution began in the late 18th century, most production was in the primary sector. During the 19th century, secondary production expanded rapidly as manufacturing grew during the Industrial Revolution.

However, in the last 60 years, the tertiary sector has started to expand at the expense of both agriculture and manufacturing. The decline in manufacturing is called **de-industrialisation**. Figure 14.2 shows the pattern of employment in the primary, secondary and tertiary sectors in Germany between 1950 and 2015. Similar patterns can be identified in other developed nations.

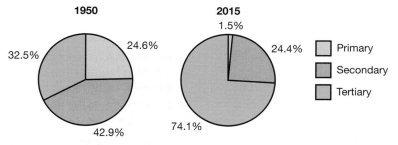

▲ **Figure 14.2** Employment by sector in Germany, 1950 and 2015

Why has manufacturing declined in developed countries while services have grown?

- People may prefer to spend more of their income on services than manufactured goods. There has also been a decline in demand for the goods produced by some of the traditional industries in manufacturing, such as shipbuilding and textiles.

- There is fierce competition in the production of manufactured goods from developing countries such as Brazil, China and India.

- As countries develop, their public sector grows. Since the public sector mainly provides services, this adds to the growth of the tertiary sector.

- Advances in technology mean that employment in manufacturing falls because machines replace people.

ACTIVITY 2

CASE STUDY: OLIVE OIL PRODUCTION

The largest olive growing region in the world is Andalucía, in southern Spain. Many of the growers in this region are owned and run by small family businesses. The Casillas family grow olives on their farm near Cordoba. Each year they sell their harvest to a local business that processes the olives into oil, much of which is exported. Harvest time between November and March is a very busy time for the family. They usually employ about 15 villagers to help out. However, Marco Casillas has recently thought about investing in some harvesting machinery to reduce labour costs and remain competitive.

▲ The olive harvest

▲ Processing olives for oil

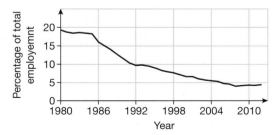

▲ **Figure 14.3** Spanish employment in agriculture (as a percentage of the total employed), 1980–2013

1 What is the difference between the primary and the secondary sectors? (Use examples from this case study.)

Look at Figure 14.3.

2 What has happened to the number of people employed in agriculture in Spain since 1980?

3 Describe **one** possible reason for the pattern described in (**2**).

DEVELOPED AND DEVELOPING COUNTRIES

There are some significant differences in the structure of economies in developed and developing countries. In most developed countries, the primary sector is much less important than the tertiary sector. Only a small percentage of the workforce is employed in the primary sector. In many developing countries, the secondary sector is now growing with some expansion of the tertiary sector. For example, many developing countries in Asia are beginning to manufacture goods on a large scale and to export them to developed countries. In very undeveloped countries, such as some African states, most people are still employed in the primary sector with weak growth in manufacturing and services.

Figure 14.4 shows employment in the different sectors of the economy for two countries – Tanzania and Japan. Clearly, Japan, which is the most developed nation of the two, employs fewer people in agriculture and many more in services than Tanzania.

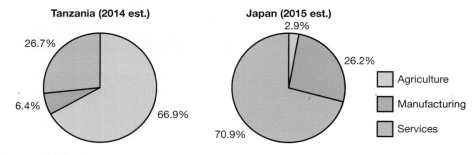

Figure 14.4 Employment by sector, Tanzania and Japan

MULTIPLE-CHOICE QUESTIONS

▶ 1 Which of the following businesses operate in the secondary sector?

   A Santander   **B** Qatar Airways

   C Ford Motor Company   **D** McDonald's

▶ 2 Which of the following is a factor of production?

   A Dental treatment   **B** Wages

   C Birthday card   **D** Enterprise

ECONOMICS IN PRACTICE

CASE STUDY: HISENSE

China is well known for its manufacturing capability. The country has many thousands of manufacturers that make a wide range of goods, which are sold all over the world. China has enjoyed a competitive advantage in manufacturing in the last 30 years due to its cheap and large supply of labour. However, producers in other parts of the world are now taking market share away from China as wages in the country are starting to rise.

One very large Chinese manufacturer is the state-owned company Hisense. Hisense makes white goods, such as washing machines and refrigerators, as well as electrical goods, such as televisions, laptops, mobile phones and many other related products. Hisense has a large number of factories in both China and overseas. However, Hisense also provides a range of services, such as product design, information technology services and property management. Hisense has recently opened two new research and development centres to help speed up product development.

In common with many other countries in the world, the pattern of business has changed in China over time. Figure 14.4 shows the proportion of people in China employed across the primary, secondary and tertiary sectors in 1990 and 2015.

▲ Products made by Hisense

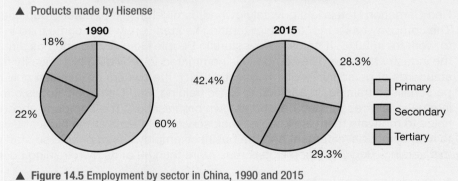

▲ Figure 14.5 Employment by sector in China, 1990 and 2015

CHAPTER QUESTIONS

1 Suggest two renewable resources likely to be used by Hisense.

2 What is the difference between secondary and tertiary production? (Use examples from the case study.)

Look at Figure 14.5.

3 What evidence is there to suggest that China's economy has become more balanced since 1990?

4 Describe what de-industrialisation is.

5 Discuss the main causes of de-industrialisation.

15 PRODUCTIVITY AND DIVISION OF LABOUR

LEARNING OBJECTIVE

- Understand how to define productivity
- Understand the factors that affect productivity: land, labour and capital
- Understand how to define division of labour
- Understand the advantages and disadvantages of the division of labour to workers and businesses

GETTING STARTED

It is important for businesses to make the best possible use of resources during production. This will help keep costs down, raise efficiency and improve their competitiveness in the market. One approach is to make better use of workers to improve labour productivity. Employing specialist labour and training workers can achieve this. Look at the example below.

CASE STUDY: RED CARNATION HOTELS

Red Carnation Hotels is a privately owned, family-run luxury hotel group with 17 hotels on four different continents. The company has a reputation for treating its staff very well. It came third in the *Sunday Times* best companies to work for in 2016. It holds an Investors in People Gold Award and has a staff turnover rate that is far below the industry average. The company is committed to providing high-quality training. The hotels offer very high standards of personal service to guests, which the owners believe can only be delivered if people are given personalised training. In addition to basic training, Red Carnation Hotels offers learning opportunities that are internationally recognised beyond its own organisation. The company encourages staff to develop new skills that helps to motivate them, so keeping their service to guests at the highest level. Workers can get additional training to help career development and the business employs extra people so staff can be released from duty to carry out this training. Red Carnation Hotels runs more than 80 of its own training courses that include:

- foundation skills for team members
- foundation skills for managers
- technical skills for specialist jobs
- developmental skills
- college sponsorships.

1 Suggest **two** possible examples of specialist workers at Red Carnation Hotels.

2 Describe **one** advantage of employing specialist workers.

3 Discuss the importance of training at Red Carnation Hotels.

▲ Training at Red Carnation Hotels

PRODUCTIVITY

SUBJECT VOCABULARY

productivity rate at which goods are produced, and the amount produced in relation to the work, time, and money needed to produce them

Businesses can produce more output if **productivity** can be raised. Productivity is the output per unit of input. For example, the productivity of labour is the *output per worker*. It can be calculated by dividing total output by the number of workers employed. If a car manufacturer produced 24 000 cars in a year with a workforce of 2000, labour productivity would be 12 cars per worker (24 000 ÷ 2000).

Raising productivity in an economy is highly desirable. It means that more goods and services can be produced with the same, or fewer, resources. Countries are likely to measure and monitor productivity levels in their economy. Figure 15.1 shows the pattern of productivity levels in the EU between 2006 and 2016. The graph clearly shows that productivity has increased over the period. The dip in productivity in 2009 was the result of the global financial crisis, which hit the EU quite hard. Over time, firms try to increase productivity because they will lower their costs and make more profit.

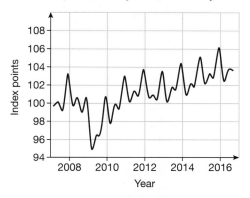

▲ **Figure 15.1** EU productivity, 2006–16

FACTORS AFFECTING PRODUCTIVITY

Productivity can be improved if businesses make better use of their resources. There are a number of ways of raising the productivity of production factors, some of which are outlined below.

LAND

The quality of land varies. Some is fertile and can be used to grow crops or farm cattle. Other land is dry or mountainous and is almost useless. However, measures can be used to make agricultural land more productive.

■ **Fertilisers and pesticides:** Fertilisers are chemicals given to plants to improve their health and appearance, and raise crop yields. Pesticides are used to kill pests. However, pesticides and some fertilisers can harm people, wildlife and the environment. This is why there are strict controls in place over their sale and use.

■ **Drainage:** Some areas of land are unproductive because they are flooded. Drainage can be used to improve the flow of water off this land and thereby make it more productive. A few years ago, with funding help from the World Bank, Uzbekistan set up a major drainage project in the Aral Sea Basin. It was hoped the project would increase the productivity of agriculture in the region and improve the water quality of the Amu Darya River.

■ **Irrigation:** This involves redirecting water from natural sources, such as rivers, lakes or streams, to land that needs more water to become more productive. In crop production, it is mainly used in dry areas and in periods of rainfall shortages but also to protect plants against frost. Irrigation systems are used in many parts of the world.

■ **Reclamation:** In some circumstances, it is possible to create new land from oceans, riverbeds or lakebeds. Clearly, if more fertile land can be found to grow crops, the productivity of the earth's land will rise. To reclaim land water is drained from wetlands. The graph in Figure 15.2 shows that China leads the world in land reclamation, with an extra 11 900 square kilometres of land to date. About 65 per cent of the tidal flats around the Yellow Sea, the Yangzi lowlands and many parts of Shanghai and Wuhan is reclaimed land. Hong Kong International Airport was also built on reclaimed land.

■ **Genetically modified crops:** Land productivity has been increased recently by using genetically modified (GM) crops. Producing GM plants involves transferring genes and DNA from one organism to another. This results in plants that are less likely to be affected by disease, may produce higher yields and, in some cases, more appealing to consumers. However, there has been some opposition to the development of GM crops because genetic engineering is unpredictable. By adding genes from organisms that have never been eaten as food, new proteins are introduced into food chains. There is concern that these could cause allergic reactions or other negative health effects.

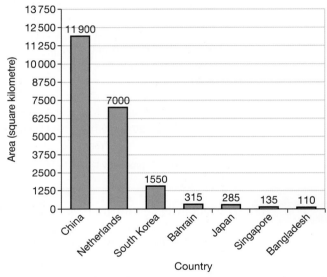

▲ **Figure 15.2** Land reclaimed by the top seven countries with reclaimed land

LABOUR

If the quality of human capital can be improved, there will be gains in labour productivity.

■ **Training:** One way to improve the quality of human capital is to invest in training. Training involves increasing the knowledge and skills of workers so they can do their jobs more effectively. Training is important because it allows employees to acquire new skills, improve existing ones, perform better and be better leaders. It also helps to improve employee motivation so productivity will be higher. It is also important since training involves, in part, teaching new staff how to work safely in their new environment.

The government can help to improve the quality of human capital by investing in the education system. This might involve providing more equipment for schools and improving the quality of teaching. To equip young people with the skills needed in the workplace, a government might invest more in vocational education. Firms can also improve the productivity of their workers by providing their own training. In 'Getting started', Red Carnation Hotels is an example of a business committed to the training of its workers. The company offers its employees about 80 different training courses.

■ **Improved motivation:** If people are motivated at work they will be more productive. One way of motivating staff is to use a financial incentive scheme such as **piece rates**, which involves paying workers according to how much they produce. However, some workers are not motivated by money so non-financial incentives might be needed. For example, a firm might use **job rotation**, which involves an employee changing tasks from time to time. If people are trained to do different jobs, their time at work may be more interesting because there is more variety. They may be less bored and therefore better motivated.

■ **Improved working practices:** The way labour is organised and managed can affect productivity. Working practices are the methods and systems of work that employees are expected to adopt when taking on a job. Labour productivity has been improved significantly by adopting new working practices. For example, it may be possible to change the factory layout by moving workstations or reorganising the flow of production. Such changes can improve labour productivity because workers may not have to move around as much, for example.

■ **Migration:** It might be possible to improve the quality of human capital by attracting skilled workers from overseas. If immigrants are well trained and highly skilled then an economy is likely to become more productive as a result of their presence in the labour market. However, many immigrants are not skilled but still make a positive contribution to productivity. This may be because an untrained migrant childminder might release a highly skilled parent for work, for example. Many countries in the world openly attract large numbers of overseas workers. Figure 15.3 shows a selection of countries and their reliance on immigrant workers. The Middle East relies particularly heavily on immigrant labour.

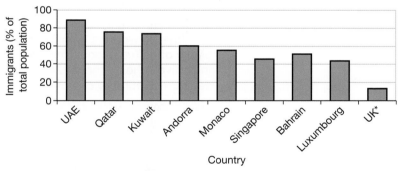

▲ Figure 15.3 Immigrant levels in a selection of countries, 2015   Note: *2014

CAPITAL

Improvements in productivity often arise because of the introduction of new technology. Improvements may occur because more capital is employed, possibly at the expense of labour, or because new technology is more efficient than existing technology. Advances in technology have helped improve productivity in all three sectors of the economy.

■ **Primary sector:** In agriculture, for example, the use of machinery such as tractors, combine harvesters, lifting equipment and irrigation systems have helped to increase output, reduce waste and improve working conditions. Chemicals and pesticides have raised crop yields and biological research has developed plants that are less likely to suffer from diseases.

■ **Secondary sector:** New technology has featured significantly in manufacturing. Many factories and production lines employ complex plant and equipment. This has led to huge increases in productivity. One example includes the use of robots that can handle a lot of the repetitive work in factories. Robots have reduced the need to employ people in jobs that were boring and demotivating. Another example is the use of computer numerically controlled (CNC) machines. These computerised machines come in a variety of forms. They may be involved in processes such as cutting, pressing, moulding, sewing and welding.

■ **Tertiary sector:** The provision of services has historically been labour intensive but the use of technology is becoming more widespread. For example, in retailing there has been a huge growth in internet shopping in the last few years. In some supermarkets there are unstaffed checkout systems. The packaging used today is lighter, stronger and more attractive. In health care, there have been dramatic technological advances in medicine and surgical techniques that have improved productivity. Developments in new vaccines and drugs have reduced patients' suffering and cured some serious diseases. Surgeons can carry out surgery using lasers, viewing the operation on a screen with the use of fibre optic cables.

ACTIVITY 1

CASE STUDY: PRODUCTIVITY IN COFFEE GROWING

The main species of coffee grown around the world are Arabica and Robusta. The world famous Kenyan Arabica, which is mild and high in quality, is grown on rich mountain soils. Here, the climate is ideal for coffee growing. The temperature range does not exceed 19°C (35°F) and the rainfall is evenly distributed throughout the year. Kenya's coffee growing regions are to be found on broad and gently rounded hills. The fertile soil is deep and well drained.

One coffee grower, Bernard Chukwu, is experienced and successful. He employs 24 workers on his estate and in 2015 produced a total of 380 sacks of coffee beans. However, in 2016, Bernard introduced a financial incentive scheme for workers and as a result production rose to 450 sacks. The number of workers he employed also fell in 2016 to 22.

▲ Coffee harvesting in Kenya

1 Calculate the labour productivity on Bernard's estate in 2015 and 2016.

2 What is the possible reason for the change in labour productivity on Bernard's estate?

3 How might farmers improve the productivity of land? Give two methods in your explanation.

THE DIVISION OF LABOUR

SUBJECT VOCABULARY

division of labour breaking down of the production process into small parts with each worker allocated to a specific task

specialisation production of a limited range of goods by individuals, firms, regions or countries

In many businesses, the production process is broken down into small parts and each worker is allocated a specific task. This is called the **division of labour**. It allows people to concentrate on the task or skill at which they are best. For example, in house construction, specialists are often employed throughout the whole construction process. A building contractor may employ specialist workers, such as bricklayers, electricians, plumbers, roofers, carpenters, painters, decorators, glaziers and labourers. It is argued that **specialisation** raises efficiency in firms and the economy.

DIVISION OF LABOUR AND THE WORKER

An individual worker will benefit from focusing on one specific work task but there will also be some disadvantages.

ADVANTAGES

Focusing on the same task allows the worker to become more skilled at doing that task. It is often said that 'practice makes perfect' and constant repetition of the same task will usually mean a worker will get better and better. Therefore, workers with well practised skills will be able to find employment more easily. Also, the more highly skilled they are, the more they are likely to get paid. Workers can also learn new skills or improve their existing ones. For example, an IT worker will need to keep updated with new technological developments. Finally, workers may enjoy more job satisfaction if they are highly skilled in a specialist task.

DISADVANTAGES

One of the main problems with specialisation is that the work can become boring because it is repetitive. This is most likely to happen if a particular task requires little skill. For example, workers employed on a production line responsible for an assembly task that only takes 30 seconds are likely to get very bored if that single task has to be repeated 120 times an hour, 960 times a day and nearly 4000 times a week! This boredom may lead to job dissatisfaction and affect motivation. Repetitive tasks can also have health implications for workers, such as joint wear. Another serious problem for workers that might be too specialised is the risk of unemployment.

DIVISION OF LABOUR AND BUSINESSES

Generally, if workers are more specialised, efficiency improves and businesses can make more profit. However, there are also some disadvantages regarding the division of labour for firms.

ADVANTAGES

- Efficiency is improved because, through specialisation, workers can perform tasks more quickly and more accurately. There are fewer mistakes and productivity (output per worker) will rise. People who try to perform a wide range of tasks may find it difficult to develop the skills needed to be excellent at each one. Therefore their productivity will be lower.

- A greater use of specialist tools, machinery and equipment is possible when workers specialise. For example, specialist CAD (computer-aided design) software is available for production designers, which they can use to improve efficiency.

- Production time is reduced because workers do not have to waste time moving from one task to another. This often involves moving around the workplace collecting tools, changing workstations and resetting machinery. Specialists are likely to remain at the same workstation repeating their task without the need to move around.

■ The organisation of production becomes easier. This is because specialist workers can fit more easily into a structured system of production, such as a production line.

DISADVANTAGES

■ One of the main problems of the division of labour is that if tasks are too repetitive and boring, people become dissatisfied and poorly motivated. This might result in poor-quality work, staff arriving at work late, increased rates of absence and high staff turnover. In the worst cases, people become detached and try to avoid work. This will obviously reduce productivity and have an impact on profitability.

■ Problems can also occur if one stage of production depends on another stage. If one stage breaks down, all other stages may also have to be stopped. For example, if a specialist supplier of parts to an assembly plant fails to deliver, the whole assembly plant may have to stop production. This is called interdependence.

■ Specialisation may result in a loss of flexibility in the workplace. For example, if a highly skilled and specialist worker is absent, and there is no one else with those skills, production may be disrupted.

ACTIVITY 2

CASE STUDY: PINTERS LTD

Pinters Ltd build catamarans and employ 20 staff. The production process has four stages.

■ **Moulding:** Production begins with the body of the catamaran. Moulds are used to shape resin, cloth and fiberglass into separate parts. These are then attached together to create the fiberglass shell of the boats.

■ **Trimming:** The windows, ports, hatches and other openings are cut out from the fibreglass shells and cleaned. Imperfections are ground out and repaired at a central inspection station.

■ **Assembly:** The boat components are joined using assembly lines. The method of bringing the pieces to the stations where workers and their tools are located is extremely efficient in reducing wasted time.

■ **Finishing:** The engine and electronics are tested as well as all the hulls for leaks. The finished boats then go to a final inspection stage where the entire craft is checked for quality.

Four workers are employed in each production stage and four in the office. One of the office workers is a specialist marketing manager, one is a specialist designer and the other two handle all the accounts and administration. The workers in each of the production stages require 2 years of on-the-job training. After that, they remain in the same area.

▲ Building a catamaran requires very specialist skills

1 What is meant by the division of labour? Use the example in this case to support your answer.

2 Suggest two disadvantages to Pinter's employees of specialising in one area of production.

3 To what extent do the advantages of the division of labour outweigh the disadvantages at Pinters Ltd?

MULTIPLE-CHOICE QUESTIONS

▶ 1 Which of the following is a non-financial method of motivating workers?

A Job rotation

B Profit sharing

C Piece rates

D Performance-related pay

▶ 2 Which of the following is a reason why specialist workers might get bored?

A The training is too lengthy

B Tasks can be very repetitive

C The pay is low

D There is no opportunity for social interaction at work

ECONOMICS IN PRACTICE

CASE STUDY: PENTANGLE PLASTICS

Pentangle Plastics makes plastic components for mobile phones. The company is based in Shanghai, China, and has recently hired a new production manager. The purpose of the new role was to improve productivity. In 2014, the company produced 25 million units with a workforce of 50. In 2015, output fell to 24 million units with the same numbers employed. As a result, Pentangle Plastics was beginning to lose its competitive edge. The new manager promised to improve labour productivity within 12 months. The manager carried out a survey among staff and discovered that they were bored and poorly motivated. The manager also promised to make further productivity gains by introducing new technology over a 3-year period.

▲ A robot operating in the plastics industry

CHAPTER QUESTIONS

1 Describe what labour productivity is.

2 Calculate labour productivity at Pentangle Plastics in 2014 and 2015 to show that it has fallen.

3 Suggest two ways in which the production manager can improve motivation at the company by reducing boredom.

4 The new manager favours the introduction of robots in the factory. How might this reduce workers' boredom?

5 Discuss the advantages to

   a Pentangle Plastics and

   b the Chinese economy, of improving productivity at the factory.

16 BUSINESS COSTS, REVENUES AND PROFIT

LEARNING OBJECTIVE

Understand how to define and calculate:

- total revenue
- total fixed costs
- total variable costs
- total costs
- average total costs
- profit

GETTING STARTED

Firms incur expenses when they produce goods and services. These expenses are called costs and are classified by economists according to how they behave when output changes. For example, when output rises some costs also rise. However, there are other costs that stay the same when output rises. Look at the example below.

CASE STUDY: GREENWAY CONSTRUCTION

Finders Construction is a specialist house builder. It is established family business with a successful 79-year trading history. The company buys plots of land and builds residential properties, which it markets to individuals. Like any other business, it incurs a wide range of costs. Some examples of costs incurred in the construction of a house include bricks, sand, cement, timber, pipes, glass, electrical wire, glass, plastic window frames and insulation materials. Other costs include: labour; machinery, such as cement mixers, lifting gear, vehicles; tools and equipment, such as spades, trowels, wire cutters, saws, power tools; protective clothing; computers; smartphones and office furniture at the company office.

▲ Construction at a building site

Finders Construction employs 140 people and builds about 350 houses each year. In 2016, its total costs were US$56 450 200 and total revenue from selling houses was US$64 340 700.

1 Suggest **four** costs incurred by Finders Construction that will rise when more houses are built.

2 Suggest **four** costs incurred by Finders Construction that remain unchanged when more houses are built.

3 Calculate the profit made by Finders Construction in 2016.

TOTAL FIXED COSTS

SUBJECT VOCABULARY

costs expenses that must be met when setting up and running a business
fixed costs (also known as overheads) costs that do not vary with the level of output

Costs can be classified according to how they behave when output changes. Some production costs remain the same whatever the level of output. These are called **fixed costs**. Examples of fixed costs include rent, business rates, advertising, insurance premiums, interest payments, and research and development costs. These costs will not increase even if a firm produces more output. However, fixed costs will still have to be met if the firm produces nothing. Fixed costs are sometimes called overheads.

Fixed costs can be shown on a graph. Figure 16.1 shows the total fixed cost for Frampton Training. This business provides training courses for HGV drivers. The business incurs total fixed costs of US$40 000 p.a. The graph shows that fixed costs stay the same at all levels of output. If the business provides 100 training places, fixed costs are US$40 000. If the number of places rises to 150, total fixed costs are still US$40 000.

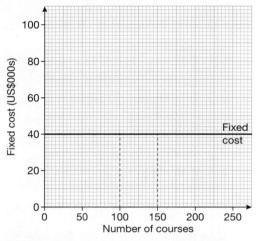

▲ **Figure 16.1** Fixed costs for Frampton Training

TOTAL VARIABLE COSTS

SUBJECT VOCABULARY

variable costs costs that change when output levels change

Production costs that change when the level of output changes are called **variable costs**. If a firm produces more output, variable costs will increase. Similarly, if output levels are cut, variable costs will fall. Examples of variable costs include raw materials, packaging, fuel and labour. If a firm produces nothing, variable costs will be zero. If the variable cost per unit is mutliplied by the number of units produced, this will give the total variable cost, ie TVC = VC × Q.

Figure 16.2 shows variable costs for Frampton Training. The business has variable costs of US$500 per course. If 100 courses are provided, the total variable costs will be US$50 000 (100 × US$500). If 50 extra courses are provided, total variable costs rise to US$75 000 (150 × US$500). The graph shows that variable costs change whenever output changes.

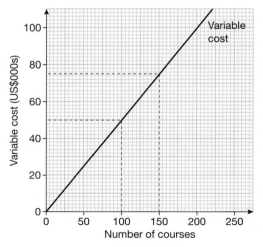

▲ **Figure 16.2** Variable costs for Frampton Training

TOTAL COSTS

SUBJECT VOCABULARY

total cost fixed costs and variable costs added together

The cost to a firm of producing all output over a period is called **total cost**. Total cost (TC) can be calculated by adding ftotal fixed costs (TFC) and total variable costs (TVC) together.

TC = TFC + TVC

If Frampton Training provides places for 100 training courses, total cost will be:

TC   = US$40 000 + (100 × US$500)

        = US$40 000 + US$50 000

        = US$90 000

The total cost graph in Figure 16.3 shows that total cost increases from US$90 000 to US$115 000 when the number of courses provided rises from 100 to 150.

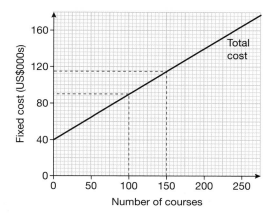

▲ **Figure 16.3** Total cost for Frampton Training

ACTIVITY 1

CASE STUDY: KANDASAN CRICKET BATS

Kandasan Cricket Bats manufactures high-quality cricket bats. The company, which is based in Colombo, Sri Lanka, employs six skilled craftsmen. Table 16.1 shows some cost information for the business in 2015.

Rent	LKR 50 000 p.a.
Business rates	LKR 5000 p.a.
Other fixed costs	LKR 25 000 p.a.
Wood	LKR 30 per bat
Other raw materials	LKR 10 per bat
Labour	LKR 50 per bat
Other variable costs	LKR 10 per bat

▲ **Table 16.1** Cost information for Kandasan Cricket Bats

▲ Making cricket bats

1   What is meant by a fixed cost? Use examples from the case to support your answer.

In 2015, Kandasan Cricket Bats produced 4800 bats.

2   Calculate the total cost of production.

In 2016, the rent increased to LKR 60 000.

3   Calculate the total cost of producing 6000 bats taking into account this cost increase.

AVERAGE COSTS

The average cost of production is the cost of producing a single unit of output. The formula for calculating average cost is:

$$\text{Average cost} = \frac{\text{Total cost}}{\text{Quantity produced}}$$

So, for example, the average cost of a training course provided by Frampton Training, if 100 places were provided, would be:

$$AC = \frac{TC}{Q} = \frac{\text{US\$90 000}}{100} = \text{US\$900}$$

This means that each course provided to trainee HGV drivers costs Frampton Training US$900.

THE AVERAGE COST CURVE

The average costs for a business can be presented graphically. An example is shown in Figure 16.4. The average cost curve is U-shaped, which means that as output increases, average costs fall at first, reach a minimum and then start to rise. At an output level of 100 units, the average cost is £20.

■   If output is increased to 300 units, the average cost falls to £7.50. This is the minimum average cost in this example.

■   If output is increased further still to 400 units, average costs are now higher at £10.

The reason for the shape of the average cost curve is discussed in Chapter 17 (pages 124–131).

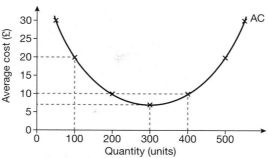

▲ Figure 16.4 Average cost curve

TOTAL REVENUE

The amount of money a firm receives from selling its output is called total revenue. Total revenue can be calculated by multiplying the price of each unit by the number of units sold:

Total revenue = Price × Quantity

If Frampton Training, in the earlier example, charged US$1500 for its HGV training courses, the total revenue from the sale of 100 courses is given by:

Total revenue = US$1500 × 100 = US$150 000

This means that Frampton Training generated US$150 000 of revenue from providing 100 places on its HGV driving course.

CALCULATING PROFIT

One of the main reasons why firms calculate their costs and revenue is to work out profit or loss. Profit is the difference between total revenue and total costs.

Profit = Total revenue – Total costs

The profit made by Frampton Training from providing 100 places is given by:

Profit   = US$150 000 × 100 – (US$40 000 + US$50 000)

         = US$150 000 – US$90 000

         = US$60 000

It is possible to calculate the profit for a firm at any level of output using this method. If total costs exceed total revenue, then a loss is made.

ACTIVITY 2

CASE STUDY: JENKINS LTD

Jenkins Ltd manufactures electronic control systems that open and shut swing gates. Its most popular product is the underground system, which sells for £250. The systems are assembled in a factory using components supplied by firms nearby. In 2015, Jenkins sold 4500 systems. Total fixed costs for the year were £160 000 and variable costs were £120 per system.

In 2015, Jenkins produced and sold 4500 control systems.

1 Calculate the total cost.

2 Calculate the total revenue.

3 Calculate the profit.

In 2016, fixed costs and the price charged remained the same. However, variable costs rose to £140 per system.

4 Calculate the profit made in 2016 if 5200 systems were sold.

MULTIPLE-CHOICE QUESTIONS

▶ 1 If total cost is US$35 000 000 and output is 100 000 units, what is average cost?

A US$100 000

B US$35

C US$350

D US$3500

▶ 2 If variable cost is £10 per unit and fixed costs are £400 000, what is the total cost of producing 50 000 units?

A £900 000

B £450 000

C £4 000 000

D £500 000

ECONOMICS IN PRACTICE

CASE STUDY: MAHABIR METALS

Mahabir Metals is a medium-sized engineering company. In the last 6 years, the business has begun to specialise in the production of signage, particularly road signs. Around 80 per cent of its business comes from government contracts. Mahabir Metals has benefitted from government investment in road building in India. One of its recent orders was for 1000 speed limit signs. Table 16.2 shows some cost information for the order. The fixed costs for the order were expected to be Rs600 000. Most of this cost was to pay for a specialist machine. The price of each sign would be Rs2500.

VARIABLE COSTS PER SIGN	RS
Sheet metal	200
Metal pipe	500
Clips and fastenings	200
Paint	100
Labour	300
Other variable costs	100

▲ Table 16.2 Cost information for an order

▲ Road signs

CHAPTER QUESTIONS

1 Describe what variable costs are.

2 For the new order, calculate **(a)** total variable cost and **(b)** total cost.

3 Plot fixed cost, variable cost and total cost on a graph. (Use a range of output of 0 to 1000 units.)

4 Calculate the profit made on the order.

5 Calculate the average cost of each sign.

Six months later, Mahabir Metals gets another order for 1500 speed limit signs. The variable costs remain the same but fixed costs are only Rs200 000. However, the government will only pay Rs1500 for each sign.

6 Consider whether Mahabir Metals should accept the order. Show all your calculations.

17 ECONOMIES AND DISECONOMIES OF SCALE

LEARNING OBJECTIVE

- Understand how to define economies of scale and internal economies of scale

- Understand the long run average cost curve and the impact economies and diseconomies of scale have on its shape

- Understand the types of internal economies of scale: purchasing, marketing, technical, financial, managerial and risk bearing

- Understand how to define external economies of scale

- Understand the types of external economies of scale: skilled labour, infrastructure, access to suppliers, similar businesses in the area

- Understand how to define diseconomies of scale

- Understand the types of diseconomies of scale: bureaucracy, communication problems, lack of control and the distance between top management and workers at the bottom of the organisation

SUBJECT VOCABULARY

scale size of a business

GETTING STARTED

Setting up a business and surviving is challenging. However, once a business is established, the owners often want it to grow. They want to increase the **scale** of the business. This means that they want to increase its size. One of the benefits of increasing the scale of operations is that certain costs start to fall. Look at the examples below.

CASE STUDY: GILLY'S SNACK SHACK

Gilly's Snack Shack sells sandwiches and other snacks from a kiosk by Grant Park, in central Chicago, Illinois, USA. It serves office workers, shoppers and tourists. Gilly's Snack Shack sells about 900 sandwiches a week. Gilly, the owner, buys sandwich ingredients from supermarkets and wholesalers. For example, the business buys about 20 loaves of bread per day at a cost of US$1.80 each. Tomatoes cost US$2.50 per kilogram and cheese is US$7.00 per kilogram. Most of their sandwiches sell for US$2.00. The business has a US$5000 loan, which was taken out to help set up the business. An interest rate of 8.9 per cent is paid on the loan.

CASE STUDY: GF FOODS

GF Foods is a large catering company based in Chicago. It supplies sandwiches to supermarkets and sells about one million sandwiches a week. GF Foods employs 110 workers and buys ingredients direct from farmers and manufacturers. For example, it buys tomatoes from a local farm for US$1.50 per kilogram and cheese for US$5.00 per kilogram. It buys thousands of loaves of bread from a Chicago baker for US$1.10 each. It sells sandwiches at an average price of US$1.40 per packet. GF Foods pays 7.5 per cent interest on a US$1 million loan.

▲ Sandwich production

1 Which of the two businesses is the largest?

2 Which business has the lowest costs?

3 Which firm is likely to be the most efficient?

4 How might GF Foods benefit from its cost advantage?

5 In groups, draw up a list of the possible advantages that very large firms have over their smaller rivals. Present your ideas to the rest of the class.

ECONOMIES OF SCALE

Large firms can usually produce goods more cheaply than small firms. The size of a firm has an important effect on the average costs of production. As a firm increases its size, average costs start to fall. This is because of **economies of scale** and is shown in Figure 17.1. When the business is producing 20 000 units of output, the average cost is US$25. If it raises output to 40 000 units, average costs fall to US$15. The firm could carry on expanding and lower its average costs until it is large enough to produce 70 000 units. At this level of output average costs are minimised at US$10 per unit. It is the ideal size because average costs are at an absolute minimum. At this level of output the firm is efficient and waste is avoided. If the firm grows beyond 70 000 units, average costs will start to rise. For example, if the firm increases its size and produces 90 000 units, average costs will now rise to US$12.50 per unit. This is because of **diseconomies of scale**, which occur because of inefficiency.

SUBJECT VOCABULARY

diseconomies of scale rising average costs when a firm becomes too big
economies of scale falling average costs due to expansion

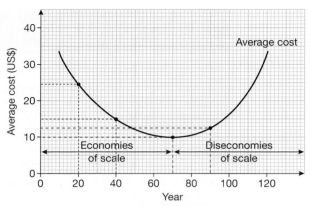

▲ **Figure 17.1** Economies and diseconomies of scale

INTERNAL ECONOMIES OF SCALE

Internal economies of scale are the cost benefits that an individual firm can enjoy when it grows. The reasons why costs fall are summarised in Figure 17.2.

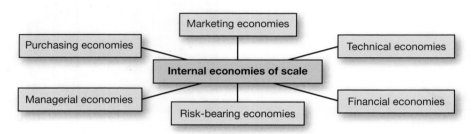

▲ **Figure 17.2** Sources of internal economies of scale

PURCHASING ECONOMIES

Large firms that buy lots of resources get cheaper rates. Suppliers offer discounts to firms that buy raw materials and components in bulk. This is similar to consumers buying multi-packs in supermarkets – they are better value for money. **Bulk buying** is a purchasing economy. In 'Getting started' above, GF Foods was able to buy bread for US$1.10 a loaf. However, Gilly's Snack Shack was having to pay US$1.80 because it was buying smaller quantities. In fact, all the purchases made by GF Foods were cheaper than those of Gilly's Snack Shack for the same products.

MARKETING ECONOMIES

A number of marketing economies exist. For example, it may be cost effective for a large firm to run its own delivery vehicles. For a large firm, with lots of deliveries to make, this would be cheaper than paying a distributor. Marketing economies can occur because some marketing costs, such as producing a television advert, are fixed. These costs can be spread over more units of output for a larger firm. Therefore, the average cost of the advert is smaller for a large firm.

TECHNICAL ECONOMIES

Technical economies occur because larger factories are often more efficient than smaller ones. There can be more specialisation and more investment in machinery. One example of a technical economy is the way a large firm will make better use of an essential resource than a smaller firm. For example, a small engineering company may buy some CAD (computer-aided design) software for US$1000. It is needed by the business but is only used for one day a week. A much larger engineering company may buy the same software but use it every day of the week. Clearly, the larger company is making better use of the software and therefore its average cost will fall.

FINANCIAL ECONOMIES

Large firms can get access to money more cheaply. They also have a wider variety of sources to choose from. For example, a large limited company can raise money by selling shares. This option is not available to a sole trader. Large firms can put pressure on banks when negotiating the price of loans. Banks are often happier lending large amounts to large companies at lower interest rates. In 'Getting started', GF Foods was paying 7.5 per cent to borrow US$1 million. In contrast, Gilly's Snack Shack was paying 8.9 per cent to borrow just US$5000.

MANAGERIAL ECONOMIES

As firms expand, they can afford specialist managers. A small business may employ a general manager responsible for finance, human resources, marketing and production. The manager may find this role demanding and may be weak in some areas of the job. A large firm can employ specialists and, as a result, efficiency is likely to improve and average costs fall.

RISK-BEARING ECONOMIES

Larger firms are more likely to have wider product ranges and sell into a wider variety of markets. This reduces the risk in business. For example, many supermarkets have extended their product ranges to include household goods, consumer durables, books, a café, financial services, garden furniture, pharmaceuticals and clothes.

ACTIVITY 1

CASE STUDY: IKEA

IKEA is a Swedish multinational that designs and sells ready-to-assemble furniture, such as tables, chairs and beds. It also sells appliances and domestic products. IKEA operates about 500 large stores in nearly 50 different countries. Its own factories manufacture many of its product lines. One of the reasons for its success has been its ability to keep manufacturing costs down. IKEA is very large and is able to exploit economies of scale.

On the technical side, IKEA benefits from specialisation. It employs specialist workers in different parts of the world to produce different products and components. This division of labour allows average costs to be reduced since specialists are more efficient. IKEA also invests heavily in research and development. This allows the business to develop cost effective products and money-saving production techniques.

IKEA also exploits risk-bearing economies. Although the business first began trading in furniture, IKEA is now involved in other markets such as appliances and domestic products. It operates restaurants and food markets with many stores serving food throughout the day. It also provides childcare with some stores offering safe and supervised play areas. This growth in the business means that IKEA can benefit from good trading conditions in different markets. It can also cope with difficult trading conditions in one market by relying on sales in others.

▲ Inside an IKEA factory

1 Discuss how IKEA is exploiting **(a)** technical economies of scale and **(b)** risk-bearing economies of scale.

EXTERNAL ECONOMIES OF SCALE

Sometimes all firms in an industry can enjoy falling average costs as the whole industry grows. This is called **external economies of scale**. External economies of scale are more likely to occur if an industry is concentrated in a particular region.

SKILLED LABOUR

If an industry is concentrated in one area, there may be a build-up of labour with the skills and work experience required by that industry. As a result, training costs will be lower when workers are recruited. It is also likely that local schools and colleges will provide vocational courses that are required by local industry.

INFRASTRUCTURE

If a particular industry dominates a region, the roads, railways, ports, buildings and other facilities will be shaped to suit that industry's needs. For example, a specialised industrial estate may be developed to help a local IT industry.

ACCESS TO SUPPLIERS

An established industry in a region will encourage suppliers in that industry to set up close by. Specialist marketing, cleaning, banking, waste disposal, distribution, maintenance and components suppliers are likely to be attracted to the area. All firms in the industry will benefit from their services, like the car industry in the Midlands in England, for example.

SIMILAR BUSINESSES IN THE AREA

When firms in the same industry are located close to each other, they are likely to cooperate with each other so that they can all gain. For example, they might work together to share the cost and benefits of a research and development centre, as high-tech businesses do in Silicon Valley, California, USA.

DISECONOMIES OF SCALE

Figure 17.1 shows that if a firm continues to expand beyond a certain point average costs eventually rise. This is because the firm suffers from diseconomies of scale. Average costs start to rise because aspects of production become inefficient. The possible reasons why this might happen are discussed below.

BUREAUCRACY

Larger business rely more on **bureaucracy**. If a business becomes too bureaucratic, it means that too many resources are used in administration. Too much time may be spent filling in forms or writing reports. Also, decision making may be too slow and communication channels too long. If resources are wasted in administration, average costs will start to rise.

COMMUNICATION PROBLEMS

Some very large organisations employ hundreds of thousands of workers. They are likely to be spread all over the world. Workers in different countries speak different languages and have different cultures. There are also time differences between different global operations. This can make communication in an organisation challenging.

LACK OF CONTROL

A very large business may be difficult to control and **coordinate**. Thousands of employees, billions of pounds and dozens of plants all over the world can make running a large organisation demanding. There may be a need for more supervision and more layers of management, which will raise costs.

DISTANCE BETWEEN SENIOR STAFF AND SHOP FLOOR WORKERS

If a firm becomes too big, relations between workers and managers may worsen. There may be many layers of management between the chairperson at the top and the shop floor workers in a factory. As a result, senior managers might be so far removed from those at the bottom of the organisation that they may not be aware of their needs. This lack of understanding may result in many workers becoming demotivated. As a result, conflicts may occur and resources may be wasted resolving them.

ACTIVITY 2

CASE STUDY: VOLKSWAGEN

In 2015, Volkswagen (VW), the very large German car manufacturer, was caught falsifying emissions data on its diesel cars. VW had been fitting some special software in its diesel vehicles called a 'defeat device'. This fine-tunes the engine's performance so that nitrogen oxide emissions are limited when being tested. However, when the cars return to the road, the emissions levels rise again. This meant that the cars would pass the strict emissions test.

It appears that around 11 million cars were fitted with this device and since its discovery VW has suffered badly. For example, the value of the company fell by around €30 000 million following a flood of bad publicity across the world. A number of theories have been suggested to explain why this scandal was allowed to happen. Some analysts have suggested that the company is now too big and suffering from diseconomies of scale. Giant companies like VW, which employs over 500 000 employees, become huge bureaucracies rather than commercial organisations. Controlling and monitoring such vast operations, with factories, offices, warehouses and other operational facilities all over the world becomes a very challenging task for managers. Although economies of scale are crucial in the mass production of cars, some people think that a number of companies are beginning to experience diseconomies of scale – particularly when managing information in the organisation.

It is possible that VW has grown too big to manage. It has been claimed that the chief executive officer (CEO) of VW did not know about this activity. In such a large organisation, this might be true. It is unlikely that any CEO, however capable, committed and well-organised, could be in complete control of such a huge quantity of resources that are located all over the world.

To conclude, as businesses grow, at some point, the disadvantages of being big are eventually greater than the benefits. These costs may include:

- loss of control
- communications problems
- the need for more supervision and extra layers of management
- the increasing amounts of delegation
- the geographical spread of resources
- the near impossibility of establishing a common business culture
- employing a single unified IT system.

This may have been the cause of VWs current problems.

▲ A VW vehicle being tested for emissions

1 What is meant by diseconomies of scale?

2 Assess whether VW has experienced diseconomies of scale in its organisation.

MULTIPLE-CHOICE QUESTIONS

▶ 1 Employing a specialist cost accountant in a growing business is an example of which type of economy?

A Technical economy

B Risk-bearing economy

C Managerial economy

D Marketing economy

▶ 2 Internal economies of scale affect costs how?

A Falling total costs

B Rising average costs

C Rising variable costs

D Falling average costs

CASE STUDY: FLAMBOYANCE

Flamboyance is a clothes chain based in Singapore. It sells high-quality clothes, shoes and fashion accessories. It has an excellent reputation for good customer service and operates 21 shops in Singapore and a further 52 in other Asian countries. In 2012, Flamboyance employed a specialist marketing manager. The new manager raised the profile of the Flamboyance brand right across Singapore. As a result, the company grew quickly and became very profitable. Flamboyance buys most of its clothes and shoes from China.

▲ Inside a high-quality clothes store

In 2015, Flamboyance bought a clothes chain in the Middle East. It was thought that the company could further exploit economies of scale and make even more profit. However, there were some problems. Communications became difficult due to language and cultural difficulties. There was also a lack of employee understanding. Many of the staff did not seem to care whether the company succeeded or not. Some of the store managers also complained that the company was becoming too bureaucratic.

CHAPTER QUESTIONS

1 Describe what the term 'scale' in business is.

2 What effect will economies and diseconomies of scale have on Flamboyance's average cost?

3 Why is employing a specialist marketing manager an economy of scale?

4 Discuss whether or not Flamboyance has benefited from purchasing economies of scale.

5 Consider the extent to which Flamboyance is experiencing diseconomies of scale.

18 COMPETITIVE MARKETS

LEARNING OBJECTIVE

■ Understand the advantages and disadvantages of competition to firms, consumers and the economy including:

- efficiency
- choice
- quality
- innovation
- price

SUBJECT VOCABULARY

competition rivalry that exists between firms when trying to sell goods to the same group of customers

GETTING STARTED

Not all markets are the same. In some markets, lots of firms compete with each other to sell their goods to customers. They use a variety of methods, such as advertising, promotions and special offers, to encourage customers to buy their products. In other markets, a firm may face very little **competition**. Look at these examples.

CASE STUDY: ONATEL

Onatel is a communications company and is the only internet provider in Burkina Faso, a small country in West Africa. In October 2016, a strike by Onatel's employees cut all internet connections in the country for over a week. Arouna Ouédraogo, an information technology specialist in Burkina Faso, said people without the internet became desperate, rushing to his internet cafe with contracts to sign and documents to send. Unfortunately, he could not help them because there was no internet anywhere in the country. Some people were so desperate to get on the internet that they flew to Bamako, in neighbouring Mali, for access. Burkina Faso is one of the few African countries that have only one internet provider. Ouédraogo said that the internet was too expensive and the service was very poor. He argued that some competition was needed.

▲ Onatel is the only internet provider in Burkina Faso

GENERAL VOCABULARY

deregulation to remove or reduce the number of government controls on a particular business activity, done to make companies work more effectively and to increase competition

CASE STUDY: MILK PRODUCTION IN AUSTRALIA

The dairy industry employs about 38 000 people in Australia in around 6000 farms. Unlike many countries around the world, there is no legal control over the price milk processing companies pay farmers for their milk. Since **deregulation** in 2000/01, all prices within the industry are set by market forces. This means that all farmers supplying the market in a particular Australian state would expect to get much the same for a litre of milk. In 2016, farmers in New South Wales were getting around 50 cents a litre. This was slightly more than they were getting in 2010 when it was 48.7 cents.

▲ Dairy farming

1 How much competition exists in each of these markets?

2 How might consumers benefit from competition in a market?

3 In groups, identify five businesses in your area where you think there is a lot of competition, and five where you think there is very little competition. Present your ideas to the rest of the class giving the reasons for your choices.

WHAT IS A COMPETITIVE MARKET?

SUBJECT VOCABULARY

barriers to entry obstacles that might discourage a firm from entering a market

Competition is the rivalry that exists between firms when trying to sell goods in a particular market. In some markets, there is a lot of competition. In 'Getting started', the market for milk in Australia is very competitive, with around 6000 farms competing for customers. However, in other markets, there is very little competition. In 'Getting started', Onatel is the only internet supplier in the country of Burkina Faso. No other firm competes with Onatel. In a competitive market, there are likely to be some common features.

■ There is a large number of buyers and sellers.

■ The products sold by each firm are close substitutes for each other.

■ Low **barriers to entry**, which means that it is fairly easy to break into the market. For example, it is not technically difficult or it does not require too much capital.

■ Each firm has almost no control over the price charged. For example, if a firm tries to charge more than its rivals it is likely to lose business.

■ There is a free flow of information about the nature of products, availability at different outlets, prices, methods of production and the cost and availability of production factors.

ACTIVITY 1

CASE STUDY: MARKET FOR CURRENCY

In any city in most countries it is possible to obtain foreign currency for a holiday abroad from a wide range of outlets. Banks, building societies, hotels, post offices, specialist exchange dealers and travel agents are some examples. It is also possible to buy foreign currency over the internet. The price charged by each supplier is very similar. Table 18.1 shows euro prices for AUD 5000 at a selection of outlets in a French city.

OUTLET	A	B	C	D	E	F
PRICE (€)	3497	3500	3509	3492	3494	3496

▲ Table 18.1 The prices of AUD 5000 in six outlets

▲ Foreign exchange outlet

1 Why is the market competitive in this case?

2 Which outlet would you recommend to someone buying Australian dollars?

COMPETITION AND THE FIRM

Generally, firms do not welcome competition. Most firms would prefer to dominate the market and operate without the threat of rivals. If there is no threat from competition, a firm can usually charge a higher price. There is also less pressure to be efficient and **innovative**. This reduces the effort needed to survive and be successful. When faced with competition, firms have to offer products that give consumers value for money. This involves:

■ operating efficiently by keeping costs as low as possible

■ providing good quality products with high levels of customer service

■ charging prices that are acceptable to customers

■ innovating by constantly reviewing and improving the product.

One aspect of innovation is **product differentiation**. This means that firms try to persuade consumers that their product is different from those of rivals. For example, in Italian towns and cities there are likely to be large numbers of restaurants offering authentic Italian food all competing for customers. However, although each one is offering the same cuisine, there are likely to be differences in the service supplied by each restaurant. There may be differences in menus, food quality, atmosphere, decoration, customer service and location. Over time, each restaurant may be trying to develop their product so that it suggests to customers that it is different and better than rivals.

The main disadvantage to a firm operating in a competitive market is that the amount of profit made will be limited. In markets where competition is fierce, prices are likely to be lower and the potential for profit also lower. The total profit in the industry has to be shared between many firms.

ACTIVITY 2

CASE STUDY: THE FUNHOUSE

Queenstown is a small tourist destination in New Zealand. It has a population of around 18 000 and is famous for its adventure activities, such as snowboarding, jet boating, white-water rafting, bungee jumping, mountain biking, skateboarding, tramping, paragliding and skydiving. The town expects to get about 2 million visitors each year, which means that providing accommodation is an important source of income for many residents. However, competition for guests is fierce. In 2016, there were 118 businesses offering accommodation. These included hotels, motels, apartments, backpackers (lower cost hostels for backpackers) and holiday parks.

Ilene Chappell owns The Funhouse, a backpacker offering affordable accommodation for young adults. Even though competition is fierce, The Funhouse generates good profits for Ilene. The average occupancy rate for backpackers in Queenstown was 73 per cent in 2016. However, occupancy at The Funhouse was 79 per cent. The Funhouse considers itself innovative. It was one of the first businesses in Queenstown to use social media in its promotion. When Ilene took over The Funhouse in 2012, she introduced free sausage sandwiches for breakfast, a free bus service to the airport, a discount bar for guests, free lockers and free Wi-Fi. Ilene said that, 'Competition is good. It keeps you on your toes, every year we sit down and review our performance and try to come up with new ideas for the future. Next year we are going to offer free sunscreen and free mosquito repellent.' The accommodation rates at The Funhouse are slightly higher than rivals. However, Ilene said, 'when you offer free this, and free that, people love it, we get loads of recommendations through social media and the freebies are always mentioned.' Ilene also explained that offering free services actually helped to keep administration costs down.

▲ Bungee jumping in Queenstown

1   What evidence is there in the case to suggest that the accommodation market in Queenstown is competitive?

2   Discuss the main disadvantage to firms of competition.

3   Assess how firms, such as the Funhouse, might benefit from competition.

COMPETITION AND THE CONSUMER

Most consumers would argue that competition in business is desirable. This is because of the advantages that consumers enjoy from healthy competition.

- **Lower prices**: In a competitive market, firms cannot overcharge consumers. If one firm tries to raise its prices, it will lose a lot of its business. This is because the market is full of good substitutes and consumers can easily switch from one supplier to another.

- **More choice**: Competition means there are many alternative suppliers to choose from. Where possible, each supplier is likely to differentiate its product from those of rivals. This helps to widen choice even more. Competitive markets will also have a constant stream of new entrants offering fresh ideas and even more choice.

- **Better quality**: Firms that offer poor goods or services in a competitive market will lose business. Consumers are rational (see Chapter 2, pages 12–17) and will look for value for money. This means they consider both the price and the quality of products when deciding what to buy. Modern consumers are more aware and better informed than ever before.

There are also disadvantages to consumers of a highly competitive market.

- **Market uncertainty**: It could be argued that there may be some uncertainty or disruption in competitive markets. This is because unprofitable firms eventually leave the market. This means that some consumers might be inconvenienced.

- **Lack of innovation**: It could be argued that innovation in a competitive market might be lacking. This is because firms make less profit in competitive markets. As a result, they may not have enough profit to invest in product development.

COMPETITION AND THE ECONOMY

One of the main advantages of competitive markets is that resources will be allocated more effectively. This is because firms have to operate efficiently to survive. They are under pressure to keep their costs down so that their prices are lower.

It is also argued that firms in competitive markets are more innovative. This is because innovative firms can get a competitive edge over their rivals. This means that firms will develop new products, new production techniques, new technologies and new materials. The economy will benefit from this because people will have a better standard of living.

One of the main disadvantages of a highly competitive market is that resources might be wasted. One of the reasons for this is that some factors of production are often immobile. When firms cease trading in a competitive market, resources are released for alternative uses. People are made redundant and resources like machines, tools, equipment, land and buildings come up for sale. However, it often takes time for these resources to be reallocated.

MULTIPLE-CHOICE QUESTIONS

▶ 1 Which of the following is likely to be a benefit to the economy of competitive markets?

A Higher interest rates

B Better resource allocation because there is less waste

C Factors of production are more mobile

D Lower unemployment

▶ 2 Which of the following is a feature of a competitive market?

   A There are a limited number of sellers in the market

   B Each firm has total control over the price charged

   C There are lots of sellers in the market

   D There are high barriers to entry

ECONOMICS IN PRACTICE

CASE STUDY: COMPETITION IN THE USA

US CORPORATE PROFITS

The graph in Figure 18.1 shows corporate profits made by companies in the USA between 1950 and 2016. The increase over the time period looks very impressive. For example, between 2000 and 2015, corporate profits rose by more than 200 per cent. The dip shown after 2015 should not be too worrying. It came during a period when the dollar was very strong (which would reduce the demand for exports) and the low oil price impacted negatively on energy firms. In the third quarter of 2016, US corporate profits were US$1 575 400 million.

Corporate profits have risen in most rich countries over this period but the increase has been much higher in the USA. Along with the fall in the number of businesses operating in many sectors, this means the benefits of economic growth in the USA are being enjoyed by a relatively small number of people. This might explain why most US residents believe that the economy unfairly favours the rich and powerful. It might also explain the statement by 2016 US election Democratic candidates Hillary Clinton and Bernie Sanders that the economy is 'rigged'.

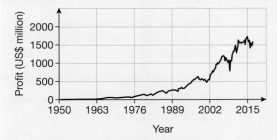

▲ **Figure 18.1** US corporate profits, 1950–2016

US AIRLINE INDUSTRY

It has been argued in the past that US airlines were famous for two things – poor customer service and weak financial management. However, recently, US airlines made an annual profit of US$24 000 million. Unfortunately, improved profits did not mean improved service for passengers. They have had to endure continued hidden charges, poor punctuality, shabby cabins, a lack of legroom in seats and poor in-flight food. Neither have customers benefitted from the recent drop in the price of aircraft fuel. Some argue that there is not enough competition in the industry. During the last decade, the number of operators in the market has fallen. Four airlines now dominate the domestic market.

US PHARMACEUTICALS INDUSTRY

The US pharmaceuticals industry was criticised in 2016 for some astonishing price increases.

- Mylan Pharmaceuticals increased the price of EpiPens (devices that deliver an emergency shot of epinephrine to someone suffering a potentially fatal allergic reaction) by 550 per cent from US$94 to US$608 since getting the selling rights in 2007.
- Turing Pharmaceuticals increased the price of Daraprim, an anti-malarial drug also used by HIV patients, by more than 5000 per cent.
- Valeant raised the price of Syprine, a blood-cleaning agent, by more than 3000 per cent.

The pharmaceutical companies blame pharmacies and the prescription system for not passing along the discounts they negotiate with manufacturers. However, it is argued that the drug companies are responsible for the massive price increases, not the middlemen. What is needed is more competition from generic drug makers (companies who produce non-branded drugs that are identical to branded drugs). Like Daraprim and Syprine, epinephrine is available in a generic form. At present, however, there is no generic version of the EpiPen injector for sale in the USA. One of the problems is that companies like Mylan keep rivals out of their market. For example, Mylan struck deals with potential competitors to delay them from seeking approval for generic versions of the EpiPen.

CHAPTER QUESTIONS

1 Describe what competition is.

2 Who might benefit from the increase in corporate profits in the USA?

3 Discuss the disadvantages to consumers when there is a lack of competition in a market. Use examples from the cases above in your analysis.

There should be more competition between businesses in the USA.

4 To what extent do you agree with this argument? Make a clear judgement in your evaluation.

19 ADVANTAGES AND DISADVANTAGES OF LARGE AND SMALL FIRMS

LEARNING OBJECTIVE

- Understand the advantages and disadvantages of large and small firms
- Understand the factors that influence the growth of firms
- Understand the reasons why some firms stay small

GETTING STARTED

In many countries around the world, the economy is dominated by small- and medium-sized enterprises (SMEs). In some countries, the number of SMEs is as high as 99 per cent. They make significant contributions to output, employment and income generation. However, large firms are also very important. The relatively small number of large firms often contribute far more to the economy than all of the SMEs put together. Also, in some sectors, small firms find it difficult to survive. Look at the example below.

CASE STUDY: THE ROLE OF SMEs IN MALAYSIA

There were an estimated 5 million private sector businesses in Malaysia in 2016. Of these around 97 per cent were SMEs. These businesses are responsible for nearly 36 per cent of the country's GDP, 65 per cent of the country's employment, and nearly 18 per cent of Malaysia's exports. The graph in Figure 19.1 shows the role played by SMEs in the Malaysian economy. SMEs play the biggest role in the agriculture sector with a share of 48.6 per cent. The SMEs in this sector produced rubber, oil palm, livestock, fish and food crops, such as vegetables and fruits.

In 2014, Malaysia's GDP was US$338 100 million.

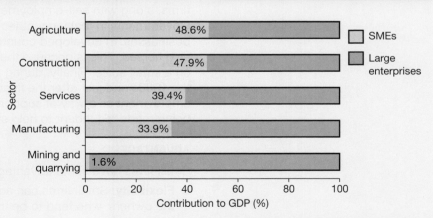

▲ Figure 19.1 GDP contributions by SMEs and large firms in Malaysia, 2017 (constant 2010 prices)

1 Calculate the contribution made by (a) SMEs in agriculture and (b) large firms in manufacturing.

2 Describe one possible advantage of operating as an SME.

3 Describe one possible reason why the mining and quarrying sector is dominated by large firms.

4 In groups, make a list of advantages that large firms might have compared to small firms. Present your ideas to the rest of the class using a poster.

HOW IS THE SIZE OF A FIRM MEASURED?

Several methods can be used to measure the size of a firm. Here are three common methods.

TURNOVER

Firms with high turnovers will tend to be larger than those with small turnovers. For example, in 2015, BP had a turnover (total revenue) of US$225 900 million. This makes BP a very large company. BP is one of the world's leading gas and oil companies.

NUMBER OF EMPLOYEES

Large firms tend to employ larger numbers of employees than smaller firms. In 2015, BP employed about 80 000 people worldwide. By this measure, again BP is classified as a large company.

BALANCE SHEET TOTAL

This measure is based on the amount of money invested in the business by the owners. Generally, more money will be invested in larger firms such as BP. In 2015, the balance sheet total for BP was US$98 300 million. Table 19.1 shows how the European Union (EU) defines different sized firms.

	MICRO	SMALL	MEDIUM	LARGE
Turnover (revenue) (€ million)	< 2	< 10	< 50	> 50
Number of employees	< 10	< 50	< 250	> 250
Balance sheet total (€ million)	< 2	< 10	< 43	> 43

▲ Table 9.1 How the EU defines the size of firms

SMALL FIRMS

The vast majority of firms in many countries are small. The number of small firms, along with self-employment, has also grown in the last 30 years. Governments in many countries have encouraged the development of small businesses. In developed countries, the growth in the tertiary sector has also helped. This is because the provision of many services is more effective on a small scale. Finally, during periods of high unemployment, such as in the 1980s and just after the financial crisis in 2008, many people saw self-employment as a way of supporting themselves. They often used money from being made redundant to help start their own business.

ADVANTAGES

Small firms have some advantages over their larger rivals.

- **Flexibility**: Small firms can adapt to change more quickly. This is because the owners, who tend to be the main decision makers, are actively involved in the business and can react to change. For example, a small baker can produce a personalised birthday cake for individual customers. A large national cake manufacturer may not be able to do this.

- **Personal service**: As firms get bigger, it often becomes difficult to offer customers an individual personal service. Some people prefer to deal with the owner of a firm directly and are prepared to pay a higher price for this benefit. Owners are far more accessible in small firms than larger ones.

- **Lower wage costs**: Many workers in small firms do not belong to trade unions. As a result, their negotiating power is weaker and the owners are often able to restrict pay to the legal minimum wage.

- **Better communication**: Since small firms have fewer employees, communication tends to be informal and more rapid than in larger organisations. The owner will be in close contact with all staff and can exchange information quicker and more efficiently. As a result, decision making will be faster and workers may be better motivated.

- **Innovation**: Although small firms often lack resources for research and development, they may be surprisingly innovative. One reason for this is that small firms face competitive pressure to innovate. For example, if they fail to come up with new ideas for products, they will lose their market share. It may also be because small firms are more prepared to take a risk. Perhaps they have less to lose than large firms.

DISADVANTAGES

There are some disadvantages to being a small firm.

- **Higher costs**: Small firms cannot exploit economies of scale because their output is limited. Consequently, their average costs will be higher than their larger rivals. This means that small firms often lack a competitive edge.

- **Lack of finance**: Small firms often struggle to raise finance. Their choice of sources is limited. For example, a sole trader cannot sell shares to raise more finance. They are also considered to be more risky than larger firms by financial institutions and other moneylenders.

- **Difficult attracting quality staff**: Small firms may find it difficult to attract highly qualified and experienced staff. One reason for this is because they lack resources. For example, they may not be able to afford the wages or the training that high-quality employees require.

- **Vulnerability**: When trading conditions become challenging, small firms may find it more difficult to survive than their larger rivals. This is because they do not have the resources to draw on when economic conditions worsen. Small firms might also be at risk of takeovers. Owners may be forced to accept unattractive takeover terms.

ACTIVITY 1

CASE STUDY: BOLT

In 2015, two entrepreneurs, Satyajeet Mohanty and Ronak Kumar Samantray, set up their own business, Bolt, in Hyderabad, India. They invented and developed a device for charging mobile phones while riding a motorbike. The device, called the Bolt Red Streak, is a compact waterproof mobile charger designed to charge any mobile phone safely and quickly on the motorbike. The unique design makes it easy to unplug and carry around when not riding. The device also tracks the entire ride on a route map and calculates total distance and average speed, using the Bolt Riders App. It sells for Rs1599 and can be purchased online or from around 30 authorised dealers.

The business, which was funded with about Rs25 million raised from family and friends, has a lot of potential. In 2015, around 16 million two-wheeled vehicles, such as scooters, motorcycles and mopeds were sold in India alone. It currently employs five people with primary focus on production quality and aftersales service with customers.

▲ The Bolt Red Streak

The business hopes to sell 350 units per month in 2016.

1   Calculate the expected revenue in 2016 if sales are realised.

2   What evidence is there in the case to suggest that Bolt is a small business?

3   Discuss two possible disadvantages for small businesses like Bolt.

LARGE FIRMS

The largest firms in the world are multinational companies. Multinationals have a great deal of power. They have huge resources and employ thousands of people. The largest firm in the world in 2016 was the US retailer Walmart.

ADVANTAGES

Large firms tend to be more powerful than smaller rivals. They enjoy a number of key advantages.

- **Economies of scale**: The main advantage to large firms is that their average costs are likely to be lower than those of smaller rivals. They can operate in large-scale plants and exploit economies of scale. For example, they can get cheaper supplies of materials and components because they buy in bulk.

- **Market domination**: Large firms can often dominate a market. They have a higher profile in the public eye than small firms and benefit from such recognition. This may mean that they can charge higher prices that enable them to make higher profits.

- **Large-scale contracts**: There are both small firms and large firms in the construction industry. However, a small firm could not compete with a large firm for a contract to build a new motorway for the government. Only large firms can win these large-scale, often highly profitable contracts because small firms do not have the resources to carry out the work.

DISADVANTAGES

Although big firms can generally produce goods more cheaply than small firms, they do have some disadvantages.

- **Too bureaucratic**: Large firms sometimes become overwhelmed by their administration systems. For example, decision making can be very slow in large firms because so many different people have to be contacted before a decision can be taken. Too many resources may be used up in administration. For example, too much time may be spent filling in forms and writing reports. Also, communication channels may be too long and too many managers may be employed.

- **Coordination and control**: A very large business may be difficult to control and coordinate. Thousands of employees, billions of pounds and dozens of plants all over the world can make running a very large organisation demanding. There may also be a need for more supervision that will raise costs.

- **Poor motivation**: In very large organisations, people can become alienated. The organisation may become so large that the effort made by a single employee seems insignificant. Personal contact between employees in large organisations may be lacking and this can result in poor worker motivation.

FACTORS INFLUENCING THE GROWTH OF FIRMS

Many owners will hope to grow their businesses. However, in some cases growth may not be easy. What might influence the growth of firms?

GOVERNMENT REGULATION

It is in the interests of consumers, and the economy in general, to have healthy competition between businesses. Competition will encourage innovation, improve efficiency and prevent consumer exploitation. Consequently, governments will monitor business activity and ensure that individual markets are not dominated by one or a small number of firms. In this role, the government may sometimes prevent the growth of some firms to stop them becoming too big. They can do this by investigating each merger and takeover, and blocking those that threaten to reduce competition. For example, in 2016, the EU prevented Three's takeover of O_2. Both are telecommunications companies and the EU said that the takeover would have reduced competition in the market.

ACCESS TO FINANCE

Businesses need finance to grow. They may need money to make acquisitions, build new factories, open new stores or develop new products, for example. Firms that can persuade money lenders and other investors to provide finance are in a better position to grow. Consequently, access to finance can have an important influence on growth.

ECONOMIES OF SCALE

One of the main motives for growth is to reduce average costs. As a firm grows, average costs will fall because it is possible to exploit economies of scale. In some industries, such as car manufacturing, air transport, power generation and water distribution, costs can be lowered significantly by producing very large quantities of output. Consequently, businesses are more likely to grow in such industries. However, in other markets it may be more difficult to exploit economies of scale. For example, there are few examples of international taxi firms, giant window cleaning operations and multinational hair salons. There are few opportunities to exploit economies of scale in these markets; therefore business growth will be limited.

THE DESIRE TO SPREAD RISK

Another motive for growth is to spread business risk. Risk can be reduced by diversifying. Selling into new markets and developing new products means that if one venture fails, success in others can keep the firm going. If business risk increases, perhaps because of growing uncertainty in certain sectors, firms are likely to diversify and grow as a result. Events like the UK's decision to leave the EU and sharp falls in commodity prices like oil are likely to result in this behaviour.

THE DESIRE TO TAKE OVER COMPETITORS

One way to grow a business is to take over rivals in the market. This is a quick way of growing and helps to reduce competition. However, over time the amount of merger and acquisition (M&A) activity tends to vary. For example, 2015 was a record year for global M&A deals. One big deal involved Anheuser-Busch InBev's US$100 000 million-plus takeover of SABMiller in the beverages industry. Globally, M&A deals totalled US$4.7 trillion during 2015, an increase of 42 per cent compared with 2014. However, over the first 8 months of 2016, global M&A fell to US$2.2 trillion. Consequently, if the desire to take over rivals falls, this can influence the growth of firms.

ACTIVITY 2

CASE STUDY: BT

In 2015, a communications giant was formed when telecoms group BT confirmed that it would buy mobile operator EE for £12 500 million. This takeover created a communications company offering a range of telecommunications services, such as broadband, fixed telephone and pay-television services. BT plan to sell these services to those EE customers who do not currently subscribe to BT. BT also hopes to speed up the sale of other services to its existing customers. The takeover was subject to approval by BT shareholders and examination by the Competition and Market Authority (CMA). However, the CMA cleared the deal in early 2016 and it went ahead.

The takeover should result in cost savings for BT. It was reported that BT could expect to save about £360 million a year in operating costs and capital costs after 4 years. BT also hoped that by combining the two businesses an extra £1600 million a year could be generated. Although BT would have to raise about £1000 million by selling some fresh shares, BT **chief executive** Gavin Patterson said, 'This is a major milestone for BT as it will allow us to accelerate our mobility plans and increase our investment in them.'

1 How can **(a)** the desire to take over rivals and **(b)** government regulation; influence the growth of firms. Use examples from the case in your explanation.

2 How is BT spreading risk as a result of the takeover?

REASONS FIRMS STAY SMALL

SIZE OF THE MARKET

Some markets are too small to sustain very large companies. For example, the market for luxury yachts is limited. Only a relatively small number of very wealthy people can afford to buy a luxury yacht. Therefore, businesses in this market will struggle to grow into very large organisations.

NATURE OF THE MARKET

In some markets, such as groceries, painting and decorating, hairdressing and taxi driving, the set-up costs are relatively low. There is little to discourage new businesses joining the market. As a result, fierce competition stops any single firm from growing.

Also, in some markets, businesses serve a particular **market niche**. Customers in niche markets have very particular needs, which are sometimes neglected by larger firms. Consequently there is a gap in the market for a business that is prepared to tailor goods or services to this small customer group. Such businesses are generally small.

LACK OF FINANCE

Some businesses would like to grow but are not able to raise the finance needed to expand. Growth usually requires investment in new resources, such as property extensions, new machinery, equipment and more labour. Unfortunately, some businesses are not able to convince money lenders that if the company grows it will be more successful and the finance will be repaid. Many small businesses that want to grow are still seen as too risky.

AIMS OF THE ENTREPRENEUR

Some business owners do not want to grow their businesses. They may be happy running a small business. They may be making enough profit to satisfy their needs and do not want the responsibility of taking on more workers, expanding operations and borrowing more money, for example. Also, some businesses are 'lifestyle' businesses. This means that the owners have interests other than their businesses and they need the time and flexibility to pursue them. As a result, such businesses are likely to remain small.

DISECONOMIES OF SCALE

Once a firm reaches a certain size, any further growth results in diseconomies of scale (see Chapter 17, pages 124–131). If a firm expands beyond the minimum efficient scale, average costs start to rise. A firm is not likely to grow any further if costs start to rise because it would have to charge more for its output.

MULTIPLE-CHOICE QUESTIONS

▶ 1 Which of the following is a reason why some firms remain small?

    A Lack of unskilled labour

    B Lack of finance

    C High tariffs on exports

    D Low interest rates

▶ 2 Look at Table 19.1. Which of the following firms is considered to be medium-sized according to the EU definitions of business size?

    A One employing 23 workers

    B One with a turnover of €23 000 million

    C One with capital employed of €2.4 million

    D One employing 202 workers

ECONOMICS IN PRACTICE

CASE STUDY: STARBUCKS AND THE COFFEE LOUNGE

STARBUCKS

Starbucks is an international coffee and coffeehouse chain based in Seattle, Washington, USA. Starbucks is the largest coffeehouse company in the world, with over 22 000 stores in 67 countries. Starbucks sells drip-brewed coffee, espresso-based hot drinks, other hot and cold drinks, snacks, and items such as mugs and coffee beans. Starbucks began trading in Seattle as a local coffee bean retailer in 1971. The company has grown rapidly, opening two new outlets every day (on average) for the last 27 years. It plans to open 3400 shops in China by 2019. Starbucks employs around 238 000 people and had a turnover of US$19 200 million in 2015.

▲ A Starbucks outlet

THE COFFEE LOUNGE

The Coffee Lounge is a small coffee shop in Trujillo, Peru. It is owned by Paolo Cueva and employs three full-time and two part-time staff. The market is competitive with Starbucks operating an outlet nearby. However, Paolo is not worried about the power of Starbucks. The Coffee Lounge opens at 5.00 a.m., several hours before its rivals, and draws in a significant number of regular early morning customers. Paolo says, 'I have been running this business for 32 years. I know it inside out. I know many people in the town and they like to do business with me. I am flexible – I give my customers whatever they want. Every day I make a special chorizo, fried egg and banana sandwich for one of my customers. Starbucks wouldn't do that.'

When asked if he would like to own a chain of stores, Paolo replied, 'Absolutely not. I do not want the responsibility of growth more staff, more decisions, more worry and more work. It's not for me – I am happy with what I have got.'

▲ Inside The Coffee Lounge

CHAPTER QUESTIONS

1 How is Starbucks spreading business risk through its growth strategy?

2 Discuss two advantages that Starbucks might have over The Coffee Lounge.

3 Why is The Coffee Lounge likely to remain a small firm? Give at least two reasons in your analysis.

4 Discuss the reasons why The Coffee Lounge can survive in the market alongside powerful rivals such as Starbucks.

20 MONOPOLY

LEARNING OBJECTIVE

- Understand how to define monopoly
- Understand the main features of monopoly: one business dominates the market, unique product, price-maker and barriers to entry (legal barriers, patents, marketing budgets, technology and high start-up costs)
- Understand the advantages and disadvantages of monopoly: efficiency, choice, quality, innovation, price and economies of scale

GETTING STARTED

In some markets, there is a lack of competition. As a result, one firm may dominate the market. The firm that dominates the market is said to be a monopolist. It is often said that where there is a **monopoly**, consumers are likely to be exploited. However, there may also be advantages when monopolies exist. Look at the example below.

SUBJECT VOCABULARY

monopoly situation where there is one dominant seller in a market

CASE STUDY: US MARKET FOR SEARCH ENGINES

One provider dominates the US market for search engines. Most people would probably guess that it is Google. Figure 20.1 shows that in the US Google had 79.88 per cent of the market for desktop searches in August 2016. Two other providers, Bing and Yahoo, had much smaller market shares, while others including AOL and DuckDuckGo shared just 1.88 per cent of the market. Google generates revenue by selling online advertising services including the delivery of targeted ads online. In 2015, Google generated US$74 500 million in revenue and made a profit of US$16 300 million.

Google has been criticised recently in many countries for avoiding the payment of tax on its profits. For example, in 2014, the company transferred €11 700 million to Bermuda in an effort to minimise the taxes it had to pay on its income. This transfer meant that Google avoided paying tax on much of its foreign income. Google paid just €2.8 million in taxes which was 0.024 per cent on the €11 700 million in revenue. Many people in the world pay up to 25 per cent tax, or more, on their own personal income! Google was also fined US$22.5 million recently because it 'placed an advertising tracking cookie on the computers of Safari users who visited sites within Google's DoubleClick advertising network' (Federal Trade Commission, 2012). This broke a privacy agreement. When powerful firms like Google dominate markets, it is often difficult for the authorities to challenge their 'misdemeanours'. Although it has to be said that Google did not break any laws with its tax avoidance.

One of the possible benefits of market domination is that large powerful firms can invest heavily in research and development (R&D). Google spent US$12 280 million on R&D in 2015. Google also has a reputation for being an innovative company and leading the market in product development.

1 What evidence is there to suggest that Google is a monopolist?

2 Using an example from this case, describe one possible advantage of monopolies for consumers.

3 Using examples from this case, discuss the possible disadvantages of a single firm dominating the market.

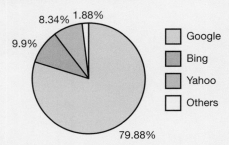

▲ **Figure 20.1** US desktop search engine market shares, August 2016 (%)

WHAT IS MONOPOLY?

A pure monopoly exists when just one producer supplies a market. However, there is also a legal monopoly. In some countries, if a firm has 25 per cent or more of a market it is said to be a monopolist. Pure monopolies are not common but they do exist. For example, in some countries, pure monopolists operate in the water and rail industries. In some markets, there might be local monopoly. This is where one firm supplies an entire local market in the way a village shop might be the only shop in the village.

FEATURES OF MONOPOLY

ONE BUSINESS DOMINATES THE MARKET

In markets dominated by one seller, a monopoly is said to exist. For example, in India there is only one supplier of rail travel in the whole country. This is Indian Railways, which employs over 1 million people and is owned and operated by the Government of India through the Ministry of Railways. However, a monopoly can exist when one firm dominates the market even though there may others operating alongside. For example, in 'Getting started' there are at least six firms providing a search engine service in the USA. But Google, with a market share fast approaching 80 per cent, dominates the market.

UNIQUE PRODUCT

The product supplied by a monopolist will be highly differentiated. There will not be another exactly like it. For example, where a pure monopoly exists there will be no rivals at all. Therefore, the product supplied is the only one available; there is no choice whatsoever for the consumer. This is often the case with rail travel and water provision, for example.

PRICE-MAKER

Although monopolists face a downward sloping demand curve, they are able to control the prices they charge. Monopolists are sometimes called **price makers**. They can force prices up by restricting the quantity supplied in the market. However, they cannot fix both price and quantity. If they try to sell larger quantities, the price will be forced down.

BARRIERS TO ENTRY

Monopolies often exist because competition is discouraged. In some markets, there are obstacles that prevent a **new entrant** from trying to compete. Barriers to entry are a common feature in monopoly and the main ones are summarised in Figure 20.2.

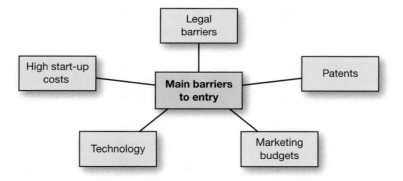

▲ **Figure 20.2** The main barriers to entry

- **Legal barriers**: In some markets, it is possible to exclude competition legally. This might happen when a government awards a contract to a single firm to provide a particular service. Two common examples are in the provision of rail travel and water supply. Governments often award contracts to a single supplier to provide rail travel on a particular route or water in a particular district. These contracts may run for between 10 and 30 years. Once a firm has a government contract to provide a service, competition is legally forbidden.

- **Patent**: A **patent** is a licence that prevents firms copying the design of a new product or new piece of technology. The new product developer can be the sole supplier in the market for a period of up to 20 years. This allows the firm to charge a higher price and recover the costs of research and development (R&D). Patents are common in the pharmaceuticals industry where firms are allowed to sell new drugs or medicines without competition. Therefore patents encourage R&D.

- **Marketing budgets**: Monopolists often have strong brand names. This makes it difficult for new entrants to compete because their products will be unfamiliar and may not be trusted by consumers. Dominant firms often spend large amounts of money on advertising to strengthen their brand names. For example, Coca-Cola, which dominates the soft drinks market, spent US$2800 million on advertising in 2014. Such high spending levels like this are very difficult, almost impossible, for new entrants to match.

- **Technology**: If an established and dominant firm has access to complex or up-to-date technology, this can act as a barrier to entry. For example, if a manufacturer develops a sophisticated new machine to improve efficiency in production, its average costs will fall and rivals might be forced out of business. Unless rivals can copy the technology, or buy it at a fair price, they might be forced to leave the market.

- **High start-up costs**: In some markets, the cost of setting up a firm to compete with the existing operators is too high. For example, in the UK, Rolls-Royce is the only producer of jet engines for aircraft. To set up a firm to compete would probably cost many hundreds of millions of pounds. In 2016, Rolls-Royce spent over £800 million on R&D alone. New competitors may find it difficult to match such financial commitment.

THE ADVANTAGES OF MONOPOLY

Many would argue that monopoly is bad for the consumer because choice is limited and prices are often higher. However, there may be some advantages.

EFFICIENCY

In some markets **natural monopolies** might exist. These are markets where it is actually more efficient if just one firm supplies all consumers. In these markets, it is often the case that the sole supplier is unable to exploit all economies of scale. Examples of such markets are those with very high fixed costs such as the utilities and rail travel. It would be highly inefficient if two or more railway operators tried to supply rail travel between the same destinations using their own railway lines. There would be a huge duplication of resources, which is wasteful.

INNOVATION

Since monopolies are often large and make high profits, they have the resources to invest in R&D. As a result they are able to develop new products and new technologies from which consumers will benefit. For example, in 'Getting started', Google spent US$12 280 million on R&D in 2015. Google also has a reputation for being innovative.

ECONOMIES OF SCALE

Since most monopolists are large, they are able to exploit economies of scale. This means that their average costs are lower. As a result, they may be able to supply products to consumers at a lower price. This will obviously benefit consumers if the cost savings are passed on. It is argued by some that if a firm has a monopoly in the domestic market, it can build strength and compete more effectively with competition from overseas. This will help to increase employment and national income in the domestic economy.

ACTIVITY 1

CASE STUDY: UK WATER INDUSTRY

In 2016, it was reported that Britain's privately owned water companies would make unexpectedly high profits of over £1000 million. The reason for this was because the industry regulator, Ofwat, had overestimated some of the costs companies would incur when setting water price limits. Consequently, the water monopolies made excess profits of £1200 million over 5 years. This was because they charged higher prices than necessary. Unfortunately, it was the poorest customers who were hit hardest. Their bills represented 5.3 per cent of their annual income compared with 2.3 per cent a few years ago. At the same time, the share prices of water companies grew by around 50 per cent on average. This was above the general rise in share prices. The supply of water in the UK is delivered by a number of private monopolies, with each company being the sole supplier in a particular region. Some of the different services provided are shown in Figure 20.3.

▲ **Figure 20.3** Services provided by water companies

The market for water provision is a natural monopoly.

1 What is meant by a natural monopoly?

2 Describe one other possible advantage of a monopoly.

3 Why is there an industry regulator in the provision of water in this case?

4 Who is likely to benefit from the mistake made by Ofwat in this case?

THE DISADVANTAGES OF MONOPOLY

Most people would consider monopolies to be undesirable. This is because of the disadvantages associated with markets that are dominated by a single firm.

HIGHER PRICES

A firm that dominates a market is able to charge more for its products. Monopolists will tend to restrict output in order to force up the price. For example, in the US some pharmaceutical companies have been heavily criticised for raising the prices of medication once they have secured sole ownership. A survey in 2014 of 3000 prescription medications found that prices more than doubled for 60 drugs and increased by at least four times for 20 drugs. On average, the cost of drugs is increasing at 10 per cent a year in the USA.

RESTRICTED CHOICE

If there is just one supplier in a market, consumer choice is obviously restricted. For example, 2.9 million households and businesses in the north-west of England have their tap water supplied by United Utilities. United Utilities is the UK's largest operator of water systems and owns and operates the entire water network in north-west England. These 2.9 million customers have no choice but to get their tap water from United Utilities. If they are unhappy with the quality of water, the prices charged or the level of customer service, they cannot switch to another provider.

LACK OF INNOVATION

It is sometimes argued that monopolists do not have enough incentive to spend money on product innovation. If they dominate the market and are able to prevent or restrict entry, there is no need to develop new products. This is because consumers are forced to buy the existing products. If monopolists are making higher profits without innovating, they may consider that resources invested in R&D are wasted.

INEFFICIENCY

It is possible to argue that monopolists may be inefficient. If a firm does not face any competition, there is no incentive to keep costs down. As a result, a monopolist might adopt a 'care-free' approach to business and incur unnecessary costs. If monopolies get too big, they might suffer from diseconomies of scale. As a result, their average costs will rise. Finally, some monopolists have been criticised for offering poor customer services. For example, because monopolists know that their customers cannot switch to another provider, they may operate call centres with too few staff.

ACTIVITY 2

CASE STUDY: AIR NAMIBIA

Air Namibia is the only airline in Namibia that offers domestic flights. In recent years, passengers have complained about high prices and poor quality service. For example, in 2015 passengers in Katima Mulilo were very annoyed when Air Namibia switched departure locations from Eros airport to Hosea Kutako International Airport (HKIA). Many passengers, particularly regular business travellers, said that it would be more expensive and inconvenient, as HKIA is over 40 kilometres outside Windhoek. They also pointed out that the local Mpacha Airport is also 20 kilometres away from Katima Mulilo. One businessman accused

DID YOU KNOW?

When senior managers travel to business meetings, they may incur unnecessary expenses that contribute to the overall inefficiency of their company. For example, they may spend a lot of money travelling first class, staying at five-star hotels and eating in Michelin star restaurants – all at the firm's expense. Some may regard this as wasteful.

Air Namibia of failing to respect its clients, stating that flight charges from Katima Mulilo to Windhoek were already very high. People living in Zambezi and Kavango are disadvantaged by this decision.

They already spend around NAD 5000 for a return ticket to Windhoek. This domestic flight was more expensive than going to Cape Town. In its defence, Air Namibia said traffic growth and the importance of minimising positioning costs were the main reasons for the switch. The current arrangement involves flying the aircraft from its original hub of HKIA to Eros Airport while empty in order to carry local passengers to their various destinations. Air Namibia said this was unsustainable.

Air Namibia has also been accused of blocking competition in the market. In September 2015, action taken by Air Namibia resulted in the high court suspending low-cost carrier Fly Africa's operations between Windhoek and Johannesburg. In response to this, Fly Africa posted a comment on Facebook saying it is 'aware of the decisions made in the High Court on Friday. Air Namibia has again used dirty tactics to stop competition so they can continue to charge unreasonable fares for bad service. It needs to stop.' Fly Africa said it wanted to introduce low cost flights on routes where overcharging was evident.

▲ An Air Namibia plane

1 Do you think that Air Namibia is a pure monopolist? Explain your answer.

2 Describe two features of monopoly. Using examples from this case to support your answer.

3 How are consumers being exploited in this case?

▶ 1 Which of the following is a barrier to entry?

    A Diseconomies of scale

    B High start-up costs

    C Low labour productivity

    D Inflation

▶ 2 Which of the following is a feature of monopoly?

    A Consumers have lots of choice

    B All firms are price takers

    C A large number of sellers in the market

    D Barriers to entry

ECONOMICS IN PRACTICE

CASE STUDY: PFIZER AND FLYNN PHARMA

Pfizer is one of the largest and most powerful pharmaceuticals companies in the world and dominates the market in a number of **market segments**. For example, in 2015, Pfizer had a 75.84 per cent share of the market to treat infectious and respiratory diseases and a 76.11 per cent share of the consumer health care and vaccines market. In 2016, Pfizer and another drugs company were fined for their involvement in what the Competition and Markets Authority (CMA) described as 'extraordinary price rises'. Pfizer and the UK firm, Flynn Pharma, were fined a total of £90 million for 'unfair' pricing after the price of an anti-epilepsy drug was increased by 2600 per cent. Around 48 000 patients rely on the drug in the UK and the NHS saw expenditure on the medication rise from £2 million in 2012 to £50 million the following year. The CMA also said that the prices of the drug in the UK were far higher than anywhere else in the EU.

Pfizer sold the rights to market the drug to Flynn Pharma in 2012. Before the sale, Pfizer was selling the medication under the brand name of Epanutin. However, once the sale went through the name of the drug was changed and the price was increased. The two firms claim that the price increase was lawful because an agreement between Pfizer and the NHS was no longer valid. Pfizer said it was going to appeal against the fine and explained that the deal with Flynn Pharma ensured that the supply of the drug would be continued. Flynn Pharma also said that it would appeal and that the CMA did not fully understand the drugs markets. A representative of Flynn Pharma said, 'We believe that left unchallenged, the CMA's decision would stunt investment in generics, eventually leading to a reduction in supply and less choice for doctors and patients.' Figure 20.4 helps to illustrate Pfizer's commitment to R&D in the pharmaceuticals industry.

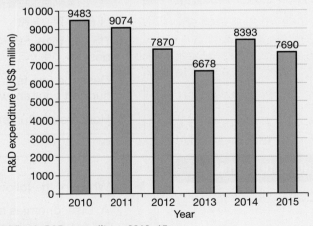

▲ **Figure 20.4** Pfizer's R&D expenditure, 2010–15

CHAPTER QUESTIONS

1 Describe what a monopoly is.

   Companies in the pharmaceuticals industry, such as Pfizer, use patents.

2 What is the purpose of patents?

3 In addition to patents, describe one other barrier to entry.

4 Consider the advantages and disadvantages of monopoly.

21 OLIGOPOLY

LEARNING OBJECTIVE

☐ Understand how to define oligopoly

☐ Understand the main features of oligopoly: few firms, large firms dominate, different products, barriers to entry, collusion, non-price competition and price competition

☐ Understand the advantages and disadvantages of oligopoly: choice, quality, innovation, collusion and cartels, fixing prices and price wars

GETTING STARTED

In many markets a few large firms dominate. For example, in Australia, just four providers – ANZ, Westpack, Commonwealth Bank and NAB – dominate the banking industry. A fraction of the market is supplied by a number of small operators. In such markets, prices tend to be fairly stable and firms find other ways of competing with each other. Look at the example below.

CASE STUDY: GLOBAL CAR SALES

In 2015, a total of 75.24 million new cars were sold worldwide. Japanese and European markets were unstable, while higher demand in the USA made up for the fall in sales in Brazil and Russia. Toyota, which has the biggest market share, had strong sales in Japan and China. Indeed, the Chinese market is growing rapidly with car sales amounting to 24.6 million vehicles in 2015.

Just six producers dominate the global car industry, as shown in Figure 21.1. The 'Big Six' compete by regularly updating their models, investing in R&D to develop new motor technology and spending heavily on advertising and other forms of promotion. For example, GM and Ford spent US$3500 million and US$2680 million, respectively, on advertising in 2015. This is called non-price competition.

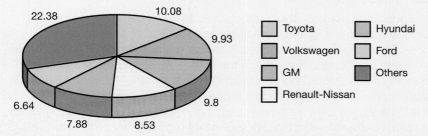

▲ **Figure 21.1** Global car sales and market shares, 2015 (vehicle sales, millions)

1 Calculate the proportion of the market served by the top six car manufacturers.

2 Describe how these companies compete with each other.

3 In groups, draw up a list of other car manufacturers that you can identify. How big do you think their global market share is?

WHAT IS OLIGOPOLY?

SUBJECT VOCABULARY

oligopoly market dominated by a few large firms

A market that is dominated by a few very large producers is called an **oligopoly**. 'Getting started' above shows that the global motor industry is dominated by just six large firms: Toyota, Volkswagen, GM, Renault-Nissan, Hyundai and Ford. These six firms supply about 70 per cent of the total market. However, in common with most other oligopolies, a fraction of the market is served by a number of much smaller firms. Such small firms can often survive alongside huge firms because they supply a market niche – a very small part of the market that is not served by the dominant firms.

> **DID YOU KNOW?**
> In the car industry, there are many smaller manufacturers, including Porsche, Rolls-Royce, Bugatti, Peugeot, BMW, Daimler, Opel, Tata, Hindustan, Fiat, Ferrari and many more.

FEATURES OF OLIGOPOLY

Oligopoly is a common market structure. However, the features in each oligopolistic market may differ slightly depending on the circumstances. The main features of oligopolistic markets are outlined briefly below.

FEW FIRMS

One of the main features of oligopoly is that the market often contains just a few firms. There is no exact number but it could be as few as three, four, five or six, for example. Oligopoly is a common market structure and there are many examples in most countries across the world. For example, just three firms dominate the music entertainment industry: Universal Music Group, Sony BMG and Warner Music Group.

LARGE FIRMS DOMINATE

When an oligopoly exists in a market, a few large firms will dominate it. They will have a large proportion of the market to themselves. For example, in 'Getting started', the 'Big Six' car manufacturers took 70 per cent of the total global market. Large firms will be highly influential in the market. For example, they are likely to set the price that the majority of consumers will pay. Smaller firms often just copy the price charged by the dominant firms.

DIFFERENT PRODUCTS

In most oligopolistic markets, the products sold by each of the large firms will be very close substitutes for each other. However, there are likely to be some differences. For example, although the big six car manufacturers all produce cars, there are some significant differences in the style, size, shape, interior, colours, performance, specifications and quality among all the manufacturers. Also, each manufacturer produces a wide product range where each product is different and aimed at a slightly different market segment. Firms in an oligopolistic market usually make a deliberate effort to differentiate its products from those of rivals.

BARRIERS TO ENTRY

The firms that dominate the market are likely to benefit from barriers to entry. For example, the set-up costs might be very high, as they are in the motorcar industry. The dominant firms are also likely to discourage entry by investing heavily in their brands. Without barriers to entry, the high profits enjoyed by the dominant firms would attract new entrants. As a result, their dominance would be reduced.

GENERAL VOCABULARY

collusion informal agreements between firms to restrict competition

COLLUSION

In some oligopolistic markets collusion might take place. This is where the dominant firms in the industry set up agreements to restrict competition. For example, firms might agree to share a market geographically. This means that each firm agrees to supply a particular region and not compete in others. Another form of collusion is price fixing, where all firms agree to charge the same (higher) price. Finally, firms may agree to restrict output. By restricting output, supply is decreased and prices rise. In many countries, collusion is illegal because it exploits consumers.

NON-PRICE COMPETITION

Since firms are keen to avoid price wars, they compete using advertising and promotions such as coupons, loyalty cards, competitions and free offers. Branding is a common feature in some markets. This is where firms give products a name, term, sign or symbol, for example. This helps consumers identify them more easily. Firms then try to create brand loyalty through advertising, so that customers carry on buying the brand. Product differentiation is also common. This is where the firm tries to persuade customers that their brands are different from those of competitors. The differences may be real or imaginary. For example, there is a real difference between a Mars Bar and a Cadbury Flake. However, the difference between Kellogg's Cornflakes and supermarket own brand cornflakes may be a product of the imagination. Imaginary differences can be created and reinforced by the work of marketing teams.

SUBJECT VOCABULARY

interdependence where the actions of one country or large firm will have a direct effect on others
price war where one firm in the industry reduces price causing others to do the same

PRICE COMPETITION

In many oligopolistic markets, prices stay the same for quite long periods of time. The market leader often sets the price and others follow. One reason for this pattern is because firms are afraid of a **price war**. If one firm cuts price, others in the market have to do the same or they will lose sales. As a result, revenue and profits would be lower for all firms. However, price wars do occur but tend to last for quite short periods of time. Firms in oligopoly are said to have **interdependence**. For example, if one firm decides to cut its price, this has an impact on the other firms in the industry. They will have to make changes of their own – perhaps match the price cut or invest in some form of promotion. They will need to do this or risk losing market share to rivals.

ACTIVITY 1

CASE STUDY: US FILM INDUSTRY

Some large and well-known distributors dominate the US movie industry. These are shown in Table 21.1. However, there are many hundreds of other smaller film distributors. Making movies is an expensive business. For example, *Finding Dory*, the most successful film for Buena Vista in 2016, cost US$200 million to make. Amazingly, *Batman v Superman: The Dawn of Justice*, which was distributed by Warner Brothers, cost US$410 million. This was one of the most expensive films ever produced. These distributors also spend huge amounts of money advertising and promoting their films. For example, Warner Bros. spent US$727 million on television advertising alone, airing close to 95 000 national ads. This was followed by Universal Studios, which spent US$395 million on 59 000 airings.

RANK	DISTRIBUTOR	MARKET SHARE	SALES (US$ MILLION)
1	Buena Vista	26.30%	3000.9
2	Warner Bros.	16.80%	1907.6
3	20th Century Fox	12.90%	1469.1
4	Universal	12.40%	1408.0
5	Sony / Columbia	8.00%	911.5
6	Paramount	7.70%	876.8
7	Lionsgate	5.80%	665.0
8	Focus Features	1.70%	196.5
9	STX Entertainment	1.70%	195.6
10	Open Road Films	0.90%	107.0

▲ **Table 20.1** Top 10 film distributors' market shares and sales from movies released in 2016

1 Calculate the percentage of the market dominated by the top six distributors.

2 What is meant by oligopoly? Use your answer in **(1)** as part of your explanation.

3 Describe the barriers to entry that exist in the movie industry.

ADVANTAGES OF OLIGOPOLY

Since there is some competition in oligopolistic markets, it is reasonable to assume that consumers will benefit in some way.

CHOICE

Competition in oligopolistic markets ensures that consumers are provided with some choice. One of the ways in which oligopolists compete is by launching new brands. These new brands provide consumers with new products, and often, an ever-growing choice in the market. Small producers also provide choice by supplying a **niche market**. For example, in the car industry, there are small operators that supply sports cars to niche markets. Morgan Cars of Malvern in England is one such example.

However, in other markets there may be little real choice. For example, in many countries, a few large companies dominate the supply of petrol. It might be argued that there is little if any difference between the quality of the petrol sold by each supplier.

QUALITY

Since non-price competition is common in oligopolistic markets, one method firms can use to differentiate their product is to make it better. Consequently, the quality of products in some markets might be superior. For example, the soft drink industry in the USA is an oligopoly dominated by the Coca-Cola Company, the Dr. Pepper Snapple Group and PepsiCo. It might be argued that these companies are able to differentiate their products (for example, by taste), and are therefore able to gain market power. However, sometimes the superior

SUBJECT VOCABULARY

niche market market for a product or service, perhaps an expensive or unusual one, that does not have many buyers, but that may make good profits for companies that sell it

GENERAL VOCABULARY

superior better in quality than other things of the same kind

quality of products might only be a matter of perception. This means that consumers just think that the quality of certain products is better because the powerful forces exerted by advertising and promotion have shaped their views.

ECONOMIES OF SCALE

If the dominant firms are able to exploit economies of scale, their average costs will be lower. Therefore, it is possible that some of the cost savings will be passed on to consumers in the form of lower prices. The smaller rivals in the market cannot exploit economies of scale. They often survive because they do not compete directly with the dominant firms.

INNOVATION

The level of innovation in oligopolistic markets might vary. On the one hand, since large and powerful firms dominate the market, it could be argued that they will have the resources to invest in R&D. It is true to say that competition can be resisted if an individual firm can develop a new model that is superior to those of rivals. On the other hand, it might be argued, from a consumer's point of view, that the large amounts of money many oligopolists spend on advertising and promotion would be better spent on innovation.

PRICE WARS

In some oligopolistic markets, prices are fairly stable for quite long periods of time. This is helpful for consumers because it provides some certainty. However, consumers might benefit from a price war. Once one firm cuts price aggressively, others in the market are forced to follow or they risk losing market share. As a result, consumers benefit from lower prices in the market. However, price wars do not normally last for very long and there is also the threat that one of the firms is squeezed out of the market. As a result, the market becomes less competitive and in the long term the survivors might push prices even higher.

A price war in the UK supermarket industry was ignited in January 2017 by Morrisons, one of the big four supermarkets dominating the market. It cut the prices of around 800 product lines including fish fingers, potatoes, meatballs, kale and avocado. A representative of Morrisons said that the price cuts were designed to help families on tight budgets and make Morrisons more competitive.

DISADVANTAGES OF OLIGOPOLY

Consumers are not likely to benefit from oligopoly if there is no competition in the market. The main disadvantage of oligopoly is the temptation among firms to collude. If firms agree to restrict competition, by price fixing, for example, consumers will end up paying higher prices. Consumers will also suffer if a market is shared out geographically. There will be a lack of choice because only one firm will supply each area.

In 2016, Colgate-Palmolive was fined AUD 18 million for colluding with rivals to fix the price of detergents in Australian supermarkets. Colgate admitted entering deals with rivals that limited the supply, and controlled the price, of laundry detergents. Colgate also agreed with the Australian Competition authorities on the size of the fine.

In a minority of oligopolistic markets, a **cartel** might exist. This is where a group of firms or countries formally join together and agree on pricing or output levels in the market. If cartels are successful, they are able to act as a monopoly. In the USA and the EU, cartels and collusion are illegal. One example of an international cartel is OPEC (Organization of the Petroleum Exporting Countries). Its members include some of the world's major oil

SUBJECT VOCABULARY

cartel where a group of firms or countries join together and agree on pricing or output levels in the market

producing countries. Their aim is to restrict the supply of oil so that the price is forced up. Members meet on a regular basis to agree on output quotas for each country. However, agreement is not guaranteed and the restriction of supply is not always achieved.

If there is genuine competition between the dominant firms in an oligopolistic market, then consumers might benefit. There may be more innovation, genuine product development, increasing choice, open pricing and lower costs. There may even be price wars where prices are cut dramatically. However, if there is collusion, too much spending on advertising and a lack of innovation, consumers will be worse off. Consumers will also lose out if a fierce price war eliminates one or more of the firms. There will be less competition between the remaining, and smaller group, of dominant firms.

ACTIVITY 2

CASE STUDY: CARTEL

In 2016, Daimler, Volvo/Renault and two other lorry manufacturers were fined a total of €2930 million for their part in a price-fixing agreement. A cartel, which also included MAN (owned by Volkswagen), Iveco and DAF, fixed prices and passed on the costs of emissions rules to customers in the EU between 1997 and 2011. The cartel, which served around 90 per cent of the market for medium-sized trucks (such as that shown in Figure 21.2), initiated delays that meant that customers missed out on new technology.

The established cartel began with a first meeting between senior managers in Brussels in 1997. After that they colluded at meetings on the fringes of trade fairs and other events. They also discussed tactics over the telephone. However, from 2004, fewer senior managers ran the cartel through the companies' German subsidiaries. Information was also exchanged online by email. MAN eventually exposed the cartel and, as a result, Volkswagen avoided a fine of €1200 billion. The biggest penalty of €1000 million was imposed on Daimler. DAF, Volvo/Renault and Iveco were fined €753 million, €670 million and €495 million, respectively. The fines were more than double the previous record for a cartel. They would also have been twice as big if the companies had not cooperated. The EU competition authorities said the size of fines depends on how large the market is and how long the cartel had been operating.

▲ **Figure 21.2** A medium sized truck

1 What is meant by a cartel? Use this case as an example in your explanation.

2 Discuss the possible impact on customers of the cartel in this case.

3 How was the size of fines determined in this case?

MULTIPLE-CHOICE QUESTIONS

▶ 1 Which of the following is a possible disadvantage of oligopoly?

    A Lower prices

    B Collusion

    C More choice

    D More innovation

▶ 2 Which of the following industries is likely to be oligopolistic?

    A Chicken farming

    B Petrol

    C Restaurant

    D Flower selling

ECONOMICS IN PRACTICE

CASE STUDY: DOMESTIC AIR TRAVEL IN INDIA

Domestic air travel in India is growing rapidly. The air travel consultancy firm Capa said domestic passenger traffic would reach 100 million by 2016–17. Airlines carried 81 million passengers in 2015, up from 15.7 million in 2003/04 when India's first low-cost airline, Air Deccan, was launched. Figure 21.3 shows the market shares of India's domestic airlines. Passenger traffic grew about 23 per cent in January 2017, compared with about 21 per cent a year ago. Much of the growth was fuelled by cheaper fares resulting from low oil prices. Flights were almost full for SpiceJet at 92.1 per cent, followed by GoAir at 84.9 per cent and IndiGo at 84.7 per cent. Even some of the smaller airlines were running at close to full capacity. For example, Air Costa was operating at 84 per cent and TruJet at 83.4 per cent.

In 2015, the competition authorities in India fined a number of carriers for fixing additional fuel charges for cargo transportation. When fuel prices fell due to the lower oil price, Jet Airways, IndiGo and SpiceJet colluded to keep additional fuel charges high. They received a total fine of Rs258 crore. Two carriers, Air India and GoAir, escaped a fine since its conduct was not the same as the three offending firms. The fines for each carrier amounted to 1 per cent of their annual turnover. The authorities suggested that the fines might have been harsher but they recognised the financial difficulties some of the carriers were experiencing.

Competition between the dominant firms in the domestic air travel market has kept prices relatively low for passengers. Figure 21.4 shows that air travel in India is some of the cheapest in the world. However, passengers often complained about poor customer service, baggage and flight problems. Market leader IndiGo understands the importance of punctuality to flyers and makes it a key priority in their service. In contrast, Air India cancelled the most flights of all airlines.

GENERAL VOCABULARY

crore ten million

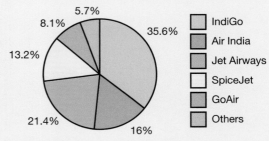

▲ **Figure 21.3** Market shares of domestic air travel in India, 2015 (%)

Pie chart segments: IndiGo 35.6%, Air India 16%, Jet Airways 21.4%, SpiceJet 13.2%, GoAir 8.1%, Others 5.7%

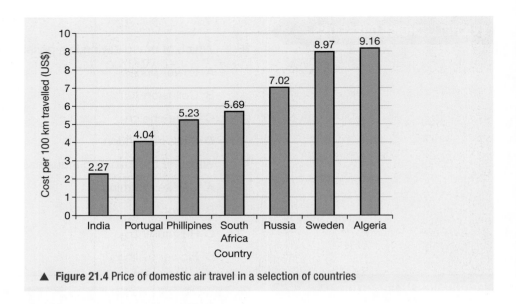

▲ **Figure 21.4** Price of domestic air travel in a selection of countries

CHAPTER QUESTIONS

1 Describe two features of oligopoly. Use examples from this case in your explanation

2 Describe one possible barrier to entry in the market for domestic air travel in India.

3 Describe one possible disadvantage to passengers if a price war broke out in the market for domestic air travel in India.

4 Consider the advantages and disadvantages to passengers of oligopoly in the market for domestic air travel in India.

22 THE LABOUR MARKET

LEARNING OBJECTIVE

- Understand the factors that affect the demand for labour: demand for the final product, availability of substitutes and its productivity
- Understand the factors that affect the supply of labour: population size, age and distribution of the population, retirement age, school-leaving age, female participation, skills and qualifications and labour mobility
- Understand the importance of labour to business
- Understand the impact of training on the quality of labour
- Understand how wages are determined

GETTING STARTED

The labour market works like any other market: there are buyers and sellers. The demand for labour comes from firms in the private sector and organisations in the public sector – these are the buyers. The supply of labour comes from the working population – these are the sellers. As the examples below show, several factors affect demand and supply of labour.

CASE STUDY: ROBOTS AT FOXCONN

Foxconn is a Taiwanese multinational electronics manufacturer. It supplies a number of high profile customers such as Apple, Samsung and Sony with components and other electronic products. In 2016, Foxconn said that it was going to reduce the workforce from 110 000 to 50 000 in one Chinese factory and replace the 60 000 workers with robots. In a statement, Foxconn said it was introducing robots and other innovative technologies to replace repetitive tasks previously done by people. The company wanted employees to retrain and focus on higher **value-added** elements in the manufacturing process, such as research and development, process control and quality control.

▲ A robot at work in a factory

SUBJECT VOCABULARY

value-added products or services have an increased value because work has been done on them, they have been combined with other products and so on; this increase in value to the buyer is what the buyer pays for

CASE STUDY: EMPLOYMENT IN US SOLAR POWER

In 2015, the US solar power industry grew by 20 per cent. By the end of the year, around 209 000 people were employed in the industry. This was greater than the number employed in the US gas and oil industry for the first time, which was 184 500. However, the growth in employment in the solar industry is not the same in all the different sectors. The most growth has come in the installation of solar power. Solar installation accounted for around 65 per cent of the jobs growth in the industry. The US solar installation sector now employs 77 per cent more people than the domestic coal mining industry.

▲ Solar power installation

1   What is happening to the demand for labour in these examples?

2   What accounts for the change in the demand for labour in each of the examples?

THE DEMAND CURVE FOR LABOUR

SUBJECT VOCABULARY

wage rate the amount of money paid to workers for their services over a period of time (that is, the price of labour)

The price of labour is the **wage rate**. This is the amount of money that has to be paid to people for them to work for a period of time. The demand curve for labour slopes downwards, from left to right. This is because the wage rate and the demand for labour are inversely related. This means that when wages rise, firms demand fewer workers and when wages fall they demand more. A demand curve for labour (DL) is shown in Figure 22.1. If the wage rate is US$600 per week, 100 workers are required. However, if the wage rate rises to US$800, the demand for labour falls and only 80 workers are required.

DID YOU KNOW?

The main reason why the demand for labour falls as wages rise is because higher wages lead to higher production costs. As a result, firms cut production and therefore need fewer workers.

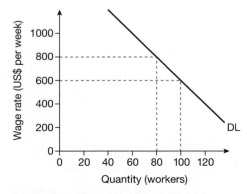

▲ **Figure 22.1** Demand curve for labour

FACTORS AFFECTING THE DEMAND FOR LABOUR

SUBJECT VOCABULARY

derived demand demand that arises because there is demand for another good

The wage rate is not the only factor that affects the demand for labour. Below are some other influences.

DEMAND FOR THE PRODUCT

The demand for labour is said to be a **derived demand**. This means that the demand for labour is derived from the demand for the goods and services supplied by firms and public sector organisations.

AVAILABILITY OF SUBSTITUTES

The demand for labour may be affected by the cost and availability of substitutes for labour. For example, in many organisations, it is possible to replace people with machines. If firms believe that machines are more efficient and cheaper than people, they will probably substitute people with machines. In 'Getting started', Foxconn was replacing labour with robots. As technology advances the opportunities for replacing labour with machines seems to increase.

PRODUCTIVITY OF LABOUR

The productivity of labour may also affect demand. If every worker is able to produce more output, demand for workers is likely to increase. This is because production becomes more profitable, provided the extra output can be sold.

OTHER EMPLOYMENT COSTS

The demand for labour may also be affected by other costs linked to employing labour. These include national insurance contributions (NICs), which are paid to the government when employing a worker in some countries; recruitment and selection costs; the costs of pensions; perks such as a company car, private health insurance and free meals; training; sick pay; maternity and paternity pay; holiday pay and the provision of childcare facilities.

Changes in these factors will have an effect on the demand curve for labour. For example, if there is an increase in the demand for air travel, there will be an increase in the demand for cabin crews. This will shift the demand curve for cabin crew workers to the right. This is shown in Figure 22.2 where the demand for cabin crew workers shifts from DL_1 to DL_2. At the wage rate of W_1, this means that the number of cabin crew workers employed rises from QL_1 to QL_2.

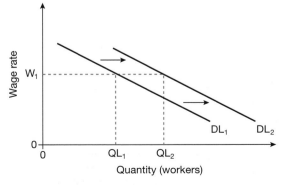

▲ **Figure 22.2** Shift in the demand curve for cabin crew workers

ACTIVITY 1

CASE STUDY: FUKOKU MUTUAL LIFE INSURANCE

In 2017, Fukoku Mutual Life Insurance, a Japanese company, said that it planned to replace 34 workers with artificial intelligence (AI). The company will purchase IBM's Watson Explorer AI system for JPY 200 million. The new technology, which can calculate payouts on insurance claims, would save the company about JPY 140 million per year. Fukoku expects the cost of the investment will be recovered in less than 2 years.

The AI system, which the manufacturers claim can think like a human, will improve productivity by around 30 per cent per year. The system is capable of analysing and interpreting a wide range of data. This includes unstructured text, images, audio and video recordings.

There have been worries about the scale of job replacement by technology in the past. Researchers say that by 2035 half of all Japanese jobs could be replaced by machines. Scientist Stephen Hawking said that AI could disrupt the economy even though it would bring huge benefits such as putting an end to disease and poverty. He said AI 'will also bring dangers, like powerful autonomous weapons or new ways for the few to oppress the many. Also, in the future AI could develop a will of its own that is in conflict with ours.'

1 Why is Fukoku Mutual Life Insurance replacing workers with technology?

2 Draw a diagram to show the effect on the demand curve for labour in this market as a result of Fukoku's decision to introduce AI.

3 Discuss one disadvantage of the introduction of new technology in business.

▲ Will humanity be taken over by AI?

THE SUPPLY CURVE FOR LABOUR

The supply curve for labour (SL) slopes upwards, from left to right. This is because wages and the quantity of labour supplied are proportionately related. So, for example, if wage rates rise, more people will make themselves available for work. A supply curve for labour is shown in Figure 22.3. This shows that if the wage rate were US$600 per week, 40 workers would want to work in that labour market. If the wage rises to US$800 per week, the number of people prepared to work in that job rises to 80.

DID YOU KNOW?

The main reason why the supply curve for labour is upward sloping is because as the wage rate rises an increasing number of people are prepared to work. Work is more worthwhile at higher wage rates.

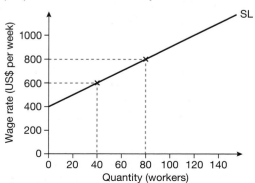

▲ Figure 22.3 Supply curve for labour

FACTORS AFFECTING THE SUPPLY OF LABOUR

In addition to wages, a number of other factors will affect the supply of labour. A country's workforce, or its working population, includes all those people over the age of 16 but under the age of retirement. A number of factors can affect the size of a nation's workforce and these are outlined below.

POPULATION SIZE

In most countries in the world, the size of the population is growing. The global population was 7400 million in 2016. However, this was predicted to rise to 9700 million by 2050. As the population grows, there will be more people available for work. Therefore, the supply of labour will tend to increase over time.

MIGRATION

Many countries welcome immigrants to help increase the working population. For example, many countries in the Middle East have a history of welcoming foreign workers. In Bahrain in 2015, 69.2 per cent of the population were immigrants. In recent years, a number of countries in the EU have welcomed the arrival of foreign workers as a result of new members enjoying the right to cross international borders (within the EU) to work.

AGE DISTRIBUTION OF THE POPULATION

The age distribution of the overall population of a country may have an effect. In most developed countries in the world there is an aging population. This means that the number of people over the age of about 65 years as a proportion of the total population is increasing. This also means that the *dependency ratio* is rising. This is the proportion of dependents (non-workers) to workers in the population. As the population ages, the dependency ratio may increase and this places a financial burden on the rest of the population.

RETIREMENT AGE

In many countries, once people reach a certain age they are entitled to a state pension. This is called the retirement age. For example, in Canada, the government announced in 2016 that the retirement age would rise from 65 to 67 – although the change is not due to be introduced until 2023. This means that people will have to work for longer before they are entitled to any state benefit. Therefore the supply of labour will increase in Canada.

SCHOOL LEAVING AGE

In most countries, children must attend school until they reach a certain age. This is called the school leaving age. Once this age is reached, children are allowed to work. Consequently, any changes to the school leaving age can affect the supply of labour. For example, in Ireland, the government announced that it would raise the school leaving age from 16 to 17 in 2016. This means that the supply of labour will be reduced because children will not be allowed to work until they are 17.

FEMALE PARTICIPATION

In the last 50 years, in many countries, there has been a change in the role of women. An increasing number of women have elected to work due to changes in society and more favourable equality legislation to work and pursue careers (see Activity 2). This has increased the size of the working population.

SKILLS AND QUALIFICATION

The supply of labour will tend to increase if people become more employable. This can happen if people have good skills and are well qualified. The quality of labour is discussed in more detail below.

SUBJECT VOCABULARY

labour mobility ease with which workers can move geographically and occupationally between different jobs

LABOUR MOBILITY

Labour mobility can have an impact on the supply of labour in a particular labour market. For example, if workers are geographically mobile, it means that they can move easily from one region to another to find work. If workers are occupationally mobile, it means they can switch from one type of job to another more easily. As workers become increasingly mobile, the supply of a labour in a particular market can be boosted. In recent years, improvements in the transport networks in many countries have improved the geographical mobility of labour.

Changes in these factors will have an effect on the supply curve for labour. For example, if there is an increase in immigration, there will be an increase in the supply of labour. This will shift the supply curve for labour to the right. This is shown in Figure 22.4, where the supply curve for labour shifts to the right from SL_1 to SL_2. At the wage rate of W_1, this means that the number of workers employed rises from QL_1 to QL_2.

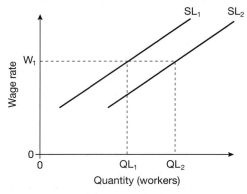

▲ **Figure 22.4** Effect of an increase in immigration on the supply curve for labour

ACTIVITY 2

CASE STUDY: WOMEN AT WORK IN CANADA

Since the early 1950s, there has been a dramatic change in the role played by women in the workplace. In Canada in 1953, about one-quarter of women aged 25 to 54 contributed to the working population. In contrast, virtually every man was either employed or looking for a job. However, the number of women entering the labour market has increased significantly since then, mainly due to changes in social norms regarding gender roles. For example, new technologies such as electrical appliances reduced the time needed to perform household tasks. This released many women from the traditional household duties associated with their gender at the time. Also, families had fewer children, which reduced the traditional need at the time for mothers to stay at home. Other possible reasons may include the following.

■ Employment opportunities in the service sector increased. This meant that mental ability became more important than physical ability (where men are perceived to have an advantage) in many of the new jobs created.

■ Economic necessity has resulted in more women seeking work to help generate more income for the family.

■ New laws that gave women equal rights in pay and opportunities have encouraged more women into work.

- The feminist movement has promoted the rights of women both in the workplace and in general.
- More women have entered higher education so they were better equipped to seek employment.

Figure 22.5 shows the labour force participation rates for Canadian men and women ages 25 and 54 for the period from 1953 to 2014.

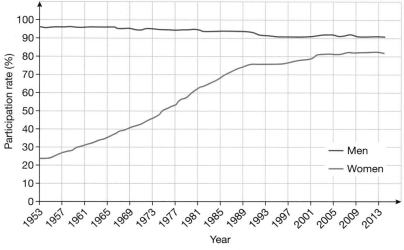

▲ **Figure 22.5** Labour force participation rates in Canada of men and women aged 25–54, 1953–2014

1 What were the labour force participation rates for men and women in 2014?

2 What has happened to the proportion of women employed in Canada over the period?

3 How might you account for the changes you identified in response to question **(2)**?

4 Use a diagram to show the effect on the labour supply in Canada of the changes shown by the data.

WAGE DETERMINATION

The wage rate in any labour market is determined by the interaction of the supply and demand for labour. The equilibrium wage is determined where the supply and demand for labour is equal. A labour market is shown in Figure 22.6. The equilibrium wage is US$800 per week and at this wage rate both the supply of labour and the demand for labour is 80 workers. The impact of changes in the supply and demand for labour on the wage rate is discussed in Chapter 23 (see pages 173–180).

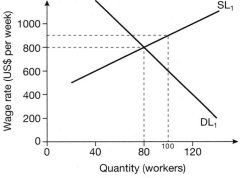

▲ **Figure 22.6** Wage determination in a labour market

THE IMPORTANCE OF THE QUANTITY AND QUALITY OF LABOUR TO BUSINESSES

When a business is considering locations for its operations, it is not just the cost of labour that is important, it is also the quantity and quality of human capital. A business is not likely to locate a factory in a particular place just because labour is cheap. A business has to consider whether the labour available meets the skills required to maintain quality standards. Businesses cannot afford the consequences of poor quality work. In some of the locations where labour is cheap, most of the workers are unskilled and often poorly educated. Consequently, a business setting up an operation in that location may have to invest substantial sums of money in training unless all the work on offer is unskilled.

When choosing a location, businesses have to ensure that there are enough workers near to the site chosen. They will also have to consider whether there would be enough workers in the future if operations needed to expand. Some businesses are beginning to find recruitment difficult in China. For example, Jenlo Apparel Manufacturing, a Canadian-owned clothing company, opened a factory in southern China in 2008. It now has recruitment problems. First, the availability of workers has been reduced due to China's one-child policy. But also, many do not want to work in factories, nor do they want to work for exporters. This is because the quality standards are more challenging than those for goods produced for the domestic market. Businesses need access to sufficient numbers of skilled workers in order to minimise costs, operate efficiently and make more profit.

IMPACT OF EDUCATION AND TRAINING ON THE QUALITY OF HUMAN CAPITAL

GENERAL VOCABULARY

recruit to find new people to work in a company, join an organisation, do a job

The quality of human capital and the quality of labour can be improved through education and training. Although the price of labour is important for businesses when making decisions about how many workers to hire, the quality of labour is also important. Generally, employers will want to **recruit** people who can read and write and have good communication skills. They will also want to recruit people with specialist skills. If the labour supply is well educated and trained, it will be more productive.

The responsibility for education and training in most countries is divided between the state and firms. Over time, a country will want to improve the quality of labour so that it is more productive. This will require investment by the state and firms in training and education.

The main reason for training is to provide workers with the skills and knowledge needed to do their jobs effectively. As a result, their productivity will increase. However, there are several other reasons. For example, workers will need training if there are changes that might affect their jobs. Some examples might include new health and safety procedures, new technology or new working practices. Some businesses train their workers in a range of different jobs so that they are multi-skilled. This provides businesses with added flexibility. Also, workers will feel secure if they have been trained to do their job effectively. Not being able to do a job properly will be a source of anxiety, frustration and dissatisfaction for workers. It is also argued that training can be used to motivate staff.

MULTIPLE-CHOICE QUESTIONS

▶ 1 Which of the following would help to increase the labour supply in a country?

A Reduce the retirement age

B Raise the school leaving age

C Encourage more people to stay on in higher education

D Raise the retirement age

▶ 2 Which of the following might be a reason for a business to invest more in training?

A Improve labour flexibility

B Increase labour turnover

C Improve the punctuality of workers

D Reduce the average cost of recruitment

CASE STUDY: LABOUR SHORTAGE IN NEW ZEALAND

In 2016, it was reported that the construction industry in Auckland, New Zealand, was very short of workers. Although the unemployment rate in the city was 6.6 per cent, which is above the national average, construction firms were struggling to recruit decent quality construction workers. During the year, over 17 000 building jobs were created in New Zealand with the majority being taken up in Auckland where there is currently a building **boom**.

One company director said that his employment agency, Labour Exchange, was being stretched with more and more work coming in. He said that other agencies were also busy and that there were lots of new construction projects planned for Auckland. He also suggested that there were people who had paid for new apartments but they were not yet completed.

Another problem faced by the construction industry is that the flow of trained and skilled construction workers was allowed to fall when there was a dip in demand. The industry did not deal with the **boom and bust** period very well. During the global financial crisis, there was limited training. The industry also needs to provide some clear routes from schools to construction sites, many say. It has been suggested with unemployment so high in New Zealand, more young people leaving school need to be pointed in the right direction – that is, towards construction.

The construction industry also failed to predict the rapid increase in growth it is now experiencing. Auckland's Chamber of Commerce said, 'I think you could sit back and look at the current growth that's in Auckland and some of the major projects that we need to undertake, and say the delayed action in completing some of this work means that it's all coming to a head quickly, and that's the reason for some of the shortages.'

One solution to the problem is to attract more immigrants. A small number of Mexican construction workers have recently been employed but some say that the government should let more in. Under the Mexico Working Holiday Scheme, 200 workers are allowed into the country for up to 12 months. It has been pointed out that immigration rules were relaxed to allow foreign workers to help with the rebuilding of Canterbury following the earthquake in 2010. Some say that the government should do the same for Auckland.

However, many say that immigration is only a short-term answer. In the long term, universities need to have a better understanding of the nation's construction needs. In particular, they need to know the planned construction projects over the next 5 to 10 years. They can then make adjustments to their curriculums in order to meet these needs. Figure 22.6 shows New Zealand's migration gains for the 2006–16 period.

SUBJECT VOCABULARY

boom time when business activity increases rapidly, so that the demand for goods increases, prices and wages go up, and unemployment falls

boom and bust when an economy regularly becomes more active and successful and then suddenly fails

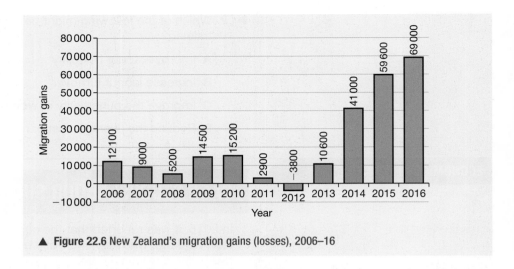

▲ **Figure 22.6** New Zealand's migration gains (losses), 2006–16

CHAPTER QUESTIONS

1 Describe what the derived demand for labour is. Use the example in this case in your explanation.

2 Describe what labour mobility is.

3 Describe what is likely to happen to the wages of construction workers as a result of the labour shortage in New Zealand.

4 Discuss the importance of education and training to improve the quality of labour.

5 Consider the measures that could be taken to increase the supply of construction workers in New Zealand.

23 THE IMPACT OF CHANGES IN THE SUPPLY AND DEMAND FOR LABOUR AND TRADE UNION ACTIVITY IN LABOUR MARKETS

LEARNING OBJECTIVE

☐ Understand the effects of shifts in the demand and the supply of labour

☐ Understand trade union involvement in the labour market: the impact of trade union activity to improve working conditions and increase wages

GETTING STARTED

Wages are determined by the supply and demand for labour in a labour market. If there is a change in the supply or demand for labour, there is likely to be an impact on wage rates and the total quantity of labour employed. Look at the example below.

CASE STUDY: WAGE RATES FOR CLEANERS

The diagram in Figure 23.1 shows the supply and demand for cleaners in a particular country. In recent years, there has been an increase in the labour supply due to rising immigration. Many of the workers arriving in the country are unskilled and have looked to the cleaning industry as a means of earning income. In Figure 23.1, the increase in supply is represented by a shift in the supply curve for cleaners to the right.

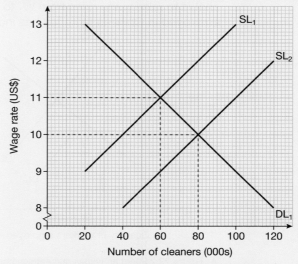

▲ Figure 23.1 Market for cleaners in a particular country

▲ Rising immigration recently has increased the labour supply of cleaners

1   What has happened to the wage rates of cleaners as a result of the increase in supply?

2   What has happened to the numbers of cleaners employed in the market as a result of the increase in supply?

3   Suggest three other factors that could increase the supply of labour in a country.

4   What impact might new legislation to reduce immigration have in the market shown in Figure 23.1?

CHANGES IN THE DEMAND FOR LABOUR

The demand for labour in a particular industry is not likely to remain constant over a long period of time. For example, since the demand for labour is a derived demand, if there is a fall in the demand for a particular product, there will be a fall in demand for workers involved in the production and selling of that product.

In some countries, the demand for certain types of labour has been growing in recent years. For example, in China, demand for factory workers in manufacturing has increased. Manufacturing output in China has been rising for many years to meet the rising demand for manufactured exports. This increase in the demand for factory workers is shown by a shift in the demand curve for labour to the right from DL_1 to DL_2 as shown in Figure 23.2. The effect of this shift is to raise wage rates from W_1 to W_2. Note also that the number of people employed in Chinese factories has increased from QL_1 to QL_2.

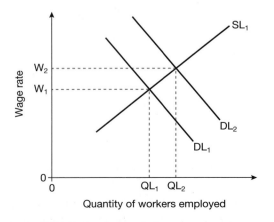

▲ **Figure 23.2** Effect on wages and employment of an increase in the demand for labour in Chinese manufacturing

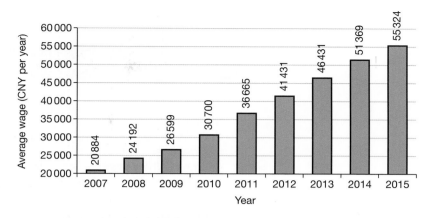

▲ **Figure 23.3** Rising wages in Chinese manufacturing

The bar chart in Figure 23.3 supports the view that the rising demand for factory workers in China has caused wages to increase. Over the time period, average yearly earnings have increased from CNY 20 884 to CNY 55 324.

CHANGES IN THE SUPPLY OF LABOUR

The supply of labour can change for a number of reasons. One of the main driving forces behind the growth in the supply of labour in many countries has been global population growth. In 2016, the world's population was 7400 million. However, in 2002, it was only 6280 million and by 2050 it is expected to be 9700 million. Naturally, if there are more people on the globe, there are more people available for work.

In some countries, governments have raised the retirement age. For example, in Greece the retirement age has been increased twice in recent years, first from 60 to 65, and then again to 67. This means that people have to work longer before they can receive any state pension. Therefore, raising the retirement age will increase the supply of labour. This is shown in Figure 23.4 by a shift in the supply curve for labour to the right from SL_1 to SL_2. This causes wage rates to fall from W_1 to W_2 and the number of people employed to rise from QL_1 to QL_2.

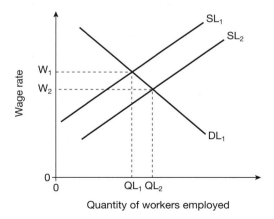

▲ **Figure 23.4** Effect on wages and employment of an increase in the supply of labour caused by an increase in the retirement age

It could be said that there is little evidence to suggest that wages have fallen over the years as both the global population and the supply of labour have grown.

ACTIVITY 1

CASE STUDY: WAGE DETERMINATION IN A DECLINING INDUSTRY

Over time, it is not unusual for an industry to decline. It may be because the products supplied in that industry have been replaced by more up-to-date versions. For example, in many countries, the coal mining industry has declined. This is because more countries are using 'cleaner' energy sources. When this happens, demand for the resources used in that industry starts to decline. Table 23.1 shows the supply and demand for labour at different wage rates in a declining industry in 2013.

WAGE RATE (US$)	4	8	12	16	20
DEMAND FOR LABOUR (000)	100	150	200	150	100
SUPPLY OF LABOUR (000)	0	100	200	300	400

▲ Table 23.1 Supply and demand for labour in a declining industry, 2013

1 Plot the supply and demand curves for labour on a graph.

2 What was the equilibrium wage rate in 2013?

3 How many people were employed in the industry in 2013?

4 Why is the supply of labour in this industry zero when the wage rate is US$4?

WAGE RATE (US$)	4	8	12	16	20
DEMAND FOR LABOUR (000)	225	175	125	75	25

▲ Table 23.2 Demand for labour in a declining industry, 2017

5 On the same graph, plot the new demand curve for labour.

6 Using the graph, describe what has happened to the wage rate and the number of people employed in the industry in 2017.

7 Describe the reason for the changes identified in response to question (6).

TRADE UNIONS

GENERAL VOCABULARY

trade unions organisation representing people working in a particular industry or profession that protects their rights

Trade unions are organisations that exist to protect the interests of workers. In most countries, there are numerous different trade unions that represent different types of workers. The main aims of trade unions are to:

■ negotiate pay and working conditions with employers

■ provide legal protection for members, such as representation in court if an employee is fighting a case against an employer (discrimination in the workplace, for example)

■ put pressure on the government to pass legislation that improves the rights of workers

■ provide financial benefits, such as strike pay whenever necessary.

THE POWER OF TRADE UNIONS

GENERAL VOCABULARY

disputes serious disagreement between two groups of people, especially a disagreement between workers and their employers in which the workers take action to protest
secret ballot way of voting in which people write their choices on a piece of paper in secret

SUBJECT VOCABULARY

closed shop company or factory where all the workers must belong to a particular trade union
secondary picketing workers in one workplace or company strike in a group at a particular location in order to support the striking workers in a different workplace or company

KEY FACTS: EXAMPLES OF SOME TRADE UNIONS IN THE UK

- The NUJ (National Union of Journalists) represents journalists.
- Equity represents actors.
- The NUT (National Union of Teachers) represents teachers.
- The largest union in the UK is UNITE. It has around 2 million members and is a general union. This means that it represents the interests of lots of different types of workers.

EFFECTS OF TRADE UNIONS ON WAGES AND EMPLOYMENT

In the 1960s and 1970s, many trade unions in the UK were involved in **disputes** with employers. There was a considerable amount of disruption to production and some people thought that trade unions were responsible. Some people felt that unions had become too powerful. As a result, in the 1980s, the government passed legislation to limit the power of trade unions. For example, new laws:

- required trade unions to have a **secret ballot** before a strike; a strike could only go ahead if the majority of members voted in favour

- allowed businesses to sue for compensation if trade unions did not obey the law

- banned **secondary picketing**

- made **closed shops** illegal.

Partly as a result of this anti-trade union legislation, trade unions became weaker in the UK. They also became less popular and as a result their membership fell. This weakened their position further. For example, in 1980 around 10 million workers belonged to trade unions in the UK. By 2015, this had fallen to about 6.5 million. Trade union membership has fallen in other countries. Figure 23.6 shows the decline in trade union membership in Australia since 1990.

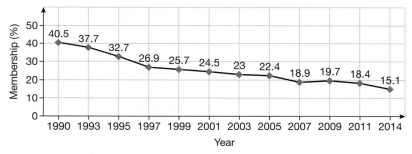

▲ **Figure 23.6** Australian trade union membership, 1990–2014

A strong trade union may be able to force wages up in some labour markets. If a union has the full support of its members, it can put pressure on employers during wage negotiations. When this happens, unions are able to affect wages and employment levels. In Figure 23.7, the equilibrium wage without trade union interference is W_1, where the supply, SL_1, and demand, DL_1, for labour is equal. If a trade union becomes involved, it will force wages up. In this case, trade unions have insisted that wages of W_2 are paid to workers. This means that an employer cannot hire workers below the wage rate of W_2. As a result, a new supply curve for labour, SL_2, emerges. This supply curve has a horizontal section, which is perfectly elastic. This means that the employer must pay W_2 for all workers employed up to QL_3. If the firm needs to hire more workers beyond QL_3, wages will rise further.

One of the effects of trade union interference here is that the higher wage of W_2 has resulted in fewer workers being employed. Employment has dropped from QL_1 to QL_2. This is because the demand for labour falls when wages increase. Therefore, it could be argued that trade union interference has increased wages at the expense of jobs for some of its members. However, job losses might be avoided:

- if labour productivity rises at the same time

- if employers are able to pass on wage increases to customers in the form of price rises

- if profit margins are reduced (which means that employers meet the cost of the wage increase).

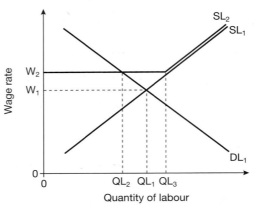

▲ **Figure 23.7** Effect on wages and employment of trade union interference in the labour market

ACTIVITY 2

CASE STUDY: IG METALL

In 2015, IG Metall, Germany's biggest trade union, secured a substantial pay increase for its members. The deal involved an annual pay increase of 3.4 per cent plus a one-off payment of €150 for workers in the southwest region of the country. The offer appears attractive since the level of **inflation** in the country was only 0.9 per cent. The union also reached an agreement with an employers' representative regarding conditions of work for some part-time workers. Specifically, the agreement related to the part-time conditions for older workers and job-related training for some employees in Baden-Württemberg. This is an industrial and car-making region in Germany, where the headquarters of Daimler and Bosch are located.

IG Metall, which has around 3.7 million members, had originally requested a 5.5 per cent pay increase. However, employers were only offering 2.2 per cent. A representative of IG Metall said that the agreement was a satisfactory compromise after very lengthy negotiations. The deal meant that workers would be getting some of the profits made by the company. A representative of the employers said that the deal was painful for companies – it represented one of biggest real pay increases for many years.

▲ Industry in Baden-Württemberg

1   Using this case as an example, describe the main purpose of a trade union.

2   How might the increase in wages secured by the trade union result in job losses?

▶ 1 Which of the following will cause wage rates to rise in a labour market?

A An increase in the supply of labour

B An increase in the demand for labour

C An increase in supply and a fall in demand for labour

D A fall in the demand for labour

▶ 2 Which of the following would reduce the power of trade unions?

A An increase in anti-trade union legislation

B Low wages

C A decrease in trade union subscriptions

D Favourable media coverage of trade union activity

CASE STUDY: AGING POPULATION IN THE USA

In many countries in the world, the population is aging. This means that a rising proportion of the population is over the retirement age. For example, Figure 23.8 shows that in the USA more than 22 per cent of the population will be over 65 by 2050. This compares with just over 10 per cent in 2010 and only 1 per cent in 1900. This may have consequences for the supply of labour in the USA. When the population ages, the amount of young people joining the workforce is smaller than the number who retire. As a result, the supply of labour is likely to fall.

An aging population also places demands on certain industries. The main one is health care. In the USA, it is estimated that by 2050 the number of people requiring health care services – such as care at home, residential care (assisted living) or skilled nursing facilities – will probably double from 13 million in 2000 to 27 million. Health care is the fastest-growing sector of the US economy, currently employing around 18 million workers. Interestingly, women represent nearly 80 per cent of the health care workforce in the USA. Figure 23.9 shows the growth in the number of health care workers in the US between 2000 and 2016.

Employment in health care increased and is expected to grow faster than any other occupation between 2010 and 2020. Historically, the USA has employed a growing number of migrants in the health care industry. The total grew from 1.5 million to 1.8 million between 2006 and 2010. Today, immigrants make up a significant proportion of the US health care workforce. In 2010, around 16 per cent of all care workers were from overseas. In some health care professions, this share was larger. For example, 27 per cent of physicians and surgeons were foreign-born, as were 22 per cent of persons working in health care support jobs such as nursing, psychiatric and home health aides.

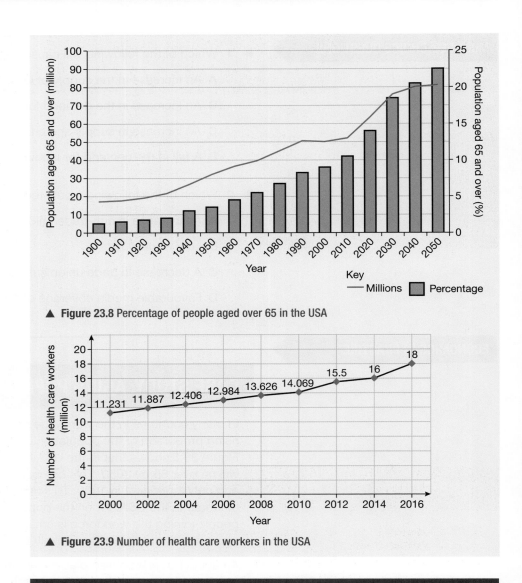

▲ **Figure 23.8** Percentage of people aged over 65 in the USA

▲ **Figure 23.9** Number of health care workers in the USA

CHAPTER QUESTIONS

1 What effect might an aging population have on a labour market? Use a diagram to support your answer.

2 Discuss whether raising the retirement age would help to compensate for a fall in the nation's labour supply due to an aging population.

3 What might happen in the market for care workers in the US in the future? Use a supply and demand diagram to support your answer.

4 What measures might the US government take to meet the growing demand for care workers? Give at least two measures in your analysis.

According to economic theory, wage increases secured by trade unions will result in lower levels of employment.

5 To what extent is this statement true? Make a clear judgement in your evaluation.

24 GOVERNMENT INTERVENTION

LEARNING OBJECTIVE

Understand government policy to deal with externalities: taxation, subsidies, fines, regulation and pollution permits

Understand government regulation of competition to: promote competition, limit monopoly power, protect consumers interests and control mergers and takeovers

Understand intervention in the labour market: reasons for the minimum wage, advantages and disadvantages of the minimum wage and the impacts of it in labour markets

GETTING STARTED

One of the roles played by the government is to ensure that business activity is conducted in a fair way. This might involve dealing with the problem of externalities, making sure that competition exists in markets and protecting consumers from exploitation. The government might also try to influence businesses in other ways, such as ensuring that workers are paid a fair wage. Look at the example below.

CASE STUDY: DU PONT

DuPont is one of the world's largest chemical companies. In 2014, it was fined over US$1 million for eight chemical releases in West Virginia, USA. The leaks happened at DuPont's Belle production plant in Kanawha County, where an employee was killed after being exposed to phosgene. DuPont was also ordered to improve safety and emergency response systems to prevent future leaks. In 2015, DuPont was fined US$531 000 for alleged Clean Air Act violations at its chemical plant in Deepwater, New Jersey. The US Environmental Protection Agency (EPA) fined DuPont for failing to maintain and repair two large refrigeration units adequately. With proper maintenance, the units should minimise chlorofluorocarbon (CFC) leaks. CFCs destroy the ozone layer, which protects the earth from harmful radiation, which can cause skin cancer. In addition to the fine, DuPont was ordered to correct the problems in its leak detection programme and comply with legal reporting requirements.

1 Why is government intervention needed? Use examples from this case to support your answer.

2 Describe the nature of government intervention in these cases.

3 What is the role of the Environmental Protection Agency in this case?

4 In groups, discuss whether you think the penalties received in these examples are adequate. Record your ideas on a poster and present them to the rest of the class.

▲ DuPont's Belle plant, Kanawha County, West Virginia, USA

THE NEED FOR GOVERNMENT INTERVENTION

Without government intervention, some businesses might neglect the needs of certain stakeholders. For example, the environment might be damaged, workers might be paid low wages, small businesses might be unduly pressurised or consumers might be overcharged. One of the roles of the government is to provide a legal system in which businesses can operate and a system of incentives and penalties to ensure that 'at-risk' groups are protected. However, it is important for the government to find the right balance. Too much intervention will discourage enterprise and reduce foreign investment. This might restrain growth in national income, reduce job creation, decrease tax revenues and reduce consumer choice. Too little, and some stakeholders' best interests might be neglected.

GOVERNMENT INTERVENTION TO DEAL WITH EXTERNALITIES

Chapter 13 (pages 89–96) explained that economic activity can have an impact on third parties such as individuals, organisations, property owners or resources such as woodlands. For example, a business might clear 200 hectares of rainforest to provide more grassland to rear cattle. This may destroy some ancient rainforest and eliminate a natural habitat for a wide range of plant and animal species. This negative impact on the environment is an example of an external cost or a negative externality. Both production and consumption can result in external costs.

It is also possible for economic activity to generate benefits to third parties. For example, if a business sets up a waste recycling operation, this is likely to encourage recycling. This will benefit the environment and the economy in general since a greater quantity of resources would be reused. These are called external benefits or positive externalities. In many countries, the government is likely to use a range of measures to reduce external costs and provide external benefits. These could include taxes, subsidies, fines, regulation and pollution permits. The nature, advantages and disadvantages of these measures are discussed in detail in Chapter 13 (pages 89–96).

GOVERNMENT REGULATION OF COMPETITION

PROMOTING COMPETITION

One of the roles of the government in the economy is to promote competition and prevent anti-competitive practices. Some examples of the action a government might take are outlined below.

Encourage the growth of small firms: If more small firms are encouraged to join markets, there will be more competition. In some countries, both central and local government have taken measures to help the growth of small firms. For example, business start-up schemes have been used to provide funds for new businesses when they first set up. There may be business services that provide information and advice on running a business and obtaining finance. Taxes are also lower for small firms.

Lower barriers to entry: If barriers are lowered or removed, then more firms will join a market making it more competitive. In recent years, many countries have removed some of these legal barriers. For example, the provision of bus services in the UK used to be the sole responsibility of local authorities. There was no competition at all. However, the law was changed so that new operators, such as Stagecoach, could join the market.

Introduce anti-competitive legislation: In many countries, legislation exists to prevent practices that result in reduced competition. For example, in India, the Competition Commission of India (CCI) acts as a regulator to:

- eliminate practices that reduce competition
- promote and sustain competition in markets
- protect the interests of consumers
- ensure freedom of trade.

LIMIT MONOPOLY POWER

If monopolies exist in markets, they need to be carefully monitored. Without government intervention, the temptation to exploit consumers may be too great for some organisations. In many countries, there is an appointed body that is responsible for overseeing monopolies. For example, in China, the State Administration for Industry and Commerce (SAIC) is responsible for developing and enforcing legislation relating to the administration of industry and commerce in the country. It has many divisions, one of which is the Antimonopoly and Anti-unfair Competition Enforcement Bureau. In 2016, SAIC found that Tetra Pak, the Swiss packaging firm, had broken anti-monopoly regulations. It was discovered to be abusing its monopoly status by forcing customers to purchase packaging materials. Tetra Pak had also prevented other suppliers from providing materials to its rivals. Tetra Pak was fined US$97 million.

In some countries, where a whole industry is dominated by just one, or a few very powerful firms, a special industry 'watchdog' is set up to monitor their activities. For example, in the UK, Ofwat (the Office of Water Services) was established to regulate the water and sewerage industry. Most tap water in the UK is supplied by monopolies. Such bodies often control the prices charged by monopolies and issue fines if quality standards are not met.

PROTECT CONSUMER INTERESTS

Consumers want to buy good quality products at a fair price and receive good customer service. They want information about products that is accurate and clear. They do not want to buy goods that may be dangerous, overpriced or sold to them on the grounds of false claims. Without government intervention, some firms may exploit consumers by using anti-competitive practices or restrictive practices. These might include:

- increasing prices to higher levels than they would be in a competitive market
- price fixing, where a number of firms agree to fix the price of a product to avoid price competition
- restricting consumer choice by market sharing
- raising barriers to entry by spending huge amounts of money on advertising, which smaller companies could not match, for example.

In some countries, there is a lot of consumer legislation. Such legislation covers a variety of consumer issues and aims to protect consumers from some of the practices mentioned above. Figure 24.1 shows some examples. Legislation exists to prevent businesses from activities such as making false claims about the performance of their products, selling goods that are not fit for human consumption and selling goods that are not **fit for purpose**. If businesses break consumer laws, they may be fined and have to compensate consumers for any loss.

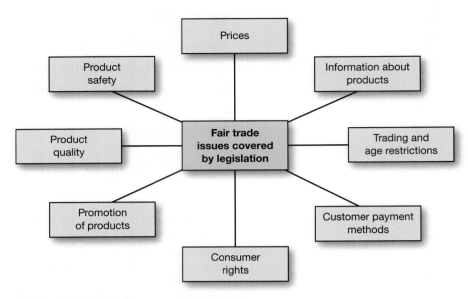

▲ **Figure 24.1** Fair trade issues covered by legislation

KEY POINT

Some examples of UK consumer legislation are:

- **Sale of Goods Act 1979:** This states that products sold by businesses must be of an appropriate quality and fit for purpose. For example, customers cannot be sold paint that peels off in the sun after 1 month or a waterproof coat that lets in the rain.

- **Food Safety Act 1990:** This law means that food should be fit for human consumption and comply with safety standards. For example, a business should not sell frozen food if it has defrosted and been refrozen or fresh produce that is decaying.

CONTROL MERGERS AND TAKEOVERS

In order to ensure that markets remain competitive, governments often monitor mergers and takeovers. Mergers and takeovers usually result in a reduction of competition in a market. Consequently, large mergers or takeovers are likely to be investigated by government bodies. They may be blocked or allowed to go ahead if certain conditions are met. For example, in 2016, the European Commission blocked Telefonica's sale of O_2 to CK Hutchison, the owner of Three. The commission ruled that the £10 300 billion deal would have left the UK with just three major mobile phone network operators. It was concerned that the takeover would reduce customer choice and raise prices. The European Commission said, 'The goal of EU merger control is to ensure that tie-ups do not weaken competition at the expense of consumers and businesses.'

In another EU ruling, Microsoft, the global technology company, was given the go ahead to take over LinkedIn, the social networking service that focuses on promoting professional connections. However, the deal, worth US$26 200 million, was subject to three key conditions relating to the preservation of competition in the industry. One of these was that PC manufacturers and distributors would be free not to install LinkedIn on Windows. Also, users would be able to remove LinkedIn from Windows if PC manufacturers and distributors install it onto new machines.

ACTIVITY 1

CASE STUDY: THE NATIONAL COMMISSION OF MARKETS AND COMPETITION (SPAIN)

In Spain, the CNMC (The National Commission of Markets and Competition) is responsible for monitoring industry in general and ensuring that markets are sufficiently competitive. The CNMC has a number of legal duties, which include:

- supervising and monitoring a range of economic sectors in Spain, such as electricity and gas, electronic communications and audio-visual, railways and airports and the postal markets
- enforcing competition law which addresses anti-competitive behaviour, merger control and state aid
- resolve trade disputes between a range of organisations
- promote competition.

In 2015, the CNMC fined 21 car manufacturers and two consultancy firms €171 million for anti-competitive practices. GM and Ford were hit hardest with fines of €22.8 million and €20.2 million, respectively. Three French firms – Renault, Peugeot and Citroen – were fined €18.2 million, €15.7 million and €14.8 million, respectively. The Spanish competition authorities said that the firms acted like a cartel. They exchanged information relating to car sales, repairs, maintenance activities and car parts to avoid competition. For example, some of the information included details of price incentives to avoid a price war for new-car sales. Volkswagen and its **subsidiaries**, including its Spanish brand Seat, avoided a penalty because they cooperated fully with the CNMC.

1 What is meant by an anti-competitive practice? Use the example in this case in your explanation.

2 Describe the role of the CNMC in Spain.

3 Discuss how consumers might benefit from the action taken by the CNMC.

SUBJECT VOCABULARY

subsidiaries companies that are at least half-owned by another company

---

GOVERNMENT INTERVENTION IN THE LABOUR MARKET

SUBJECT VOCABULARY

minimum wage minimum amount per hour which most workers are legally entitled to be paid

One way in which governments intervene in the labour market is to set a **minimum wage**. This involves passing legislation that means no employer is allowed to pay their workers an hourly rate below the limit set. In some countries, governments appoint a body to review minimum wage levels every year. Employers face a penalty if they pay wages that are lower than the national minimum wage. Also, workers will be entitled to have money owed repaid at current rates.

Canada introduced minimum wages many years ago to help reduce poverty in the country. It uses a region system so that wages can reflect local conditions. For example, in 2016, the following rates applied:
- Alberta CAD 12.20 per hour
- Manitoba CAD 11.00 per hour
- Nova Scotia CAD 10.70 per hour
- Quebec CAD 10.75 per hour

REASONS FOR A MINIMUM WAGE

The general reason for introducing minimum wages is to raise the incomes of low paid workers. However, some specific reasons are also given.

Minimum wages will benefit disadvantaged workers. It is argued that people such as women, ethnic minorities and low-income families benefit from minimum wages since they reduce inequality and increase fairness. In many countries, the gap between the rich and the poor is rising and it is argued that minimum wages might help to close this gap.

In some countries, many workers on low incomes are entitled to claim welfare benefits from the state. However, if their incomes are increased by the minimum wage, the amount they are entitled to claim will fall. This will save the government money. Also, as incomes rise, workers may pay more tax, which will benefit the government.

Higher wages may serve to motivate many workers. If people know that their work is going to be rewarded with higher pay, they may work harder. This will help to boost productivity in the economy.

If minimum wages are enforced, employers might respond by making their workers more productive to justify the higher wages. They may invest more in training, for example. They may also replace inefficient labour with more efficient machinery. Both of these responses would increase the productivity of the economy.

THE IMPACT OF A MINIMUM WAGE ON WAGES AND EMPLOYMENT

Supply and demand analysis can be used to show the effects of a minimum wage on wages and employment in labour markets. Figure 24.2 shows a labour market and the equilibrium wage is W_1. If the government imposes a minimum wage of W_2, above the equilibrium wage, by law all workers will receive at least W_2. Unfortunately though, economic theory suggests that the minimum wage of W_2 will have a negative effect on the level of employment. According to the diagram, at a wage of W_2, the number of workers employed falls from QL_1 to QL_2. Therefore, in theory, a minimum wage will result in job losses.

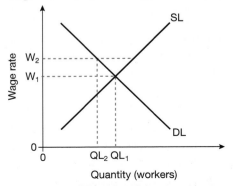

▲ **Figure 24.2** Effect of a minimum wage on wages and employment in a labour market

DO MINIMUM WAGES CAUSE JOB LOSSES?

Some have argued that minimum wages do not reduce the level of employment in the economy, as shown in Figure 24.2. There is some evidence to support this view. For example, since the introduction of the minimum wage in the UK in 1999, the number of people employed has actually risen. Figure 24.3 shows that in 1999 employment was 71.9 per cent. However, this rose to 74.5 per cent in 2016. There was a dip for a few years but this was almost certainly due to the global financial crisis when employment fell in many countries during a global recession.

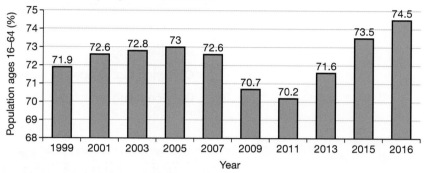

▲ **Figure 24.3** UK employment rates since the introduction of the minimum wage in 1999, 1999–2016

Furthermore, in the USA, a study by the Economic Policy Institute (EPI) found that the 1996/97 minimum wage increases did not reduce employment in the economy. In fact, after the increase, the low-wage labour market performed better than it had in many years (for example, lower unemployment rates, increased average hourly wages). However, it is important to note that both the UK and the US economies grew strongly during this period, which means that demand for labour would have been increasing.

ACTIVITY 2

CASE STUDY: IMPACT OF MINIMUM WAGE

Figure 24.4 shows a labour market for a country. The government has imposed a minimum wage of US$10 per hour.

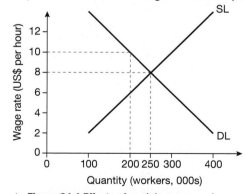

▲ **Figure 24.4** Effects of a minimum wage in a country

1 What is the equilibrium wage in this labour market?

2 What happens to the number of people employed in the market when the minimum wage is imposed?

3 Describe two reasons why a government would impose a minimum wage.

▶ 1 The introduction of a minimum wage in a labour market will:

    A Raise employment and lower the wage rate

    B Raise the wage rate and increase employment

    C Raise the wage rate and increase unemployment

    D Reduce the wage rate but boost employment

▶ 2 Which of the following is an example of an anti-competitive practice?

    A Product differentiation

    B Advertising

    C Paying high wages to workers

    D Price fixing

ECONOMICS IN PRACTICE

CASE STUDY: THE MINIMUM WAGE AND THE BAYER-MONSANTO MERGER

In 2016, Bayer, the German chemical company, said it would take over Monsanto, the giant US seed company, in a deal worth US$66 000 million. Bayer is known mainly for its pharmaceuticals and was linked with the development of Aspirin and Alka-Seltzer. However, its connection with Monsanto would make the company heavily involved in agriculture. In particular, it would have an important influence in the market for agricultural chemicals, crop supplies, pesticides and weed killers. Monsanto is the world's largest supplier of genetically modified (GM) seeds. These dominate the US farming industry but are still a major source of environmental protests overseas.

Many have objected to the merger in the belief that it would not be in the interests of consumers. The merger would mean that the new company would control about 25 per cent of the world's seed and pesticide market. It would also mean that about 90 per cent of the world's food supply would be in the hands of just four giant multinationals. Opponents of the merger say that food would be sprayed with more pesticides and produced with more GM seeds. They also say that food choices would be restricted and prices all over the world would rise. Senator Bernie Sanders, one leading opponent of the merger, said, 'these mergers boost the profits of huge corporations and leave Americans paying even higher prices. Not only should this merger be blocked, but the DOJ should reopen its investigation of Monsanto's monopoly over the seed and chemical market.'

In India, Monsanto has been accused of exploiting its monopoly power in the supply of GM cotton seeds. Unlike the seeds farmers can collect from this year's crop to use the following year, farmers have to buy GM cotton seeds every year. Monsanto's cotton seeds can sometimes cost up to four times more than traditional varieties. Monsanto has a 90 per cent market share in cotton seeds, Monsanto has a tight grip on cotton growing in India as farmers become dependent on expensive seeds and chemicals.

After the merger, Bayer has promised to keep all of Monsanto's 9000 plus US employees. The company also hopes to add 3000 new jobs – most of which will be in R&D. Bayer and Monsanto plan to spend about US$16 000 million on agriculture R&D over the next 6 years if the merger goes ahead – at one least half of which will be in the USA. In a joint statement, the companies said, 'The United States is a global leader in agriculture, and the combination of Bayer-Monsanto will underscore that role and ensure the United States retains a pre-eminent position as the anchor of the industry.'

▲ Protests against Monsanto's influence in agriculture

CHAPTER QUESTIONS

1 Describe what a minimum wage is.

2 Describe two possible benefits to the economy of the introduction of a minimum wage.

3 How might mergers and takeovers result in less competition? Use an example in this case in your explanation.

4 Discuss whether government intervention is needed in the merger between Bayer and Monsanto. Make a clear judgement in your evaluation.

EXAM PRACTICE: 1.2 BUSINESS ECONOMICS

Khan Enterprises is a small packaging manufacturer based in Rawalpindi in Pakistan. It produces a range of crates and other wooden packaging for engineering companies. The total fixed costs and the total variable costs at different levels of output for one of its products are shown in Table 1.

OUTPUT	FIXED COSTS (PKR)	VARIABLE COSTS (PKR)
0	500 000	0
50	500 000	50 000
100	500 000	100 000
150	500 000	150 000
200	500 000	200 000

▲ Table 1

1 With reference to the data in Table 1, what is the value of variable costs per unit? **(1)**

A PKR 500 000   B PKR 700 000   C 0   D PKR 1000

2 With reference to the data in Table 1, what is the value of total costs if output is zero? **(1)**

A PKR 500 000   B 0   C PKR 1000   D PKR 50 000

A01 **3** (i) State the formula for calculating total revenue. **(1)**

A02 (ii) Calculate the profit made by Khan Enterprises if 150 units are sold for PKR 5000 each. You are advised to show your working. **(2)**

A01 **4** State **one** example of an internal economy of scale. **(1)**

Colt Fuels is a large distributor of petrol. It has 457 petrol stations and operates in an oligopolistic market.

SKILLS CRITICAL THINKING, **A01** **5** What is meant by an oligopolistic market? **(2)**

SKILLS CRITICAL THINKING REASONING ADAPTIVE LEARNING CREATIVITY

A02 **6** Explain **one** advantage to consumers of oligopoly. **(3)**

In 2017, a US judge put a block on a proposed merger between two health care insurance firms, Aetna and Humana. The judge said that the merger would result in a lack of competition in the market. The two companies, the largest in the industry, claimed that the deal would not reduce competition. They responded by saying that the US$37 000 million deal would actually benefit consumers. This was because the two companies had complementary strengths in technology and relationships with health care providers.

A02 **7** With reference to the data above and your knowledge of economics, assess the impact of the US court decision on consumers. **(9)**

A03

A04 **(Total = 20 marks)**

2.1
GOVERNMENT AND THE ECONOMY

Assessment Objective AO1

Recall, select and communicate knowledge of economic terms, concepts and issues

Assessment Objective AO2

Demonstrate understanding and apply economic knowledge using appropriate terms, concepts, theories and calculations effectively in specific contexts

Assessment Objective AO3

Select, organise and interpret information from sources to investigate and analyse economic issues

Assessment Objective AO4

Evaluate economic information to make reasoned judgements and draw conclusions

Macroeconomics looks at the performance, structure and behaviour of the entire economy. This section addresses the key macroeconomic objectives of a government, such as growing income, keeping prices stable, keeping unemployment low, redistributing income and protecting the environment. It looks at the various tools and measures that a government might use to achieve its objectives, such as adjusting levels of spending, taxation and interest rates in the economy. Finally, this section also looks at the impact on the economy of using these tools and measures and the possible trade-offs that might exist between different macroeconomic objectives.

25 ECONOMIC GROWTH

LEARNING OBJECTIVES

- Understand macroeconomic objectives
- Understand how to define economic growth
- Understand how GDP is used to measure economic growth
- Understand the limitations of using GDP to measure economic growth
- Understand the economic cycle: boom, downturn, recession and recovery
- Understand the impact of economic growth on employment, standards of living, poverty, productive potential, inflation and the environment

SUBJECT VOCABULARY

budget deficit amount by which government spending is greater than government revenue

GETTING STARTED

In most countries, it is the government's job to manage the economy. This usually involves making sure that output grows, that prices do not rise too quickly and that people are in work. If the economy performs well, people's living standards will improve and a government might be re-elected. Look at the example below.

CASE STUDY: CANADA

In 2015, the Canadian Liberal party led by Justin Trudeau, made a number of economic promises before being elected with a significant majority. Prior to the election, the Canadian economy had been a little 'sluggish' with a mild recession and rising unemployment. However, Trudeau promised to change this. Some of the policies promised by the government included the following.

▲ Justin Trudeau at a political rally

- Raise taxes for the wealthiest 1 per cent of Canadians and redistribute income in favour of low-income families. For example, child benefit to support middle-class parents would be introduced. A typical family of four will get an extra CAD 2500 every year.

- Help low-income students to pay for university by increasing the maximum grant (to CAD 3000 per year for full-time students, and to CAD 1800 per year for part-time students). Also, students would not be required to repay student loans until they are earning at least CAD 25 000 per year.

- Cap the **budget deficit** at CAD 30 000 million over the first 3 years.

- Spend CAD 6000 mlion on 'green' infrastructure over 4 years.

- Double the spending on infrastructure to CAD 120 000 million over the next 10 years. This included CAD 3400 million for public transit and CAD 5000 million for water and wastewater facilities. A further CAD 3400 million would be spent on affordable housing, early learning and childcare, and cultural and leisure facilities.

Trudeau wanted to grow the economy by investing in public infrastructure projects. By the end of 2016, it was too early to say whether the economy was starting to benefit. However, it was clear that Canada's economy had not 'taken-off' under Trudeau. National income had grown by just 1.2 per cent in 2016 – up slightly from 0.9 per cent in 2015.

1 Discuss whether Trudeau's policies are working.

2 How might Trudeau's policies create jobs in Canada?

3 Describe how this case emphasises the importance of the economy to governments.

4 Involve yourself in a classroom discussion about the general state of the economy in your own country.

WHAT IS MACROECONOMICS?

SUBJECT VOCABULARY

macroeconomics study of large economic systems such as those of a whole country or area of the world

microeconomics study of small economic systems that are part of national or international systems

The study of economics can be divided into two areas. One of these involves looking at the economy as a whole. It looks at the performance, structure and behaviour of the entire economy. For example, it involves analysing patterns of total income or spending, total employment, the general price level and the total value of all goods traded with other countries. This is **macroeconomics**. In contrast, **microeconomics** looks at individual parts of the economy. It looks at how individuals, households or firms make decisions when allocating resources. It often involves analysing specific markets, such as the markets for rail travel, teachers, oil, health care, package holidays or wheat.

WHAT ARE MACROECONOMIC OBJECTIVES?

When managing the economy, the government has certain aims. These aims are called macroeconomic objectives. They focus on four key economic measures but include other aims that have become increasingly important in recent years. These are all summarised in Figure 25.1.

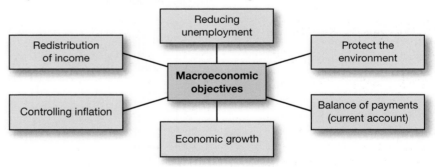

▲ **Figure 25.1** Macroeconomic objectives

SUBJECT VOCABULARY

economic growth increase in the level output by a nation

One of the key aims is to promote **economic growth**. This means that the government introduces policies designed to help grow incomes, output and employment in the economy. However, at the same time as creating more jobs and improving living standards, the government must ensure that prices do not rise too quickly and that imports are not significantly greater than exports. Also, in recent years, governments have been under pressure to introduce measures that protect the environment and redistribute income in the economy. This chapter is about economic growth.

WHAT IS ECONOMIC GROWTH?

SUBJECT VOCABULARY

national income value of income, output or expenditure over a period of time

Over a period of time, most economies will grow. This means that **national income** will rise. National income is the value of all incomes in the economy added together. It includes income from wages, profits, royalties, dividends, interest and income generated abroad. National income is also equal to the value of all output or production in the economy. It is also equal to the value of all spending in the economy.

If the economy is producing more, businesses are more profitable and share prices rise. This makes it easier for businesses to raise more capital and employ more workers. As more jobs are created, incomes rise. This means that consumers will have more money to spend on goods and services, which will drive economic growth even higher. Consequently, economic growth is desirable.

MEASURING ECONOMIC GROWTH

SUBJECT VOCABULARY

gross domestic product (GDP) market value of all final goods and services produced in a period (usually yearly), an internationally recognised measure of national income

The most common measure of national income is **gross domestic product (GDP)**. This measures a country's total output for the year. It measures the value of all goods and services that are produced in a country for sale. It includes both goods that are sold domestically (within a country) and those sold overseas. However, GDP only measures final production. The manufacture of parts and components used to make another product are not included. Exports are included because they are part of domestic production. However, imports are subtracted because they represent the output of another country.

GDP is used to measure economic growth all over the world. Using this standard definition means that meaningful comparisons can be made between the growth rates of different countries.

Figure 25.2 shows GDP growth in the EU between 1996 and 2016. For most of the period, economic growth was between zero and one per cent. This shows that many European economies have struggled to grow in the last 20 years. Also, just after 2008, the growth rate fell sharply and actually became negative. When the growth rate is negative, the value of GDP falls. In the last quarter of 2008, the EU growth rate was –3 per cent. This sharp decline was caused by the global recession.

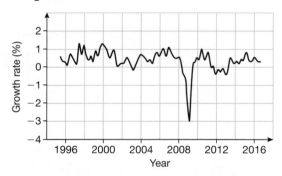

▲ **Figure 25.2** Economic growth in the EU, 1996–2016

LIMITATIONS OF GDP AS A MEASURE OF GROWTH

Although GDP is a common measure of economic growth, it does have some limitations.

INFLATION

Price increases can mean growth rates are misleading. For example, if an economy grows by 2.6 per cent in a year and prices also rise by 2.6 per cent, the economy has not grown. It has remained the same because the 2.6 per cent increase in *money GDP* is matched by a 2.6 per cent increase in prices. However, this problem can be overcome by using real GDP to measure growth. This involves adjusting GDP for inflation. For example, if inflation is 2.3 per cent and money GDP grows by 4.4 per cent, real GDP has grown by 2.1 per cent (that is, 4.4 – 2.3).

POPULATION CHANGES

Population growth must be taken into account when analysing growth patterns. For example, if GDP grows by 2.8 per cent in a year, and the population also rises, this increase in population will offset the growth in GDP. GDP will therefore be difficult to calculate. To overcome this problem, changes in *GDP per head or per capita* can be calculated. GDP per capita can be calculated by dividing GDP by the size of the population. In 2015, GDP per capita in the EU and in Kenya, for example, was US$35 079 and US$1133, respectively.

STATISTICAL ERRORS

Gathering the data needed to calculate national income is a huge task. The government collects millions of documents from firms, individuals and other organisations. Unfortunately, errors are made because the information has been entered inaccurately or left out. Therefore, the true value of GDP is never really known.

THE VALUE OF HOME PRODUCED GOODS

Some goods and services are not traded and therefore economic activity is not recorded. Examples might include people growing their own produce in gardens and the work done by DIY enthusiasts. In undeveloped countries, people rely almost entirely on their own produce to live. It is not traded and therefore not recorded. As a result, if such activities are not recorded, the value of national income is underreported.

THE HIDDEN ECONOMY

Sometimes paid work goes unrecorded. For example, a friend may drive a family to an airport for US$25 cash. This US$25 will not be recorded. The transaction becomes part of the hidden, 'black' or informal economy. Certain paid services go unrecorded in this way. People may do a variety of jobs for cash and not record transactions.

GDP AND LIVING STANDARDS

GDP is used to measure living standards. However, just because GDP rises, it does not automatically mean that living standards have also risen. Other factors have to be taken into account such as:

■ the amount of leisure time people have

■ the way extra income is shared between the population

■ whether growth has resulted in pollution

■ the quality of goods and services.

EXTERNAL COSTS

GDP does not take into account external costs such as environmental costs. For example, the price of plastic is cheap because it does not include the cost of disposal. As a result, GDP does not measure how these costs impact on the well-being of society.

ACTIVITY 1

CASE STUDY: ECONOMIC GROWTH IN USA, EU AND EAST ASIA AND PACIFIC

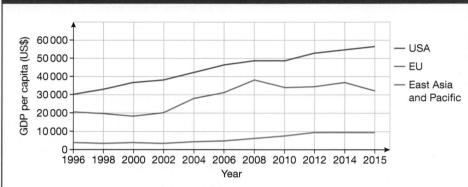

▲ **Figure 25.3** GDP per capita for the USA, EU and East Asia and Pacific, 1996–2015

1 What is meant by (a) GDP and (b) GDP per capita?

2 Which country/region has performed the best over the period? Explain your answer.

3 Which country/region had the lowest GDP per capita in 2015?

4 Which country/region had the most inconsistent economic growth over the period?

THE ECONOMIC CYCLE

Over a period of time, GDP is expected to grow. However, the rate of growth is not likely to be smooth. There is likely to be some variation and it is also possible for GDP to fall. This variation is often referred to as the economic, trade or business cycle. Figure 25.4 shows these variations and identifies four different phases: boom, downturn, recession and recovery.

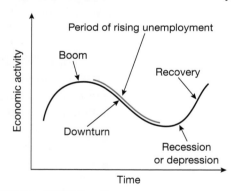

▲ **Figure 25.4** Economic, trade or business cycle

THE IMPACT OF THE ECONOMIC CYCLE ON GROWTH, EMPLOYMENT AND INFLATION

BOOM

The peak of the cycle is called a **boom**. During a boom, GDP is growing fast because the economy is performing well. Existing firms will be expanding and new firms will be entering the market. Demand will be rising, jobs will be created, wages will be rising and the profits made by firms will be rising. However, prices may also be rising.

SUBJECT VOCABULARY

boom peak of the economic cycle where GDP is growing at its fastest

DOWNTURN

A boom will be followed by a **downturn**. The economy is still growing but at a slower rate. Demand for goods and services will stop increasing or begin to fall, unemployment will start to rise and wage increases will slow down. Many firms will stop expanding, profits may fall and some firms will leave the market. Prices will rise more slowly.

RECESSION OR DEPRESSION

At the bottom of the economic cycle, GDP may be flat. If GDP starts to fall, the bottom of the cycle may be referred to as a **depression** or **slump**. Such a period is often associated with widespread poverty. Demand will start to fall for many goods and services – particularly non-essentials. Unemployment rises sharply, business confidence is very low, bankruptcies rise and prices become flat. The prices of some things may even fall. A less severe version of a depression is a **recession**.

RECOVERY

When GDP starts to rise again, there is a recovery or an upswing in the economy. Businesses and consumers regain their confidence and economic activity is on the increase. Demand starts to rise, unemployment begins to fall and prices start to rise again.

SUBJECT VOCABULARY

depression or **slump** bottom of the economic cycle where GDP starts to fall with significant increases in unemployment

downturn period in the economic cycle where GDP grows, but more slowly

recession period of temporary economic decline during which trade and industrial activity are reduced, generally identified by a fall in GDP in two successive quarters

THE IMPACT OF ECONOMIC GROWTH

Promoting growth is one of the government's key macroeconomic objectives. Generally economic growth is beneficial, but not always. The different impacts that economic growth can have are outlined below.

EMPLOYMENT

Economic growth is the result of businesses generating more output. As businesses produce more, they need more workers. Consequently, economic growth raises employment levels, and thus reduces unemployment. Governments also tend to spend more during periods of economic growth. This will also help to create more jobs – in education, health care and infrastructure development, for example.

STANDARDS OF LIVING

Increases in GDP mean that on average people have more income. With more disposable income, people can buy more goods and services. They can buy better quality food, improved housing and more leisure goods. Also, as the economy grows, it is possible to spend less time working. This is because there have been significant improvements in efficiency. Fifty years ago, many people worked a six-day week. Today most people work for 35 hours over just 5 days. People may also retire earlier. Finally, owing to economic growth, people are living longer. People can afford healthier diets and there have been advances in medical technology, which have all helped to increase life expectancy. Consequently, economic growth brings improved living standards.

POVERTY

Rapid economic growth in some developing countries has helped to reduce poverty. The expansion of existing businesses and the development of new businesses create jobs, some of which will be taken by the poor. For example, in India after 1991, GDP per capita grew nearly two-and-a-half times faster than in the previous 35 years. During this time, the fall in poverty also accelerated. In addition, a growing economy means that the government is able to collect more tax revenue. Most tax revenues are linked to income and spending, which both increase when the economy grows. Therefore, the government can spend more on services such as health care, education and provision for the poor. Extra government spending is often targeted at the poor, which can help reduce poverty.

PRODUCTIVE POTENTIAL

Economic growth can raise the productive potential of a country. This means that a country can produce more goods and services. This can be shown using production possibility curves (PPCs). Figure 25.5 shows that economic growth will shift the PPC out to the right from PPC_1 to PPC_2. In this example, it means the country can produce more of both capital goods and consumer goods.

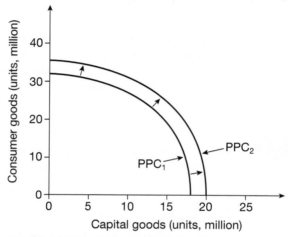

▲ **Figure 25.5** Economic growth and the PPC

INFLATION

If economic growth is too fast, the economy may **overheat**. This can cause inflation, which is bad for an economy (see Chapter 26, pages 203–210). In many parts of the world in the late 1990s and 2000s, there was a house price boom. House prices rose so sharply that many people could not afford to buy a house. In the last 10 years, inflation has not been a serious problem in many countries. This could be because of the relatively low levels of economic growth in most of these countries.

THE ENVIRONMENT

Environmental groups believe that the benefits of growth are lower than the costs of generating that growth. For example, as economies grow, more cars are purchased and more flights are taken. Both car and air transport contribute to greenhouse gases which cause global warming. In some countries, such as China and India, very high levels of pollution have accompanied high levels of economic growth. Also, economic growth uses up non-renewable resources such as oil, gas, gold and iron ore. Once they have been used, they cannot be replaced. Economic growth means that future generations will have fewer resources. This is referred to as **unsustainable growth**.

ACTIVITY 2

CASE STUDY: ECONOMIC GROWTH AND UNEMPLOYMENT IN BRAZIL

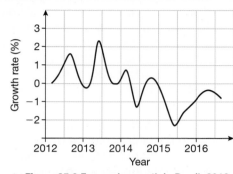

▲ **Figure 25.6** Economic growth in Brazil, 2012–16

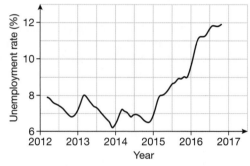

▲ **Figure 25.7** Unemployment in Brazil, 2012–16

Look at Figure 25.6 and Figure 25.7.

1 Describe the possible relationship between economic growth and unemployment in Brazil between 2012 and 2016.

2 What is the likely cause of the relationship identified in your anser to question **(1)**?

3 What happened in the Brazilian economy in 2015? Use a PPC diagram to support your answer.

MULTIPLE-CHOICE QUESTIONS

▶ 1 The value of GDP for a country in 2015 was US$980 000 million. In 2016, the value was US$1 020 000 million. What is the rate of economic growth over these 2 years?

A 40.8 per cent

B US$1 020 000 million

C US$408 000 million

D 4.08 per cent

▶ 2 Which of the following is a benefit of economic growth?

A Higher cost of living

B Higher levels of employment

C Higher levels of taxation

D Lower government spending

ECONOMICS IN PRACTICE

CASE STUDY: ECONOMIC GROWTH IN INDIA

India has enjoyed some very high levels of economic growth in the last 10 years or so. For example, Figure 25.8 shows growth in GDP reached 11 per cent in 2010. During this period, it is clear that some of the benefits have helped the poor. For example, there has been an increase in the percentage of people who can read and write and a fall in the number of children under the age of one year who die throughout the country. Census data showed that literacy improved from 64.8 to 74.04 per cent of the population between 2001 and 2011. Also, the infant mortality rate (per 1000 live births) fell from 80 in 1991 to 50 in 2009. Life expectancy (the average period that a person may live) in India has also improved from 55.7 in 1981–85 to 64.2 in 2002–06.

With the high rates of economic growth, the government has enjoyed a significant boost in tax revenues. As a result, the Indian government has introduced policies to reduce poverty and generate employment. Two of the schemes include the Rural Health Mission and Mahatma Gandhi National Rural Employment Guarantee Scheme. The latter aims to provide at least 100 days of guaranteed wage employment each year to every Indian household including women. As a result, 52.6 million households were provided with jobs in 2009–10. Evidence also suggests that the poorest Indian states benefitted the most.

The government has also invested heavily in infrastructure development. For example, the government is committed to a huge road construction programme. The country's road network has expanded at rate of 4 per cent, which has added more than 4.8 million kilometres of additional roads since 1951. However, more is needed since the network is still underdeveloped. India now has the second-largest road network after the USA, with 5.23 million kilometres of roads, of which 3.17 million are surfaced.

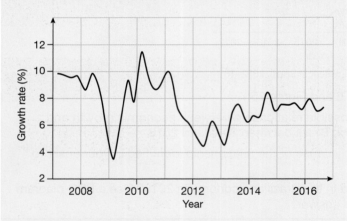

▲ Figure 25.8 Economic growth in India, 2008–16

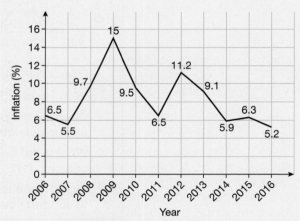

▲ Figure 25.9 Inflation in India, 2006–16

CHAPTER QUESTIONS

1 How is economic growth measured?

2 Describe two limitations of using GDP as a measure of economic growth.

3 What was happening in the Indian economy over the period shown in Figure 25.8. Use a drawing of the economic cycle to support your answer.

4 Discuss the possible link between economic growth and inflation in India.

5 Consider the possible benefits of economic growth to India.

26 INFLATION

LEARNING OBJECTIVES

- Understand how to define inflation and deflation
- Understand how inflation is measured
- Understand the different types of inflation: demand pull and cost push
- Understand the relationship between inflation and interest rates
- Understand the impact of inflation on: prices, wages, exports, unemployment, menu costs, shoe leather costs, uncertainty, business confidence, consumer confidence and investment

GETTING STARTED

It is unlikely that the prices of the goods and services bought by households and firms will stay the same over a period of time. For example, over a period of one year, the prices of many items will probably rise. Look at the example below.

CASE STUDY: THE SAMUELSEN HOUSEHOLD

Stefan and Omar Samuelsen and their two children live in Trondheim, Norway. In 2016, they noticed that the prices of certain goods and services had changed. For example, the annual gas bill had risen from NOK 8000 to NOK 8340. The weekly grocery bill for essentials had also increased. Two till receipts are shown in Table 26.1. Olga Thompson also noticed that the price of her annual gym membership had risen from NOK 2000 to NOK 2300. However, her brother Julian pointed out the price of petrol for his car had fallen from NOK 150 per litre to NOK 140 per litre.

1 Calculate the percentage change in (a) the gas bill and (b) the grocery bill.

2 Which of the bills in (1) have increased the most?

3 Describe **one** possible reason why the gas bill may have risen by so much.

4 Describe **one** possible reason for the change in the price of petrol for Julian's car.

	2015 KRONE		2016 KRONE
Bread (5 loaves)	150	Bread (5 loaves)	155
Milk (7 l)	120	Milk (7 l)	115
Fish (2 kg)	210	Fish (2 kg)	220
Chicken (2 free range)	190	Chicken (2 free range)	180
Rice (1 kg)	19	Rice (1 kg)	17
Cheese (2 kg)	220	Cheese (2 kg)	230
Butter (1 kg)	20	Butter (1 kg)	21
Coffee (250 g)	44	Coffee (250 g)	48
Bran Flakes (750 g)	24	Bran Flakes (750 g)	25
Krumcakes (12)	120	Krumcakes (12)	130
Cola (4 l)	80	Cola (4 l)	83
Chocolate	60	Chocolate	64
Total	**1257**	**Total**	**1288**

▲ Table 26.1 A comparison of the Samuelsen family's grocery bills from 2015 and 2016

WHAT IS INFLATION?

Inflation can be defined as a general and continuing rise in prices. If the prices of goods and services are going up generally in the economy over a period of time, inflation is said to exist. For example, according to Figure 26.1, in 2016, the inflation rate in Peru was 3.2 per cent. So prices rose on average by 3.2 per cent during the year. This means that PEN 4000 of goods purchased in 2015 would cost PEN 4128 (PEN 4000 + 4000 × 3.2 per cent) in 2016.

Sometimes prices fall over time. In 'Getting started', the price of petrol for Julian's car fell from NOK 150 per litre in 2015 to NOK 140 in 2016. However, falling prices are not as common as rising prices. **Deflation** is the term used to describe a fall in average prices. However, deflation may also be used to describe a slowdown in the economy – a period where **aggregate demand** is falling. Aggregate demand in the economy is total demand from consumers, businesses, the government and foreign buyers (but excludes demand for goods purchased from overseas). It includes consumption, investment, government expenditure and exports minus imports.

Governments usually measure and monitor the rate of inflation. In the EU and many other counties, inflation is measured using the **consumer price index (CPI)**. The CPI is a measure of average prices calculated from the same price information. Every month, the government records the prices of about 600 goods and services purchased by over 7000 families. An average monthly price is then worked out from all the information gathered. This average price is then converted into an index number. This allows comparisons to be made between two different periods. The CPI is the measure used worldwide and is the measure used in Figure 26.1.

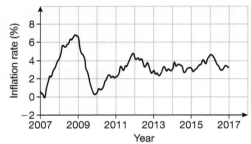

▲ **Figure 26.1** Inflation in Peru, 2007–16

ACTIVITY 1

CASE STUDY: EU INFLATION

Figure 26.2 shows the EU inflation rate between 2006 and 2016. The CPI increased by 1.1 per cent at the end of 2016. This was the highest inflation rate since September 2013. Inflation was boosted by the rising prices of fuel. The highest rate was in Estonia, where CPI rose by 2.4 per cent. In contrast, negative inflation rates were recorded in a number of countries – Bulgaria and Ireland, for example, where the rates were –0.5 per cent and –0.2 per cent, respectively.

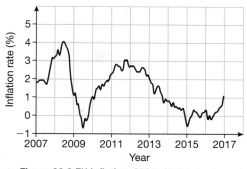

▲ **Figure 26.2** EU inflation, 2007–16 (percentage change in the CPI)

1 Describe what has happened to the EU inflation rate over the time period.

2 When did the EU experience deflation?

3 How is the EU inflation rate measured in this case?

4 In pairs, find out the inflation rate in your country for the last 3 years. Compare this with inflation rates in three other countries of your choice. Present your findings on a poster to the rest of the class.

TYPES OF INFLATION

Inflation may be caused by different factors and there is often some disagreement about the importance of each one. This is because different economists have different views about the causes of inflation.

DEMAND-PULL INFLATION

Some economists argue that inflation can be caused by too much demand in the economy. This is called **demand-pull inflation**. Chapter 7 (see pages 41–48) explained that in any market, if demand increases, there would be an increase in price. This will be the same for the whole economy. If aggregate demand increases, there will be an increase in the general price level. Aggregate demand is the total demand in the economy. So, demand-pull inflation could be caused by:

- rising consumer spending encouraged by tax cuts or low interest rates
- sharp increases in government spending
- rising demand for resources by firms
- booming demand for exports.

> **SUBJECT VOCABULARY**
>
> **demand-pull inflation** inflation caused by too much demand in the economy relative to supply

DID YOU KNOW?

Demand-pull inflation is most likely to occur if the economy is close to full employment. As consumers, businesses, foreigner visitors and the government increase their spending levels, total demand in the economy will begin to rise. If businesses are close to full capacity, they will find it difficult to produce the extra output to meet this demand. As a result, they are likely to respond by raising their prices. In sectors where businesses find it almost impossible to produce more, and where the increase in demand is at its greatest, prices are likely to rise more sharply.

> **SUBJECT VOCABULARY**
>
> **cost-push inflation** inflation caused by rising business costs

COST-PUSH INFLATION

Another theory is that inflation can be caused by rising costs. This is called **cost-push inflation**. When businesses are faced with rising costs, they put up their prices to protect their profit margins. As a result, inflation is caused.

For example, a retailer buys goods from a supplier for £10 per unit. The retailer then adds 10 per cent of the cost to get the selling price. This is £11 (£10 × 0.10). If the cost of this product from the supplier rises to £12, the new price will be £13.20 (£12 × 0.10). The retailer has increased the price of the product from £11 to £13.20 because costs have risen. This is cost-push inflation. If the retailer did not increase the price when the cost rose, profits would be reduced. Costs might rise for a number of reasons.

It has been suggested that cost-push inflation in the UK has been caused by the rising costs of imported goods, such as oil. For example, in the early 1970s, the price of imported oil went up by around 400 per cent. Shortly after, inflation in the UK reached heights of almost 25 per cent.

Wage increases might also cause cost-push inflation. For example, in the 1970s, trade unions became quite strong and were able to put pressure on employers to increase wages (see Chapter 23, pages 173–180). Employers recovered the extra money paid to workers by increasing prices.

Increases in taxation can also cause cost-push inflation. For example, in 2010, the Greek government increased VAT from 13 per cent to 23 per cent, and then again to 24 per cent in 2016. If entrepreneurs try to increase the amount of profit they make, this can also cause cost-push inflation. This is because raising the selling price can return higher profits.

ACTIVITY 2

CASE STUDY: DEMAND PULL INFLATION

The global demand for zinc has been rising since the beginning of 2016. One of the main contributors to the rising demand has been growth in the motorcar industry in China. The rising demand has resulted in higher prices for zinc. Figure 26.3 shows the price of zinc between 2016 and 2017. It has risen from around US$1500 per tonne in January 2016 to US$2600 per tonne in April 2017.

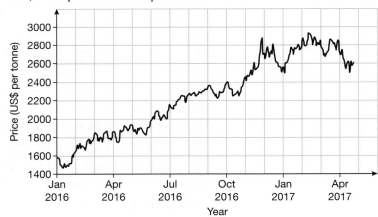

▲ **Figure 26.3** Changes in the price of zinc

1 Calculate the percentage increase in the price of zinc between January 2016 and April 2017.

2 What is meant by demand-pull inflation? Use this case as an example in your explanation.

3 Explain how zinc mining companies might respond to the rising price of zinc in the market.

THE RELATIONSHIP BETWEEN INFLATION AND INTEREST RATES

SUBJECT VOCABULARY

interest rates price paid to lenders for borrowed money; it is the price of money
monetarists economists who believe there is a strong link between growth in the money supply and inflation

Another theory of inflation is held by a group of economists called **monetarists**. Monetarists believe there is a strong link between inflation and growth in the money supply. The money supply is the stock of notes and coins, bank deposits and other financial assets in the economy. This is explained in Chapter 32 (pages 259–265). Inflation may be caused when households, firms and the government borrow more money from banks to fund extra spending. This adds to the money supply because there are now more bank deposits (the borrowed money increases bank balances). The extra money lent by the banks creates more demand and prices are driven up. This type of inflation is more likely to happen if **interest rates** are low. This is because borrowing is likely to increase when interest rates are low.

In the past, some governments have raised interest rates to bring down the rate of inflation. If interest rates rise, borrowing will fall as it becomes more expensive, the money supply will grow less quickly and demand will fall. As a result, the pressure on prices is relieved so inflation will fall.

THE IMPACT OF INFLATION

SUBJECT VOCABULARY

purchasing power of money amount of goods and services that can be bought with a fixed sum of money

PRICES

One of the main problems of inflation is that prices are rising. As a result, inflation reduces the **purchasing power of money**. This means that people cannot buy as much with their income. Therefore, households will experience a fall in their living standards. However, if incomes are rising as fast, or faster than prices, this may not be a problem for individuals.

WAGES

When prices are rising, workers need to increase their wages to compensate for the loss in purchasing power. If workers can negotiate higher wages with their employers, they will get more money. However, as a result of the higher wages, firms may need to raise their prices because costs have risen. If this pattern is repeated, a wages/prices spiral develops. This means that higher prices lead to higher wages, which then leads to higher prices and so on. Demands for higher wages when there is inflation can cause conflict between employers and trade unions. Such conflict could result in a strike and both workers and firms would lose out.

EXPORTS

If inflation is higher at home than in other countries, firms may find it difficult to sell in overseas markets. This is because the prices of exports rise. As a result, demand for exports is likely to fall which means that the balance of payments (see Chapter 28, pages 220–227) is affected negatively. Falling demand for exports will also result in job losses for those people employed by businesses that sell goods abroad.

UNEMPLOYMENT

High levels of inflation usually mean that aggregate demand is rising. As a result, firms will be keen to increase output since the prices of goods is increasing. This means that firms will need to recruit more workers, which reduces unemployment. It has been suggested in the past that a trade-off exists between inflation and unemployment. This means that if the government wants to reduce inflation, it will have to accept higher levels of unemployment. However, some economists suggest that this relationship is not always found. For example, in countries where inflation is very high indeed, such as Venezuela and Iran, unemployment has also risen sharply.

MENU COSTS

If inflation is rapid, firms will have to increase their prices frequently. This will cost money because customers have to be told. New brochures will have to be printed, websites updated and sales staff informed. These are called **menu costs** because, for a restaurant, when prices are increased a new menu has to be printed.

SHOE LEATHER COSTS

When prices are changing frequently consumers and firms will have to spend more time looking for the lowest prices or the best value for money. This involves 'shopping around', which is a cost because it takes time and wears out the leather on your shoes. Hence, these are called the **shoe leather costs** of inflation.

UNCERTAINTY

If inflation is high and varying, firms do not know what prices will be in 3 or 6 months' time, and predicting years ahead becomes impossible. However, decisions have to be made now which will affect the business in the long term. Inflation creates uncertainty, which makes planning for the future very difficult. Making investment decisions is particularly difficult. This is discussed below. Another problem with uncertainty is linked to entering long-term contracts. A customer might approach a firm wanting to buy goods on a regular basis for the next 3 or 4 years. How can a supplier set a price for this contract if it does not know what the inflation rate will be over this time?

BUSINESS AND CONSUMER CONFIDENCE

The uncertainty caused by inflation may have an effect on the confidence of consumers and businesses. For example, inflation might make consumers anxious. They may become more cautious – less willing to borrow money, for example. They may start to save more, so they have reserves for unforeseen circumstances. This behaviour will reduce demand, which may not be good for job security in the economy. Businesses may lose their confidence during periods of high inflation as well. They may postpone growth plans or reduce their spending on product development. When businesses lack confidence, they are less likely to take risks. As a result, economic growth rates tend to fall.

If **hyperinflation** exists, where price increases are out of control, rising at several hundred or thousand per cent a year, for example, money may not be accepted as a means of payment. As a result, both consumers and businesses become very worried indeed. Hyperinflation can destabilise a country.

INVESTMENT

Inflation often results in a decline in business investment. This is because investment requires spending quite large amounts of money now in the hope of returns over a future period of time – perhaps up to 5, 10 or more years. Owing to the uncertainty about future prices created by inflation, and the lack of business confidence among decision makers, investment projects are likely to be postponed or cancelled. This will have a negative impact on economic growth and the future level of employment in the economy.

MULTIPLE-CHOICE QUESTIONS

▶ **1** Inflation caused by firms raising prices owing to increased wages, for example, is called:

   A Demand-pull inflation

   B Hyperinflation

   C Deflation

   D Cost-push inflation

▶ **2** Which of the following is likely to cause demand-pull inflation?

   A Falling consumer spending fuelled by higher taxes

   B A substantial fall in exports

   C Rapid increases in government spending

   D A rise in interest rates

ECONOMICS IN PRACTICE

CASE STUDY: INFLATION IN VENEZUELA

One of the government's macroeconomic objectives is to keep inflation down. This is because inflation can be harmful. Inflation can cause problems for consumers, firms and the economy. In recent years, Venezuela has seen some unbelievable price increases. Some economists predicted that inflation would reach 1600 per cent in 2017. Figure 26.4 shows the rate of inflation in Venezuela between 2012 and 2016.

Inflation at this level (hyperinflation) can have serious consequences. In Venezuela, the government declared a state of emergency. Venezuelans are dying of treatable illnesses caused by shortages of medical supplies. There are regular shortages of basic foods, such as milk, eggs and vegetables. Inflation has become so bad that the government ordered millions of pounds of provisions to be airdropped across the country. The army now controls food supplies and people have to queue up for hours in the hope that they can buy something. In December 2016, Venezuela's credit card and cash machine system froze. This meant that businesses could not process **transactions** and had to ask for cash or delay payment. Venezuela is now distributing new higher-value notes to deal with some of the practical problems of sky high inflation. For example, a backpack full of cash is often needed to pay supermarket bills. The central bank has now introduced six new bills ranging from VEF 500 to 20 000. Before this, the largest note was VEF 100 and worth about 2 US cents. One person interviewed by the media said, 'I still go to the open market to buy fruit but even there it is ridiculous. In April 2015, I bought some fruit and vegetables for 430 bolivars. Last Saturday the same items cost me 14 000 bolivars. Isn't that crazy?'

The economy is now in a deep recession with rising unemployment and huge government debt. One of the problems is that the falling oil price in 2014 resulted in a loss of earnings for businesses and lower tax revenues for the government. Venezuela's economy relies very heavily on oil production. For example, oil sales account for nearly 90 per cent of the nation's exports. Many feel that the only hope now is to receive assistance from the International Monetary Fund (IMF). However, Venezuela cut links with the IMF many years ago.

SUBJECT VOCABULARY

transactions payment, or the process of making one

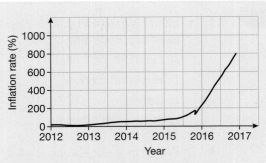

▲ **Figure 26.4** Inflation in Venezuela, 2012–16

▲ Shortages of produce in Venezuela

CHAPTER QUESTIONS

In 2016, some goods purchased in Venezuela cost VEF 50 000.

1 Calculate how much these goods would cost a year later if inflation reached 1600 per cent.

2 Comment on the scale of inflation in Venezuela.

3 Describe two negative impacts that households in Venezuela have experienced as a result of inflation.

4 Describe the difference between the menu costs and the shoe leather costs of inflation.

5 Discuss the impact that inflation in Venezuela might have on business confidence and investment.

27 UNEMPLOYMENT

LEARNING OBJECTIVES

Understand how unemployment is measured

Understand the different types of unemployment: cyclical, structural, seasonal, voluntary and frictional

Understand the impact of unemployment on: output, use of scarce resources, poverty, government spending on benefits, tax revenue, consumer confidence, business confidence and society

GETTING STARTED

It is important for a government to keep as many people as possible in work. If people do not work, they make no contribution to national production and their labour is wasted. Also, the living standards of those out of work are not as good as those with jobs. People can be without jobs for a number of reasons. Look at the examples below.

CASE STUDY: KOSTAS MANTALOS

Kostas Mantalos is married with a one-year old son. He lives on the Greek island of Kos. He works at one of many tourist hotels on the island. He is employed as a waiter and works 12 hours a day, 6 days a week between April and October. Unfortunately, he is not required from November to March. He earns €12 000 a year (plus tips) and is used to this pattern of work. However, he struggles financially when not working.

▶ A hotel in Kos

CASE STUDY: MAUREEN CONTE

Maureen was employed as a cost accountant by a construction company specialising in the building of oilrigs. However, in January 2015, she was made redundant as the company struggled to survive in an increasingly competitive market. Owing to a fall in the global oil price, there was a huge reduction in the number of oil-related construction projects being started. As a result, Maureen and four of her colleagues were laid off. Maureen hopes to get another job, but she is not confident because she has quite a specialised set of skills.

▶ An oilrig under construction

1 Why is Kostas Mantalos not employed after the end of October each year?

2 Why was Maureen was made redundant?

3 Why should a government be concerned about unemployment?

4 In pairs, find out the level of unemployment in your country and make comparisons with three other countries of your choice.

WHAT IS UNEMPLOYMENT?

Unemployed people are defined as those who want a job but cannot find work. **Unemployment** is a waste of resources. If people are not working, they are not making any contribution to economic output in their country. Therefore, that country's GDP will be lower. Unemployment will also cause hardship to those who cannot find work. Their living standards will be very low compared to most of those in work. Economists might define unemployment as those without a job but who are actively seeking work at current wage rates.

SUBJECT VOCABULARY

unemployment when those actively seeking work are unable to find a job

HOW IS UNEMPLOYMENT MEASURED?

In 2016, Portugal had a population of just over 10 million. However, many of these people were not able to work – they were children or retired, for example. The number of people able to work was just over 5 million. But in November 2016, 549 000 of these were not in work. They were unemployed. This means they were actively seeking work but were not able to find a job.

One method used to measure unemployment in much of the world is to carry out a survey. The survey used (in the EU) is called the Labour Force Survey (LFS) and is carried out every month. In the survey, the International Labour Organisation (ILO) defines unemployment. This definition is used internationally so that comparisons can be made. Figure 27.1 shows unemployment in Portugal between 2006 and 2016. The rate is expressed as a percentage of the workforce. It was 10.5 per cent in the third quarter of 2016.

KEY FACTS

Unemployed people
The ILO defines unemployed people as:
- without a job, want a job, have actively sought work in the last 4 weeks and are available to start work in the next 2 weeks, or
- out of work, have found a job and are waiting to start it in the next 2 weeks.

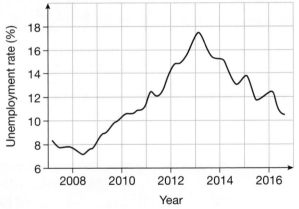

▲ **Figure 27.1** Unemployment in Portugal, 2006–16

In general, anyone who carries out at least one hour's paid work in a week, or who is temporarily away from a job (for example, on holiday), is in employment. Also counted as in employment are people on government-supported training schemes and people who do unpaid work for their family's business. Those who are out of work but do not meet the definition of unemployment are said to be *economically inactive*. Figure 27.2 shows examples of different individuals' employment status.

Examples: Individuals' employment status

Example	ILO Classification
Mr A worked 36 hours last week as a lorry driver.	In employment
Mrs B lost her job as a secretary 3 months ago. Every week she visits an employment agency to try to find a new job, which she would be able to start immediately.	Unemployed (out of work, wants job, has actively sought work in the last 4 weeks and is available to start work within 2 weeks)
Ms C looks after her one-year-old son. She neither holds a job, nor wants a job.	Economically inactive – she does not want or have a job
Mr D has no job from which he receives any pay or profit. However, he helps in his parents' shop for around 20 hours per week.	In employment
Mrs E is currently receiving training at a local hairdresser. This is being partly paid for by the government. She works 28 hours a week and goes to college for one day.	In employment
Ms F is out of work, but stopped looking for new job a year ago as she does not believe any jobs are available.	Economically inactive

▲ **Figure 27.2** Examples of individual employment status

DID YOU KNOW?

In some countries, a second method is used to measure unemployment. This is the claimant count and includes all those people who claim Jobseeker's Allowance (as it is known in the UK), or some other form of state unemployment benefit. The claimant count will always be lower than the ILO count because it excludes some groups. For example, unemployed women who are actively seeking work but are not entitled to benefits are not included.

TYPES OF UNEMPLOYMENT

SUBJECT VOCABULARY

cyclical or demand deficient unemployment unemployment caused by falling demand as a result of a downturn in the economic cycle

laying off to stop employing someone because there is no work for them to do

People are unemployed for a number of reasons.

CYCLICAL OR DEMAND DEFICIENT UNEMPLOYMENT

Cyclical or demand deficient unemployment is linked to the economic cycle. When an economy moves from a boom into a downturn, business activity slows down and people are laid off. This will continue and worsen if the economy goes into a recession or depression. People lose their jobs because demand for goods and services starts to fall. Firms often react to falling demand by **laying off** staff. Figure 27.3 shows the economic cycle and the position where cyclical unemployment starts to rise.

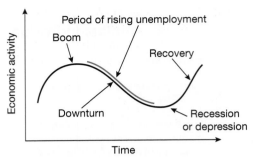

▲ **Figure 27.3** Economic cycle and unemployment

STRUCTURAL UNEMPLOYMENT

Over a period of time, the structure of an economy changes. For example, in most developed countries, over time, the manufacturing sector declines and the service sector grows. Changes in the structure of the economy can result in **structural unemployment**. There are three main types.

■ **Sectorial unemployment** occurs when people are laid off because the industry they work in is in decline.

■ **Technological unemployment** occurs when jobs that were previously done by people are now done by machines. The development and introduction of computers in the last 20 years or so has made a huge difference to production methods in many industries. These new methods usually involve replacing some labour with technology. For example, banks have cut their workforces because people can bank online and get their cash from automatic teller machines (ATMs).

■ **Regional unemployment** Unemployment in a particular country is not likely to be the same in all regions. For example, in the UK, unemployment has tended to be much lower in the south-east of England than in the north-east of England. One reason for this is linked to the decline in certain industries. For example, the north-east has suffered owing to the decline in the shipbuilding and mining industries. At the same time, the south-east has benefited from the growth in financial services.

SEASONAL UNEMPLOYMENT

Some types of workers are only required for certain times of the year. For example, in holiday resorts, hotels, restaurants and tourist attractions take on more staff during the holiday season. In most of Europe this would be the summer. People who do this work are seasonal workers and are unemployed when the season ends. There is little that can be done to reduce **seasonal unemployment** because it is usually linked to the climate.

VOLUNTARY UNEMPLOYMENT

Most people are unemployed against their wishes. They are victims and want to work if they are given the opportunity. However, there are a minority of people in society who choose not to work. These people are said to be **voluntarily unemployed**. They may choose not to work because they are not prepared to work for the wages offered or perhaps because they do not like the idea of work in general.

FRICTIONAL UNEMPLOYMENT

Frictional unemployment is short-term unemployment. It occurs when people are unemployed as they move from one job to another. Frictional unemployment will always exist in an economy but it is not considered to be a problem. For example, some people deliberately take an extended break between jobs, treating it like a holiday. Others have to wait a short while because their new employment is not due to start immediately. Unemployment for periods of up to 8 weeks is considered to be frictional.

ACTIVITY 1

CASE STUDY: MARINE D'ARCY

'How unlucky can you get?' This is what Marine D'Arcy said when she was made redundant for the second time in 2 years. In 2015, Vent Plastique, a manufacturer of plastic household products based in Lyon, France, laid her off. Marine worked on the factory floor but the company was taken over and production was switched to the Far East. However, Marine managed to get another job in Lyon working in a warehouse for a mail order company. She helped to 'pick stock' and process customer orders. Unfortunately, after 18 months the company automated the warehouse resulting in 12 redundancies. Marine was one of the unlucky ones because she was a recent recruit.

▲ Warehouse work

1   What is the difference between sectorial and technological unemployment? Use the example in this case to support your explanation.

2   How might Marine improve her mobility in the labour market?

IMPACT OF UNEMPLOYMENT

OUTPUT

If people are unemployed, the productive potential of a country is not being fully exploited. As a result, levels of output are lower than they could be. This means that national income and living standards will be lower (on average). However, if most of the unemployment is a result of new technology being introduced, output might not fall. Output could actually increase if productivity rises.

USE OF SCARCE RESOURCES

People who are out of work do not make any contribution to production. This is a waste of resources and results in lower levels of national income. If there is full employment in an economy, output will be higher and income per head will be higher. In some countries, youth unemployment is very high. Many consider that this is particularly wasteful.

POVERTY

In some developing countries, many people have never worked in their lives. There have never been any employment opportunities for them. As a result, they have to live in poverty. They may try to support themselves at a minimum level by growing some food on a plot of land, for example.

Even in developed countries, most people who find themselves without a job have to suffer hardship. Their incomes fall because state benefits are generally lower than wages. In extreme cases, unemployed people lose their homes because they cannot afford mortgage payments. Sometimes the costs can extend to family break-ups and a lower self-confidence for those who are long-term unemployed.

GOVERNMENT SPENDING ON BENEFITS

In most developed countries, when people are unemployed they are entitled to receive some financial benefit from the state. If unemployment levels rise, the government has to allocate more money to unemployment benefit. This extra expenditure will incur an opportunity cost. For example, the money could be better spent on education or health care, for example.

TAX REVENUE

When unemployment rises, tax revenues will fall because most taxes are linked to income and spending. This means the government has less to spend and may have to cut public sector services. Alternatively, it may borrow more, which will increase national debt or it may have to increase tax rates. For example, taxes on incomes, corporate profits and spending may have to rise.

CONSUMER CONFIDENCE

During periods of high unemployment, consumer confidence is likely to fall. Most people who find themselves without a job have to suffer hardship. Their incomes fall because state benefits are generally lower than wages. As a result, these people lose confidence and play a less significant role in the economy. Also, people who remain employed may start to worry about their own job security. Their confidence is also negatively affected. They become more cautious, which will result in lower levels of spending and probably more unemployment.

BUSINESS CONFIDENCE

When firms lay off workers, they have to pay them redundancy money. Also, the remaining workers may be demotivated because they may fear that they will be the next to be made redundant. A firm will be left with spare capacity when laying people off and there is likely to be a fall in demand. Sales are likely to fall for most businesses when unemployment starts to rise in the economy. This is because people have less to spend. However, firms producing non-essential goods and services are likely to be hit harder. All these effects are likely to reduce the confidence of business decision makers. As a result, they are less likely to take risks and may postpone or cancel investment projects.

SOCIETY

Sometimes unemployment can have an impact on local communities. For example, in some towns and villages, a large proportion of the population may be employed by the same business. If this business closes down, local unemployment can be very high indeed. As a result, the spirit in many of these communities worsens. Such areas become run down. Smaller businesses start to struggle and fail because their customers are suffering hardship. Households do not have enough money to maintain their houses and gardens and the residential environment starts to look uncared for.

There may also be an impact on the wider society. For example, losing a job can be psychologically hard on workers. Individuals may doubt their value as a person. This can lead to stress within relationships. Unemployed people are less likely to get married and more likely to get divorced as their lack of work raises stress levels. Stress can also lead to poorer health. Finally, unemployment can potentially lead to crime. The unemployed still need the necessities of life. In some cases, they may turn to crime to meet their material needs.

ACTIVITY 2

CASE STUDY: UNEMPLOYMENT IN SOUTH AFRICA

▲ Statue of South African leader Nelson Mandela in London, UK

Like many African states, South Africa suffers from very high levels of unemployment. Figure 27.4 shows the unemployment rates for the last 10 years. In 2016, unemployment reached 27 per cent. Many firms were laying off workers. For example, FNB, a South African bank, laid off 589 employees when it closed 34 branches. This was down to automation and the computerisation of some of its services. The volume of electronic transactions at FNB has increased by 14 per cent. In addition, online transactions rose by 15 per cent and the use of its app for banking services by 69 per cent. Another company, RCL Foods, laid off 1350 factory workers in the Kwazulu-Natal province. This was the result of rising cheap imports. Reports said that the chicken industry is battling for survival due to fierce competition from producers in Brazil, the EU and the USA. The long period of low rainfall in South Africa had also raised costs in food production.

Although the number of people living in poverty in South Africa fell during the Nelson Mandela government over 35 per cent of the population still live below the poverty line. The evidence is everywhere in the growing townships that surround Johannesburg, Cape Town and Durban, where millions live in extreme poverty. In one report, a taxi driver who lives in one of Cape Town's settlements, explained how dangerous it was when he returned home from work late at night. He has been robbed of his daily wages several times. However, he considers that he is lucky because he has a job. One problem in South Africa is the distribution of wealth. Between 60 and 65 per cent of the wealth belongs to the wealthiest 10 per cent of the nation.

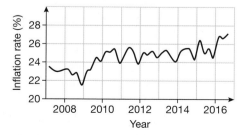

▲ **Figure 27.4** Unemployment in South Africa, 2006–16

One worrying issue is the scale of youth unemployment in the country. It has been greater than 50 per cent for most of the last 10 years. Employment for young people is very important. It is needed to help support career development. Young people in employment develop the skills such as confidence, discipline, work ethic, accountability and interpersonal skills. These are necessary to make a success of life and survive in the job market. Such high levels of youth unemployment is a dreadful waste of resources.

1 What might happen to business confidence in South Africa if the pattern of unemployment shown in Figure 27.4 continues?

2 Discuss how unemployment has impacted on **(a)** poverty levels and **(b)** resource use in South Africa in recent years.

MULTIPLE-CHOICE QUESTIONS

▶ 1 Which of the following refers to people out of work when moving between jobs?

   A Seasonal unemployment

   B Frictional unemployment

   C Voluntary unemployment

   D Structural unemployment

The diagram shows four positions, W, X, Y and Z, on and around a production possibility curve for a country.

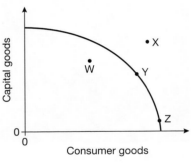

▶ 2 Which of the positions illustrates that the country has unemployment?

   A Position W

   B Position X

   C Position Y

   D Position Z

ECONOMICS IN PRACTICE

CASE STUDY: UNEMPLOYMENT IN GREECE

The global recession in 2008 hit many countries very hard. However, one of the hardest hit was Greece. In addition to falling demand resulting from the global recession, Greece had other economic problems. Both private sector and public sector debt was too high. From 1999 to 2008, private sector debt as a proportion of GDP more than doubled from 59 per cent to 126 per cent. The ratio of public sector debt to GDP was around 100 per cent over the same period. During this period, consumers, businesses and the government spent heavily. This was reflected in the booming level of imports. However, when the financial crisis hit the world in 2008, those with debt struggled to repay what they owed. In an effort to reduce debt, households and businesses cut their spending. This resulted in a huge increase in unemployment, which is shown in Figure 27.5. The government's debt also rose as they were faced with rising social security payments to the unemployed and lower tax revenues from falling spending and lower corporate profits.

Another problem in Greece was the nation's culture of early retirement and low tax collection. Historically, Greece spent around 17.5 per cent of its GDP on pension payments. This is the highest in the EU. The average Greek man retires at 63 and the average woman at 59. Also, some police and military workers have retired as early as age 40 or 45 in the past. The government has always struggled to collect taxes in the country. There have been reports of large-scale illegal underpayment and avoidance of tax.

The situation in Greece got so bad that the country was on the verge of bankruptcy. It was saved by large loans from the EU. However, the country was forced take a number of measures to reduce government debt. These included raising taxes, cutting government spending and selling off state assets. Also, in 2013, Greece's retirement age was raised to 67 in common with many other countries in the world.

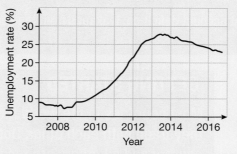

▲ **Figure 27.5** Unemployment in Greece, 2006–16

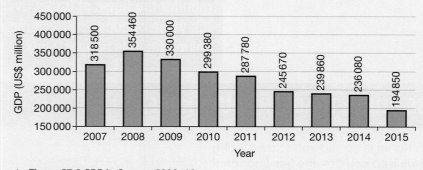

▲ **Figure 27.6** GDP in Greece, 2006–16

CHAPTER QUESTIONS

Look at Figure 27.5.

1 Describe the pattern of unemployment in Greece over the period shown.

2 How is unemployment measured?

3 What are the possible causes of unemployment in Greece. Give at least two reasons in your analysis.

4 Describe the effect on unemployment of the government raising the retirement age in Greece.

5 Consider the impact of high unemployment in Greece on (a) output and (b) the government.

28 BALANCE OF PAYMENTS ON THE CURRENT ACCOUNT

LEARNING OBJECTIVES

- Understand how to define the current account
- Understand current account deficits and surpluses
- Understand visible and invisible trade
- Understand the relationship between the current account and exchanges rates
- Understand examples of real-world exchange rates
- Understand the reasons for deficits and surpluses: quality of domestic and foreign goods, prices of domestic and foreign goods, and exchange rates between countries
- Understand the impact of a current account deficit on: leakages from the economy, inflation, demand for domestic exports and deficit funding

GETTING STARTED

Most countries in the world have open economies. This means that they trade with each other. Details of the transactions between one country and all others are recorded so that the government can monitor the flows of trade. Over a period of time, it is desirable for the value of goods sold overseas to be roughly the same as the value of goods bought. Look at the example below.

CASE STUDY: TRADE IN SOUTH KOREA

South Korea is considered to be a highly industrialised country and has important trade links with many foreign countries. Examples of goods that it sells overseas include semiconductors, petrochemicals, automobile/auto parts, ships, flat display screens, steel, electronics, plastics and computers. The country also sells iron, steel and many products made using those metals. South Korea buys goods such as crude oil/petroleum products, semiconductors, natural gas, coal, steel, computers, automobiles, fine chemicals and textiles, from overseas. Its main trading partners include the EU, China, Japan and the USA.

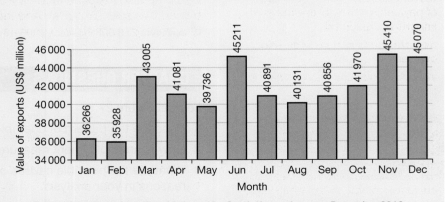

▲ Figure 28.1 Value of goods sold abroad by South Korea, January–December 2016

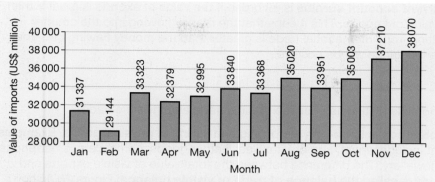

▲ Figure 28.2 Value of goods bought by South Korea from abroad, January–December 2016

South Korea has an open economy.

1 What does this mean?

2 What is the difference between the value of goods bought and the value sold by South Korea in the last quarter of 2016?

Look at the difference between the value of goods sold (Figure 28.1) and the value bought (Figure 28.2) by South Korea over the whole period.

3 Do you think South Korea benefits from trading with other nations? Account for your answer.

4 In groups, make a list of the goods and services that your country buys and sells abroad. Compare your list with those of other groups in the class.

THE CURRENT ACCOUNT ON THE BALANCE OF PAYMENTS

SUBJECT VOCABULARY

balance of payments record of all transactions relating to international trade

capital and financial account that part of the balance of payments where flows of savings, investment and currencies are recorded

current account part of the balance of payments where all exports and imports are recorded

exports goods and services sold overseas

imports goods and services bought from overseas

Goods and services which are sold overseas are called **exports**. In 'Getting started', examples of South Korea's exports included semiconductors, petrochemicals, automobile/auto parts and ships. Those goods and services which are bought from other countries are called **imports**. In 'Getting started' examples of South Koreas' imports included crude oil/petroleum products, semiconductors, natural gas, coal, steel and computers. A country will keep a record of all transactions relating to international trade. This record is called the **balance of payments**. It is divided into two parts.

The **current account** shows the value of all imports and exports over a period of time. It includes both visible trade and invisible trade. (This is explained below.) It also includes income from interest, profits and dividends on assets owned overseas (exports). And income paid in the form of interest, profits and dividends to the foreign owners of assets at home (imports).

The **capital and financial accounts** record flows of money into and out of a country resulting from transactions relating to savings, investments and speculation, for example.

CURRENT ACCOUNT DEFICITS AND SURPLUSES

SUBJECT VOCABULARY

current account deficit when value of imports exceeds the value of exports

current balance difference between total exports and total imports (visible and invisible)

It is very unlikely that in any given period of time, the value of a countries exports will be exactly the same as the value of its imports. The difference between the two values is called the **current balance**. The current account balance can be in deficit or surplus.

A **current account deficit** occurs when the value of imports is greater than the value of exports. This means that the money flowing out of the economy resulting from international trade is greater than the money flowing in. The current balance will be negative.

SUBJECT VOCABULARY

current account surplus when value of exports exceeds the value of imports

A **current account surplus** is recorded if the value of exports is greater than the value of imports. This means that the money flowing into the country resulting from international trade is greater than the money flowing out. The current balance will be positive.

VISIBLE AND INVISIBLE TRADE

SUBJECT VOCABULARY

balance of trade or visible balance difference between visible exports and visible imports

invisible trade trade in services

primary income money received from the loan of production factors abroad

secondary income government transfers to and from overseas agencies such as the EU

visible trade trade in physical goods

Economists distinguish between visible trade and invisible trade.

Visible trade is to do with the buying and selling of physical goods. Examples might include wheat, iron ore, textiles, leather goods, gems, cars, smartphones and jewellery. The difference between the total value of visible exports and imports is called the **balance of trade** or **visible balance**. Figure 28.3 shows the visible trade for a country in 2016. The balance of trade is –US$69 181 million (US$96 732 – US$165 913). It has imported more goods than it has exported.

Invisible trade involves the exchange of services. Examples include tourism, trade in financial services, transport such as shipping and business consultancy fees. Invisible trade also includes flows of money resulting from the ownership of assets overseas. Examples might include interest, rents and profits. This is called **primary income**. Finally, invisible trade also includes **secondary income**, which results mainly from government transactions. Examples might be the money flowing between a government and other organisations such as the EU.

GENERAL VOCABULARY

beneficiary someone who gets advantages from an action or change

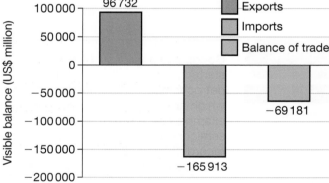

▲ **Figure 28.3** Visible balance for a country, 2016

Figure 28.4 shows the balance on the current account for a country in 2016. The current balance is the balance of trade and the invisible balance added together. It is –US$22 332 million. This is a current account deficit.

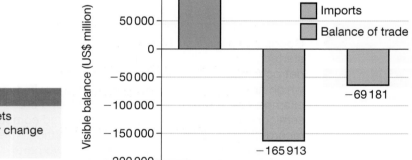

▲ **Figure 28.4** Current balance for a country, 2016

ACTIVITY 1

CASE STUDY: NIGERIA'S BALANCE OF TRADE

Nigeria has the largest economy in Africa and an estimated population of 186 million. It has a range of trading partners including China, India, the Netherlands, Spain, Brazil and South Africa. Its main exports are petroleum, petroleum products, cocoa and rubber. However, about 95 per cent of Nigeria's exports are petroleum. The country was hit quite hard when the price of oil fell in 2014. In contrast, Nigeria's imports include machinery, chemicals, transport equipment, manufactured goods and food. The balance of trade for Nigeria in 2015/16 is shown in Figure 28.5.

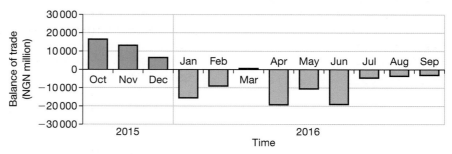

▲ **Figure 28.5** Nigerian balance of trade, 2015/16

Most of Nigeria's trade is in visible items.

1   What is meant by visible trade?

2   What is meant by the balance of trade?

3   Describe what has happened to Nigeria's balance of trade over the time period.

4   Describe **one** possible reason for the pattern of trade shown in Figure 28.5.

THE RELATIONSHIP BETWEEN THE CURRENT ACCOUNT AND EXCHANGE RATES

The pattern of international trade can be influenced by changes in the **exchange rate**. If a country's exchange rate gets stronger (which means that one unit of a currency can buy more units of another currency), exports become more expensive and imports become cheaper. This might result in fewer exports being sold and more imports being bought. This will have a negative impact on the current account. For example, if a country already has a current account deficit, the size of the deficit is likely to increase.

The balance on the current account may also have an impact on the exchange rate. For example, if a country has a surplus on the current account resulting from rising sales of goods abroad, demand for that country's currency will rise (foreigners will need to buy that country's currency to pay for the goods). This increase in demand for currency could drive up the exchange rate. Therefore that country's exchange rate gets stronger. Exchange rates, and the impact of changing exchange rates on the current account, are discussed in more detail in Chapters 41 (see pages 333–339) and 42 (see pages 340–346).

EXAMPLES OF REAL-WORLD EXCHANGE RATES

Exchange rates rarely remain stable over a period of time. The rate at which one country's currency exchanges against that of another is determined by market forces. Therefore, when there is a disturbance in the market, the exchange rate is likely to change. For example, when the UK voted to leave the EU in June 2016, the value of the pound fell quite sharply. Figure 28.6 shows the value of the pound against the US dollar. Just before the Brexit vote the exchange rate was £1 = US$1.50, however, in January 2017 it was around £1 = US$1.24. This is a fall of about 17 per cent. Sharp changes like this can have an impact on international trade. This is discussed in detail in Chapter 42 (pages 340–346).

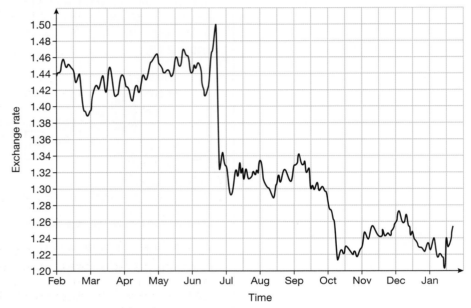

▲ **Figure 28.6** Pound : dollar exchange rate, 2016/17

REASONS FOR DEFICITS AND SURPLUSES

Most governments would prefer to have a healthy current account on the balance of payments. This might mean that over a period of time a large deficit is avoided. Some countries, like China and Japan for example, have often enjoyed quite large current account surpluses. What are the reasons for deficits and surpluses?

QUALITY OF DOMESTIC GOODS

If a country develops a reputation for high-quality goods, it is likely to enjoy rising sales from overseas buyers. This will drive up the demand for exports and help to improve a current account balance. For example, the UK has a reputation in China for the production of high-quality goods. Also, if the quality of domestic goods is high, demand from the home market will rise as consumers will prefer them to imports. This will also help to improve the current account.

QUALITY OF FOREIGN GOODS

If goods and services from overseas are superior to those produced domestically, there will be an increase in demand for these imports. Clearly this will have a negative impact on the current balance. The size of a current account deficit, for example, would get bigger. There will also be less demand for home produced goods, which could result in lower domestic output and employment.

PRICE OF DOMESTIC GOODS

Demand for goods and services is heavily influenced by the price. If domestic goods are expensive, owing to rapid inflation, for example, then demand from overseas buyers is likely to fall. This will see a progressive worsening of the current balance.

PRICE OF FOREIGN GOODS

If foreign goods are cheaper than those produced at home, there will be a rapid in demand for imports. This will have a negative effect on the current account, reducing the size of a surplus, for example. In recent years, Chinese manufactured goods have been cheaper than those produced at home in many Western countries. The resulting high demand for them has had a negative effect on the current accounts of many of these countries.

EXCHANGE RATES BETWEEN COUNTRIES

Since the exchange rate affects the prices of domestic goods and foreign goods, any changes in the exchange rate can have an impact on the current account. For example, when the value of the pound fell after the Brexit vote, there was an increase in demand for holidays in the UK. This helped to boost invisible exports and had a positive effect on the UK's current account.

ACTIVITY 2

CASE STUDY: FERRARI

Ferrari, the Italian car manufacturer, produces high performance luxury supercars. Although there are only a few people in the world who can afford to buy a Ferrari, it is a famous global brand name. In 2015, it produced 7664 cars and made a record profit. Few people buy Ferraris as a means of transport. Most Ferrari owners have several cars and as a brand Ferrari is a status symbol. Enthusiasts say that Ferrari is a special car because it has a soul. Red stands for passion and the horse logo represents aggression. For many, Ferrari symbolises power, strength, speed, confidence and boldness.

Ferrari is targeted at a niche market – the luxury segment of the car market where performance, quality and exclusivity are highly valued. Most Ferrari sales are in overseas markets. For example, in 2015, only 285 of the cars produced were sold in Italy. The other 7379 were exported to markets all over the world. Total revenue for Ferrari in 2015 was €2854 million.

▲ Ferrari 488

1   What impact will Ferrari sales have on Italy's current account?

2   Using this case as an example, discuss the importance of product quality in relation to a country's current account.

THE IMPACT OF A CURRENT ACCOUNT DEFICIT

GENERAL VOCABULARY

persistent continuing to exist or happen, especially for longer than is usual or desirable

If a nation has a **persistent** current account deficit, it may experience a number of effects. For example, if consumers buy increasing quantities of imports, domestic output and employment may be negatively affected.

LEAKAGES FROM THE ECONOMY

A persistent current account deficit suggests that a country is becoming increasingly dependent on imports. This means that consumers are buying goods produced outside the domestic economy. As a result, money flows out of the economy to overseas businesses. This represents a leakage from the economy. It means that output and employment levels in the domestic economy are under threat.

INFLATION

A country running a high current account deficit might be exposed to inflationary pressures. If the prices of imports go up, this will be reflected in the general price level since many imported goods will be counted when the CPI is calculated. Consequently, rising import prices will result in higher domestic inflation levels. The greater the reliance on imports, the greater the threat of inflation when import prices rise.

LOW DEMAND FOR EXPORTS

A country with a high current account deficit might be struggling to sell goods and services abroad. If demand for exports is low, it might mean that the quality of goods and services is poor or the price is too high. Unless the demand for exports can be reversed, a country may suffer a progressive decline in economic growth and a rise in unemployment. A current account deficit may reflect structural weaknesses in the economy. This means that domestic firms may struggle because they are not competitive in certain industries.

FUNDING THE DEFICIT

If a country has a continuing current account deficit, it will need foreign currency to pay for the rising quantity of imports that are being purchased. If the foreign currency reserves of a country run low, it may be necessary to borrow. However, persistent borrowing may cause long-term problems. Sometimes, a current account deficit can be financed by a capital account surplus. For example, flows of foreign currency can be attracted by a country if its interest rates are high.

DID YOU KNOW?

In relation to the amount of international trade done by the UK, the size of the country's deficit is insignificant. It is like someone earning £25 000 a year and spending £25 005. The person has overspent by £5; it is very small in relation to the total amount spent.

MULTIPLE-CHOICE QUESTIONS

▶ 1 Which of the following is an example of an invisible item of trade?

   A Machinery

   B Cars

   C Insurance

   D Confectionery

▶ 2 The sale of Renault cars from the Morocco factory to Spain, France and Germany result in which?

   A Increase imports

   B Reduce exports

   C Improve the current account

   D Improve the invisible balance

CASE STUDY: THE MOROCCAN CURRENT ACCOUNT BALANCE

The North African state of Morocco has taken advantage of its location close to Europe and cheap labour to develop a diverse and open market economy. In 2012, the French car company Renault opened a €1600 million factory in the north of the country. It employs over 7000 people and has a capacity to produce 340 000 vehicles. Most of the output is exported to Spain, Germany and France. The Renault plant is the biggest car production facility in Africa. However, despite this positive development in the economy, in the last few years Morocco has experienced several deficits on its current account. Figure 28.7 shows Morocco's current account balance from 2014 to 2016.

Morocco exports a wide range of goods such as clothing and textiles, automobiles, electrical components, inorganic chemicals, transistors, crude minerals, fertilisers, petroleum products, citrus fruits, vegetables and fish. Morocco also has a well-developed tourist industry with destinations such as the ancient cities of Marrakesh and Fez attracting thousands of overseas visitors every year. Morocco's imports include crude petroleum, textile fabric, telecommunications equipment, wheat, gas, electricity, transistors and plastics.

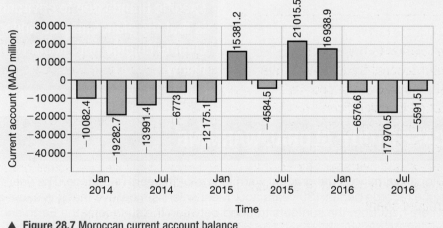

▲ Figure 28.7 Moroccan current account balance

CHAPTER QUESTIONS

1 What is the difference between visible and invisible exports? Use examples from this case to support your answer.

In November 2016, Morocco's balance of trade was MAD –13 866 million.

2 Describe the difference between the balance of trade and the balance on the current account.

3 During which period did Morocco have a current account surplus?

4 Discuss how a current account deficit might affect the Moroccan exchange rate with other currencies.

5 Consider the possible impact on the Moroccan economy of a persistent current account deficit. Make a clear judgement in your evaluation.

29 PROTECTION OF THE ENVIRONMENT

LEARNING OBJECTIVES

- Understand the business activity that damages the environment
- Understand the ways that businesses damage the environment
- Understand the government intervention to protect the environment

GETTING STARTED

Unfortunately, some business activity may damage the environment. For example, chemical-processing plants may discharge dangerous emissions into the atmosphere and oil companies may spill crude oil into the seas and oceans. However, consumers are becoming increasingly aware of this and are changing their consumption. Two-thirds of consumers now avoid specific brands due to environmental concerns. One major concern is that the planet may be under threat. This threat comes from climate change and global warming. Look at the information below.

CASE STUDY: GLOBAL WARMING

Global warming is the gradual warming up of the earth's surface. The year 2016 was the hottest year on Earth since records began 130 years ago. Most scientists believe that it is caused by the 'greenhouse effect'. This is where heat from the sun gets trapped between the surface of the Earth and a layer of greenhouse gases, such as carbon dioxide, methane and nitrous oxide. However, some scientists believe that over a long period of time, hundreds of millions of years, for example, the temperature of the Earth is subject to natural variations. So they conclude that the planet is getting warmer naturally.

Global warming is predicted to have some alarming effects on the planet.

- Sea levels will rise because the ice caps will melt, which will cause flooding in parts of the world.
- The amount and pattern of rain, snow and hail will change. Some areas will get more and others less.
- Insufficient rainfall in some areas will see the expansion of some deserts.
- Permafrost (the thick layer of soil that remains frozen throughout the year in the polar regions) will melt releasing trapped methane. This will add to the greenhouse gases in the atmosphere.
- The Amazon rainforest and boreal forests will be reduced.
- There will be more extreme weather systems such as storms and floods.
- Many species will become extinct.
- Agricultural yields will be affected.

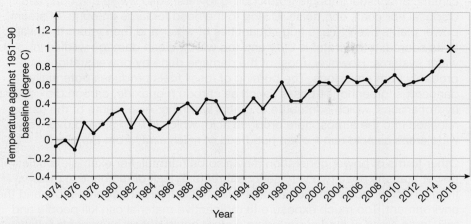

▲ **Figure 29.1** Global temperatures, 1974–2016

1 What evidence is there to suggest that global warming is occurring?

2 Why do you think governments are becoming more concerned about the environment?

3 How might the agriculture industry be affected by global warming?

4 In groups, make a list of the reasons why it is important to protect the environment. Record your ideas on a poster and present them to the rest of the class.

BUSINESS ACTIVITY THAT DAMAGES THE ENVIRONMENT

A wide range of business activity has the potential to damage the environment. However, heavy industry, such as chemical processing, oil refining, mining, power generation and steel production, in particular, can have a harmful impact on the environment. Some examples of the way certain business activity damages the environment are described below.

MINING

Open-cast mining, where materials are extracted from a giant hole in the ground, is one of the most damaging mining activities of all. One problem is that many of the minerals and other useful materials that are mined are only available in very small quantities. This means that huge quantities of earth and rock have to be extracted from a site and then processed to recover the small fraction of valuable material. This often involves crushing rocks, which may release harmful materials, such as radioactive elements, asbestos-like minerals and metallic dust. During the separation process, something called **tailings** is produced. This is a mixture of crushed rock and liquid. It is possible for toxic and radioactive elements from tailings to leak slowly through the ground into water systems if not managed effectively. In addition to this, huge open-cast mines scar the countryside and destroy wildlife habitats. The mining of coal, iron ore, gold, diamonds, copper and many other minerals can have this effect. Another problem is that most modern mining techniques use large quantities of water. Wastewater from these activities may find its way into waterways and threaten the supply of fresh drinking water.

POWER GENERATION

The generation of electricity can be very damaging to the environment. This is particularly the case when it is produced by burning fossil fuels, such as coal and oil. A wide range of harmful environmental impacts can result from fossil fuel power plants, such as emissions, the release of hot water,

GENERAL VOCABULARY

tailings waste material left over once the useful content has been removed from an ore, can be toxic

climatic and visual impacts from cooling towers, solid waste disposal, ash disposal (for coal), and noise. Owing to the need for large amounts of steam, power plants need to use huge quantities of water and then return that water to its source. It the water is dirty and too warm, it can damage wildlife in water systems. However, most of the damage done by power stations is probably from emissions. The burning of fossil fuels produces potentially dangerous 'greenhouse gases', such as carbon monoxide, carbon dioxide and hydrocarbons, which contribute to global warming. Also, some of the gases released into the atmosphere produce acid, which is then spread over very wide areas as acid rain – often hundreds of miles away from the plant.

Other forms of power generation may also be harmful. For example, nuclear power stations pose two very serious threats. A leak of radioactive material from a nuclear power station could have a disastrous effect on people and the environment. Too much exposure to radioactive material can kill people and very large areas of land surrounding a plant could become unusable following a leak. There is also the problem of waste disposal. Radioactive waste has to be stored underground for thousands of years before it is safe.

CHEMICAL PROCESSING

Chemicals are used to make the majority of synthetic materials and play an important role in everyday life. For example, chemicals are used in products to provide protection for crops and increase yields, prevent and cure disease, provide insulation to reduce energy use and provide countless other benefits that help improve living standards and the quality of life. However, chemicals can also create a negative impact on human health and the environment when their production and use are not managed responsibly. The range of chemical processes and applications in business is huge. The examples below are just two of the potential threats on the environment posed by the chemicals industry.

- Some refineries and chemical processing plants release hazardous air pollutants (HAPs). These can cause cancer and other health problems. For example, petrochemical plants use benzene, a chemical known to cause cancer in humans. People can breathe in benzene if they are close to industrial plants.

- Some chemical processes release volatile organic compounds (VOCs), such as ethylene and propylene, into the atmosphere. VOCs react with oxygen and nitrogen oxides, which are produced when burning fossil fuels, to form ozone. Contact with VOCs and ozone may result in increased rates of asthma, lung and respiratory infections and heart problems. The list of products from which VOCs may be produced includes fuels, paints, stains and lacquers, cleaning supplies, **pesticides**, plastics, glues, adhesives and refrigerants.

AGRICULTURE

Farming can have a variety of negative environmental effects. One of the main problems results from the use of pesticides and fertilisers. Although fertilisers can increase crop yields, after heavy rainfall some always ends up in rivers, lakes and the sea where it can kill aquatic life. For example, nitrogen (a key element in fertiliser) feeds an algal bloom, but when the algae die, rotting bacteria then consume most of the available oxygen, which kills aquatic life by preventing it from breathing. Also, some fertilisers can starve soil of organic matter. As a result, the soil cannot hold sufficient water and is subject to erosion. It is possible that pesticides can cause ill health. The long-term effects of exposure to pesticides on humans is still very much unknown. However, farmers who face regular exposure to pesticides have been found to suffer symptoms, such as headaches and hand tremors.

GENERAL VOCABULARY

pesticides chemical substances used to kill insects and small animals that destroy crops

Farming can also contribute to global warming. One reason is because factory farming, in particular, generates about 37 per cent of global methane emissions. This is a greenhouse gas and can impact on global warming. Deforestation also contributes to global warming. This is where areas of woodland or rainforest are cleared to grow crops. For example, clearing 100 million hectares of forest to grow soybeans in the Amazon rainforest is responsible for releasing enough carbon dioxide into the atmosphere to increase the rate of global warming by 50 per cent.

▲ Algal bloom caused by water pollution

CONSTRUCTION

The construction industry produces more waste material than any other industry. For example, in the UK the construction industry produces 109 million tonnes of construction waste each year. Of this, about 24 per cent is total waste. The industry produces three times more waste than all households combined. About one-half of the waste is recycled but huge amounts still end up in landfill sites or other disposal points. Waste on this scale uses up resources and causes disposal problems.

Construction activities such as land clearing, operation of diesel engines, demolition, burning and working with toxic materials contribute to air pollution. Also, construction sites generate high levels of dust from materials such as concrete, cement, wood, stone and silica. The air can carry the dust for large distances and this can cause health problems including respiratory illness, asthma, bronchitis and cancer.

Water pollution can also result from construction. Diesel and oil, paint, solvents, cleaners and other harmful chemicals and construction waste and dirt can be washed into water systems. Also, when land is cleared it causes soil erosion. As a result, silt and soil runs into natural waterways, restricts sunlight and can destroy aquatic life.

Most business activity tends to have a negative impact on the environment. For example, most businesses use electricity. If this is generated by burning fossil fuel, environmental damage will be caused. Most businesses also produce waste. If it cannot be reused or recycled, it might be burnt, which will cause emissions. Alternatively, it might find its way into landfill sites, which cause other problems.

ACTIVITY 1

CASE STUDY: ENVIRONMENTAL DAMAGE

▲ Environmental damage (scarring) caused by coal mining

▲ Pollution caused by burning fossil fuels

The generation of electricity by burning fossil fuels, such as coal, has a 'dual' negative impact on the environment.

1 Describe the dual environmental impacts of using coal to generate electricity.

2 Discuss how the construction industry might impact on the environment.

WAYS BUSINESSES DAMAGE THE ENVIRONMENT

VISUAL POLLUTION

Business activity may cause some visual pollution. This is where business activity results in something physical that looks very unattractive. For many people, the sight of smoke flowing from power stations might be regarded as visual pollution. Other examples might include giant office blocks, advertising hoardings, bright illuminated signs advertising products and businesses, wind farms, electricity pylons, slag heaps, overflowing skips next to construction sites, disused factories and smog. Finally, most people would also regard litter as visual pollution. Litter is a more serious problem in countries where there is no orderly collection system. In some countries, refuse is often left in piles on the street. Although visual pollution may not be as severe as other types of pollution, it is likely to have a negative impact on people's well-being and reduce living standards.

▲ Piles of uncollected refuse in an Indian street

NOISE POLLUTION

If excessive noise results from a business activity, this could be regarded as noise pollution. If noise causes disturbance to everyday life, then it can be a problem for people and reduce their quality of life. Some common examples of business-related noise pollution may be caused by:

- jet engines, as aircraft fly over residential areas
- music and loud conversations in pubs, bars, night clubs and discos if located too near residential areas
- machinery, vehicles and power tools on construction sites
- heavy industrial machinery, such as compressors, generators, exhaust fans, presses and grinding mills, in factories
- the constant sound of commercial traffic on a road or motorway.

Constant exposure to loud noise can have a negative impact on people and wildlife. For example, noise can damage eardrums and lead to loss of hearing. Loud noise can also disrupt sleeping patterns and raise stress levels.

AIR POLLUTION

Factories, machines and vehicles that discharge emissions into the atmosphere are responsible for most of the world's air pollution. Air pollution is dangerous. In 2012, the World Health Organization (WHO) estimated that, globally, toxic gases caused around 6.5 million deaths per year. The WHO also said that around 90 per cent of these deaths occur in low- to middle-income countries; two out of every three deaths occur in Southeast Asia and the Western Pacific. Figure 29.2 shows the levels of pollution in some of the world's most polluted cities. The most polluted city at the time of measurement was Onitsha in Nigeria. The air in Onitsha contained around 30 times more than the WHO's recommended levels of PM10 particles (particulate matter of less than 10 millionths of a metre in diameter).

The main causes of air pollution differ around the world. For example, in China, the main cause is particle emissions from coal burning. In India, a lot of the air pollution is indoors and comes from the burning of wood, dung, crop residues and other materials for cooking and heating. In other cities, it is the combination of industrial emissions and combustion gases from vehicles. A summary of the way businesses might cause pollution is given below.

- **Burning of fossil fuels:** Sulphur dioxide, which comes from burning fossil fuels, such as coal and petroleum, is one the major causes of air pollution. Emissions from vehicles, such as lorries, buses, cars, trains, auto rickshaws and aeroplanes, are responsible for a huge amount of pollution.

- **Emissions from factories and other business activities:** Manufacturing and processing businesses discharge carbon monoxide, hydrocarbons, organic compounds and chemicals into the air, which contribute to pollution. The burning of waste, heavy manufacturing, chemical processing, power generation and petroleum refining, which release high levels of carbon monoxide, organic compounds and chemicals into the air, are some of the worst causes.

- **Agricultural activities:** Ammonia is one of the most dangerous gases in the atmosphere. It is often a by-product from a range of agriculture activities. Crop dusting with insecticides, pesticides and fertilisers in farming is the main cause of air pollution in agriculture.

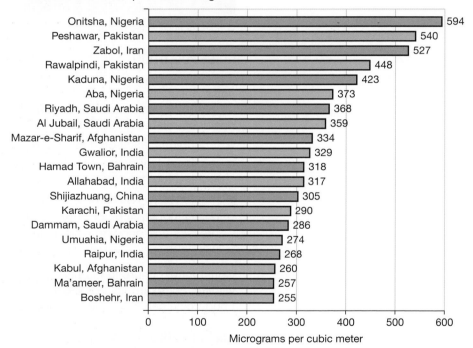

▲ **Figure 29.2** Selection of the most polluted cities in the world

Note: PM10 particular concentration, micrograms per cubic metre, annual mean

WATER POLLUTION

Around two-thirds of the planet is covered in water. However, only about 2.5 per cent of this water is drinkable. Unfortunately, in many countries the supply of safe drinking water is diminishing due to water pollution. Water pollution is the **contamination** of oceans, rivers, lakes, groundwater and other bodies of water by harmful substances. These substances often find their way into the waterways as a result of business activity. Some of the main causes of water pollution by businesses include the following.

- **Industrial waste:** Many industries, such as power generation, brewing and chemical processing, use very large quantities of water in their manufacturing processes. Often their plants are located right next to rivers where waste water is discharged directly into the waterways. In most countries, businesses are required to treat this waste to make it safe before it enters the river. However, some waste water still contains harmful substances such as lead, mercury, nitrates, sulphur, phosphates and petrochemicals. If these materials are discharged in high enough quantities, waterways will be polluted.

■ **Marine and ocean dumping:** the dumping of waste materials into the sea causes this form of water pollution. It comes from the waste dumped by shipping, leaks from oil extraction and waste dumped from the land into the sea. In some countries, refuse collected from households containing paper, aluminium, rubber, glass, plastic and food is dumped directly into the sea. Some of the materials dumped can take many years to rot or break down. For example, foam and Styrofoam can take 50 and 80 years, respectively.

■ **Sewerage:** Sometimes the businesses responsible for collecting and disposing of sewerage discharge large quantities into the sea. In most developed countries it is treated before it reaches the sea. However, in others, untreated sewerage may be released directly into the sea. Although most sewerage is 90 per cent water, it also contains other materials such as chemicals from pharmaceutical drugs, and paper, plastic, and other waste that is flushed down the toilet. Also, when people contract viruses, the sewage they produce transports those viruses into the environment. It is possible to catch illnesses such as hepatitis, typhoid and cholera from contaminated river and sea water.

The harm resulting from water pollution can be serious. All marine life, such as plants and fish, is threatened. Water pollution is responsible for loss of species and loss of habitat. Perhaps more importantly, at least 320 million people in China do not have access to clean drinking water; in Bangladesh about 85 per cent of the total area has groundwater contaminated with arsenic (arsenic is very toxic, an acute poison and known to cause cancer in humans) every year 250 million people worldwide contract diseases and 15 million young children die from causes related to water pollution.

ACTIVITY 2

CASE STUDY: The Hachiuma Steamship Co. Ltd

In 2015, The Hachiuma Steamship Co. Ltd., a Japanese shipping company, was fined £1.8 million for dumping waste into the ocean. The waste contained oil residue and waste water and was discharged into the ocean via a 'magic pipe', which was used to illegally avoid the ship's pollution control equipment and dump the oily waste into the sea.

A **whistle-blower** (a member of the crew) notified the coast guard of the violation when it boarded the ship in Baltimore, Maryland, USA. He received a US$250 000 reward for his part in the reporting of the crime. Another US$450 000 was given to the National Fish and Wildlife Foundation for projects benefiting the Chesapeake Bay. The shipping company was also put on probation for 3 years during which it was instructed to produce an environmental compliance programme.

At a later date, the chief engineer of the ship was jailed for 8 months when he pleaded guilty to obstruction of justice and violating the Act to Prevent Pollution from Ships. He tried to obstruct the coast guard's investigation and hide the illegal discharges by keeping false records, destroying documents, lying to the investigators and ordering crew members to lie.

GENERAL VOCABULARY

whistle-blower someone working for an organisation who tells the authorities that people in the organisation are doing something illegal, dishonest, or wrong

▲ Dumping waste at sea

1 What is meant by water pollution? Use the example in this case to support your answer.

2 Describe the role of a 'whistle-blower'.

3 Discuss some of the possible consequences of water pollution.

GOVERNMENT INTERVENTION TO PROTECT THE ENVIRONMENT

A number of measures are used to help reduce environmental damage resulting from business activity.

TAXATION

Many governments impose taxes on those that damage the environment. The aim of taxation is to ensure that those who cause social costs through business activity meet them. In 2016, Canadian Prime Minister Justin Trudeau announced a new carbon tax in Canada. The tax, which will come into effect in 2018, will help to raise the prices of energy sources that use fossil fuels. These will then be more expensive than clean energy, such as wind and solar power. The advantages of this tax are that emissions would be reduced, new jobs will be created in the production of clean energy and tax revenues will be boosted.

Another common tax designed to protect the environment is the landfill tax. This is imposed on the disposal of waste in landfill sites. The EU reckons that about 80 per cent of the solid waste produced by households is recyclable or compostable. Figure 29.3 shows the various components of solid waste produced in the EU. The EU aims to reduce landfill to almost zero by 2020. The landfill tax should help achieve this aim.

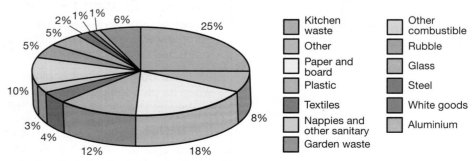

▲ **Figure 29.3** The components of EU refuse (solid waste)

GENERAL VOCABULARY

tax allowances amounts of money
that firms are allowed by the
government to offset against tax

SUBSIDIES

The government can offer grants, tax allowances and other subsidies to firms
as an incentive to reduce activities that damage the environment. For example,
a firm might receive a subsidy if it builds a plastics recycling plant. This might
encourage households and firms to recycle their plastic waste instead of
dumping it. The government can also give subsidies to firms or activities that
generate positive externalities. For example, one reason why rail companies
are subsidised in many countries might be because they take traffic off the
road and therefore help to reduce congestion and carbon emissions.

REGULATION

A range of legislation, regulations, guidelines and codes of practice exist
in many countries, which is designed to help protect the environment. For
example, in 2016, the Chinese government demonstrated some commitment
to dealing with businesses that damage the environment. It will ban industrial
plants, paper mills and refineries that pollute the country's water supplies.
This was part of a wider plan to improve water quality in rivers, lakes, coasts
and aquifers. The government has already blocked some industrial projects,
such as coal gasification plants, because they use up too much water or
pollute water systems. The plan will focus on small-scale paper factories,
leather, printing and dying, oil refineries, electronic plating, and pharmaceutical
factories.

Many governments employ specialist agencies to help monitor pollution
levels. Such agencies are responsible for taking action against those who
break environmental laws. Other duties include giving advice to firms about
protecting the environment, helping firms reduce waste, working with farmers,
looking after wildlife and helping people get the most out of enjoying the
environment.

DID YOU KNOW?

There is legislation to protect the environment in the UK.

- **Air legislation** controls emissions of gases, dark smoke and other
  airborne pollutants that harm the atmosphere. It includes systems
  of permits, authorisation and financial incentives to switch to less
  polluting ways of working. For example, the **Clean Air Act 1993**
  bans emission of dark smoke from chimneys and furnaces, sets
  minimum chimney heights, and creates smoke control zones.

- **Water legislation** aims to control water quality. It covers discharges
  to sewers, surface water and groundwater, water confinement and
  the protection of water against agricultural nitrate pollution. For
  example, the **Water Resources Act 1991** is designed to preserve,
  manage and control pollution of water resources.

FINES

The use of fines for those who break environmental laws are common in many
countries. Many firms are responsive to financial penalties when imposed.
This is because fines will reduce their profits. Fines should therefore act as
an incentive to comply with environmental laws. In 2016, Harley-Davidson,
the famous motorcycle manufacturer, was fined US$18 million by a US court

for selling motorbikes that exceeded emissions limits. The bikes were fitted with 'defeat devices' that avoided emissions controls. As a result, the bikes discharged higher levels of harmful air pollutants such as nitrogen oxide from their exhausts. The Environmental Protection Agency in the US said, 'Anyone else who manufactures, sells or installs these types of illegal products should take heed of Harley-Davidson's corrective actions and immediately stop violating the law.'

In some cases, those that cause environmental damage are forced by the law to pay compensation to the victims. For example, people living by airports may receive payments to pay for soundproof windows and other types of insulation.

POLLUTION PERMITS

Governments can issue pollution permits. These documents give businesses the right to discharge a certain amount of polluting material – say 1 tonne per year. These permits are 'tradable'. This means that a business can sell its pollution permit to another business if it has found a way of reducing its own level of pollution. Therefore, a business that is struggling to control levels of pollution can buy them and discharge more polluting material legally. An incentive in the market exists to introduce new technology that reduces pollution because pollution permits can be sold for cash. This can also help to raise profits.

PARK PROVISION

In many countries the government establishes national parks where business development and other commercial ventures are completely illegal. The parks, often very large areas of land, aim to preserve and protect areas of outstanding natural beauty. They may contain wildlife, historic sites, beautiful scenery and areas of special interest. They welcome visitors but there may be restrictions on their activities. For example, the lighting of fires may be prohibited and selected areas will be provided for camping and other accommodation. Examples of national parks around the world include Yellowstone Park in the USA, Kruger Park in South Africa and the Lake District in the UK. The largest national park in the world is the Northeast Greenland National Park, which was established in 1974.

MULTIPLE-CHOICE QUESTIONS

▶ 1 Which of the following tax changes is most likely to help protect the environment?

  A Decrease in income tax

  B Increase in income tax

  C Increase in carbon tax

  D Decrease in excise duty on petrol

▶ 2 Which of the following might be an example of visual pollution caused by a business?

  A Wind farm

  B Cattle grazing

  C Rain forest

  D Coastal mist

CASE STUDY: DEALING WITH ENVIRONMENTAL PROTECTION

SUBSIDIES

In some countries, subsidies are used to encourage businesses to produce renewable energy such as wind power and solar power. In 2014, a total of US$112 000 million was given in subsidies to businesses involved in renewable energy technologies worldwide. A further US$23 000 million was given to support biofuels. Germany provides more subsidies to producers of renewable energy than any other country in the world. However, in 2016, it announced that subsidies to the production of green energy would be cut sharply due to the strain that wind and solar power were placing on the nation's electricity grid. Unfortunately, Germany's wind and solar power generators have provided too much power at unpredictable times. This has damaged the national grid and caused power cuts. The government now plans to cap wind energy to 40–45 per cent of the national capacity. Despite the reduction in subsidies, the German government will still provide a massive €1.1 trillion in subsidies to support wind power.

FINES

In 2016, Enter Air, a Polish airline, was fined €1.1 million by the French noise reduction authority. The airline was responsible for 83 noise violations between 2013 and 2014. However, there was some confusion when an aircraft belonging to Enter Air was held for five hours at Paris CDG airport for allegedly not paying the fines. It turned out that the fines had been paid and the plane was released for service very quickly. The French authorities said that fines for noise violations were owed by 159 different airlines and that it was not ruling out legal action to enforce payment.

LANDFILL TAX

Landfill taxes are designed to reduce the amount of waste that is dumped in landfill sites. Disposing of waste in this way can damage the environment. For example, rotting waste at landfill sites produces the gases methane and carbon dioxide, which contribute to climate change. Also, much of the waste that goes into landfill can be recycled or reused. As a result, resource use could be reduced. This has an obvious environmental benefit where people are encouraged to recycle waste rather than throw it away. Finally, people do not like to live near landfills. They take up a lot of space, they are a source of visual pollution and can create unpleasant smells, water discharges and pests. Figure 29.4 shows the amount of waste going to landfill sites in the UK between 2000/01 and 2015.

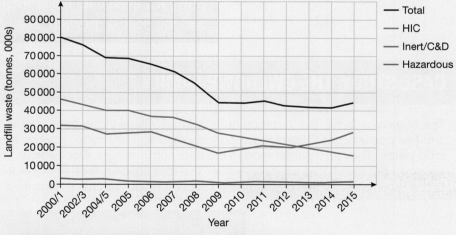

▲ Figure 29.4 Waste going to landfill sites in the UK, 2000–15

CHAPTER QUESTIONS

1 Describe how increased energy consumption might damage the environment.

2 Draw a supply and demand diagram to show the effect of granting a subsidy to renewable energy producers in the market for renewable energy.

3 Why is Germany planning to cut subsidies to producers of renewable energy?

4 How can fines be used to reduce noise pollution?

5 What is the purpose of a landfill tax?

6 Discuss whether the landfill tax in the UK has worked.

30 REDISTRIBUTION OF INCOME

LEARNING OBJECTIVES

- Understand how to define income inequality, absolute poverty and relative poverty
- Understand the reasons for reducing poverty and inequality
- Understand the government intervention used to reduce inequality and poverty: progressive taxation, redistribution through benefits and investment in education and health care

GETTING STARTED

In some countries, people enjoy a good standard of living. They may own a house, a car, lots of consumer durables, enjoy meals out and take regular holidays. In contrast, in many countries, people may own very little. They may live in a slum, eat very basic food, have very few clothes and have no access to safe drinking water. Many would describe the living standards of these people as desperate. In some countries, the government tries to help those with very poor living standards by redistributing income. However, even with government help, the gap between the rich and the poor is growing. Look at the examples below and overleaf.

CASE STUDY: THE GWENGWE FAMILY

The Gwengwe family live in a mud hut in a small village in the poor African state of Malawi. They have no income and few possessions. Their food supply is irregular. They try to grow cereals but all too often the dry weather limits crop yields. They also gather food in the rural surroundings. Occasionally, they receive a food parcel from an aid agency – but these are increasingly rare. The four children receive no education and no health care. Last year, one of the Gwengwe children died from an infection thought to have originated from contaminated drinking water.

▲ The Gwengwe family in Malawi

CASE STUDY: THE BIRNBAUM FAMILY

The Birnbaum family live in Florida, USA. They own a six-bedroom house with four bathrooms and a swimming pool. It cost US$4.1 million in 2012. Mrs Birnbaum is an investment banker and earns between US$1 million and US$1.6 million p.a. Mr Birnbaum is a partner in a firm of accountants and earns about US$700 000 p.a. Their two children go to private schools where the fees are US$40 000 per term. They also own four cars and a yacht, which is moored in a nearby marina.

▲ The Birnbaum family in Florida

1 Describe how these examples illustrate the inequality of income that exists in the world.

2 Describe two possible reasons why the Gwengwe family is so poor.

3 In groups, identify a number of measures that could be taken to close the gap between the very rich and the very poor. Record your ideas on a poster and present them to the rest of the class.

INCOME INEQUALITY

In a market economy, individuals receive different levels of income. For example, in France, a shop assistant might earn €17 600 p.a. (equivalent to the national minimum wage), a teacher might earn €48 000 p.a. and a company director might receive €2.4 million p.a. The difference here between the company director, who is a high-income earner, and the shop assistant, who is a low-income earner, is considerable. Many would also argue that the difference between the teacher's income and that of the shop worker is also significant. However, what is clear is that income is distributed very unevenly in this example. In most countries in the world, the distribution of income is very unequal.

The USA is an example of a country where **income inequality** is severe. The information in Figure 30.1 supports this view. The graph shows that the top 0.1 per cent of the population enjoyed a massive average annual income of US$6 087 113 in 2014. In contrast, the bottom 90 per cent of the nation's population earned an average of just US$33 068 in that year. US earners at this top level earn over 184 times the income of the bottom 90 per cent.

SUBJECT VOCABULARY

income inequality differences in income that exist between the different groups of earners in society, that is, the gap between the rich and the poor

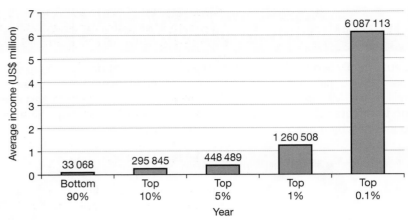

▲ **Figure 30.1** Income inequality in the USA (US$)

These huge differences in incomes may arise for a number of reasons.

■ Workers with natural talent, a good education, valuable work experience or who can offer labour in a market where there is a shortage of qualified labour, will tend to earn more.

■ People who do not work, such as pensioners, receive lower incomes than those in employment.

■ The extent to which a government redistributes income through taxes and welfare payments is influential.

■ People who own assets such as property, shares and capital will enjoy additional income such as rents, dividends and interest, respectively.

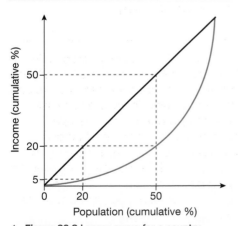

▲ **Figure 30.2** Lorenz curve for a country

DID YOU KNOW?

The income distribution in a country can be measured using a **Lorenz curve**. This shows the percentage of income earned by a certain percentage of the population. An example is shown in Figure 30.2. The 45° line shows the hypothetical, perfectly equal distribution of income. For example, if this line did represent the distribution of income in a country, it would show that 50 per cent of the population enjoyed 50 per cent of the income. However, the red Lorenz curve shows that 50 per cent of the population only enjoy 20 per cent of the income. This means that the other 50 per cent of the population enjoy a disproportionate 80 per cent of the income. The further the Lorenz curve is away from the 45° line, the greater the degree of inequality.

ABSOLUTE POVERTY

The unequal distribution of income in countries often means that a proportion of the population live in poverty. This means that people are living in an environment where their needs are not fully met. However, there are two definitions of poverty. One of these is **absolute poverty**. This is where people try to survive in an environment where even their basic needs are not adequately met. People living in absolute poverty may be deprived of food, shelter, safe drinking water, sanitation facilities, education, basic health care and information. In 2015, the World Bank defined absolute poverty as those people who are required to survive on less than US$1.90 per day. The Gwengwe family in 'Getting started' are living in absolute poverty. They have no income and have to search in the countryside for much of their food. Their shelter is built from mud and straw.

In developed nations, levels of absolute poverty are very low. In most of these countries, the government provides welfare payments to those in need – the unemployed, sick, disabled and the elderly, for example. However, the World Bank estimated that 702 million people (9.6 per cent of the world's population) were living in absolute poverty in 2015. However, this was down from 902 million people (12.8 per cent of the global population) in 2012. Many of these people are to be found living in African and Asia. Figure 30.3 shows levels of absolute poverty between 1981 and 2013.

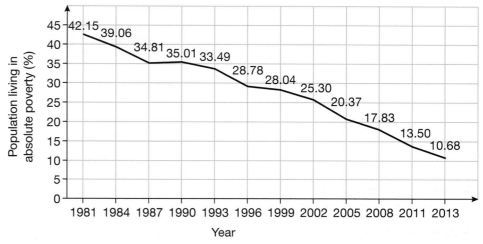

▲ **Figure 30.3** Percentage of the world's population living in absolute poverty

RELATIVE POVERTY

A second definition of poverty is **relative poverty**. This is always present in society. Relatively poor people are to be found at the bottom end of a nation's income scales. Their incomes will fall short of the levels needed to provide an average living standard in their country where they live. There is no precise measurement of relative poverty. However, one approach is to measure the number of households whose total income is at a certain level below the median income for that country. This certain level will vary according to different definitions. In the EU, the level is 60 per cent. Therefore, if the median income in an EU country was €21 500, a household living on an income of €11 400 would be living in relative poverty. This is because 60 per cent of the median income in this country is €12 900 (60% × €21 500).

Relative poverty will vary between different countries. This is because the median income level in a particular country determines relative poverty. Each country is likely to have a different median income level. Richer countries will have higher median income levels than poorer countries. Generally, people are considered to be living in poverty if they are unable to attain the average living standard in their society.

Relative poverty will also change over time. This is because income levels change over time. They usually rise. Therefore, if an individual receives an increase in income that is higher than the average increase, that individual might move out of poverty altogether, or further away from the poverty line, for example.

ACTIVITY 1

CASE STUDY: GLOBAL INCOME INEQUALITY

Figure 30.4 shows the global population by income group. It illustrates the inequality of income in the world.

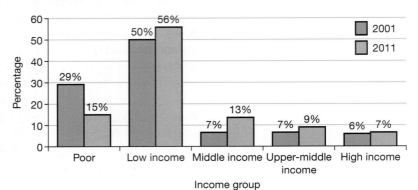

▲ **Figure 30.4** Global population by income group, 2001 and 2011

1 Calculate the proportion of the global population living on incomes below the middle-income group in 2001 and 2011.

2 What is meant by inequality of income? Use the information in Figure 30.4 to support your explanation.

3 Assess whether incomes have become more or less equal over the time period.

REASONS TO REDUCE POVERTY AND INEQUALITY

MEET BASIC NEEDS

Just under 10 per cent of the world's population still live in absolute poverty according to the World Bank. This means that around 700 million people struggle to survive. In some countries, many people are undernourished. For example, in Zambia and the Central African Republic, 47.8 per cent and 47.7 per cent of the population, respectively, do not have enough to eat. They are unable to consume enough calories per day to sustain an active and healthy life.

In some cases, people in absolute poverty are starving to death. Young children are particularly at risk. According to one study, 3.1 million children died of starvation in 2011. This was 45 per cent of the total number of child deaths in that year. Also, undernutrition worsens the effect of many diseases, such as measles and malaria. The estimated proportions of deaths in which undernutrition is a fundamental cause are 61 per cent for diarrhoea, 57 per cent for malaria, 52 per cent for pneumonia and 45 per cent for measles. It is also reckoned that, in 2013, 161 million children in the world under the age of five were unable to fully develop physically.

If absolute poverty can be completely eliminated, the basic needs of people will be met. This would avoid the loss of life from starvation and help children to grow up healthily.

RAISE LIVING STANDARDS

If poverty can be reduced, living standards across the world would rise. If absolute poverty is eliminated, the basic needs of people would be met and clearly their living standards would improve. However, average living standards would also increase if relative poverty were reduced. Although relative poverty will always exist, it is still possible to bring people out of relative poverty. It is also possible to improve the living standards of those living in relative poverty. This is because as a nation's income rises, the median income will also rise. Therefore, many of those living on less than 60 per cent of the median income will still have a higher income and a better living standard.

Even with relative poverty, ill health and early death are still problems. Studies show that people living in relative poverty are more likely to get ill and have a lower life expectancy. This may be because those living in relative poverty have poorer housing, less nutritious diets and reduced access to health care. People living in relative poverty also consume fewer goods and services such as vehicles, consumer durables, entertainment services and education. They may also have low self-confidence, less control over their lives and less choice.

If reducing poverty can raise living standards, more people would be educated. This would help to boost global economic growth. As a result, there would be more employment, more income and more tax revenue for the government. This could be spent improving public services for everyone.

ETHICAL REASONS

Many people think that poverty and income inequality should be reduced for ethical reasons. This means they believe it is the moral duty of both people and governments to help reduce poverty. It could be argued that the sacrifice needed by the relatively better off to reduce poverty is very small indeed. Take the two families in 'Getting started'. If the wealthy Birnbaum family gave US$2300 (just 0.01 per cent of their annual income) to the poverty-stricken Gwengwe family, it would be enough to lift them out of absolute poverty. Further, the Birnbaum family would probably not even miss their loss of income.

Many people are concerned by the vast inequalities of income around the world – some are even disgusted by it. In 2015, the GDP per head in Qatar, the USA and Germany, three of the richest countries in the world, was US$73 653, US$56 116 and US$41 318, respectively. In contrast, the GDP per head in three of the poorest countries in the world, Burundi, Central African Republic and Malawi, was US$227, US$323 and US$372, respectively. Also, in 2016, it was estimated that the 62 richest people in the world owned more wealth than one-half of the world's poorest people – that is over 3600 million other people.

Millions of ethically minded people do give money to charities, such as Oxfam and Save the Children, to help reduce poverty. It is also fair to say that some of the world's richest people donate large sums to help the poor. However, despite this there is still a need to reduce poverty and income inequalities in the world.

GOVERNMENT INTERVENTION TO REDUCE POVERTY AND INCOME INEQUALITY

Generally, if a country enjoys more economic growth, the level of poverty in that country should fall. However, even if poverty did fall there is still likely to be considerable income inequality. According to a report by the OECD in 2014, the gap between rich and poor is now at its highest level in 30 years in most OECD countries. If a government is committed to reducing poverty and achieving a fairer distribution of income, a number of measures could be used.

PROGRESSIVE TAXATION

A **progressive tax** system is one that places the **burden** of taxation more heavily on the rich – that is, those who can afford to pay. A progressive tax is a tax where the proportion of income paid in tax rises as the income of the taxpayer rises. For example, if a person earning US$10 000 paid US$600 in tax, the proportion of their income paid in tax is 6 per cent. In the same country, if a person earning US$100 000 pays US$30 000, the proportion paid in tax is 30 per cent. This is a progressive tax system. In many countries, taxes on personal income tend to be more progressive. This is often because people on very low incomes do not have to pay any tax at all. For example, in France people do not pay any tax at all on the first €9700 they earn.

In contrast, a **regressive tax** system places the burden of the tax more heavily on the poor. With such a system, the proportion of income paid in tax actually falls as income rises. Taxes on spending, such as VAT tend to be more regressive.

If a government uses a progressive tax system, the gap between the rich and the poor might be closed. This is because people on higher incomes will be paying more tax. However, if average incomes are rising rapidly, the people at the top of the income scales will benefit more so the gap might widen. The gap is also more likely to close if the government gives poorer sectors of society some of the tax it collects from those on higher incomes.

REDISTRIBUTION THROUGH BENEFIT PAYMENTS

In most developed countries, governments have a welfare system, which is used to redistribute income in favour of the poor. Most systems involve using tax revenues to make direct payments to those on low incomes and those who cannot work at all. For example, in many European countries payments are made to the unemployed, the disabled, the sick, single-parent families, the elderly and those on very low incomes. These payments help to boost the incomes of some of the most at-risk people in society. Such payments help to reduce both absolute poverty and relative poverty. In countries where large numbers of people live in absolute poverty, there are rarely any systems that redistribute income in this way. This is mainly because the governments in these countries do not have enough money. GDPs are low so the tax revenues collected are also low.

In recent years, some developing countries have been able to reduce poverty and close the gap between the rich and the poor. For example, in 2000, about 20 per cent of the population in Ecuador were living in absolute poverty. By 2015, this had fallen to just 4 per cent. One of the reasons for the improvement was the government's commitment to highly redistributive social policies brought about by Rafael Correa when his party was elected in 2007. However, booming oil sales, lower unemployment, rising wages and investment in public services also helped.

INVESTMENT IN EDUCATION AND HEALTH CARE

One route to reducing poverty is through education. Clearly, if people are educated and are able to develop a range of skills, such as reading and writing, numeracy, communication, analysis, problem solving, evaluation, critical thinking and language, they are more employable. However, according to UNICEF, schooling has other benefits. 'Education will give the next generation the tools to fight poverty and conquer disease. School also offers children a safe environment, with support, supervision and socialisation. Here they learn life skills that can help them prevent diseases, including how to avoid HIV/AIDS and malaria. Children may receive lifesaving vaccines, fresh water and nutrient supplementation at school.'

Unfortunately, investment in education is very expensive and the returns on the investment often take many years to realise. Consequently, funds for education in many developing countries are inadequate. For example, in most developing countries:

- public school is not free – the costs of books, uniforms and teachers are met by the students or their families

- 67 million 5–11 year olds receive no primary education

- more than 226 million children do not attend secondary school.

It is reckoned that in many developing countries, every additional year of education can increase a person's future income by an average of 10 per cent. It is easy to see that several years of education could help to reduce poverty.

Investment in health care will also help to reduce poverty. Health programmes can reduce child mortality rates, increase life expectancy and reduce suffering. These are some of the key indicators of poverty. If children are healthier, their attendance at school is higher. If people live longer, they are more likely to save for their retirement, which increases the flow of funds for investment. Finally, if people are healthy, they will be more productive in the workplace, which will help to increase economic growth.

ACTIVITY 2

CASE STUDY: PROGRESSIVE TAX IN FRANCE

France has few, if any, people living in absolute poverty. However, as in all societies, there are examples of relative poverty. To help redistribute income in the country, France has one of the most progressive tax systems in the world. Table 30.1 shows the tax rates on different bands of income in France in 2016.

INCOME	TAX RATE (%)
Up to €9700	0
Between €9701 and €26 791	14
Between €26 792 and €71 826	30
Between €71 827 and €152 108	41
Above €151 108	45

▲ **Table 30.1** Tax rates for income tax in France, 2016

1 Calculate the amount of tax payable on earnings of **(a)** €15 000 and **(b)** €50 000.

2 What is meant by a progressive tax system? Use your answers to question **(1)** to support your explanation.

3 Describe the main purpose of a progressive tax system.

4 What is meant by relative poverty?

MULTIPLE-CHOICE QUESTIONS

▶ **1** The median income in an EU country is €19 400. Which of the following incomes is below the relative poverty line?

     A €19 200

     B €19 400

     C €11 200

     D €13 200

▶ **2** Which of the following might increase income inequality?

     A A fall in regressive taxation

     B A more progressive tax system

     C A fall in GDP per capita

     D A cut in state benefits

ECONOMICS IN PRACTICE

CASE STUDY: POVERTY IN INDIA

India has more people living in poverty than anywhere else in the world. In 2016, the World Bank reported that about 30 per cent of India's population were living in absolute poverty. This means that 224 million people in India do not have enough resources to meet their basic needs. This is more than one-quarter of the world's total. Many of them live in slums like the one shown in Figure 30.5. However, the number of people living in poverty in India has fallen.

▲ **Figure 30.5** An Indian slum

Figure 30.6 provides some evidence of the improvement in living standards in India. The graph shows that India's GDP per head has risen very sharply from about US$300 per capita in the 1960s to nearly US$1800 per capita in 2016. Life expectancy in India has also increased. In the last 16 years, it has risen from 62.3 years to 68.5 years. Literacy rates have also improved. In 1995, only 52 per cent of adults were literate. By 2016, the national literacy rate was 75 per cent. However, in some individual states it was as high as 90 per cent.

One reason for the fall in poverty is improved infrastructure. The World Bank said improved infrastructure, specifically the expansion of the electricity network into rural areas, has had extremely positive effects. The Bank argued that electrification had changed earnings, consumption and even encouraged schooling for girls. Nearly 96 per cent of villages in India are electrified but only 69 per cent of homes have electricity connections according to a report. However, there are variations across different states. For example, in Uttar Pradesh, 99 per cent of villages are electrified, but only 60 per cent of households have access to electricity.

Another possible reason why India is lifting many of its citizens out of poverty is because of the government's commitment to education. Although the data is incomplete there have been increases in government expenditure on education in recent years. For example, in 2016, the government announced an allocation of Rs72 394 crore compared with Rs68 963 crore for the previous year, which is a 4.9 per cent increase in the education budget. The government has also introduced a number of measures to increase the literacy rate in India. Some examples are listed below.

- It provides free education programmes to poor people living in villages and towns.
- It is setting up new schools and colleges at district and state levels.
- Committees check that funds allotted to improve literacy rate are spent appropriately.
- Door-to-door surveys are used to monitor literacy rates.

Finally, in November 2016, the government made some radical changes to the nation's monetary system. It withdrew all Rs500 and Rs1000 notes from use and replaced them with new Rs500 and Rs2000 notes. This caused chaos at the time but forced most of the population to open bank accounts. This was because people in possession of the old notes could only pay them into bank accounts. They could not be used as a medium of exchange. One of the reasons for the change was to improve accountability in the country. Before the changes, the overwhelming majority of transactions in India were conducted in cash. The government wanted to encourage more electronic transactions, which meant that people and businesses would have to declare their incomes. This meant the government would collect more tax and be able to invest more heavily in public services in the future. It was hoped that this would help to reduce poverty even further.

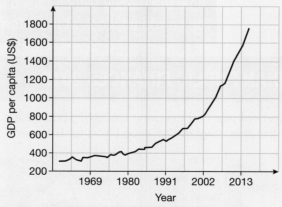

▲ Figure 30.6 Indian GDP per capita, 1960–2013

CHAPTER QUESTIONS

1 Describe what absolute poverty is.

2 Why has poverty in India fallen? Give two reasons in your analysis.

3 Discuss how investment in education might reduce poverty.

4 Why should poverty in India be reduced further? Give at least two reasons in your analysis.

31 FISCAL POLICY

LEARNING OBJECTIVES

- Understand how to define fiscal policy
- Understand the nature of government revenue: direct and indirect taxes
- Understand the nature of government expenditure: main areas of focus
- Understand fiscal deficits and fiscal surpluses
- Understand the impact of a fiscal deficit and fiscal surplus
- Understand the impact of fiscal policy on macroeconomic objectives

GETTING STARTED

A government has a number of measures it can use to achieve its macroeconomic objectives. These measures might be used to control inflation, bring down unemployment or promote economic growth, for example. One of the measures it can use is to adjust levels of government expenditure on public services, such as defence, education and health care. Each year, the government has to decide how much will be spent on each service and how much will be spent in total. The government also has to decide how the money will be raised through taxation and how much will be borrowed. Look at the information below.

CASE STUDY: CANADIAN PUBLIC FINANCES 2015

In 2015, the Canadian government planned to spend CAD3 688 000 million on a range of government services. Figures 31.1 and 31.2 show the spending and revenue plans for the year.

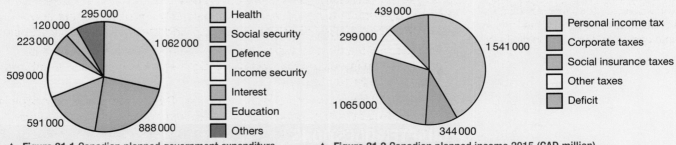

▲ Figure 31.1 Canadian planned government expenditure 2015 (CAD million)

▲ Figure 31.2 Canadian planned income 2015 (CAD million)

1 What is meant by government expenditure? Use examples from this case to support your answer.

2 Which item of government expenditure in Canada is the most expensive?

3 Which is the most important source of income for the Canadian government?

POLICY INSTRUMENTS

SUBJECT VOCABULARY

policy instruments tools governments use to implement their policies, such as interest rates, rates of taxation, levels of government spending

The government can use a number of tools to help achieve its macroeconomic objectives. These are called **policy instruments**. Policy instruments are economic variables such as the rate of interest, rates of taxation and levels of government expenditure. The government can adjust them directly or indirectly. Changes in policy instruments can affect other variables in the economy, such as aggregate demand, inflation, unemployment and GDP. For example, if the government increases income tax rates, there is likely to be a fall in aggregate demand because people will have less disposable income to spend.

FISCAL POLICY

SUBJECT VOCABULARY

budget government's spending and revenue plans for the next year

fiscal policy decisions about government spending, taxation and levels of borrowing that affect aggregate demand in the economy

One important policy instrument is **fiscal policy**. This involves adjusting levels of government expenditure and taxation to influence aggregate demand in the economy. Fiscal policy can be used to influence the behaviour of firms and individuals. For example, many governments place heavy taxes on cigarettes to discourage consumption of this harmful product.

Every year, the government plans how much it is going to spend on each category of expenditure. The government also shows how the money is going to be raised and states how much it plans to borrow. These plans are published in the government's **budget**. In 'Getting started', Figures 31.1 and 31.2 showed the spending and revenue plans for the Canadian government in 2015.

GOVERNMENT REVENUE

The main source of revenue for a government is taxation. Governments all over the world impose taxation for the following reasons.

- To pay for public sector services.
- To discourage certain activities. For example, in some countries, taxes are imposed on cigarettes to discourage smoking because it is dangerous. There is also a tax on dumping rubbish in landfill sites. This is to encourage everyone to reduce waste.
- Taxes can be used to help to control aggregate demand in the economy. This is discussed in more detail later.
- The distribution of wealth in the economy can be made fairer. Taxing the wealthy more heavily than the poor achieves this. This is discussed in Chapter 30 (pages 240–249).

DIRECT TAXES

SUBJECT VOCABULARY

direct taxes taxes levied on the income earned by firms and individuals

Most government taxes fall into two categories. **Direct taxes** are taxes imposed on firms and individuals. They are usually linked to income and wealth. Some of the key direct taxes used around the world are outlined below.

- **Income tax** is a direct tax on the amount earned by an individual. It is a common and important tax worldwide. Both employed and self-employed people have to pay this tax.
- **Social insurance taxes** are like income tax. They are imposed on people's income. However, the money collected is used specifically for pensions, benefits and health care. In 'Getting Started', Canada planned to raise CAD1 065 000 million in social insurance taxes in 2015.
- **Corporation taxes** are levied on the profits made by limited companies. Other types of business, such as partnerships and sole traders, are likely to pay income tax.
- **Capital gains tax** is levied on any financial gains made when selling assets at a profit. Assets such as shares, businesses and properties attract capital gains tax.

■ **Inheritance tax** is paid on money that is inherited from people who die. However, in most countries where this tax is used, a certain amount of money can be passed on to relatives, friends and other benefactors before this tax applies.

INDIRECT TAXES

Any tax on spending is an indirect tax. Some of the main **indirect taxes** used around the world are described briefly below.

■ **Sales taxes** are taxes on spending. For example, EU countries use **value-added tax**. In Denmark, Belgium and Italy, the standard rates of VAT are 25 per cent, 21 per cent and 22 per cent, respectively. However, some goods such as food, books, drugs and medicines and public transport may be zero rated (VAT = 0 per cent). Also, firms with a small turnover do not have to charge VAT.

■ **Duties** are often heavy taxes on a select range of goods. In some countries, goods such as petrol, cigarettes and alcohol attract quite heavy duties.

■ **Customs duties** are taxes levied on imports. In the UK, goods coming in from a country that is not a member of the EU attract customs duties.

■ **Council tax** is collected by local authorities to help pay for local services such as refuse collection. It is levied according to the value of residential property and is paid by the occupants.

■ **Business rates** are also collected by local authorities and contribute to the provision of local community services. However, they are paid by businesses and are levied according to the value of business property.

■ **Stamp duties** are paid when buying certain assets, such as houses and shares.

ENVIRONMENTAL TAXES

These are designed to protect the environment. Below are some examples.

■ **Landfill tax** is imposed on the disposal of waste in landfill sites. The charge is usually linked to the weight of waste dumped in a landfill site.

■ **Climate change levies are used to help countries** meet their commitment to reducing greenhouse gases. It is paid mainly by the suppliers of electricity, gas and coal, for example.

■ **Aggregates levy** is a tax on sand, gravel and rock that is dug from the ground. The tax is designed to reduce the environmental damage caused by quarrying.

SUBJECT VOCABULARY

indirect taxes taxes levied on spending, such as VAT

valued-added tax (VAT) tax on some goods and services – businesses pay value-added tax on most goods and services they buy and if they are VAT registered, charge value-added tax on the goods and services they sell

---

ACTIVITY 1

CASE STUDY: TAXATION IN GHANA

In 2016, the government of Ghana planned to raise GHS 38 000 million to help fund its spending plans. Figure 31.3 shows the main sources of this revenue. Ghana uses both direct and indirect taxes to generate government revenue. Ghana's tax regime include the following features.

■ A fairly progressive income tax system is used with tax rates of 0, 5, 10, 17.5 and 25 per cent on rising bands of income.

■ Companies have to pay a standard rate of 25 per cent in corporation tax on their profits.

- Some business activities, such as mining and petroleum activities, are taxed more heavily at 35 per cent.
- Companies exporting non-traditional goods and those involved in waste management are taxed less at 8 per cent and 1 per cent, respectively.
- A standard rate of VAT is charged at 15 per cent. Some goods and services, such as food, water and education services, are exempt.
- A national health insurance levy (NHIL) of 2.5 per cent is also charged on spending.
- Other taxes used by Ghana include customs and excise duties, airport tax, and environmental taxes on the production of plastics and a special petroleum tax.

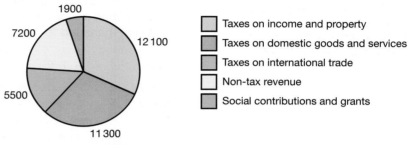

▲ Figure 31.3 Planned sources of government revenue, Ghana, 2016 (GHS million)

1 What is the difference between direct taxes and indirect taxes?

2 What is meant by (a) VAT and (b) customs duties?

3 Discuss which of Ghana's taxes might help protect the environment.

GOVERNMENT EXPENDITURE

Total planned expenditure and the amount to be spent on each category is announced every year in the budget. Figure 31.1 in 'Getting started' shows the amount of money the Canadian government planned to spend in 2015. Some countries divide government spending into *mandatory spending* and *discretionary spending*. The levels of mandatory spending are determined by current systems. For example, when someone is made redundant they are entitled to claim Jobseeker's Allowance. These payments are made automatically. The government is legally obliged to meet them. Discretionary spending is 'extra' or 'new' spending. An example would be money provided for a new motorway. The main areas of focus for government spending in most countries are outlined in Table 31.1.

CATEGORIES	MAIN EXAMPLES
Social protection	State benefits, pensions, child benefits, jobseekers allowances and disability allowances
Health care	Salaries of nurses, doctors and admin staff; drugs and medicines; equipment and care programmes
Education	Teachers' salaries, equipment for schools and student grants
Defence	Maintenance of the armed forces (army, navy and air force)
Interest	The interest paid on government borrowings such as the national debt
Public order/safety	Spending on the police force, fire service, prison service, the justice system and health and safety
Social services	Spending on the care of children, the elderly and people with learning disabilities
Other	Transport, housing and the environment, industry, agriculture, training, and recreation

▲ Table 31.1 Government expenditure – main focus areas

FISCAL DEFICITS AND FISCAL SURPLUSES

In most years, many governments plan to spend more than they receive in tax revenue. This results in a **fiscal deficit** and means that the government must borrow money to fund the deficit. For example, in 'Getting started', Figure 31.2 showed that Canada planned to borrow CAD439 000 million. This money might be borrowed from both domestic and foreign banks and possibly other governments.

If the government were to spend less than it received in tax revenues, there would be a **fiscal surplus**. This may be used to repay government debts. Figure 31.4 shows the pattern of fiscal deficits and surpluses for Sweden between 2008 and 2015. At the beginning of the period, Sweden enjoyed a number of fiscal surpluses. However, from 2009 to 2014, the government spent more than it received in revenues. Finally, in 2015, the Swedish government managed to generate another surplus.

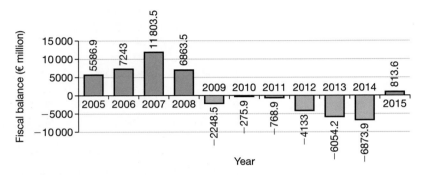

▲ **Figure 31.4** Fiscal balances for Sweden, 2005–15 (€ million)

IMPACT OF A FISCAL DEFICIT AND A FISCAL SURPLUS

FISCAL DEFICITS

Over a long period of time, most governments would prefer to avoid running a fiscal deficit. In a year when the government plans to overspend, it will have to borrow money to fund the deficit. Consequently, if deficits build up over a period of time, the **national debt** gets bigger and bigger. This means that the government has to spend more and more of its revenue on paying off the debt. Many would argue that money spent on interest payments has a high opportunity cost. For example, the money could be spent on lower taxes or extra spending on social provision or infrastructure development.

Another problem with persistent fiscal deficits and rising national debt is that future generations may be burdened with the debt of 'today'. Many would argue that this is not really fair on those people that have not even been born yet. They will be paying for the excesses of previous generations.

FISCAL SURPLUSES

The impact of a fiscal surplus is likely to be positive. If a government collects more revenue than it spends in a year, the surplus could be used in a number of ways. For example, it could be used to spend on the future provision of public services or used to lower taxes in the economy. However, most governments would use it to pay off some of the national debt. This would reduce future interest payments and strengthen the nation's finances.

Finally, when analysing the size of fiscal deficits, it is more important to focus on the size of the deficit in relation to the nation's GDP. This is because the amount that needs to be borrowed to cover the deficit is only a serious problem if it is a large percentage of the GDP. It is like an individual taking out a loan. If an individual has an income of US$80 000, a US$5000 loan is fairly easy to pay back over a few years. However, someone earning just US$15 000 a year may struggle to meet the interest and loan repayments on US$5000. This is because the loan is equal to one-third of the person's annual income. It might be quite a burden. Therefore, when analysing fiscal deficits and making international comparisons, it is best to express the deficit as a percentage of GDP.

ACTIVITY 2

CASE STUDY: FISCAL BALANCES IN LUXEMBOURG

The small European state of Luxembourg has a population of just under 600 000. However, it has a high GDP per capita at just over €89 000 per head, a stable economy with low unemployment and sound economic growth. About one-third of Luxembourg's GDP is generated from banking services. The country had a reputation for banking secrecy until 2015 when the EU forced Luxembourg to reveal tax information on savings accounts held in Luxembourg's banks. Other EU rulings relating to the way Luxembourg collected tax revenues meant that the government had to raise additional levies and cut its expenditure by reducing some social benefits. Figure 31.5 shows the fiscal balances for Luxembourg between 2005 and 2015.

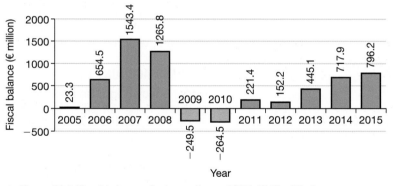

▲ Figure 31.5 Fiscal balances for Luxembourg, 2005–15 (€ million)

1 In which years did the Luxembourg government overspend? Account for your answer.

2 Comment on the pattern of Luxembourg's fiscal balances over the period.

3 Describe the possible impact of the balances described in (2) on Luxembourg.

THE IMPACT OF FISCAL POLICY ON MACROECONOMIC OBJECTIVES

GENERAL VOCABULARY

stimulate to encourage an activity to begin or develop further

Fiscal policy is also used to influence aggregate demand in the economy. In some years, a government may increase the size of a budget deficit (or reduce a surplus), by spending more or taxing less, to **stimulate** the economy. This is called **expansionary fiscal policy**. In contrast, it may be necessary to reduce aggregate demand. In this case, the government will plan to reduce the size of a deficit (or increase a surplus) by spending less or taking more in tax. This is called **contractionary fiscal policy**. Some examples of the impact of fiscal policy on macroeconomic objectives are outlined below.

INFLATION

Contractionary fiscal policy can be used to reduce inflation. If it is thought that inflation is being caused by aggregate demand growing too quickly, measures can be taken to reduce demand. The government could cut its own spending levels or raise taxation. Increases in taxes will reduce disposable income and therefore reduce demand, relieving inflationary pressure.

ECONOMIC GROWTH

Expansionary fiscal policy can be used to help stimulate economic growth. Increases in government expenditure will increase aggregate demand. For example, if more civil servants and council workers are employed, there will be more demand for most goods and services as people who were previously unemployed take up the new jobs. Cuts in taxes will also generate more demand because firms and households will have more money to spend. Economic growth is more likely to result from extra government expenditure on capital projects, such as new schools, transport links and airports. This is because money spent on investment is the key to economic growth.

UNEMPLOYMENT

Expansionary fiscal policy can help to reduce unemployment. Again increases in government expenditure and tax cuts can help to stimulate demand. To meet this extra demand, firms will have to produce more. This means more staff will be taken on and unemployment will fall. The government could help by directing its extra spending on construction projects, such as building new hospitals, motorways and rail links. The construction industry is labour intensive, which means that job creation will be higher.

CURRENT ACCOUNT DEFICIT

Fiscal policy might be used to help influence the balance on the current account. For example, if there is a large deficit on the current account, contractionary fiscal policy will help reduce aggregate demand. This will help to reduce the demand for imports.

FISCAL POLICY AND THE ENVIRONMENT

More recently, governments have used fiscal policy to tackle environmental problems. For example, taxes such as landfill tax, the climate change levy and the aggregates levy, have been used to help reduce environmental damage. These are explained above. Some governments also use subsidies to encourage activities that are environmentally friendly. For example, in the USA, subsidies have been given to the producers of environmentally friendly fuels.

MULTIPLE-CHOICE QUESTIONS

▶ 1 In 2016, a government spends €654.5 million and collects €631.6 million in revenue. As a result, the fiscal balance for the year would be which of the following?

A €654.5 million deficit

B €22.9 million surplus

C €1286.1 million surplus

D €22.9 million deficit

▶ **2** Which of the following fiscal measures is likely to increase a fiscal deficit?

  A An increase in spending on education

  B A rise in VAT

  C A cut in pension payments

  D A rise in corporation tax

ECONOMICS IN PRACTICE

CASE STUDY: RECENT FISCAL POLICY IN GREECE

In recent years, Greece has used contractionary fiscal policy in an effort to achieve a specific macroeconomic objective. The aim of Greek fiscal policy has not been to reduce aggregate demand to reduce inflation but to cut its huge fiscal deficit. The global recession in 2008 hit Greece very hard, however, Greece also had other problems. Both private sector and public sector debt was very high indeed. From 1999 to 2008, private sector debt as a proportion of GDP more than doubled from 59 per cent to 126 per cent. The ratio of public sector debt to GDP was around 100 per cent over the same period. During this period, consumers, businesses and the government spent heavily. This was reflected in the booming level of imports. However, when the financial crisis hit the world in 2008, those with debt struggled to repay what they owed. In an effort to reduce debt, households and businesses cut their spending and unemployment rose. Greece was forced to borrow from the EU and the IMF. Figure 31.6 shows the Greek and EU fiscal balances between 2005 and 2015.

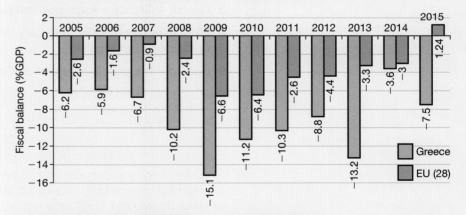

▲ **Figure 31.6** Greece and EU fiscal balances, 2005–15 (%GDP)

The loans granted to Greece came with conditions. The country had to raise revenues and cut government spending. Greece has raised many of its taxes many times in the last few years. Some examples are shown below.

■ In 2013, corporation tax rates rose from 20 per cent to 26 per cent and a top rate of income tax of 42 per cent was to be imposed on incomes above €42 000.

■ In 2016, corporation tax was increased again to 29 per cent.

■ Rates of VAT increased from 19 per cent in 2010 to 24 per cent in 2016.

■ New property taxes were introduced and existing ones increased.

■ A range of other taxes and duties were increased.

The government also agreed to cut its spending. Figure 31.7 shows the levels of government spending in Greece between 2007 and 2016. Spending was reduced from around €14 000 million to just under €10 000 million over the period. This is quite a significant cut and was achieved by making cuts to most of the various government departments. For example, the government raised the retirement age to reduce pension payments and made big cuts in benefits, education, defence and many other areas.

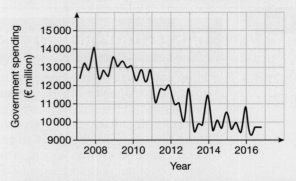

▲ **Figure 31.7** Greek government spending, 2007–16 (€ million)

CHAPTER QUESTIONS

1 Describe what fiscal deficit is.

2 Why is it important to express a fiscal deficit as a percentage of GDP?

3 Describe Greece's fiscal position between 2005 and 2015.

4 What is meant by contractionary fiscal policy? Use the example in this case to support your answer.

5 Consider the possible impact on Greece of a persistent fiscal deficit.

32 MONETARY POLICY

LEARNING OBJECTIVES

Understand how to define monetary policy and interest rates

Understand the role of central banks in setting interest rates

Understand the impact of changes in interest rates on macroeconomic objectives and how consumers and business are affected

Understand the use of asset purchasing by central banks

GETTING STARTED

Interest rates are one policy instrument that governments can use to help control the economy. A lot of spending by firms and households is funded by borrowed money and is therefore influenced by interest rates. Look at the examples below.

CASE STUDY: FRANCESCA PANICO

Francesca is employed in a museum in Naples. She is single and enjoys spending money. She relies heavily on credit cards to fund her spending. However, she was shocked when she found out that her credit card company had increased interest rates by nearly 2 per cent at a time when interest rates all over the world had fallen. She was going to write a letter of complaint but instead decided to cut her spending on credit cards from €500 per month to just €300.

CASE STUDY: ANTON AUTOBRAKES

Anton Autobrakes manufactures braking systems for car makers based in northern Italy. In 2016, the company decided to invest in new tooling technology and upgrade its computer systems. Owing to the low interest rates in the EU, the firm's interest payments on current loans had fallen from €150 000 p.a. to around €87 000 p.a. The senior management team decided to take out new loans to fund the investment.

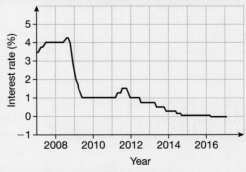

▲ Figure 32.1 EU interest rate, 2007–16

1 What has happened to the EU interest rate since 2007?

2 What effect is the pattern in (1) likely to have on firms like Anton Autobrakes?

3 What relationship exists between interest rates and consumer spending? Use the Francesca Panico example to support your answer.

MONETARY POLICY

Chapter 31 (pages 250–258) looked at how a government could influence aggregate demand by adjusting levels of taxation and government expenditure. Another way of controlling aggregate demand in the economy is to adjust interest rates or the money supply. This approach to demand management is called **monetary policy**.

Aggregate demand in the economy is affected by growth in the **money supply**. The money supply is the total amount of money that circulates in the economy. It is quite difficult to define the money supply. Economists use a number of methods. One simple way is to remember that the money supply includes all notes and coins in the economy plus any money held in bank accounts.

INTEREST RATES

Interest is the price paid to lenders for borrowed money. It is the price of money. For example, a firm borrowing US$100 000 from a bank to buy a new machine might pay interest of 7 per cent to the bank. This means that until the loan is completely repaid, the firm must pay 7 per cent on the amount owed. Interest rates can affect aggregate demand because some spending by households and firms is funded by borrowed money.

In most countries, there are many different rates of interest. There are a number of reasons for this.

- Different banks charge different rates as they compete with each other for business. For example, if a particular bank lowers rates on a particular loan product, it would expect to attract more customers because the loan becomes cheaper.

- Rates are higher if money is borrowed without security. For example, the rate charged on a **mortgage** to buy a house will be lower than the rate charged on an unsecured loan to pay for a holiday. This is because mortgages are secured loans. This means that the borrower gives permission to the lender to take control of the property if repayments cannot be met. With unsecured loans there is no such arrangement. Therefore, lenders might not get their money back if the borrower cannot meet the repayments. The interest rate charged is linked to the risk faced by lenders.

- The amount paid to borrowers is higher than the amount given to savers. This allows moneylenders such as banks to make a profit.

- Some of the highest rates of interest are charged to credit card users. For example, in February 2017, the **rate of interest** charged for one particular Barclays credit card product was 18.9 per cent (in the UK). In contrast, the rate charged by Barclays on some of its mortgage products was 3.4 per cent. All rates of interest in a country are affected by the **base rate**, which is set by the authorities. This is explained in the next section.

THE ROLE OF CENTRAL BANKS IN SETTING INTEREST RATES

In many countries, interest rates are set by a central bank. Central banks play an important role in the economy by:

- implementing the government's monetary policy and regulating the banking system
- acting as a lender of last resort to commercial banks
- controlling inflation and stabilising a nation's currency
- setting interest rates.

For example, in the EU, interest rates are set by the European Central Bank (ECB), which is based in Brussels, Belgium. In the UK, the Monetary Policy

Committee (MPC) sets the interest rate. This is a group of nine experts in economics and monetary policy led by the governor of the Bank of England. The aim of the MPC is to set interest rates at a level that keeps inflation under control. In the UK, the government sets a target for the rate of inflation – this was 2 per cent in 2016. The MPC has to set an interest rate that prevents inflation from exceeding this target. However, a central bank may also consider other economic variables when setting rates. For example, the rate of economic growth and the level of unemployment might be considered.

The rate of interest set by central banks is called the base rate. This is the rate of interest charged by a central bank when it lends overnight to commercial banks. When the base rate is changed, most other interest rates in the economy also change. Table 32.1 shows the base rates in a selection of countries around the world.

CENTRAL BANK INTEREST RATE	REGION	PERCENTAGE
FED interest rate	USA	0.75
RBA interest rate	Australia	1.50
BACEN interest rate	Brazil	13.00
BoE interest rate	UK	0.25
BOC interest rate	Canada	0.50
PBC interest rate	China	4.35
ECB interest rate	Europe	0.00
BoJ interest rate	Japan	0.00
CBR interest rate	Russia	10.0
SARB interest rate	South Africa	7.00

▲ Table 32.1 Interest rates set by a selection of central banks around the world in 2016

ACTIVITY 1

CASE STUDY: INTEREST RATES IN SOUTH AFRICA

Despite weak economic growth in South Africa, the South African Reserve Bank (SARB) increased interest rates twice in 2016 (Figure 32.2). It is now 7 per cent. The role of the SARB is to achieve and maintain price stability to promote balanced and sustainable economic growth in South Africa. The SARB is required by the

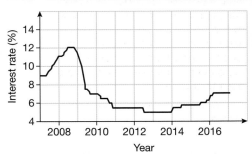

▲ Figure 32.2 South African interest rate, 2007–17

government to deliver a rate of inflation between 3 to 6 per cent. Despite the recent increases, interest rates were still considerably lower than they were in 2009 when the base rate reached 12 per cent.

1 What is meant by the interest rate?

2 How are interest rates determined in South Africa?

3 What is meant by the 'base rate'?

4 Describe the effect that interest rate changes might have on aggregate demand in the South African economy.

> ## IMPACT OF INTEREST RATE CHANGES ON MACROECONOMIC OBJECTIVES

Changes in the level of interest rates can have an impact on a number of economic variables and help to achieve a government's macroeconomic objectives.

INFLATION

Monetarists believe that inflation is caused by the money supply growing too quickly. They say that the way to reduce inflation is to slow down the speed at which the money supply is growing. This is likely to involve raising the rate of interest. When interest rates are higher, borrowing is likely to fall and the money supply grows less quickly. This will help to reduce aggregate demand in the economy and limit price increases.

UNEMPLOYMENT

A government might use lower interest rates to reduce unemployment. If interest rates were cut, there would be an increase in demand for loans. As a result, spending by firms and households would increase. This would increase aggregate demand and firms would respond by producing more goods and services. This means they would need to recruit more staff and therefore unemployment would fall.

ECONOMIC GROWTH

Monetary policy might be used to help smooth out the small variations in the economic cycle. For example, monetary policy might be used to help get an economy out of recession. In the last 10 years, interest rates in many countries around the world have been very low indeed. Table 32.1 shows that in some regions, such as the EU and Japan, two huge economic regions, the base rates set by central banks have been zero. The reason for this is to stimulate more economic growth. Since 2008, the global economy has been weak and many countries such as Japan and the EU have experienced low or negative growth rates.

THE CURRENT BALANCE

A government could use monetary policy to adjust the balance on the current account. For example, to reduce a deficit, a government might decide to tighten monetary policy. This would lower aggregate demand and reduce spending on imports. However, if interest rates are raised, the exchange rate might also increase. This would make exports more expensive, imports cheaper and worsen the current balance. The overall effect on the current balance of higher interest rates depends on the following.

- **The income elasticity of imports:** If demand for imports were income elastic, higher interest rates would reduce demand for them. This would improve the current balance.

- **The strength of the link between interest rates and exchange rates:** If the link is strong, higher interest rates will raise exchange rates. Exports will become expensive and imports will become cheaper. The current balance would worsen.

- **The price elasticity of demand for imports and exports:** If they are both price elastic and the exchange rate does rise when interest rates rise, imports will be cheaper and exports will be dearer. This would worsen the current balance.

THE MECHANISM BY WHICH INTEREST RATE CHANGES AFFECT CONSUMERS AND FIRMS

Changes in the interest rate can have an impact on aggregate demand. The impact occurs because of the way consumers and firms respond to changes in the interest rate.

CONSUMERS

When interest rates fall, demand for loans from households will rise. Consumers are likely to borrow money to buy goods, such as cars, furniture and holidays, because borrowing is cheaper. Also, when interest rates fall, consumers with a mortgage may find that their mortgage payments fall. This means they have more money to spend, which will also increase aggregate demand. Finally, if interest rates are lower, the reward to savers is also lower as a result. This might encourage people to spend rather than save. In contrast, when interest rates rise, consumers try to reduce borrowing because it becomes expensive. As a result, demand for goods using borrowed money will fall. Also, mortgage payments will rise automatically. Therefore, households will have less disposable income to spend and will have to cut some of their expenditure or reduce their saving.

FIRMS

Firms using borrowed money, such as mortgages, loans and overdrafts, to fund their business activity are likely to respond to changes in the interest rate. For example, when interest rates fall, the interest payments on current borrowings will also fall. This will help to boost their profits because costs will be lower. Lower interest rates are also likely to raise levels of business confidence and stimulate more investment. Since a large proportion of business investment is funded through borrowing, lower interest rates mean that the returns on investment are likely to be higher. Therefore, more investment is likely to be undertaken. In contrast, higher interest rates will raise costs, lower profits, reduce business confidence and make entrepreneurs more cautious. As a result, investment in the economy is likely to fall.

There is also a link between the interest rate and the exchange rate. When the interest rate falls, the exchange rate is also likely to fall (see Chapter 41, pages 333–339). If the exchange rate falls, the prices of exports become cheaper. This means that demand for them will rise. Firms will benefit because they will sell more goods and services. Also, the price of imports will rise, which means domestic consumers and firms will buy fewer. An increase in exports and a fall in imports will increase aggregate demand. This will also help to improve the balance on the current account

THE USE OF ASSET PURCHASING BY CENTRAL BANKS

In recent years, many countries have tried to control the money supply using a method called **quantitative easing**. This involves central banks buying financial assets, such as government bonds, from commercial banks. This results in a flow of money from the central bank to commercial banks. This extra cash can be used by commercial banks as a basis for making new loans to consumers and businesses. When more loans are granted, aggregate demand will increase.

This approach was used in the USA, EU, UK and Japan when historically low interest rates failed to stimulate demand during the global recession. However, one possible problem with quantitative easing is that it can be inflationary. This is because the money used by the government does not exist – it is created electronically. The government buys financial assets from commercial banks and increases the cash balances in their accounts without actually giving them any cash. It is like printing money. Whether this approach has worked or not may not be determined for several years.

ACTIVITY 2

CASE STUDY: MONETARY POLICY IN JAPAN

The Japanese economy has really struggled to grow in the last few decades. Figure 32.3 shows that growth has often been negative and has rarely risen above 2 per cent since 1981. For example, in 2009, GDP in Japan fell by around 5 per cent. In an effort to stimulate growth, interest rates have been reduced to –0.5 (base rate) and the Bank of Japan (Japan's central bank) has been buying JPY 80 trillion of government bonds per year for several years. The government wants to raise inflation in the economy, which has also been negative recently, to bring it up to its 2 per cent target.

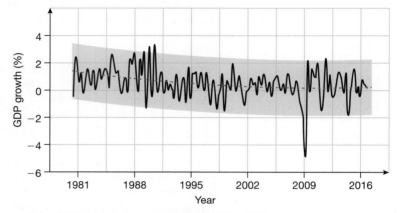

▲ Figure 32.3 Japanese economic growth, 1981–2016

1 What is meant by quantitative easing?

2 Why has Japan used quantitative easing?

3 Why might quantitative easing be inflationary?

MULTIPLE-CHOICE QUESTIONS

▶ 1 Which of the following is most likely to rise if the money supply grows too quickly?

A Inflation

B Supply of labour

C Voluntary unemployment

D Current account surplus

▶ 2 An increase in interest rates is likely to bring about which of the following?

A Increase inflation

B Reduce unemployment

C Increase the demand for imported cars

D Increase savings

CASE STUDY: MONETARY POLICY IN RUSSIA

In Russia, monetary policy is an important part of the nation's overall economic policy. Current monetary policy is aimed at improving the well-being of Russian citizens. In common with many other countries in the world, the Bank of Russia uses monetary policy to maintain price stability – or currently to bring down inflation to its 2017 target of 4 per cent. In February 2017, the Bank of Russia decided to keep the interest rates fixed at 10 per cent. In 2015, rates were as high as 15 per cent so the current trend is downwards (Figure 32.4). It was expected that high interest rates in Russia would reduce inflation further and encourage savings (Figure 32.5). The central bank also says that it will maintain what it calls its 'moderately tight monetary policy' – a policy that is giving Russia the highest real interest rates of any major economy in the world.

However, Russia's economy is not in good health. Economic growth rates are low and the country is suffering from the low global oil price. A significant proportion of Russia's earnings is from the sale of oil overseas. Government revenue also relies heavily on oil proceeds and the fiscal deficits of the last 8 years are likely to be repeated. However, according to a report by the Bank of Russia, growth in industrial production is positive. Output in several industries is growing and business investment is gradually rising.

Finally, the governor of the Central Bank of Russia was critical of the policies used by other central banks around the world. Elvira Nabiullina said that quantitative easing activities had failed to increase investment in the **real economy**. 'Because of the continued easing of monetary policy in many countries there is also the possibility that a higher level of financial market volatility will persist,' Nabiullina warned. She also believed that many central banks were being cautious in an effort to keep financial markets stable.

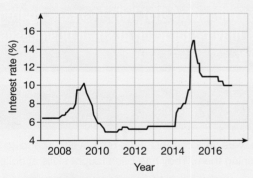

▲ **Figure 32.4** Russian interest rate, 2007–16

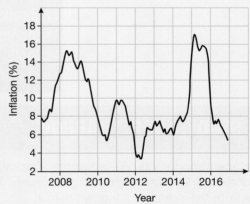

▲ **Figure 32.5** Russian inflation rates 2007–16

SUBJECT VOCABULARY

real economy part of the economy that is concerned with actually producing goods and services, as opposed to the part of the economy that is concerned with buying and selling on the financial markets

CHAPTER QUESTIONS

1 Describe what monetary policy is.

2 Why are there so many different rates of interest in an economy?

3 Describe the mechanism by which high interest rates in Russia affect consumers and firms.

4 Discuss the effect Russia's monetary policy might have on unemployment in the economy.

5 Consider whether Russia's monetary policy is working. Make a clear judgement in your evaluation.

33 SUPPLY SIDE POLICIES AND GOVERNMENT CONTROLS

LEARNING OBJECTIVES

- Understand how to define supply side policies
- Understand the impact supply side policies have on productivity and total output
- Understand the impact supply side policies have on macroeconomic objectives: privatisation, deregulation, education and training, regions, infrastructure, business taxes and income taxes
- Understand the advantages and disadvantages of government controls such as regulation, legislation, fines and pollution permits

GETTING STARTED

Fiscal policy and monetary policy is generally used to manage aggregate demand in the economy. For example, if a government wants to reduce inflation, it might raise interest rates to reduce aggregate demand. However, another approach to managing the economy is to introduce measures that help increase aggregate supply. Such measures may be targeted at small businesses. Look at the information below.

CASE STUDY: ANDREI KARPOV

A newspaper reporter interviewed Andrei Karpov, the owner of a small Russian engineering company. Some extracts from the interview are given below.

Reporter: When did you start to feel good about your business?

Andrei: I suppose a few years ago. I got some financial help from the government. They gave me some money towards a new machine. The old machine was almost useless and I couldn't really afford a new one. After this, I was able to produce more efficiently and lower my prices. This, of course, led to more business.

Reporter: Did you get any other help from the government?

Andrei: Yes. Not financial help but highly valuable. As my business grew I needed more staff. I found that the new recruits were very capable. I did not have to spend so much time training them. They had been taught skills at college.

Reporter: Has the nation's privatisation programme helped you at all?

Andrei: Yes, it has. I sometimes make parts for automobiles. After privatisation, I was given the opportunity to supply parts to the newly privatised AutoCo. Before privatisation, the company would not have considered me. They just stuck with their old suppliers. They had no incentive to look around for cheaper and better quality parts.

Reporter: Do you think the new tax cuts will help your business?

Andrei: Oh, definitely yes. At the moment, I pay 35 per cent tax on my business profit. When it falls to 20 per cent I will have more profit to invest and grow my business.

1 What financial support has Andrei received from the government to help his business develop?

2 How has privatisation helped Andrei's business?

3 How do you think tax cuts help to increase aggregate supply?

WHAT ARE SUPPLY SIDE
POLICIES?

SUBJECT VOCABULARY

aggregate supply total amount of
goods and services produced in a
country at a given price level in a given
time period

supply side policies government
measures designed to increase
aggregate supply in the economy

GENERAL VOCABULARY

obstacle something that makes it
difficult to achieve something

Supply side policies are used to help increase **aggregate supply** in the
economy. Aggregate supply is the total amount of goods and services
produced in a country at a given price level in a given period of time. Supply
side policies tend to be 'business friendly' and aim to increase economic
growth. They can be targeted at the whole economy or at those parts where
an **obstacle** exists that prevents economic growth. In many countries, supply
side policies have aimed to:

- improve flexibility in labour markets by removing restrictions
- restore the incentive to work by lowering taxes on work and enterprise
- promote competition through privatisation, deregulation and helping small
  firms
- increase investment by improving the flow of capital in capital markets.

> **DID YOU KNOW?**
> - Supply side policies became popular in the 1980s because trying to
>   control the economy using demand management policies was too
>   difficult.
> - It was thought that the economy would perform better if aggregate
>   supply could be increased.
> - With greater productive potential, the economy would grow,
>   unemployment would be lower and inflationary pressures would ease.

IMPACT OF SUPPLY SIDE POLICIES
ON PRODUCTIVITY AND TOTAL
OUTPUT

PRODUCTIVITY

Supply side policies generally improve the productivity of production factors.
This means that resources are used more effectively and the productive
potential of the economy can be increased. A number of supply side policies
have attempted to increase labour productivity using the following approaches.

Improving flexibility: In the past, many believed that labour markets were too
inflexible. For example, trade unions were often criticised for forcing up wages
and resisting the introduction of new working practices and new technology.
This prevented labour productivity from improving. To deal with the problem in
the UK, in the 1980s, the government introduced a range of anti-trade union
legislation to weaken unions and help labour markets work more freely. For
example, closed shops and secondary picketing were made illegal. As a result
of these measures, and many others, there was less disruption when new
working practices and new technology were introduced. There were also fewer
strikes relating to wages.

Training and education: If people receive more education and training, the
quality of the workforce will improve. This will help improve labour productivity
and increase aggregate supply. This is discussed in more detail below.

Some supply side policies are designed to promote more competition. If
a government can make markets more competitive, there will be pressure
on firms to be more cost effective and innovative. This will help to raise
productivity. Privatisation and deregulation can play a role in this aim.

Finally, productivity can be increased with more investment. If businesses
purchase new technology and update their production facilities, efficiency
will improve.

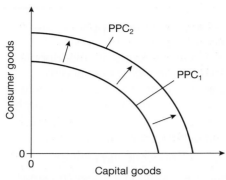

▲ **Figure 33.1** Impact of supply side policies on total output in the economy

TOTAL OUTPUT

Supply side policies aim to increase the productive potential of the economy. With increased volumes of output, national income will rise and living standards will be improved. Also, if the government can increase supply, there is less chance of demand-pull inflation and more jobs would be created. Therefore unemployment will be lower.

The production possibility curve (PPC) can be used to show the impact of supply side policies on total output. Figure 33.1 shows the PPC shifting out from PPC_1 to PPC_2. This is the effect that supply side policies will have on the total output in the economy. In this example, the country will be able to produce greater quantities of both capital goods and consumer goods when supply side policies are used to increase aggregate supply.

ACTIVITY 1

CASE STUDY: SUPPLY SIDE POLICIES IN CHINA

In 2017, China announced plans to modernise its agriculture sector and switch focus away from basic grains, such as rice, towards meat, dairy and value-added products. The purpose of this was to meet the changing needs of China's population. The state said it would use supply side policies to help increase the output of soybeans, corn silage and alfalfa for livestock. It also said it wanted to improve the quality of agricultural products. The measures announced included:

■ lower taxes for business start-ups in rural areas

■ the development of innovation centres to support high-quality produce

■ encouraging exports and supporting companies that set up overseas production bases

■ using anti-dumping and other measures to protect domestic food producers (see Chapter 38, pages 312–318)

■ increasing farmers' incomes (there were no specific details as to how this would be achieved).

The plans also emphasised the importance of making agriculture more environmentally sustainable. For example, it was stated that major water-saving programmes, such as drip irrigation, would be used. The overuse of pesticides would also be addressed as would the strict standards on handling manure. Finally, it was hoped that the

▲ **Chinese farmers**

increased use of technology, such as large-scale biogas digesters, would help to increase supply.

1 What is meant by supply side policies?

2 Describe the main aim of supply side policies.

3 Discus how some of the supply side policies in this case might help to increase total output in China.

IMPACT OF SUPPLY SIDE POLICIES ON MACROECONOMIC OBJECTIVES

Most governments use supply policies to increase economic growth. A wide range of supply side measures is available and they can have a variety of effects on the economy. Some examples of the policies used by governments, and the impact they might have, are outlined below.

PRIVATISATION

Many governments have privatised state assets in recent years (see Chapter 12, pages 81–88). Privatisation breaks up state monopolies and promotes competition because once they are part of the private sector, businesses have to make a profit to survive. They cannot rely on public money, if they make a loss. In the private sector, if they fail to provide services that give customers value for money, they may go out of business. Competitive pressure should improve quality and reduce prices.

Also, some services that were once provided by the public sector have been contracted out. For example, private sector firms in some countries have been invited to bid for contracts to provide meals and cleaning services in schools, hospitals and government offices.

One of the problems with privatisation is that state monopolies often become private monopolies. As a result, consumers might be exploited. This has led to price increases and poor quality services in some countries – particularly in industries like water supply and energy distribution.

DEREGULATION

Regulation, often called 'red tape', involves government controls in markets. Deregulation in business generally means tackling problems such as:

- excessive of paperwork
- obtaining unnecessary licenses
- having lots of people or committees to approve a decision
- various 'trivial' rules that slow down business development.

Many governments have addressed these problems by relaxing regulations that restrict competition. However, inadequate or insufficient regulation may bring problems. For example, over recent years, the world financial system has been significantly deregulated. Many have argued that a lack of regulation in financial services caused the financial crisis in 2008 and the global recession that followed.

GENERAL VOCABULARY

contracted out to arrange to have a job done by a person or company outside your own organisation

ACTIVITY 2

CASE STUDY: DEREGULATION IN THE USA

Before being elected in 2017, US President Trump said he would cut 75 per cent of business regulations in a 'bonfire' of red tape. After being elected, he signed an order that said that for every new regulation introduced, two must be cut. The main agencies affected were the Environmental Protection Agency and the Food and Drug Administration.

The system implemented by Trump is based on the one used in the UK. This started in 2010 as 'one in, one out', grew to 'one in, two out', and then became 'one in, three out'. The government reckoned that between 2010 and 2015, there were savings of £2200 million, and since May 2015 there have been annual savings to businesses of £800 million. As a result of this success in the UK, Australia and Canada plan to launch their own versions. Now the USA plans to do the same.

1 What is meant by deregulation?

2 How will deregulation help to increase aggregate supply in the US economy?

3 Describe one possible problem with deregulation.

EDUCATION AND TRAINING

If the quality of human capital can be improved, workers will be more productive. Investment by governments and firms in education and training will help to improve the quality of human capital. Clearly, if people are educated and are able to develop a range of skills such as literacy, numeracy, communication, analysis, problem solving, evaluation, critical thinking and language, they are more employable. Improving the skills of a nation's workforce is a key element of supply side policies. Governments can help by investing more in schools, universities and colleges. They can also provide firms with incentives to invest in training. They could offset training costs against tax, for example – or perhaps by meeting some of the training costs.

Unfortunately, investment in education is very expensive and the returns on the investment are not seen for many years. Consequently, funds for education in many countries are often inadequate. In many developing countries, for example, state school is not free – the students or their families meet the costs of books, uniforms and teachers. Globally, more than 226 million children do not attend secondary school.

DID YOU KNOW?

In the UK, the following measures have been used over the past 30 years to improve the quality of labour.

■ More young people were encouraged to stay in education until age 16.

■ More people were encouraged to enter university.

■ More vocational courses were introduced into schools and colleges. National Vocational Qualifications (NVQs) and more applied courses were offered in addition to academic courses.

■ AS levels (a qualification taken after 1 year of study after 16 years of age) were introduced so that students studied more subjects between the ages of 16 and 18).

■ Modern apprenticeships were introduced in 1994 (now called Apprenticeships). These are on-the-job training schemes partly funded by the government.

POLICIES TO BOOST REGIONS WITH HIGH UNEMPLOYMENT

One of the advantages of supply side policies is that they can be targeted or used selectively. In some countries, it is likely that certain regions will have far higher unemployment than others. For example, the unemployment rate in Spain in 2015 was 24.4 per cent. However, in some regions it was considerably higher. Andalusia had the worst rate at 34.8 per cent, followed by the Canary Islands (32.4 per cent), the north African Spanish territory of Ceuta (31.9 per cent) and Castilla-La Mancha (29 per cent). The Spanish government recognised these regional imbalances and introduced policies designed to reform labour markets. These helped to control wages and make it easier for firms to 'hire and fire' people. Spain also attracted EU funding for job creation projects in some of the worst hit regions. For example, a specialist technology park was built in Andalusia, which focused on the needs of the aeronautic and aerospace industries. The EU funding allocated to this project helped to create jobs, particularly in small businesses.

INFRASTRUCTURE SPENDING

The productive potential of the economy will increase if the quality of the infrastructure is improved. The government can help by investing more in infrastructure, education and health care, for example. Investment in infrastructure will improve transport and communications systems. This will help private sector firms because people will be more geographically mobile and the distribution of goods will be easier. Investment in education and health care will improve the quality of human capital. This will also help private sector firms because workers will be better educated and healthier.

The Indian government has invested heavily in infrastructure development. For example, it is committed to a huge road construction programme. The country's road network has expanded at the rate of 4 per cent since 1951. India now has the second-largest road network after the USA. There are now 5.23 million kilometres of roads, of which 3.17 million kilometres are surfaced. However, more is needed since the network is still underdeveloped.

One important infrastructure development is the provision of superfast broadband networks. For example, in 2015, China said it would accelerate the development of its high-speed broadband network. China's internet connection rate was only 47.9 per cent in 2015, with especially low connectivity in smaller cities and rural areas. This compares with about 75 per cent of people in the USA and 73 per cent in the UK. It was estimated that around CNY 2 trillion would be spent on high-speed broadband by 2020.

LOWER BUSINESS TAXES TO STIMULATE INVESTMENT

The pace of economic growth in a country can be accelerated if businesses can be encouraged to invest more. Supply side measures can help with this. Investment in the private sector can be increased if firms are confident about the future and there are funds available for investment. The government can also play a role by maintaining a stable economy and helping to increase the flow of investment funds to firms. Examples of measures that could be used include the following.

- About one-half of all private sector investment is funded from profits. Therefore by taxing profits less, more will be available for investment. In the last 20 years, many governments have reduced taxes paid by businesses. For example, in Ireland the rate of corporation tax has been cut to just 10 per cent. This is one of the lowest rates in the world.

- Firms can **offset** the cost of investment against tax. They can claim capital allowances when buying machines and equipment, for example.

- Tax incentives have been used to encourage people to save more and buy shares in companies. In some countries, tax relief may be given to individuals who invest in new companies or IT companies, for example.

SUBJECT VOCABULARY

offset if something, such as a cost or sum of money, offsets another cost it has the effect of reducing or balancing it, so that the situation remains the same

LOWER INCOME TAXES TO ENCOURAGE WORKING

Some people argue that high taxes on income and profit will reduce output in the economy. This is because high taxes reduce the incentive to work and discourage people from setting up or developing businesses. For example, some workers will take more holidays, retire earlier or refuse overtime. Also, entrepreneurs are less likely to undertake risky business opportunities. As a result, many countries have reduced taxes on personal earned income and business profits. For example, in the UK, the top rate of income tax was reduced from 83 per cent to 60 per cent in 1983 and then to 40 per cent in 1988. Corporation tax (tax on company profits) has also been reduced in the UK.

GOVERNMENT CONTROLS

GENERAL VOCABULARY

vulnerable those in need of special care, support, or protection because of age, disability or risk of abuse or neglect

In addition to fiscal policy, monetary policy and supply side policies, governments can use other controls when managing the economy and trying to achieve its macroeconomic objectives. For example, it can pass new legislation to help protect the environment, impose fines on firms that exploit consumers and workers and introduce controls as means of maintaining standards in business conduct. On the one hand, these controls have advantages because they reduce the exploitation of **vulnerable** groups or sectors. However, they may impose costs on firms that might inhibit their growth and development. Such controls are discussed in detail in Chapter 13 (pages 89–96) and Chapter 24 (pages 181–189).

MULTIPLE-CHOICE QUESTIONS

▶ **1** Which of the following is a supply side measure designed to help firms to increase investment?

   A Privatisation

   B Tax breaks for people who buy shares in businesses

   C Deregulation

   D An increase in the provision of vocational courses

▶ **2** Which of the following measures will help to improve occupational mobility?

   A Investment in government training schemes

   B Increase in unemployment benefit

   C Lower rates of income tax

   D Privatisation

ECONOMICS IN PRACTICE

CASE STUDY: SUPPLY SIDE POLICIES IN ARGENTINA

At the end of 2015, a new government was elected in Argentina. When it came to power, the economic position was highly uncertain. For example, inflation was over 20 per cent, government spending was out of control, economic growth was negative and unemployment was high. Faced with this difficult situation, the authorities began an attempt to repair the damage and develop better economic policy. Some of the measures introduced by the government were designed to increase supply in the economy to help reduce inflation.

The government began by removing a number of controls in the economy. For example, it removed foreign exchange controls so that Argentina's currency would fall in value. Further deregulation included:

- eliminating minimum interest rates for time deposits and maximum rates for consumer loans
- simplifying procedures for opening bank accounts
- eliminating bank transfer fees
- eliminating savings maintenance fees
- lifting restrictions on insurance companies that forced them to invest in infrastructure projects approved by a political committee
- lifting restrictions that limited foreign investment.

To help specific industries, the government gave subsidies to oil exporters to encourage more exploration and financial help to struggling dairy farmers. The government also made some changes to a range of taxes, for example:

- eliminating export taxes on most products
- cutting VAT
- raising personal tax allowances (this meant that people paid less income tax)
- reducing corporation tax
- phasing out the financial transaction tax.

It also plans to simplify the tax system. There are over 35 different taxes that contribute only a very small amount to government revenues. However, some of them impose high compliance costs on businesses. Simplification will help to reduce business costs.

Measures were also introduced to promote competition, for example:

- trade barriers were lowered to raise competitiveness, encourage new investment, and increase productivity
- the National Competition Commission was given powers to carry out investigations, impose fines and bring cases to court
- whistle-blowing to reveal anti-competitive practices was encouraged.

In the last 15 years, investment in infrastructure has been lacking, particularly in transport and energy production. The government is aware of this but is currently limited by a lack of funds. However, it has outlined an ambitious plan to double the supply of electricity in the next 20 years. It also aims to do this using 25 per cent renewable sources.

It is too early to say whether these measures, and many others, are working yet. As showed in Figure 33.2, inflation has continued to rise – soaring to around 40 per cent. However, economic growth is forecast to increase from 1.8 per cent to 2.7 per cent in 2017 – rising to 3 per cent per annum in the medium term.

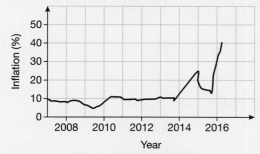

▲ **Figure 33.2** Argentina inflation, 2006–16

CHAPTER QUESTIONS

1   How might supply side policies help to reduce inflation in Argentina?

2   Describe the possible effects of the planned tax changes on the economy.

3   Discuss how the government plans to promote competition in the economy.

4   Discuss how **(a)** education and training and **(b)** spending on infrastructure might help to increase supply in Argentina.

34 RELATIONSHIPS BETWEEN OBJECTIVES AND POLICIES

LEARNING OBJECTIVE

■ Understand the impact of policies and the trade-off between macroeconomic objectives:
- unemployment and inflation
- economic growth and inflation
- economic growth and the environment
- inflation and the current account on the balance of payments

SUBJECT VOCABULARY

austerity official action taken by a government in order to reduce the amount of money that it spends or the amount that people spend

GETTING STARTED

Economic policies are designed to help achieve a government's macroeconomic objectives. However, when a particular policy instrument is used for a specific purpose, the effects might be both positive and negative. Look at the example below.

CASE STUDY: SAUDI ARABIA ECONOMIC POLICIES

The fall in the global oil price in 2014 hit Saudi Arabia quite hard. Both the residents and the government of Saudi Arabia rely very heavily on the oil industry for income. The government ran up a record fiscal deficit and the International Monetary Fund warned the government that it would run out of money within 5 years if it did not reduce its expenditure. As a result, a number of 'austerity measures' were announced in the 2016 budget with the aim of reducing the fiscal deficit. The government ran a deficit of SAR 367 000 million in 2015. The 2016 budget plan aimed to cut that to SAR 326 000 million. This would help the government avoid borrowing more and selling off overseas assets to pay its bills. Examples of the fiscal measures the government planned to use included:

■ cutting subsidies for water, electricity and petroleum products

■ introducing a value-added tax in line with many other countries around the world

■ raising taxes on soft drinks and tobacco

■ raising money from the privatisation of some state assets

■ cutting the government's spending projects from SAR 975 000 million to SAR 840 000 million.

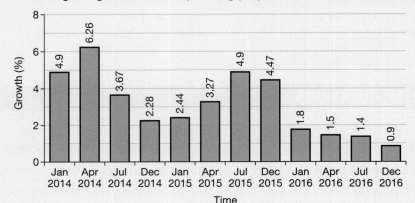

◀ **Figure** 34.1 Saudi Arabia economic growth, 2014–16

It was expected that economic growth would fall in Saudi Arabia from the current rate of 3.3 per cent. According to Monica Malik, chief economist at Abu Dhabi Commercial Bank, 'We see real GDP growth decelerating sharply in 2016, albeit remaining positive.'

1 Calculate the planned cut in the fiscal deficit of Saudi Arabia as a percentage.
2 What is the aim of Saudi Arabia's economic policies?
3 Describe one possible negative effect of Saudi Arabia's economic policies.
4 In pairs, find out the key macroeconomic objectives in your country.

IMPACT OF POLICY MEASURES ON MACROECONOMIC OBJECTIVES

Governments use policy instruments to achieve their macroeconomic objectives. The policies used will depend on the economic circumstances at the time. Ideally, a government will want to promote economic growth, keep inflation and unemployment down, prevent a large deficit on the current account and protect the environment. The use of fiscal policy, monetary policy and supply side measures will have an impact on economic variables such as inflation and economic growth. However, because there are both positive and negative effects of using different policies, it is often difficult for the government to achieve its macroeconomic objectives. For example, the use of contractionary fiscal policy to reduce inflation in the economy may increase unemployment. If the government cuts expenditure on social care, for example, fewer social workers will be required. This suggests that governments may have to accept trade-offs between macroeconomic objectives. For example, a government may have to tolerate higher levels of inflation if it wants lower levels of unemployment.

UNEMPLOYMENT AND INFLATION

POLICIES TO REDUCE INFLATION

Inflation, particularly if it gets out of control, can be very harmful for an economy. Consequently, most governments are likely to take action to reduce inflationary pressures in the economy as soon as inflation threatens to become a problem. Governments often favour the use of monetary policy to reduce inflation. One reason for this is because a government can quickly raise interest rates to reduce demand. In many countries, central banks will automatically raise interest rates if they have been given an inflationary target to meet. When interest rates are high, there will be a decrease in aggregate demand. This will help to reduce inflation but there may be some serious negative effects, such as the following.

■ Higher interest rates will discourage consumers and businesses from borrowing. As a result, there will be a fall in consumption and investment. This will reduce aggregate demand and lower economic growth. Unemployment is likely to rise.

■ Higher interest rates will result in higher mortgage payments for many households. This will reduce their spending power and lead to a fall in aggregate demand. Firms will react by reducing capacity and laying off staff.

■ Firms will incur higher interest charges. This will raise their costs and reduce their profits. They may invest less, which will reduce aggregate demand.

■ Higher interest rates will also discourage firms from borrowing to invest in new technology and expansion. This will hamper their long-term development. They may also lose their competitive edge in foreign markets.

- If higher interest rates result in higher exchange rates it may be harder for firms to sell abroad. Exporters are likely to react by laying off staff.

Even if a government favours the use of fiscal policy to reduce inflation, there will still be some negative effects.

- Higher taxes and lower government spending could result in unemployment. For example, if consumption falls as a result of higher taxes, businesses will see a fall in demand for their products. They may react by cutting production and laying off workers. Lower government spending means that some services are likely to be cut. As a result, civil servants, teachers and nurses may be laid off.

- People may suffer as a result of poorer government services after the cuts in expenditure, for example, waiting times for NHS treatments may rise, university places may fall and repairs to the infrastructure may be reduced.

POSSIBLE TRADE-OFF

It is clear from above that both anti-inflationary fiscal policy and anti-inflationary monetary policy can have some unwelcome effects on the economy. In the past, when governments have tried to reduce inflation, unemployment rises. This suggests that a trade-off exists between inflation and unemployment. Many economists recognise this trade-off and suggest that a government will have to accept higher levels of unemployment if it wishes to reduce inflation. Some economists also say that if a government tries to reduce inflation very quickly, levels of unemployment will be even higher.

However, the use of supply side measures to reduce inflation may avoid rising unemployment. This is because they are designed to increase the supply of output rather than decrease aggregate demand. Unfortunately, supply side measures are often very slow to have an impact on the economy. Consequently, governments are more likely to use them together with other measures to reduce inflation, rather than a sole measure.

ECONOMIC GROWTH AND INFLATION

POLICIES TO PROMOTE GROWTH

Governments around the world will be keen to see the economy grow when they are elected. This is because economic growth usually means that living standards will improve and therefore the voters will be satisfied. To promote economic growth, the government can use expansionary fiscal policy. This would involve lowering taxes or increasing government expenditure. If taxes on households are lowered, people will have more disposable income. If they spend this extra money, aggregate demand will rise and businesses will be encouraged to produce more. If businesses raise output levels, the economy will grow. Similarly, if the government spends more, by employing more teachers, social workers and health workers, for example, extra demand in the economy will be created. Again, firms should respond to this by producing more and national income will grow.

The government could also use expansionary monetary policy. If interest rates are lower, people will usually borrow more and spend more. Also, firms might decide to invest more. If the cost of investment funds is lower, this will encourage businesses to develop new products, expand their existing activities and set up new ventures. Extra investment will help to drive economic growth. A government might also use quantitative easing to stimulate growth. This will help to increase the money supply and therefore aggregate demand.

POSSIBLE TRADE-OFF

One of the dangers of policies designed to increase economic growth is that they may be too expansionary. As a result, the economy might become 'overheated'. This means that firms will not be able to meet the rising aggregate demand and respond by raising their prices instead of producing more. This will cause demand-pull inflation in the economy. Therefore, governments need to be cautious. If they stimulate the economy too much, they will cause inflation. This suggests there is another trade-off between rapid economic growth and inflation.

Inflation is more likely to be caused if there is limited capacity in the economy or if factors of production are immobile. If firms are close to capacity and are finding it difficult to acquire resources, such as skilled labour, then inflation is more likely to occur. However, the use of supply side policies to promote growth might help to reduce inflationary pressures. This is because supply side measures are usually 'business friendly', which means that they will help firms increase supply. For example, more government training schemes might increase the supply of skilled labour to help businesses meet rising demand.

ECONOMIC GROWTH AND ENVIRONMENTAL PROTECTION

GROWTH AND THE ENVIRONMENT

Economic growth is often associated with environmental damage, especially if the growth is very rapid like that seen in China and India over the last 10–15 years. As businesses produce more output there are likely to be more emissions from power generators, chemical processers and other manufacturers. Also, the extra wealth and income that comes along with economic growth means that increasing numbers of people buy cars and other vehicles. This results in more emissions and increasing congestion on road networks around the world. Pollution resulting from rapid business expansion in places like China and other developing nations is especially dangerous to health. For example, according to a government report, more than 80 per cent of China's underground water drawn from wells used by farms, factories and mostly rural households is not safe to drink due to pollution.

Also, as more land is taken for business development, less is available for wildlife. The Earth's rainforests, swamps, plains, lakes and other habitats continue to disappear as they are cleared to make way for agriculture, housing, roads, pipelines and other industrial uses. For example, according to a report by the Australian Conservation Foundation, Bird Life Australia and Environmental Justice Australia successive governments have failed to protect the habitat of the country's most endangered creatures. The report said that 90 per cent of the 120 most endangered animals living in Australia have no safeguards to protect their habitat.

POSSIBLE TRADE-OFF

In developing countries, it is unlikely that the majority of people would want to prevent economic growth that delivers less poverty, longer life expectancy, lower infant mortality and improved living standards. If the environment is damaged along the way, many people in these countries might argue that this is a price worth paying. Some evidence certainly suggests this is the case. However, in some of these developing countries, governments are beginning to recognise that environmental damage can be costly and that measures are needed to protect the environment even if it means limiting business development. For example, in 2015, India planned to introduce tougher measures to punish those polluting the environment. Currently, offences under the Environment Protection Act are punishable by a fine up to Rs100 000, up to 5 years imprisonment, or both. There were plans to increase the severity of these penalties.

In developed countries, where environmental issues are perhaps more pressing, many governments have used a range of measures, such as legislation, regulations, fines and pollution permits (see Chapter 29, pages 228-239) to protect the environment. However, many of these do restrict business development and governments have to ensure that measures do not discourage the entrepreneurial spirit too much. It is often difficult to find the right balance in this trade-off.

KEY FACTS

- Some environmental projects may be cancelled if government funds are short.
- New projects may be approved as part of a wider policy to increase government expenditure.
- Revenues collected from environmental taxes will add to government funds.
- Some environmental measures may constrain businesses and impose additional costs. This might result in business closures and job losses.

ACTIVITY 1

CASE STUDY: TRADE OFF BETWEEN ECONOMIC GROWTH AND ENVIRONMENTAL PROTECTION IN AUSTRALIA

Most governments recognise that rapid economic growth can have a negative impact on the environment. Most governments have also agreed that there is a need to reduce emissions to slow down or reverse the effect of global warming. In light of this, a number of measures have been introduced around the world to generate more power using 'green' energy. As global economic growth becomes stronger, more energy is needed. This is because businesses need more energy to fuel their operations. Also, consumers become wealthier and can afford to burn more energy heating (or cooling) their homes and fuelling their vehicles.

Australia generates most of its electricity by burning fossil fuels. However, the government is committed to reducing this. By 2020, it hopes that Australia will produce 22.5 per cent of its power from renewable sources, rising to 51 per cent by 2050. Also, the burning of brown coal and oil to generate electricity is set to end completely by 2050.

Australia's policy to increase power production using renewable energy is called the Renewable Energy Target (RET). The government plans to invest AUD40 400 million (Australian dollar) between now and 2030. Between 30 and 50 major projects are likely to be developed in the next few years to help boost the production of 'green' energy. This will be supported by numerous smaller-scale solar projects from businesses looking to manage their own electricity production and consumption. This should create over 15 000 jobs.

The coal mining industry in Australia has been in decline. In 2014, it employed 57 800. However, 5 years before that, total employment was over 80 000. The switch to 'greener' energy is likely to add to the decline.

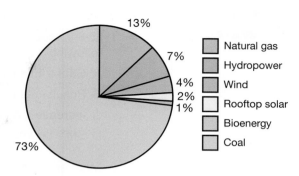

▲ **Figure 34.2** Sources of electricity generation in Australia, 2015

1   Describe the possible trade-off between economic growth and environmental protection.

2   To what extent do you think Australia needs to switch to 'green' energy?

3   Assess the possible impact on the Australian economy of switching to the production of 'greener' energy.

INFLATION AND THE CURRENT ACCOUNT ON THE BALANCE OF PAYMENTS

MEASURES TO REDUCE INFLATION

There is a possible link between inflation and the current account on the balance of payments. When inflation is high and persistent, governments will try to reduce it because of the harmful effects associated with high levels of inflation. If prices are rising, the price of exports will also be rising. This will reduce demand for exports creating pressure on the current account balance. It is also possible that consumers might switch from expensive domestic goods to relatively cheap imports. This would make the current account balance even worse. Consequently, high inflation rates have a damaging effect on a country's current account balance.

If a government uses monetary policy to reduce inflation, the balance of payments situation could actually become worse This is because monetary policy that uses higher interest rates to reduce inflation might strengthen the exchange rate. When interest rates are high, the demand for a domestic currency might rise and drive up the exchange rate (see Chapter 41, pages 333–339). If this happens exports become dearer and imports cheaper. This would create further pressure on the current account balance.

POSSIBLE TRADE OFF

A government trying to reduce inflation by raising interest rates may have to accept that the current account will worsen for a period of time. Although, the impact of price changes on the demand for exports and imports will depend on the elasticity of demand for imports and exports (see Chapter 42, pages 340–346). However, if the government uses fiscal policy alone to reduce inflation, a worsening of the current account might be avoided. For example, if the government cuts spending and/or raises taxes, there will be a fall in demand in the economy with no real direct effect on the exchange rate. Therefore, the prices of exports and imports will be fairly stable and the current account relatively unaffected. The use of supply side policies to reduce inflation will also avoid a negative impact on the current account. Supply side policies are not likely to affect the exchange rate and are also 'business friendly'. As a result, businesses might be able to produce more output at lower prices. This would help to boost exports and therefore benefit the current account.

MULTIPLE-CHOICE QUESTIONS

▶ 1 Low interest rates to promote economic growth might do which of the following?

    A Cause inflation

    B Result in higher levels of unemployment

    C Increase a current account deficit

    D Stifle private sector investment

▶ 2 More environmental protection is likely to be needed if the government follow which cause of action?

    A Drives inflation down too quickly

    B Stimulates the economy to grow faster

    C Tries to cut inflation

    D Tries to cut a current account deficit

ECONOMICS IN PRACTICE

CASE STUDY: ANTI-INFLATIONARY POLICIES IN IRAN

In 2013, when the Rouhani administration took power in Iran, a clear commitment was made by the government to reduce inflation. Figure 34.3 shows that the inflation rate in 2013, at around 40 per cent, was unacceptably high. The Central Bank of Iran (CBI) and other authorities created a clear strategy to bring price increases down. A key element of the plan was very tight monetary policy. It aimed to keep a very strict control on the money supply. As a result, interest rates were increased from around 15 per cent in 2013 to 22 per cent in 2014. In 2017, interest rates were still high at 20 per cent.

The government also reversed some of the policies introduced by the previous administration. For example, several years ago, Mahmoud Ahmadinejad (Iranian President from 2005 to 2013), introduced a subsidy reform plan that handed out cash to people without considering their financial means. This money was spent in the economy, which drove up demand and caused inflation. However, the new administration identified those that did not really need the handouts and redirected the money into the production sector.

Finally, the government also aimed to reduce the fiscal deficit. The authorities put together a carefully considered spending plan that avoided the need to go heavily into debt. This also helped to bring down inflation, which is now under 10 per cent.

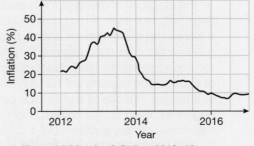

▲ **Figure 34.3** Iranian inflation, 2012–16

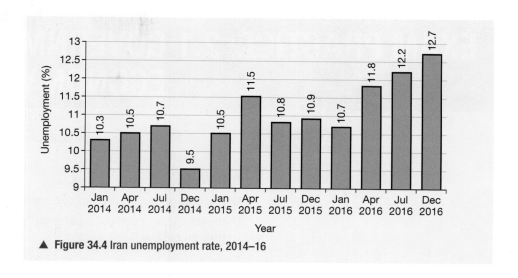

▲ **Figure 34.4** Iran unemployment rate, 2014–16

CHAPTER QUESTIONS

1 Describe the possible trade off that might exist between inflation and unemployment.

Look at Figures 34.3 and 34.4.

2 Is there any evidence to suggest that a trade-off between inflation and unemployment exists in Iran?

3 Discuss how Iran's use of anti-inflationary policies might affect its current account balance.

4 Discuss how the need for environmental protection might be affected by Iran's use of anti-inflationary policies.

EXAM PRACTICE: 2.1 GOVERNMENT AND THE ECONOMY

A01 | **1** Which of the following is an example of a macroeconomic objective? **(1)**

A Increase interest rates.

B Stimulate economic growth.

C Encourage businesses to use more capital intensive production methods.

D Invest more in education and training to increase the quality of human capital.

Table 1 shows four different income levels and four different tax rates paid on those income levels.

Income (€)	A Tax paid (€)	B Tax paid (€)	C Tax paid (€)	D Tax paid (€)
10 000	1000	0	500	1000
30 000	3000	3000	3000	2000
70 000	7000	5000	12 000	5000
200 000	20 000	12 000	45 000	10 000

▲ Table 1

A02 | **2** Which of the tax rates is a progressive system? **(1)**

A

B

C

D

A01 | **3** State **one** way in which a business might damage the environment. **(1)**

A02 | **4** What is meant by fiscal policy? **(2)**

In January 2017, Singapore had a balance of trade surplus of SGD 3287.37 million.

A02 | **5** Explain what is meant by a balance of trade surplus. **(3)**

In 2017, Ghana had an inflation rate of 13.3 per cent. This was the lowest inflation has been since November 2013.

SKILLS CRITICAL THINKING **A02** | **6** Explain how the use of monetary policy might help to reduce inflation. **(3)**

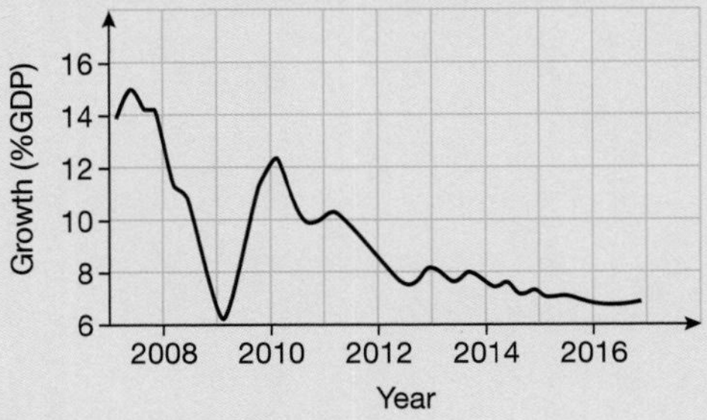

▲ Figure 1 Chinese economic growth rates, 2007–17

China has enjoyed some of the highest economic growth rates in the world in the last 10 years. In 2007, economic growth exceeded 14 per cent, however, in recent years, rates have been lower at around 7 or 8 per cent. Much of China's growth has resulted from a booming manufacturing sector. Chinese firms have flooded many Western economies with cheap manufactured goods. The income generated by these high growth rates have helped to raise living standards and reduce poverty in China. However, at the same time, China has suffered some of the most serious levels of pollution in the world.

SKILLS   CRITICAL THINKING REASONING ADAPTIVE LEARNING CREATIVITY

A02

A03

A04

7   Assess the impact of rapid economic growth on the people of China.   **(9)**

(Total = 20 marks)

2.2
THE GLOBAL ECONOMY

Assessment Objective AO1

Recall, select and communicate knowledge of economic terms, concepts and issues

Assessment Objective AO2

Demonstrate understanding and apply economic knowledge using appropriate terms, concepts, theories and calculations effectively in specific contexts

Assessment Objective AO3

Select, organise and interpret information from sources to investigate and analyse economic issues

Assessment Objective AO4

Evaluate economic information to make reasoned judgements and draw conclusions

Over time, the connectedness of different countries and their economies has increased. This is called globalisation. This section looks at the impact that globalisation, and multinational companies, can have on countries, governments, producers, consumers, workers and the environment. It also covers the importance of international trade, the development of trade blocs, the role of the World Trade Organization and protectionism. Finally, the importance of exchange rates is discussed – how they are determined, the factors that influence the supply and demand for currencies and the impact on exports and imports of changes in the exchange rate.

35 GLOBALISATION

GETTING STARTED

In recent years, economies all over the world have become more open. For example, since the break up of the Soviet Union, a large number of countries, such as Estonia, Poland, Ukraine, Latvia and many others, have started to trade with other nations. This has led to more trade, more cooperation, more communication between countries and more movement of resources such as labour and capital. Look at the example below.

CASE STUDY: THE GLOBAL CAR INDUSTRY

A few large firms, such as Toyota, General Motors (GM), Ford, Volkswagen, Hyundai and Nissan, dominate the global car industry. All of these firms produced over 6 million cars each in 2015. Three of them – Toyota, Volkswagen and GM – produced over 9 million each. Many of these firms sell their cars in global markets and have factories and suppliers in many countries. For example, Ford has factories in the USA, UK, Spain, Portugal, Australia, Brazil, France, Thailand and many others. These companies think globally. They will sell their products anywhere and operate production plants and other facilities wherever costs can be minimised. Fifty years ago, US producers like GM, Ford and Chrysler, dominated the world car industry. However, from the 1980s, their market share fell as Japan made an entrance into the global market. The market shares of the US producers declined dramatically as new and more efficient producers like Toyota entered the market.

As shown in Figures 35.1 and 35.2, the global demand for cars is growing. In 2015, global sales reached 72.37 million cars. It is expected that total sales in 2016 will reach 75 million cars. In particular, demand for cars is growing fast in emerging economies. Sales of cars in China, for example, were around 25 million in 2015.

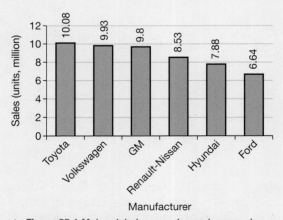

▲ Figure 35.1 Major global car producers by annual sales, 2015

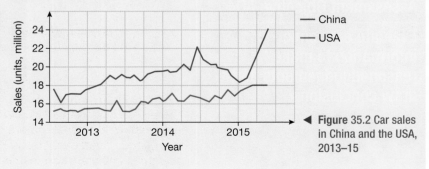

◀ Figure 35.2 Car sales in China and the USA, 2013–15

1 What do you think is meant by a global market?

2 Describe the pattern of global demand for cars.

3 Calculate the global market share of the major car producers shown in Figure 35.1.

4 Why do you think Japanese car manufacturers have started to dominate the world market?

5 Is there any evidence of globalisation in your country? Make a list of your ideas and present them to the rest of the class on a poster.

WHAT IS GLOBALISATION?

SUBJECT VOCABULARY

globalisation growing interconnection of the world's economies

interdependence where the actions of one country or large firm will have a direct effect on others

DID YOU KNOW?

It should be noted that the process of globalisation is not complete. This is because some **restrictions** still exist. For example, it may not always be possible to live and work in any country in the world. Many countries, such as Australia and the USA, restrict the number of immigrants entering the country. There are also some trade barriers that make it more difficult to sell goods in some countries.

GENERAL VOCABULARY

restrictions rule or law that limits or controls what people can do

Many markets today are global. This means that some firms expect to sell their products anywhere in the world. Today, the same firm could have a head office in London, borrow money from a bank in Japan, manufacture products in China, deal with customers from a call centre in India and sell goods to countries all over the world. Firms and people are behaving as though there is just one market or one economy in the whole world. This development is called **globalisation**. It is often defined as the growing interconnection of the world's economies. Some of the key features of globalisation are outlined below.

■ Goods and services are traded freely across international borders. There are no government laws that prevent firms from selling goods in overseas markets. This means that a firm such as Coca-Cola can sell its products as easily in Qatar as in the USA.

■ People are free to live and work in any country they choose. This has resulted in more and increasingly multicultural societies in which people from many different nations live and work in the same city, for example.

■ There is a high level of **interdependence** between nations. This means that events in one economy are likely to affect other economies. For example, the financial crisis in the USA in 2008 had an impact in many economies all over the world.

■ Capital can flow between different countries. This means that a firm or consumer in Australia can put their savings in a bank in the USA. This also means that investors can buy shares in foreign companies and firms can buy companies that operate in other countries. For example, in 2016, Dutch multinational Randstad Holding NV, a human resource consulting firm, bought Monster Worldwide Inc., a US employment website, for around US$430 million.

■ There is a free exchange of technology and intellectual property across borders. This means, for example, that patents granted in the USA are recognised in other countries.

REASONS FOR GLOBALISATION

There is a general agreement that modern globalisation began in the 1980s and has grown rapidly. There are a number of reasons for this trend.

FEWER TARIFFS AND QUOTAS

Countries use tariffs and quotas (see Chapter 38, pages 312–318) to restrict the flow of imports so that domestic industries are protected. Consequently, they restrict the development of foreign businesses when they try to sell their goods overseas. This is because it is more difficult to sell exports when countries impose trade restrictions. However, one way to avoid tariffs and quotas is to set up production facilities inside the countries that use trade restrictions. This helps to explain why large companies are growing by developing operations in other countries. In recent years, a lot of trade barriers have been dropped. An increasing number of economies are more open and many countries have stopped protecting domestic industries. Many countries have also simplified their monetary and legal systems to make international trading easier.

REDUCED COST OF TRANSPORT

International transport networks have improved in recent years. In particular, the cost of flying has fallen and the number of flights and destinations has increased. This means that people can travel to business meetings more easily and goods can be transported more cheaply. For example, in India the government has invested heavily in the construction of roads and motorways in the last 10 years. This development has reduced the cost of transporting goods in India because carriers can move goods far more quickly and easily for their customers.

REDUCED COST OF COMMUNICATION

Developments in technology have helped globalisation to accelerate. Modern computing allows firms to transfer complex data instantly to any part of the world. It also means that more people can work at home, or any other location that they choose. Many people do not have to be based in an office to do their jobs. This makes it easier for firms to have operations all over the world. The internet also allows consumers to gather information and buy goods online from firms located in different parts of the world.

INCREASED SIGNIFICANCE OF MULTINATIONALS

Many firms want to sell abroad, perhaps because domestic markets have been **saturated**. Large **multinational corporations (MNCs)**, which have a global reach, dominate some markets. They benefit considerably from having international markets and producing goods anywhere in the world where costs can be minimised. The development of multinationals and their importance is discussed in Chapter 36 (pages 295–303).

SUBJECT VOCABULARY

multinational corporations (MNCs) that operate in many different countries

saturated market in which there is more of a product for sale than people want to buy

DID YOU KNOW?

An increase in tourism has also helped globalisation to advance. Consumer tastes have changed as a result of their experiences when travelling abroad. People are more willing to try goods and services produced in other countries. For example, many people are happy to fly with a Middle Eastern Airline, drive a car made in South Korea, eat at a Bangladeshi restaurant and dress in clothes made in China.

ACTIVITY 1

CASE STUDY: AIR TRANSPORT AND GLOBALISATION

One industry that has benefited from globalisation is the airline industry. The numbers of people using air transport have grown significantly. Figure 35.3 shows the growth in passengers carried between 1980 and 2015. Air travel has risen for a number of reasons, including an increase in tourism, more business travel and the arrival of budget airlines around the world. For example, in India, airlines such as Indigo, GoAir, JetLite and Simplifly Deccan, have emerged and all offer cheap air travel in the country.

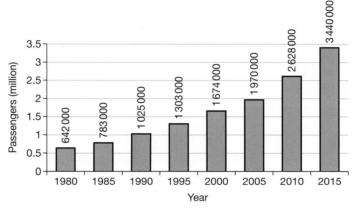

▲ **Figure 35.3** Global air transport, 1980–2015

1   Calculate the percentage increase in passengers carried between 1980 and 2015.

2   Describe **two** features of globalisation that have supported the growth of the airline industry.

3   Discuss **two** reasons for the development of globalisation.

4   Produce an illustrated poster that shows what is meant by globalisation.

IMPACT OF GLOBALISATION AND GLOBAL COMPANIES

INDIVIDUAL COUNTRIES

The impact of globalisation on individual countries is likely to vary. It depends on whether a country is the base for a global company or whether a global company selects a country as a site for a new factory, for example.

The countries where multinationals are based will benefit from globalisation. Most multinationals are based in developed countries and the gains generated from business development overseas, such as growth, will contribute to an increase in the wealth of that country. Even though many traditional industries, such as shipbuilding, mining, steel production and manufacturing, are declining in the West, other types of jobs are being created at a faster rate. For example, in the UK huge numbers of manufacturing jobs have been lost but the total number of people working has increased from 20 million to 32 million over about 30 years.

The countries that provide sites for global companies generally benefit from globalisation. It should result in higher levels of GDP. The extra output and employment resulting from new business development will increase economic growth and should raise living standards for people in these countries. The output generated by a multinational in a foreign country is recorded as output for the host country. Therefore, if this output is sold out of the host country, it is counted as an export. This helps countries to increase their foreign currency reserves and improves their current balance. Globalisation often means that new technologies and modern working practices are introduced into developing countries. For example, multinationals often provide technical assistance, training and other information to their suppliers located in the host country. Many multinationals also assist local suppliers in purchasing resources and in modernising production facilities.

Finally, increasing globalisation means that economic events in one country can have an impact on many other countries. This interdependence was demonstrated in 2008 when the world economy went into recession. Financial problems in America, where loans had been given to people who could not afford to repay them, spread rapidly to other countries. The financial crisis in the USA affected other countries because capital now flows easily between most nations. As a result, banks in other countries bought some of the bad debt generated in the USA. Eventually this caused a global banking crisis and led to a world recession. Without globalisation, this probably could not have happened.

GOVERNMENTS

The profits made by global companies are taxed by the host nation. This increases tax revenue for the government. This money can be spent to improve government services or lower taxes. Some argue that globalisation has resulted in more people setting up businesses. The arrival of global companies may have provided the encouragement and the skills required to develop new businesses. For example, a new multinational may encourage locals to supply commercial services such as transport, accommodation, restaurants, property maintenance, cleaning and leisure activities. This will help to support government economic policy in the provision of employment. Finally, globalisation can only advance if governments are committed to it. For example:

■ countries cannot trade if the government keeps international borders closed

■ international trade will be very limited if governments use protectionism

■ people cannot be free to live and work overseas unless borders are kept open

■ firms cannot develop overseas if planning permission is denied.

Governments can aid globalisation by relaxing laws and regulations that prevent, restrict or complicate trade and business.

PRODUCERS

Many would argue that the main winners from globalisation are the global companies that develop business interests overseas. Some specific benefits include the following.

■ **Access to huge markets:** Global markets are much bigger than domestic markets. If a business has access to billions rather than millions of customers this provides huge opportunities to increase sales. This should result in higher sales revenue and increased profits for businesses.

■ **Lower costs:** If businesses are able to grow by selling more output to larger markets, they may be able to lower their costs. This is because as firms grow they can exploit economies of scale. These are the cost reductions that firms enjoy as they grow.

DID YOU KNOW?
It could be argued that globalisation has reduced the likelihood of nations going to war. If an increasing number of countries are trading with each other, it suggests that diplomatic relations are good and that military conflict is unlikely.

■ **Access to labour:** One of the benefits of globalisation is the free movement of labour. This means that people are free to move around the world and find employment in other countries (subject to border controls that still exist in some countries). As a result, businesses will have access to a larger pool of labour. This is important because if a business is growing fast, there may be a shortage of domestic labour. Globalisation means that workers from overseas can help to boost the labour supply. Also, a rising labour supply might help to prevent wages from rising. It is often said that the arrival of larger numbers of foreign workers holds wages down – particularly in markets where unskilled labour is needed. Lower wages will help businesses to lower their costs.

■ **Reduced taxation:** Global businesses can reduce the amount of tax they pay. They can do this by locating their head office in a country where business taxes are low. Ireland has proved a popular destination for businesses in recent years since its rate of corporation tax is just 12.5 per cent (on trading income). This is well below other rates in the world, which are generally higher than 20 per cent.

ACTIVITY 2

CASE STUDY: GLOBALISATION AND SMARTPHONE PRODUCERS

Global sales of smartphones have grown sharply in recent years. The growth in sales of handsets between 2009 and 2015 is shown in Figure 35.4. The global market is dominated by three large multinational corporations: Samsung, Apple and Huawei with shares of 21.4 per cent, 13.9 per cent and 8.7 per cent, respectively. However, in recent years, market leaders Samsung and Apple have lost market share to emerging competitors, such as those from China.

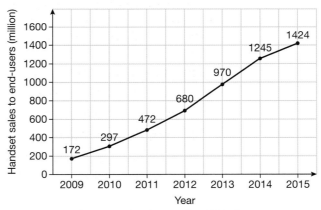

▲ **Figure 35.4** Global mobile phone sales, 2009–15

1 Calculate the number of mobile phones sold by Samsung in 2015, assuming it had a market share of 21.4 per cent.

2 Discuss two benefits of globalisation for mobile phone producers such as Samsung, Apple and Huawei.

CONSUMERS

If a multinational can produce goods more cheaply in foreign factories, prices are likely to be lower. One of the main benefits of the movement of some manufacturing from the West to countries like China and India is that many goods are cheaper for consumers. Globalisation has also resulted in a much wider range of goods and services for consumers, particularly in developed countries. For example, improved and cheaper transport communications have opened up huge numbers of new destinations for tourists. Another example is the cuisine available in restaurants today. Enormously wide-ranges are available in most towns and cities in the West. Few would have thought about organising holidays in places like Argentina, Chile, China, Fiji, Mozambique, Nicaragua Thailand and Vietnam 30 years ago. These are now common holiday destinations. Generally, globalisation has improved the living standards of billions of people worldwide.

WORKERS

Globalisation creates new jobs, particularly in developing countries when multinationals open new factories. However, local suppliers might also benefit if they get contracts with a new business venture set up by a multinational in their region.

Greater freedom of movement has allowed workers from less developed nations to look for jobs in developed countries. For example, as a result of new EU legislation, and the growth in EU members, large numbers of workers have migrated to the West. The UK has benefited from large numbers of Eastern Europeans seeking work. They are often prepared to work for the minimum wage and have proved to be reliable and hard working. Also, when economic growth was fast, they helped to reduce labour shortages in some areas. Workers in less developed countries often learn new skills as a result of training and on-the-job learning given when employed by multinationals. Also, governments in less developed countries often spend more on education and training to help attract foreign investment.

However, some workers lose out as a result of globalisation. This is because global companies will tend to locate operations where labour costs are low. This has resulted in a trend called **offshoring**. Offshoring means that some companies shift production from factories in the West to alternative locations in the Far East, such as China, Vietnam and Bangladesh. This is because key resources like labour and land are cheaper. When this happens, workers in the original factories are made redundant.

THE ENVIRONMENT

Many environmentalists oppose globalisation because global economic growth usually means more environmental damage. For example, as economies grow, more cars are purchased and more flights are taken. Both car and air transport increase greenhouse gases that cause global warming. Also, global economic growth will use up resources. Some of these resources such as oil, gas, gold and iron ore are non-renewable so once used they cannot be replaced.

Some global companies have been criticised in the past for the environmental damage they cause. For example, a report by the United Nations reckoned that the estimated combined damage to the environment by the 3000 largest companies around the world was £1.4 trillion in 2008. This is more than the national economies of all but seven countries in the world that year. The impact that businesses have on the environment is discussed in more detail in Chapter 29.

SUBJECT VOCABULARY

offshoring practice of getting work done in another country in order to save money

---

DID YOU KNOW?

Globalisation means that future generations will have fewer resources. Also, certain species are becoming extinct because their habitats are being destroyed and used instead for production.

MULTIPLE-CHOICE QUESTIONS

▶ 1 Which of the following is a reason for increasing globalisation?

   A Lower exchange rates

   B Reduced cost of communication

   C An increase in environmental legislation

   D An increase in the world's population

▶ 2 Which of the following is a feature of globalisation?

   A The high level of interdependence between nations

   B Higher levels of unemployment

   C Increased barriers to trade

   D Less scope for exploiting economies of scale

ECONOMICS IN PRACTICE

CASE STUDY: GLOBALISATION AND KENYA

Kenya is the major economic force in east Africa. Like a number of African nations, it has welcomed globalisation. Kenya's economy is dominated by the agricultural sector, which employs around 60 per cent of the working population. Productivity in the sector is very poor but more recently Kenya has seen the development of a garment industry and the creation of export processing zones. Flower production is also very successful, as is tea. Kenya is a major 'exporter' of nurses, doctors and teachers. Some of the income earned by these professionals is an important source of income from abroad.

Globalisation has helped develop manufacturing in Kenya. For example, Orbit Chemical Industries is a fast-expanding producer of soap, detergents, make-up and packaging.

The company produces goods for a number of multinationals such as Colgate-Palmolive, L'Oréal and Unilever. Orbit says that individual companies cannot effectively exploit economies of scale alone. However, by taking on orders from a number of multinationals, Orbit can produce large enough quantities to enjoy cost advantages. As a result, Orbit's revenue has increased by more than five times in the past 6 years, to US$100 million a year. Some of Orbit's produce is sold as far away as Angola, South Africa and Afghanistan. Orbit also plans to develop its operations in South Africa, Nigeria and Ethiopia next year.

Unfortunately, the benefits of globalisation are arriving in Africa very slowly indeed. One global corporation based in east Africa said that there had been no consumer boom like in China. A spokesman said, 'The middle class is coming quite quickly, but it remains relatively small and hasn't really grown yet to the level that people talk about. A lot of companies that focused on this idea of Africa as the next Asia have burnt their fingers and pulled back.' Although some of the economic data from Kenya is very positive, unemployment levels are very high at around 40 per cent and corruption is still a major barrier to growth.

African states have attracted multinationals after growing at an average of 5 per cent p.a. over the past several years. Multinationals believed they could supply a growing middle class in Africa with everything from phones to toothpaste. However, recently some established companies have started to scale back development due to the recession in Russia and the slowdown in Chinese growth. For example, Nestlé released 46 employees in Kenya and its regional hubs. More than 300 people lost jobs following the closure of Cadbury Kenya's plant and a further 99 were laid off after Eveready East Africa, the dry-cell battery maker, shut its Nakuru factory. Also, Hong Kong Shanghai Banking Corporation (HSBC) left Nairobi 3 years after failing to develop its business effectively.

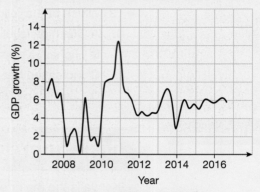

▲ Figure 35.5 Kenya GDP growth, 2006–16

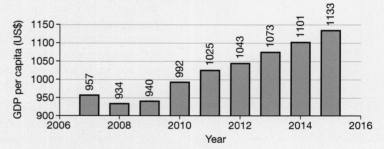

▲ Figure 35.6 Kenya GDP per capita, 2006–15

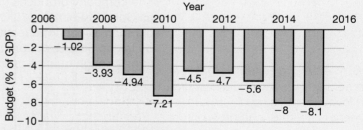

▲ Figure 35.7 Kenya fiscal deficit, 2006–15

CHAPTER QUESTIONS

1 Describe what globalisation is.

2 Why have fewer tariffs and quotas helped to foster globalisation?

3 Describe how (a) consumers and (b) producers in Kenya might be affected by globalisation.

4 Consider whether Kenya has benefited from globalisation in recent years. Make a clear judgement in your evaluation.

36 MULTINATIONAL COMPANIES (MNCs) AND FOREIGN DIRECT INVESTMENT

LEARNING OBJECTIVES

- Understand how to define multination companies (MNCs) and Foreign direct investment (FDI)

- Understand the reasons for the emergence of MNCs/FDI: to benefit from economies of scale, to access natural resources/cheap materials, to lower transport and communication costs and to access customers in different regions

- Understand the advantages and disadvantages of MNCs/FDI: creating jobs, investing in infrastructure, developing skills, developing capital, contributing to taxes, avoiding paying taxes, environmental damage and moving profits abroad

GETTING STARTED

It is very common for governments to encourage overseas firms to develop business interests in their country, which brings a number of benefits. For example, a foreign firm building a factory to assemble cars will create jobs in the factory, provide business for constructors and suppliers and pay tax on any profits made. Look at the example below.

CASE STUDY: FOREIGN INVESTMENT IN INDIA

India is keen to encourage foreign firms to set up operations in their country. It started in the 1990s when the government began to welcome globalisation. They ended regulation at home and lowered barriers to foreign investment. The government deliberately targeted the IT services sector for growth, giving it special subsidies. As a result, large numbers of foreign MNCs invested in India. They were eager to take advantage of the cheap labour and the new opportunity to trade in one of the world's biggest markets.

In 2016, foreign investment in India rose by 29 per cent to US$40 000 million. One reason for the increase was the government's decision to relax controls in industries such as defence and civil aviation. The government considers foreign investment as crucial to help support future economic growth. It reckons that around US$1 trillion of investment is needed to improve its infrastructure that includes ports, airports and road networks.

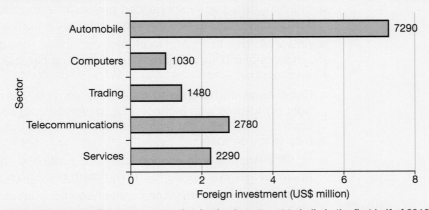

▲ **Figure 36.1** Top five sectors attracting foreign investment to India in the first half of 2016

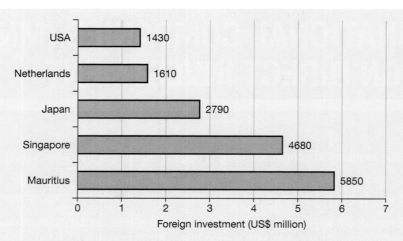

▲ **Figure 36.2** Top five source nations for foreign investment in India in the first half of 2016

1 Calculate the proportion of total foreign investment in India contributed by the top five source nations.

2 How were MNCs originally attracted to India?

3 How might the MNCs benefit from locating operations in India?

4 How might India benefit from the arrival of MNCs?

WHAT ARE MULTINATIONAL COMPANIES?

One of the reasons why globalisation has been successful in recent years is because a growing number of firms – called MNCs – have developed significant business interests overseas. These firms are very large and powerful. They sell goods and services into global markets and have production plants and other operating facilities all over the world. MNCs play a large and growing role in the world economy. They contribute about 10 per cent to world GDP and about two-thirds to global exports. Examples include McDonald's, Toyota, British Petroleum, Microsoft and Coca-Cola. Some of the key features of MNCs include:

■ huge assets (land, buildings, plant, machinery and money, for example) and revenue: MNCs are extremely well-resourced and can often afford to take on large-scale contracts and projects that many other firms could not cope with

■ highly qualified and experienced professional executives and managers: MNCs can afford to hire the very best people from anywhere in the world

■ powerful advertising and marketing capability: they can invest huge amounts of money in impressive advertising campaigns to outcompete smaller rivals

■ highly advanced and up-to-date technology: MNCs can afford to keep right up-to-date with technological developments so that they always have the most efficient factories, machinery and equipment, which can help to lower costs

■ highly influential both economically and politically: they can be very powerful and even influence government decision making

■ very efficient since they can exploit huge economies of scale: because MNCs are so large, they have the ability to reduce their costs significantly – they can buy huge quantities of raw materials more cheaply, for example.

Table 36.1 shows some information about the ten largest companies in the world.

	COMPANY	REVENUE (US$ MILLION)	SECTOR	COUNTRY
1	Walmart	482 000	Retailing	USA
2	State Grid	330 000	Power	China
3	China National Petroleum	299 000	Oil	China
4	Sinopec Group	294 000	Oil	China
5	Royal Dutch Shell	272 000	Oil	UK/Netherlands
6	Exon Mobil	246 000	Oil	USA
7	Volkswagen	237 000	Auto	Germany
8	Toyota	237 000	Auto	Japan
9	Apple	234 000	Technology	USA
10	BP	226 000	Oil	UK/Netherlands

▲ Table 36.1 The top ten companies 2016 (by revenue)

ACTIVITY 1

CASE STUDY: SONY

Sony is a huge Japanese-based MNC. It manufactures and markets a range of electronic goods including televisions, digital cameras, video cameras, Blu-ray Disc™ players and recorders, video games, semiconductors and other electronic components. In 2016, Sony employed over 125 000 people across the world and enjoyed sales of about US$80 000 million. Sony has factories, offices and technology centres in many countries around the world including Japan, China, Europe, America and India. The value of Sony's assets at the end of June 2016 was US$159 450 million.

Sony is a highly recognised global brand. The strength of the brand has been developed over many years of successful trading. However, to support the brand, Sony continues to invest heavily in global advertising. Figure 36.3 shows the amount of money Sony spent on advertising worldwide between 2011 and 2014.

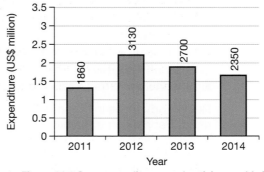

▲ Figure 36.3 Sony expenditure on advertising worldwide, 2011–14

1   What is meant by the term MNC?

2   What evidence is there to suggest that Sony is a MNC?

3   Describe **two** features of MNCs. Use examples from the case study to support your answer.

WHAT IS FOREIGN DIRECT INVESTMENT (FDI)?

FDI, or inward investment, occurs when a company makes an investment in a foreign country. This may involve the construction of a factory, distribution centre or store or the development of a mine or tea plantation, for example. Another part of FDI is the purchase of shares in a foreign business (10 per cent or more). Most FDI comes from MNCs.

A common approach to FDI is for a foreign company to work with a company in the host nation to develop a business venture. For example, GM, the giant US car MNC has a total of 11 joint ventures in China. In 2016, GM and its joint ventures sold over 3.8 million vehicles in China. This was 7.1 per cent more than in 2015. China is GM's largest market in terms of retail sales for 5 years.

REASONS FOR THE EMERGENCE OF MNCS/FDI

ECONOMIES OF SCALE

In some industries, firms that exploit economies of scale can reduce costs. MNCs will be in a better position to exploit economies of scale because they are so large. Firms that sell to global markets will produce more than those who just sell to domestic markets. They can therefore lower costs. Such firms are so powerful they can place a lot of pressure on suppliers to lower their prices. One of the main reasons why MNCs have emerged is because as companies get bigger and bigger, their costs get lower and lower – provided they avoid diseconomies of scale.

ACCESS TO NATURAL RESOURCES/CHEAP MATERIALS

Many large companies are happy to invest overseas because they need to buy huge quantities of resources. A significant proportion of FDI is targeted at the mining industry. Many African states have attracted FDI because they have large **reserves** of valuable resources. For example, in 2014, the French oil company Total went ahead with a US$16 000 million project to extract oil off the coast of Angola.

Many countries import significant quantities of food from overseas. This is because in some countries the food needs of the population are not met by domestic producers. For example, in the UK 46 per cent of the food consumed is imported. This shows that the UK needs access to natural resources abroad.

LOWER TRANSPORT AND COMMUNICATION COSTS

Developments in transport and communications have helped to drive the growth in MNC/FDI activity. Transportation costs have come down and the speed with which goods can be delivered has gone up. This makes distribution in overseas markets much more attractive. Air travel is now relatively cheap with the number of destinations growing. This means that managers and other staff can travel around the world more easily to discuss and organise business activity.

Recent advances in communications technology have been particularly rapid. People can transmit a wide range of different information, such as text, drawings, video clips, photographs and financial documents, instantly using electronic devices. Both individuals and groups can talk face-to-face even though they might be 15 000 kilometres apart from each other. Improved and cheaper communication links have made global business much more efficient.

ACCESS TO CUSTOMERS IN DIFFERENT REGIONS

One of the main reasons why MNCs have developed successfully is because they can sell far more goods and services in global markets than they can in domestic markets. Companies can make considerably more profit selling to

SUBJECT VOCABULARY

reserves amount of something valuable, such as oil, gas or metal ore

the 7000 million people worldwide than they can selling to perhaps 50 million people at home. For example, Sony, the Japanese company mentioned in Activity 1, generated more than 70 per cent of its revenue outside of Japan. This is very common among MNCs. As the global economy continues to grow, more and more companies are likely to target overseas markets to help increase revenues, profits and returns to shareholders.

ACTIVITY 2

CASE STUDY: MNCS/FDI IN AFRICA

Africa has 8.6 per cent of the world's proven oil reserves and 7.2 per cent of its natural gas. It also has a large share of the world's minerals such as bauxite, copper, chromium, cobalt, gold, manganese, phosphate, titanium and diamonds. The African Development Bank forecasts that the continent's natural resources will contribute more than US$30 000 million a year to government revenues by 2030. Although investment in Africa is starting to diversify into a wider range of sectors, the attraction of the continent's natural resources is still highly significant. Figure 36.4 supports this view. It shows results from a survey that asked business people which factors were 'very attractive', when investing in Africa. 53.2 per cent said that Africa's natural resources were very attractive. This was the highest score.

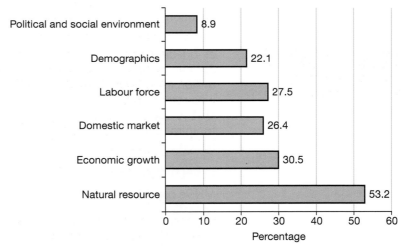

▲ **Figure 36.4** Factors that attract FDI to Africa

1 How has access to natural resources/cheap materials helped the emergence of MNCs/FDI?

2 How important is access to natural resources for foreign investors in Africa?

3 Describe two other reasons for the emergence of MNCs/FDI.

ADVANTAGES OF MNCS/FDI

Many countries are keen for foreign MNCs to develop business interests in their countries. Indeed, many governments actively seek FDI by:

■ offering tax breaks, subsidies, grants and low interest loans

■ lifting restrictions and relaxing regulations to make it easier for foreign firms to invest

- investing in their own infrastructure
- investing in education so that people can get jobs with foreign companies.

Governments are prepared to do this because the advantages of FDI are generally so attractive.

JOB CREATION

One of the main benefits of FDI is the employment created when MNCs arrive and establish factories, warehouses, shops and other business facilities. When MNCs set up operations overseas, income in those countries rises. Local suppliers are also likely to get work when a multinational arrives. The extra output and employment generated by MNCs will increase economic growth and raise living standards for people in these countries. Also, from the worker's point of view, jobs created by FDI are often good because they pay higher wages. For example, evidence from Hungary and Brazil suggests that wages offered by foreign businesses are between 4.5 and 6 per cent higher than those offered by domestic employers.

INVESTMENT IN INFRASTRUCTURE

Countries with poor infrastructure often struggle to attract FDI. If a country has inadequate road networks, ports, railway networks, bridges, power distribution, airports, telecommunications, industrial parks and other facilities, it is more difficult to do business in that country. Consequently, owing to the attractiveness of MNCs/FDI, governments are more likely to invest in infrastructure in order to attract the attention of investors. If this investment is forthcoming, everyone will benefit.

Also, sometimes foreign investors contribute to a nation's infrastructure, such as building a new road, if it is allowed to develop a specific business interest. For example, China's investment in Africa has increased from US$7000 million in 2008 to US$26 000 million in 2013. A significant proportion of this was targeted at mining. Also, in 2016, the Chinese government announced a US$60 000 million package of aid (in the form of interest free loans) to Africa for infrastructure development. This example shows that MNC/FDI can help a nation develop its infrastructure.

DEVELOPING SKILLS

MNCs provide training and work experience for workers when they locate operations in foreign countries. Also, governments in less developed countries often spend more on education to help attract MNCs. This happened in India, where the government invested heavily in IT education and training. The arrival of MNCs may also encourage local people to set up businesses. MNCs may have provided the skills and motivation needed for enterprise. For example, a new MNC may encourage locals to supply services, such as transport, accommodation, maintenance, cleaning and leisure activities. MNCs may also provide foreign suppliers with technical help, training and other information. They may also help local suppliers to learn new skills, methods and working practices.

DEVELOPING CAPITAL

The arrival of MNCs will help to boost the stock of capital in host countries. One reason is because when a business sets up a new facility, such as a factory, it is likely to install up-to-date technology. For example, BMW, the giant German car producer, is currently building a new plant in Mexico. The new plant in San Luis Potosí will contain a body shop, a paint shop and a full assembly operation. BMW will be investing in an innovative production system and comprehensive sustainability standards. It has been reported that when it opens in 2019, the plant will be BMW's most resource-efficient plant in the world. For example, the plant will use renewable energy sources which means that it is supplied with 100 per cent carbon-free electricity. The plant will generate most of its own electricity using a solar system located on the factory site.

The arrival of MNCs might also encourage local suppliers and other businesses to invest in new capital projects. This will help them win orders to supply the MNC, for example.

CONTRIBUTING TO TAXES

The profits made by MNCs are taxed by the host nation. This increases tax revenue for the government that can be used to improve government services. For example, in Mumbai, the Income Tax Department (which is responsible for collecting about one-third of India's tax revenue) claimed that it had collected Rs23 000 crore from foreign companies in 2016. However, it also said that there was at least another Rs8000 crore outstanding. If MNCs/FDI did not operate businesses in such countries, this valuable source of revenue would not exist.

DISADVANTAGES OF MNCS/FDI

Unfortunately, there are some disadvantages associated with MNCs/FDI. Some might argue that the benefits are exaggerated and that MNCs are only interested in maximising profits for their shareholders. As a result, MNCs locate operations overseas merely to exploit a nation's resources. However, some specific disadvantages include the following.

TAX AVOIDANCE

Tax avoidance, particularly by powerful MNCs, has attracted the attention of the world's media in recent years. Also, political leaders, particularly in the USA and EU, have accused MNCs, such as Apple and Google, of failing to pay their fair share. However, the MNCs have frequently responded to these accusations by saying that they pay their taxes and have done nothing wrong. For example, Apple chief executive officer Tim Cook said that his company pays 'all the taxes we owe – every single dollar'. One company, the coffee chain Starbucks, was the subject of media attention in the UK over its use of tax avoidance schemes to avoid paying any British corporation tax. Starbucks generated sales of £399 million in 2013 and eventually paid about £10 million – perhaps owing to the pressure of protests and a customer boycott. If MNCs can avoid paying taxes in countries with well-developed legal systems, it may suggest that less developed nations have little chance of getting their 'fair share' of taxes from MNCs.

ENVIRONMENTAL DAMAGE

Many environmentalists are suspicious of MNCs because they may cause environmental damage. One reason is because MNCs are heavily involved in the extraction industries such as coal, oil and gold mining. Mining is often destructive. A few years ago, according to a report by the United Nations, the cost of pollution and other damage to the natural environment caused by the world's biggest companies would wipe out more than one-third of their profits if they were held financially accountable. This amounted to about US$2.2 trillion. Issues relating to the environmental damage done by businesses are discussed in Chapters 13 (pages 89–96) and 29 (pages 228–239).

MOVING PROFITS ABROAD

The profits made by MNCs abroad are often subject to **repatriation**. This means that profits are returned to the country where the MNC is based. As a result, the host country loses out. This suggests that MNCs bring more benefits to developed countries than to less developed countries. This is because the headquarters of most MNCs are based in developed countries.

SUBJECT VOCABULARY
tax avoidance practice of trying to pay less tax in legal ways

GENERAL VOCABULARY
boycott to refuse to buy something, use something, or take part in something as a way of protesting

SUBJECT VOCABULARY
repatriation (of profit) where a multinational returns the profits from an overseas venture to the country where it is based, typically from a developing country to a developed country (not often the other way around)

▶ 1 Which of the following is a benefit of FDI in a country?

   A Lower interest rates

   B Lower exchange rate

   C Higher employment levels

   D Lower economic growth

▶ 2 Which of the following is an example of FDI?

   A The takeover of a parts supplier in Japan by Nissan

   B The construction of a factory in Shanghai by a US MNC

   C A large clothes manufacturer in Bangladesh selling clothes to a German retailer

   D A US$200 000 million investment by a government in the nation's infrastructure

CASE STUDY: FDI IN NIGERIA

FALLING FDI IN NIGERIA

In recent years, Nigeria has been the most popular destination for FDI in Africa. However, very recently, the flows of investment coming into the country have started to fall. One of the main reasons for this was the fall in the price of oil. A significant proportion of FDI arriving in Nigeria is used to develop oil production. Oil accounts for 90 per cent of Nigeria's exports.

However, the low oil price is not the only problem. Nigeria's poor infrastructure has often held back economic development in the country. The value of Nigeria's stock of infrastructure is about 25 per cent of GDP. For a middle-income country the size of Nigeria, it should be more like 70 per cent. Inside Nigeria's main port at Apapa, boats queue for days waiting to dock. Then, once the cargo is unloaded, the trucks leaving the port are held up for hours in congested streets. It is time consuming and expensive but typical of the way infrastructure works in Nigeria.

It has been estimated that about US$3 trillion will be needed over the next 30 years to improve Nigeria's infrastructure adequately. However, the government has begun to take action. A plan has been created which identifies the key investment requirements: energy; transport; agriculture, water and mining; housing and regional development; information and communication technology; social infrastructure and security. Energy and transport are currently the priorities.

In 2016, US MNC General Electric (GE) announced that it would be investing US$150 million in Nigeria's railway system. GE said that it was the beginning of a long-term US$2000 million investment project in Nigeria's infrastructure.

MNC ENVIRONMENTAL DAMAGE IN NIGERIA

Sometimes, FDI results in damage to the environment. This happened in Nigeria between 2008 and 2009 when two significant oil spills damaged the environment in the Niger Delta. The spills, which were the largest ever in the Niger Delta, caused very serious damage to thousands of hectares of mangrove forests in the southern Ogoniland region. This contaminated water supplies, crops and destroyed the livelihoods of thousands of farmers. Following the spills, which were caused by MNC Shell, there was a lengthy legal battle between communities and the company. Shell would not take responsibility for the damage. However, in 2015, the case was settled. Court documents showed that Shell knew for years that poorly maintained pipes and equipment were at risk of failure. Shell admitted that its figures were wrong and that it had underestimated the amount of oil spilled in Bodo. Shell tried to cover up the level of its involvement as it had too much control over the investigation process after the spills. The court forced Shell to pay out US$84 million in compensation. The 15 600 farmers and fishermen affected by the spills were to receive about £2000 each. However, the money will not undo the damage to the environment, which the community relies on for their water, food and livelihood.

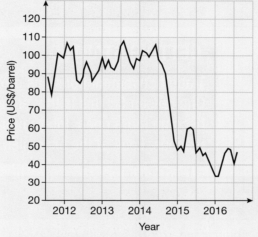

▲ **Figure 36.6** Oil price, 2012–16

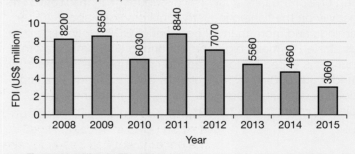

▲ **Figure 36.7** Nigeria FDI, 2008–15

CHAPTER QUESTIONS

1 Describe what FDI is.

2 Describe the pattern of FDI in Nigeria in recent years.

3 What are the possible benefits of MNCs/FDI to Nigeria? Give at least two benefits in your analysis.

4 Discuss one of the main disadvantages of MNCs/FDI. Use an example from this case to support your explanation.

5 Consider the factors that have resulted in the recent pattern of FDI in Nigeria.

37 INTERNATIONAL TRADE

LEARNING OBJECTIVE

Understand the advantages and disadvantages of free trade:

- Lower prices and increased choice for consumers
- Lower input costs
- Wider markets for businesses
- Foreign competition for domestic businesses
- Increasing unemployment

GETTING STARTED

Trade between nations has grown significantly in recent years. One reason for this is that an increasing number of countries have become more open. International trade takes place for a number of reasons. Look at the examples below.

CASE STUDY: ICELAND

Iceland is a small nation but has a high standard of living with low unemployment and one of the fairest income distributions in the world. The economy relies heavily on the fishing industry. This provides about 40 per cent of export earnings and more than 12 per cent of GDP. However, since 2010, tourism has started to make big contributions to economic growth. The number of tourists is expected to be around 4.5 times the Icelandic population (just under 332 000) in 2016. Iceland's cold, northerly position makes food production difficult. Foodstuffs, along with machinery and equipment, petroleum products and textiles, are Iceland's main imports.

▲ Food is one of Iceland's main imports

CASE STUDY: SEYCHELLES

The Seychelles is a group of 115 islands in the Indian Ocean off the coast of Africa. It is a very popular tourist destination and about 25 per cent of its GDP is generated from tourism. Holidaymakers are attracted by the year-round warm climate, attractive beaches and stunning coastal scenery. In recent years, the government has encouraged foreign investment to upgrade hotels and other services. At the same time, the government has moved to reduce the dependence on tourism by promoting the development of farming, fishing and small-scale manufacturing. In 2016, the Seychelles imported an estimated US$873.7 million of goods and services. Some of the main imports included machinery and equipment, foodstuffs, petroleum products, chemicals, other manufactured goods.

▲ The Seychelles is a major world tourist destination

CASE STUDY: QATAR

Qatar has one of the highest GDP per capita in the world. In 2015, it was US$73 653. GDP is driven largely by the oil and gas sector (Figure 37.1). Oil and gas account for 92 per cent of export earnings and 56 per cent of government revenues. However, in recent years, growth in manufacturing, construction and financial services have lifted the non-oil sectors. Qatar has oil reserves in excess of 25 000 million barrels and should continue to generate income for another 50 years.

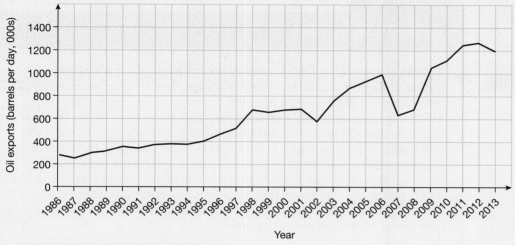

▲ Figure 37.1 Qatari oil exports, 1986–2013

1 Why does Qatar sell so much oil abroad?

2 Why does Iceland import so much food?

3 Why does the Seychelles rely so heavily on tourism for its foreign income?

4 Do you benefit from international trade? In pairs, draw up a list of products that you regularly buy and think might come from overseas. Present your list to the rest of the class.

INTERNATIONAL TRADE

International trade benefits the world. It helps to raise living standards and results in higher levels of output and income. However, there are some specific reasons why countries trade with each other.

OBTAINING GOODS THAT CANNOT BE PRODUCED DOMESTICALLY

Many countries are unable to produce certain goods. This is because they lack the natural resources that enable such production. In 'Getting started', we see that Iceland cannot produce many foodstuffs because it does not have the right climate. France cannot produce gold or diamonds because the country does not have any deposits.

OBTAINING GOODS THAT CAN BE BOUGHT MORE CHEAPLY FROM OVERSEAS

Some countries can produce goods more efficiently than others. This may be because countries have cheaper resources or because they have become experts through specialisation. For example, China can produce manufactured goods more cheaply than many countries because it has a cheap labour force. It makes economic sense to buy goods from other countries if they are cheaper.

SELLING OFF UNWANTED COMMODITIES

Some countries have large amounts of certain commodities. Indeed, in some cases, countries have so much of a resource they could never use it all themselves. In 'Getting started', you learned that Qatar has huge reserves of oil. Most of the oil produced is sold abroad. Qatar consumes just a tiny proportion of its oil output each year.

ACTIVITY 1

CASE STUDY: ESTONIA

Estonia is the smallest, least corrupt and most **prosperous** of all the former Soviet republics. The Baltic state became an open economy and developed a market system after the break-up of the Soviet Union in 1991. Estonia's economy has done very well since then, driven by its highly successful telecoms and electronics industries. By 2013, Estonia had become a world leader in information technology (IT). Estonian IT engineers developed the code behind Skype and Kazaa (an early file-sharing network). It has one of the world's fastest broadband speeds and it only takes five minutes to register a firm. Entrepreneurs wishing to start a firm log in with their national electronic identity card and a few clicks later the confirmation arrives by email.

Estonia's major export goods are textiles/clothes, machinery/equipment, food, wood/wood products and chemicals, which are exported mostly to neighbouring countries (Figure 37.2). The major imports include machinery/equipment, minerals, vehicles, textiles/clothes and food. Estonia has an open economy with few import restrictions. Duties are levied only on tobacco products, such as cigarettes, alcohol and luxury items. Export licenses are only required for a handful of natural resources, such as oil shale. The lack of trade barriers, the favourable exchange rate, and Estonia's positive attitude toward free trade contribute to the country's reputation as a respected trading nation.

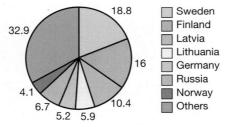

Legend:
- Sweden
- Finland
- Latvia
- Lithuania
- Germany
- Russia
- Norway
- Others

Values: 18.8, 16, 10.4, 5.9, 5.2, 6.7, 4.1, 32.9

▲ **Figure 37.2** Estonia's exports by destination, 2015 (%)

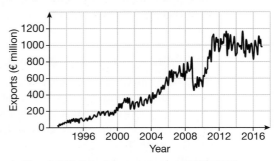

▲ **Figure 37.3** Estonia's export value, 1991–2016

Look at Figure 37.3.

1 Describe the pattern of exports in Estonia over the period shown.

2 What might account for the pattern identified in your answer to question (1)?

Before 1991, nearly all of Estonia's exports were to Russia and other Soviet partners.

3 Why has Estonia redirected its exports since then?

4 Discuss why Estonia has developed a reputation for being a respected trading nation.

DID YOU KNOW?

If domestic producers face competition from those abroad, they will be under more pressure to keep costs down and produce high-quality goods. Firms may be more innovative, more efficient and offer consumers better value for money if they face competition from abroad.

ADVANTAGES OF FREE TRADE

SUBJECT VOCABULARY

free trade situation in which the goods coming into or going out of a country are not controlled or taxed

More and more countries encourage **free trade**. This is where the government allows open access to the markets in its country. The government does not place any restrictions on the amount of goods coming in. At the same time, it encourages firms to sell goods and services abroad. The main advantages to free trade are outlined below.

LOWER PRICES AND INCREASED CHOICE FOR CONSUMERS

One of the main benefits of free trade is that consumers get more choice. For example, consumers in Norway will be able to buy goods that are impossible to produce in their climate, such as tropical fruits and wine. They will also be able to buy goods made from materials that are not available in Norway, such as gold, diamonds and other minerals. Finally, Norwegian consumers will be able to buy goods that other countries produce more cheaply, such as cars and many other manufactured consumer durables. If consumers can buy goods more cheaply, their standard of living will improve because they will have greater purchasing power. Another reason why there is increased choice for consumers is because many countries both buy and sell the same products. For example, Cadbury Schweppes produces a huge range of confectionery in its UK factories, which is sold both at home and in the USA. The US firm Mars also produces a wide range of confectionery, which it sells in the USA and in the UK. Although both firms produce confectionery, many of their products have slight differences and consumers welcome the choice they provide.

LOWER INPUT PRICES

Through international trade, countries can obtain essential inputs for its industries at a much lower cost. For example, China imports a lot of raw materials from Australia and Africa. Australia and Africa have very large deposits of the minerals coal, iron ore, copper and zinc. One of Australia's main exports is iron ore. It sells cheap iron ore to countries like China where it is used as an important input for many industries. Figure 37.4 shows the growth in exports of iron ore from Australia between 2000/01 and 2014/15.

Annual exports have risen by around 400 per cent over the period.

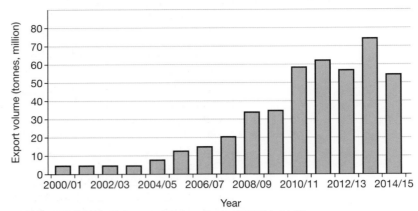

▲ **Figure 37.4** Australia iron exports by volume, 2000/01–14/15

Generally, international trade allows the advantages from specialisation to be extended. If countries specialise in the production of goods in which they are more efficient, the global economy will benefit. Goods and services all over the world will be produced in locations where costs are minimised. This means that consumers all over the world can buy goods at the lowest possible prices. This will help the world economy to grow and make better use of the world's resources.

WIDER MARKETS FOR BUSINESSES

If countries are free to specialise and trade, firms will be selling to larger markets. For example, many companies sell their goods and services in a wide range of different countries. This helps to reduce the risk of business enterprise. If sales in one country start to decline, a company can rely on sales in other countries to offset the decline. Figure 37.5 shows where Toyota, the Japanese carmaker, sells its cars in global markets. Only about 24 per cent of its output is sold in Japan. Therefore, three-quarters of its cars are sold in other countries around the world.

If a company is able to sell much larger quantities in a wider range of markets, they will be able to exploit economies of scale. This is because their output will be higher than if they were just selling to the domestic market. This will help to lower costs and improve efficiency.

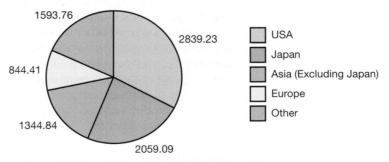

▲ **Figure 37.5** Toyota sales by region, 2016 (units, 000s)

DID YOU KNOW?

Most economists believe that free trade will boost global GDP and help the world economy to grow. This will create more income, output and employment for the benefit of the world.

DISADVANTAGES OF FREE TRADE

Unfortunately, there may be some drawbacks to free trade. Some of these are outlined below.

COMPETITION FOR DOMESTIC BUSINESSES

If countries have open economies, it means that imports from anywhere in the world can flow into the economy. If these imports are good in quality and competitively priced, domestic producers might struggle to compete. For example, when China and other emerging economies started to export manufactured goods to the West, manufacturers in Europe and the USA started to struggle. Manufacturing in these countries started to decline because a lot of companies were unable to match the prices of the new foreign goods entering the market. For example, for the first time in 2014, Chinese manufacturing output was the highest in the world at US$1.9 trillion. Many economies around the world have seen a decline in manufacturing. According to OECD data, the UK and Australia have seen their share of manufacturing drop by around two-thirds since 1971. Germany's share halved, and manufacturing's contribution to GDP fell from 30 per cent in 1980 to 22 per cent today. Not all the decline can be blamed on cheap imports though. Other factors are important, such as the booming growth in the service sector.

UNEMPLOYMENT

One of the main problems with international trade is the threat to employment levels when domestic industries are threatened by cheap imports. The USA lost 5 million manufacturing jobs between January 2000 and December 2014. One of the main reasons for this was greater foreign competition. Specifically, between 2000 and 2007, growing trade deficits in manufactured goods led to the loss of 3.6 million manufacturing jobs in that period. Between 2007 and 2009, the massive collapse in overall US output hit manufacturing particularly hard. However, it was not just the USA that suffered from huge job losses in manufacturing. Figure 37.6 shows that employment in manufacturing in several countries fell significantly between 1990 and 2015. This is the period in which China and other emerging economies started to flood the world with cheap manufactured goods. The UK is one of the worst hit with employment in manufacturing falling by 49 per cent over the period.

Countries can suffer increases in unemployment when demand patterns change. If a country is too dependent on a narrow range of goods, it will be particularly at risk. For example, some of the developing nations may rely too much on primary goods. If demand or prices fall for these goods, nations will suffer a loss of trade and income. Primary goods also have low income elasticity and when the global economy grows, demand for them will not increase at the same pace. Countries need to avoid overspecialisation and try to diversify in some way.

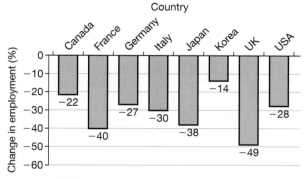

▲ **Figure 37.6** Employment in manufacturing: selected countries, 1990–2015

DID YOU KNOW?

Free trade may increase the development gap where rich nations grow more prosperous much faster than developing countries. There may also be a loss of culture in some countries if foreign ideas and products are allowed to dominate. For example, some countries may become too 'Americanised'. Countries may also lose their sovereignty. This means they do not have complete control over matters that affect them. For example, in the UK, the EU now determines many laws. This was one of the reasons why the UK voted to leave the European Union in 2016.

MULTIPLE-CHOICE QUESTIONS

▶ 1 Which of the following is an important reason why countries trade with one another?

    A To obtain goods that cannot be produced domestically

    B To reduce inflation

    C To reduce exports

    D To reduce FDI

▶ 2 What is meant by free trade?

    A Exports are transported free of charge

    B Commissions for changing currency are waived for international trade transactions

    C A government allows open access to all markets in its country

    D International transactions are free of indirect taxes such as VAT

ECONOMICS IN PRACTICE

CASE STUDY: MALAYSIA

Malaysia is an open economy with a positive attitude towards international trade. It is a middle-income country and its economy has become more diversified since the 1970s, when it was heavily reliant on the production of raw materials. Under current Prime Minister Najib, Malaysia is attempting to become a high-income nation by 2020. It also wants to develop a more sophisticated economy by attracting investments in Islamic finance, high technology industries, biotechnology and services.

Malaysia's main exports are semiconductors and electronic equipment, palm oil, petroleum and liquefied natural gas, wood and wood products, palm oil, rubber, textiles, chemicals and solar panels. It imports electronics, machinery, petroleum products, plastics, vehicles, iron and steel products and chemicals. Malaysia's main trading partners are China, Singapore, the USA and Japan.

Malaysia is also developing its tourist industry. The numbers of tourists arriving in the country increased from 16.43 million in 2005 to 25.70 million in 2015. Some say that Malaysia is like two countries in one. West (Peninsular) Malaysia is home to lively cities, colonial architecture, tea plantations and relaxing islands. In contrast, East Malaysia (on the island of Borneo) is covered in wild jungles and home to orang-utans, rocky peaks and remote tribes. It also has very impressive diving sites. Malaysia is known for its beaches, rainforests and mix of Malay, Chinese, Indian and European cultural influences. The capital, Kuala Lumpur, is home to colonial buildings, busy shopping districts and stunning skyscrapers, such as the Petronas Twin Towers. Figure 37.7 shows Malaysia's current account balance over the 2014–16 period.

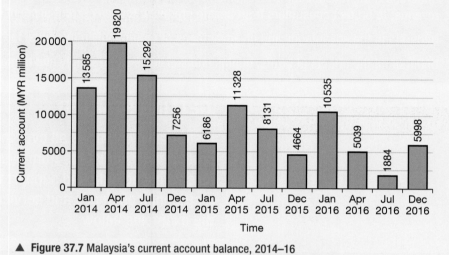

▲ **Figure 37.7** Malaysia's current account balance, 2014–16

CHAPTER QUESTIONS

1 Describe the state of Malaysia's current account balance.

2 What impact will the recent pattern of tourism have on Malaysia's current account balance?

3 Discuss one possible disadvantage to Malaysia of international trade.

4 How does international trade help firms to exploit economies of scale?

5 Consider the possible advantages to Malaysia of international trade.

38 PROTECTIONISM

LEARNING OBJECTIVES

☐ Understand the reasons for protectionism: prevent dumping, protect employment, protect infant industries, to gain tariff revenue, to protect consumers from unsafe products, reduce current account deficits and retaliation

☐ Understand the advantages and disadvantages of protectionism methods: tariffs, quotas, subsidies

☐ Understand the effects of tariffs, quotas and subsidies using supply and demand diagrams

GETTING STARTED

Historically, countries all over the world have taken measures to protect their industries from overseas competition. Such measures involve giving help and support to domestic producers or placing restrictions on goods and services coming in from abroad. Look at the examples below.

CASE STUDY: HELP FOR RWANDAN EXPORTERS

In 2016, the Rwandan horticulture industry received a boost when the government announced that exporters in the industry would get some financial help. The government said it would meet half of the transport costs when flying exports to overseas customers through Kigali International Airport. The subsidies were designed to boost the sale of high value, low volume products to help diversify exports. They would also make Rwanda's horticulture exporters competitive in the region. Before the subsidies, Rwandan horticulture exporters were paying more in transport charges to European markets than close rivals in Kenya. According to the National Export Strategy, the horticulture industry is expected to bring in more than RWF 96 000 million (US$129 million) per year by 2018, up from the current level of RWF 7000 million (US$10 million).

▲ Horticultural activity in Rwanda

CASE STUDY: CANADIAN TAXES ON US GYPSUM BOARD

In 2015, the Canadian government placed a 276 per cent tax on gypsum board products coming into the country from the USA. As a result, the price of drywall products, which are made from gypsum board, rose alarmingly. Builders said that the tax is likely to disrupt building projects and threaten the survival of construction companies that had agreed fixed-price contracts with some of their customers. One gypsum supplier said that the tax could have serious consequences for the construction industry. For example, there could be delays in the rebuilding efforts in Fort McMurray, where thousands of buildings were destroyed by fire.

▲ Stocks of gypsum board used in construction

1 Describe the measures being taken in Rwanda to protect domestic industry.

2 How will taxes on Canadian imports of gypsum board products impact on (a) Canadian builders and (b) US exporters?

WHAT IS PROTECTIONISM?

SUBJECT VOCABULARY

protectionism approach used by governments to protect domestic producers

trade barriers measures designed to restrict imports

Most economists would argue that free trade will benefit the global economy. However, sometimes countries believe that it is in their interests to restrict trade. For example, governments may think it is necessary to protect their domestic producers from overseas competition. They may also give financial help to exporters. This is called **protectionism**. Governments can use several measures to restrict trade. They are called **trade barriers** and some examples are outlined below.

REASONS FOR PROTECTIONISM

Chapter 36 (pages 295–303) outlined the benefits from free trade. However, there are a number reasons why governments feel that the use of trade barriers is sometimes justified.

PREVENTING DUMPING

SUBJECT VOCABULARY

dumping where an overseas firm sells large quantities of a product below cost in the domestic market

A government may use trade barriers if it feels that an overseas firm is **dumping** goods. Dumping is where foreign producers sell goods below cost in a domestic market. They may do this to deliberately destroy overseas competitors. In some cases, businesses that dump products are heavily subsidised by their government. Consequently, they have an unfair advantage over foreign rivals.

Dumping is considered to be unfair competition for domestic producers. If very cheap imports are being sold below cost in a country, domestic producers will find it very difficult to survive in the long term. One example of dumping was reported in 2016 by the US authorities. The US Commerce Department said that tyres for trucks and buses were being dumped in the US at below market prices. The department said the tyres were being dumped by Chinese manufacturers at margins ranging from 20.87 per cent to 22.57 per cent. It was also suggested that China was giving unfair subsidies to producers. It was claimed that 9 million tyres had entered the US market – worth about US$1000 million.

PROTECTING EMPLOYMENT

Trade barriers may be used if domestic industries need protection from overseas competitors to save jobs. Unemployment is always unwelcome and a government may be criticised if jobs are being lost because of cheap imports. In a documentary broadcast by Netflix, based on Peter Navarro's book *Death by China: Confronting the Dragon,* cheap Chinese imports were blamed for the loss of 57 000 American factories and 25 million jobs.

PROTECTING INFANT INDUSTRIES

SUBJECT VOCABULARY

infant industries new industries yet to establish themselves

It is often argued that **infant industries** need protection. Infant industries are new industries that are yet to become established. Many argue that infant industries should be protected from strong overseas rivals until they can grow, become established and exploit economies of scale. However, it is also argued that this approach may not be successful because governments have a poor record of successfully identifying infant industries with potential.

TO GAIN TARIFF REVENUE

A government can raise revenue if it imposes tariffs on imports. This money can be spent on government services to improve living standards. It is reckoned that when the UK leaves the EU, if there is no trade deal between the two, the UK government could collect around £12 900 million on imports coming in from the EU. However, the EU will also collect around £5200 million from UK exports.

PREVENTING THE ENTRY OF HARMFUL OR UNWANTED GOODS

A government might be justified in using protectionism if it is felt that overseas producers are trying to sell goods that are harmful or unwanted. For example, recently, the EU banned all beef from cattle raised using growth hormones because it felt that it was not safe for human consumption. Administrative barriers might be used to prevent this type of international trade.

REDUCE CURRENT DEFICITS

A country might need to use trade barriers because it has a very large current account deficit. A country has to pay its way in the world and if a current account deficit gets out of control, action may be needed. A government might try to reduce imports and increase exports at the same time to reduce the deficit. For example, in 2014, the Indian government used trade barriers to restrict the amount of gold coming into the country. One of the main reasons for this move was to help reduce India's growing current account deficit.

RETALIATION

One motive for imposing trade barriers is to **retaliate** against dumping. If a foreign business dumps large quantities of goods below cost, a government may feel obliged to retaliate by imposing heavy taxes on those goods when they come into the country. Retaliation may also occur if a country imposes trade barriers on exporters. That country may retaliate by imposing trade barriers on that nation's imports. This can result in a trade war that will tend to reduce trade between two nations and have a negative impact on both nations. In 2017, China said it would retaliate if the USA used trade barriers to block Chinese goods entering the US market. A US commerce secretary said, 'The Chinese leadership said to me if you guys put an import duty on us we are going to do it to you and that will be bad for both of us.'

KEY FACTS

A few years ago, there was a trade war between the USA and Mexico. The USA banned Mexican lorries used to deliver goods in the US because they were considered unsafe. In retaliation, the Mexican government imposed tariffs of 10–45 per cent on some US products such as cell phones, pears and cherries.

ACTIVITY 1

CASE STUDY: RAINBOW CHICKEN FOODS

In 2016, Rainbow Chicken Limited Foods (RCL Foods), a South African company, said it was cutting about 1200 jobs in Hammarsdale, outside Durban. It added that more job cuts may follow as the company struggled to compete with cheap imports from the USA, Brazil and EU countries.

Job cuts caused by cheap imports have occurred in the region before. Historically, the industrial area had a big textile industry. However, as a result of the new democracy, and the relaxation of trade barriers between SA and other countries, the Hammarsdale area lost more than 40 000 textile jobs, mainly because of cheap imports from China.

These new job losses hit Mpumalanga township (in Hammarsdale) hard, leaving thousands of households without a livelihood. A representative of RCL Foods said, 'Tens of thousands of tons of surplus chicken are dumped in the South African market monthly, and the EU is one of the main sources of this meat.' It was also pointed out that smaller slaughterhouses and poultry farmers would be forced to close down. This was because costs were rising and they could not charge enough to recover their costs. Chickens dumped in the market from overseas were driving down prices.

1 Describe the impact imports have had on employment in South Africa.

2 What is meant by dumping?

SUBJECT VOCABULARY

tariffs or customs duties tax on imports to make them more expensive

TARIFFS

One way of restricting trade is to make imports more expensive. This will reduce demand for imports and increase demand for goods produced at home. Imports can be made more expensive if the government imposes a special tax on them. For example, if a government adds £50 to the price of an imported camera, demand would switch from foreign cameras to home-produced cameras. Taxes on imports are called **tariffs or customs duties**.

Even though the pace of globalisation is accelerating and an increasing number of countries are opening up their economies to foreign businesses, there are many examples of countries imposing tariffs on imports. For example, in 2015, Ecuador imposed tariffs of 21 per cent and 7 per cent on imports from Colombia and Peru, respectively. The main purpose of these tariffs was to offset the effects of a stronger US dollar. Colombian and Peruvian officials claimed that the tariffs were a protectionist move and that their imposition broke the principles agreed in the Andean Community (CAN), a customs union formed by Bolivia, Ecuador, Colombia and Peru.

One of the main advantages of tariffs is that in addition to reducing imports to protect domestic industries and improve the current account, they also raise revenue for the government. However, if tariffs are set too high, imports may cease and government revenue will be zero. Also, consumers will not benefit from tariffs in the short term since they raise prices.

QUOTAS

SUBJECT VOCABULARY

embargo official order to stop trade with another country

quota physical limit on the quantity of imports allowed into a country

Another way of reducing imports is to place a physical limit on the amount allowed into the country. This is called a **quota**. By restricting the quantity of imports, domestic producers face less of a threat. They will have more of the market for themselves. However, quotas will raise prices because fewer of the cheaper imports are available. Placing physical limits on the flow of imports means that domestic producers will meet some demand for those goods. This will help to protect employment.

In 2014, Indonesia imposed a quota on wheat-flour imports. The quota was designed to protect domestic producers from further financial losses. The authorities planned to restrict imports of wheat flour to 441 141 tonnes from May until the end of the year. Turkey, which is the largest importer, will be restricted to the sale of 251 450 tonnes, while Sri Lanka and Ukraine will be able to import up to 136 754 tonnes and 22 057 tonnes, respectively. The rest will go to other trading partners.

One of the main advantages of quotas is that they physically limit the supply of imports. Foreign companies cannot easily get round quotas by adjusting prices. Also, in the short term, the impact on prices might be limited. It may take a while for shortages to force the price up. In the meantime, domestic producers might be able to increase supply to 'plug the gap' in the market. One disadvantage is that consumer choice is likely to be restricted and domestic producers might be overprotected and fail to improve efficiency.

> ### DID YOU KNOW?
> An extreme form of quota is an **embargo**. This is where imports are completely banned from a country. Most embargos are imposed for political reasons. For example, in 2015, an arms embargo had been imposed on Libya to prevent military goods being exported to the country. A number of embargos exist between Russia and the EU as a result of Russia's involvement in the war between the Ukraine and Russian-speaking rebels.

SUBSIDIES

Quotas and tariffs aim to reduce imports. Another approach to protectionism is to give a subsidy to domestic producers. This involves giving financial support, such as grants or tax breaks, to exporters or domestic producers that face fierce competition from imports. If subsidies are given to domestic producers, this will lower prices for consumers because subsidies reduce production costs and increase supply. This forces equilibrium prices down. If subsidies are given to exporters, it makes it easier for domestic businesses to break into foreign markets. However, in many cases government subsidies to either domestic producers or exporters may break the terms of free trade agreements. Even so, governments still use subsidies as a method of protectionism. A few years ago, the Indian government announced that it would re-introduce subsidies to help boost exports of textiles and engineering goods. It proposed to hand over around Rs2411 crore of subsidies to producers. The aim was to support India's weakening export industry and to help reduce the widening trade deficit.

One of the main advantages of export subsidies is that more domestic firms might be encouraged to enter the market. This will help to boost exports, employment and improve the current account. However, the main disadvantage of subsidies is that it costs the government money. Export subsidies might have a high opportunity cost. The money spent on subsidies might be spent more effectively on alternative government projects such as building new schools and hospitals.

Generally, if governments restrict free trade, consumers will end up paying more for products and their choice will be limited. If domestic producers are not exposed to competition, the quality of their goods may be inferior and the incentive to innovate will be reduced. Global growth will slow down and people's living standards all over the world will suffer. Fewer jobs will be created.

▲ Coal mining is Australia

ACTIVITY 2

CASE STUDY: CHINESE COAL TARIFFS

The falling price of coal has resulted in some protectionism from a number of countries in the world. In 2014, China imposed tariffs of 6 per cent and 3 per cent on Australian thermal coal and coking coal, respectively. The Australian coal industry said that the effects would be felt more harshly by Australia because Indonesian coal producers, who also export to China, would not be affected by the tariffs. This is because China and Indonesia have a **bi-lateral free trade agreement**. The Minerals Council for Australia argued that the tariffs would raise the price of energy in China and threaten the current trade talks between China and Australia.

China's decision to impose the tariffs was designed to protect the domestic industry in the face of falling global prices. The price of coal has fallen from US$136 in 2011 to US$65 in 2015. China reckons that 70 per cent of its coal mining companies are making a loss. However, some analysts suggest that too much coal is being produced in relation to demand. China's growth has slowed and it is making some effort to use cleaner fuels.

1 What is meant by a tariff?

2 Why has China imposed tariffs on Australian coal?

IMPACT OF TARIFFS, QUOTAS AND SUBSIDIES ON MARKETS

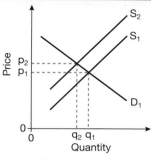

▲ **Figure 38.1** Effect of a tariff or a quota on a market

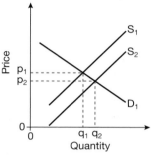

▲ **Figure 38.2** Effect of a subsidy on a market

The imposition of trade barriers by a government can have an impact on markets. For example, if a government imposes a tariff on imports, the prices of imports will rise. The impact of the different trade barriers on markets is explained below.

TARIFFS AND QUOTAS

Figure 38.1 shows that when the government imposes a tariff, the price rises from p_1 to p_2. As a result, the amount traded in the market falls from q_1 to q_2. These changes are caused by a shift in the supply curve from S_1 to S_2. The effect of the tariff on the supply curve is the same as that of indirect taxes (see Chapter 6, pages 34–39).

The effect of a quota in the market is the same as that of a tariff. The supply curve shifts to the left from S_1 to S_2 forcing a price increase from p_1 to p_2. This is also shown in Figure 38.1.

SUBSIDIES

The effect of a subsidy in a market is shown in Figure 38.2. Before a subsidy is granted, the equilibrium price in the market is p_1. The effect of a subsidy is to lower production costs, which means that producers will increase supply. This is shown by a shift in the supply curve from S_1 to S_2. The new equilibrium price is p_2, which is lower than p_1. The amount traded in the market rises from q_1 to q_2. Subsidies will lower prices for consumers.

MULTIPLE-CHOICE QUESTIONS

▶ 1 Which of the following is a reason for protectionism?

    A Protect low paid workers

    B Protect the environment

    C Prevent dumping

    D Protect monopolies

▶ 2 Which of the following is a method of protectionism?

    A Quota

    B VAT

    C Product differentiation

    D A minimum wage

ECONOMICS IN PRACTICE

CASE STUDY: US TARIFFS ON FOREIGN STEEL PRODUCERS

In 2014, the US government announced that it would impose tariffs worth several hundred millions of dollars on imports of steel. The US Commerce Department imposed tariffs of 16 per cent on imports from South Korea of steel pipe and tubes used for oil drilling. The department claimed that these products were being dumped in US markets – being sold at unfair prices. The US imposed even higher duties, up to 118 per cent, on nine other countries, including Thailand, Turkey, Saudi Arabia and Taiwan, who were all accused of dumping steel in the country.

It was hoped that the tariffs would help the US steel industry by raising prices and protecting hundreds of jobs that had been threatened by cheap imports. Steel workers in the USA had been holding demonstrations around the country to demand the government to do something about cheap imports. However, some industry analysts said that the tariffs would only have a short-term impact. This was because of the worldwide overproduction of steel caused by the slowdown in the Chinese economy and the 'softening' of the US shale gas boom (shale gas production uses a lot of steel).

Just after the announcement by the USA, South Korea said it would take action against the USA in order to protect its US$818 million of exports of steel products to the country. South Korean officials said the US steel producers charge higher than market prices for South Korean products. The South Korean trade ministry said it 'will come up with appropriate counter measures based on legal reviews and discussions with the local industry' when commenting on the US trade barriers. Officials also added that steel is a tariff-free item in US–South Korean trade according to WTO rules. South Korea was considering whether ask the WTO to investigate the claims or press charges in a US court.

One of the dangers of imposing trade barriers is that an all-out trade war breaks out between nations. This is where a country retaliates to the imposition of trade barriers by imposing some of their own. This can then lead to further rounds of more severe trade restrictions and, eventually trade between nations stops completely. This will obviously have negative consequences for both parties. In this case, the argument comes just a couple of years after the USA and South Korea signed a bi-lateral trade agreement.

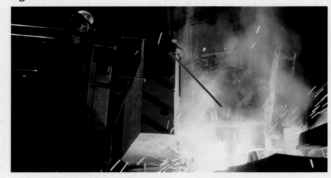

▲ Steel production

CHAPTER QUESTIONS

1 What is the difference between a quota and a tariff?

2 How might the dumping of steel products by foreigner companies impact on US steel producers?

3 Use a supply and demand diagram to show the effect of imposing a tariff in a market.

4 Describe **(a)** one advantage and **(b)** one disadvantage of using subsidies as a trade barrier.

5 Consider the possible effects of the US imposing tariffs on steel imports. Make a clear judgement in your evaluation.

39 TRADING BLOCS

LEARNING OBJECTIVES

- Understand the impact of trading blocs on member and non-member countries
- Understand some examples of trading blocs

GETTING STARTED

In recent history, the pattern of world trade has changed. An increasing number of countries have opened up their economies and many trade barriers have been relaxed. Groups of nations have joined together to form trading agreements and world trade is no longer dominated by single nations, such as the UK and the USA. Look at the information below.

CASE STUDY: CROATIA AND THE EU

In 2013, Croatia joined another 27 countries in the EU. The EU was formed just after the Second World War with the aim of developing economic cooperation. However, since then, membership has grown from six countries to 28. Also, the EU now has common policies in a wide range of areas in addition to trade agreements. The EU has developed common policies on matters such as climate, the environment, health, migration, justice and security. Since it was formed in 1958, the EU has delivered more than half a century of peace, stability and wealth. It has helped to drive economic growth in the region and raised living standards for its members. It also introduced its own currency – the euro. In 2012, the EU was awarded the Nobel Peace Prize for advancing the causes of peace, reconciliation, democracy and human rights in Europe.

Croatia first applied for membership of the EU in 2003. However, it had to gain approval over a 10-year period to ensure that Croatia could meet the conditions of membership. After 12 months of membership, Croatia was still in recession and awaiting access to EU development funds. The billion euros per year promised by the EU would be used to help SMEs develop new products. A government official said that Croatia was 'illiterate in business' and

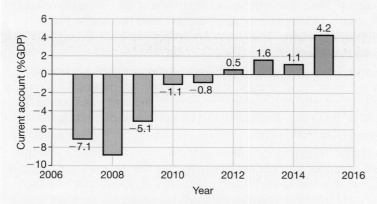

▲ Figure 39.1 Croatia's current balance, 2006–16 (%GDP)

that people had low expectations regarding the benefits of joining the EU. However, on the positive side, exports to the EU had risen by 15 per cent and business owners reported that it was now much easier doing business with EU countries. One business owner, an olive oil producer in the north of the country, said that the EU was working in their favour. It was now easier to sell larger quantities to the EU, there was less paperwork and Croatian businesses are being pressured to be more professional. The owner also said that the outlook for the younger generation is much better. For example, they realise that investment and support for rural products is beginning to emerge.

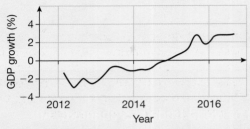

▲ **Figure 39.2** Croatia's economic growth rate, 2012–16

1 What is the purpose of the EU?

2 Assess the possible impact on Croatia of joining the EU.

3 How might businesses in Croatia benefit from EU membership?

4 In pairs, find out if your country, or one near to you, belongs to a regional trading organisation. List three possible benefits of membership.

WHAT IS A TRADING BLOC?

SUBJECT VOCABULARY

trading blocs groups of countries situated in the same region that join together and enjoy trade free of tariffs, quotas and other forms of trade barrier

The world is generally divided into a number of **trading blocs**. These are groups of countries situated in the same region that join together to form a free trade area. This means that trade between all the members will be completely free of tariffs, quotas and other forms of trade barrier. It is also common for trading blocs to have a common tariff on imports from non-members. However, not all trading blocs are the same. They may differ in size and nature.

- **Preferential trading areas (PTAs):** This type of arrangement means that members agree to remove trade barriers on a range of goods and services. However, not all goods and services are covered and some trade restrictions still exist. India has these agreements with Nepal, Mauritius and Chile, for example.

- **Free trade areas (FTAs):** Trade between members of an FTA is completely free of trade barriers. However, members are allowed to impose trade restrictions on non-members. The North America Free Trade Area (NAFTA) is one example. Its members are the USA, Canada and Mexico.

- **Customs unions:** These are similar to FTAs but members of a customs union impose a common set of trade barriers on non-members. This means that products imported by one member can be resold and transported to other members in the union. The European Union is one of the biggest customs unions in the world.

- **Common markets:** These operate like customs unions but also allow the free movement of labour and capital between member countries. Common markets will also have the same trading standards and regulations, which makes transactions between members easier. Mercosur is an example of a common market. Its members are Argentina, Brazil, Paraguay and Uruguay (Venezuela was suspended in 2016).

■ **Economic unions:** These are the most developed type of trade blocs. Economic unions adopt the arrangements of common markets and customs unions but also aim for even more integration. For example, members are likely to adopt closer economic, political and cultural ties. The Gulf Cooperation Council is an example. Its member states are Bahrain, Kuwait, Oman, Qatar, Saudi Arabia and the United Arab Emirates.

IMPACT OF TRADING BLOCS ON MEMBER STATES

ADVANTAGES

Trading blocs provide many benefits to their members. Belonging to a trading bloc brings much the same benefits as those that result from free trade anywhere. If members of the bloc abolish all trade barriers, goods will be cheaper, and there will be more consumer choice and faster economic growth. Firms will be able to exploit economies of scale because they have access to larger markets and extra competition will improve the quality of goods and encourage innovation.

It is argued that the formation of trading blocs invites FDI. This may be because foreign firms are keen to locate operations within a trading bloc to get access to a larger and barrier-free market. This was the case in Mexico where FDI more than doubled the year after it joined NAFTA.

The formation of a trading bloc should result in closer cooperation between members. For example, countries may share resources, help each other out and introduce common standards, laws and customs.

Studies have shown that trade blocs can reduce cross-border conflict, promote peace, and achieve substantial social and economic gains. For example, Argentina and Brazil have used the Southern Common Market to end their historic rivalry.

DISADVANTAGES

Unfortunately, membership of a trade bloc does have some disadvantages. Indeed, in June 2016, the UK voted to leave the EU. The UK voters decided that the disadvantages of belonging to the EU were greater than the advantages.

Those in favour of worldwide free trade generally oppose trading blocs. By their nature, trading blocs encourage regional as opposed to global free trade. However, there is no real agreement as to whether regional trade blocs result in less free trade in the world or encourage further globalisation.

One problem with belonging to a trade bloc is the financial cost to the government and therefore the taxpayer. For example, in 2015, the UK made a net contribution of £8500 million to the EU. Figure 39.3 shows the money paid to the EU each year, the money it gets back and the UK's net contribution between 1973 and 2015.

It is also possible for firms within a trading bloc to merge and become too powerful. This may result in the formation of regional monopolies that might exploit consumers in the bloc. It is also possible that certain countries get far more out of membership than others. For example, some people argue that Germany has benefitted far more than other nations in the EU.

Countries may start to rely too heavily on trade within the bloc. This would make them more vulnerable to changes in prices and demand patterns within the bloc. They may also miss out on opportunities in other world markets. Also, inefficient producers may be protected from competition from businesses outside the trade bloc. As a result, consumers might end up paying more for goods and services in some industries.

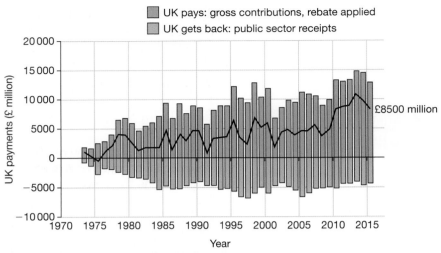

▲ **Figure 39.3** UK financial contributions to the EU, 1973–2015

Members of a trading bloc may start to standardise trading practices, laws and other customs within their bloc. Some people may not like this because they may be happy with the traditional ways of their own country. Changes in laws and customs may also threaten a nation's culture.

IMPACT OF TRADING BLOCS ON NON-MEMBER STATES

Countries that do not belong to trading blocs will face common trade barriers when selling goods to any member inside the bloc. They will obviously be at a disadvantage and may be forced to find new markets. However, it is still not clear whether non-members will suffer in the long run. For example, since joining the EU, the UK has reduced trade with some members of the British Commonwealth. However, there is little evidence, if any, to suggest that these nations have suffered as a result.

EXAMPLES OF TRADING BLOCS

NAFTA (NORTH AMERICAN FREE TRADE AGREEMENT)

NAFTA is made up of three countries: the USA, Canada and Mexico. It is the biggest trading bloc in the world. In 2017, NAFTA had a population of 450 million and a GDP of over US$20.08 trillion. The three countries have common arrangements relating to trade and investment, labour, financial dealings, intellectual property and environmental issues.

The formation of NAFTA has helped trade between the three members to grow from US$297 000 million to US$1.14 trillion. This increase in trade has helped to raise economic growth, profits, and jobs for all three countries. It also lowered prices for consumers when tariffs were removed.

However, despite these benefits, there have been some problems. First, it led to the loss of 500 000–750 000 US jobs, mostly in manufacturing. Some US companies in the automotive, textile, computer and electrical appliance industries relocated to Mexico to exploit cheap labour. Another problem was that job migration reduced or held down wages. Sixty-five per cent of companies in the affected industries threatened to move to Mexico. Also, NAFTA put Mexican farmers out of business. It allowed cheap, heavily subsidised US farm products into Mexico. Finally, it was alleged that some US companies damaged the Mexican environment to keep costs low.

ASEAN (ASSOCIATION OF SOUTHEAST ASIA NATIONS)

ASEAN has ten members from the Southeast Asian region. Some of the largest members include Thailand, Vietnam, Malaysia, Indonesia, the Philippines and Singapore. Its key aims are to:

- accelerate economic growth, social progress and cultural development in the region
- promote regional peace and stability through respect for justice and the rule of law
- promote cooperation on matters of common interest in the economic, social, cultural, technical, scientific and administrative fields
- help each other in the provision of training and research facilities
- increase cooperation so that regional improvements in agriculture, industry, trade, transport and communication can lift living standards
- promote Southeast Asian studies
- maintain close cooperation with other international and regional organisations.

SACU (SOUTH AFRICAN CUSTOMS UNION)

Formed originally in 1910, SACU is the world's oldest trading bloc. Its members include Botswana, Lesotho, Namibia, Swaziland (the BLNS states) and South Africa. SACU applies common customs and excise duties on goods imported from non-member countries. The BNLS states also impose extra duties on agricultural produce. Trade between SACU members is totally free of barriers. Trade between members is also simple and the distances to the markets are short and frequent.

MULTIPLE-CHOICE QUESTIONS

▶ 1 Which of the following is a benefit of a trading bloc?

    A Employment will fall

    B Inflation will be lower

    C Exchange rates will fall

    D More FDI is attracted

▶ 2 Which of the following statements about trading blocs is true?

    A They discourage political cooperation

    B Countries that do not belong to the bloc will face trade barriers

    C Members of trading blocs all use the same currency

    D Members of trading blocs speak in a common language

ECONOMICS IN PRACTICE

CASE STUDY: EAST AFRICAN COMMUNITY

In 2016, South Sudan became the sixth member of the East African Community (EAC). It joined Kenya, Burundi, Tanzania, Rwanda and Uganda. In 2015, before welcoming South Sudan, the total population of the region was 145.5 million and GDP was US$147 500 million. The stated mission of the community is 'To widen and deepen economic, political, social and cultural integration in order to improve the quality of life of the people of East Africa through increased competitiveness, value added production, trade and investments.'

Established in 1967, the EAC operates as a customs union. This means that the members have agreed to trade freely and impose a common external tariff (CET) on imports from non-members. Goods moving freely within the EAC must also comply with EAC trading rules.

In 2010, the EAC became a common market in an effort to speed up economic growth and development. This means that EAC members all agree to:

- free movement of goods
- free movement of labour/workers
- right of residence
- free movement of capital.
- free movement of persons
- right of establishment
- free movement of services

In the future, the EAC also wants to establish a common currency like the euro. Monetary union will enable members to trade in the same currency and thus avoid the uncertainties created by varying exchange rates. The cost of changing currencies when trading will also be avoided.

The EAC's economic performance has been very good in recent years compared with the rest of Africa. Real GDP in the EAC increased by 5.8 per cent in 2014 compared with a 5.3 per cent growth in 2013. Economic growth in the region was driven by better agricultural production, sound domestic demand and investment in the EAC's infrastructure. The rest of Africa recorded a growth of 4.5 per cent in 2014 compared with 4.0 per cent in 2013. However, the region's current account deficit (as a percentage of GDP) worsened slightly to 12.4 per cent in 2014 from 11.8 per cent in 2013.

The future of the EAC looks promising due to infrastructure developments right across the region. Further investment is planned in roads, railways and ICT. There will also be more integration of systems. The EAC region is expected to record real growth of 6.2 per cent in 2015.

▲ Members of the EAC

CHAPTER QUESTIONS

1 Describe what a trading bloc is. Use the example in this case to support your answer.

2 Describe one possible benefit to EAC of sharing a common currency.

3 Describe one impact on non-members of the EAC.

4 Consider the benefits to EAC members of belonging to the trading bloc. Make a clear judgement in your evaluation.

40 THE WORLD TRADE ORGANIZATION AND WORLD TRADE PATTERNS

LEARNING OBJECTIVES

- Understand the role of the World Trade Organization
- Understand the actions by the World Trade Organization
- Understand the trade patterns of developed and developing countries

SUBJECT VOCABULARY

World Trade Organization international organisation that promotes free trade by persuading countries to abolish tariffs and other barriers. It polices free trade agreements, settles trade disputes between governments and organises trade negotiations

GETTING STARTED

Although most countries want to increase international trade and remove trade barriers, trade disputes are common. Such disputes may cause difficulties and lead to trade wars. However, one approach to resolving a dispute is to involve the World Trade Organization. Look at the example below.

CASE STUDY: BRAZIL v THAILAND TRADE DISPUTE

In 2016, Brazil complained to the **World Trade Organization** (WTO) that Thailand had given subsidies to sugar cane producers and sugar mills. The effect of these subsidies was to dramatically reduce the global price of sugar and reduce Brazil's share of the market from 50 per cent to 44.7 per cent in 4 years. Brazil and Thailand are two of the world's largest sugar producers so the market is of vital importance to both countries. Brazilian sugar producers gathered evidence that showed that they were losing US$1200 million p.a. in revenue as a result of subsidies paid to Thailand and India. They also argued that Thailand's share of the global market had risen from 12.1 per cent to 15.8 per cent in the past 4 years.

Thailand replied to the accusation by saying that Brazil's claim was unjustified. An official from Thailand's Industry Ministry said that there were no subsidies and that trade had been conducted within the agreed conditions. The official said that the money had come from the country's Cane and Sugar Fund, which raised the money itself. In 2004, Brazil challenged the EU over sugar subsidies and won. This resulted in a complete reworking of the EU's policies for sugar production, which had an impact on the global sugar market.

The WTO will have to look at the claims made by Brazil. It will have to analyse the information that Brazil presents and also consider any defence provided by Thailand. The WTO will then have to make a judgement and decide on a course of action. This might involve imposing penalties on Thailand if the case is judged to be correct.

1 What is this dispute about?

2 What role will the WTO play in this dispute?

3 What might be the consequences if trade agreements did not exist?

▲ Sugar cane harvesting in Brazil

THE WORLD TRADE ORGANIZATION

The WTO was established in 1995, replacing a similar body called GATT (General Agreement on Trade and Tariffs). The WTO has 164 members and employs over 600 people including lawyers, economists, statisticians and communications experts. In 2015, the WTO had a budget of over US$195 million. The WTO promotes free trade by persuading countries to abolish tariffs and other trade barriers. It has become closely associated with globalisation. The WTO is the only international agency overseeing the rules of international trade. It polices free trade agreements, settles trade disputes between governments and organises trade negotiations. WTO decisions are final and every member must abide by its rulings. So, when the USA and the EU are in dispute over bananas or beef, it is the WTO that acts as judge and jury. WTO members have the power to enforce WTO decisions by punishing countries that have broken the rules. The main activities of the WTO are outlined below.

TRADE NEGOTIATIONS

The WTO aims to reduce or eliminate trade barriers through negotiation. It does this by encouraging countries to draw up trading agreements covering matters such as anti-dumping, subsidies and product standards. The WTO aims to bring about **trade liberalisation** and lays down procedures for settling disputes. The agreements reached between countries may change over time. Changes are needed because businesses operate in a dynamic world with new products and new technologies being developed at an accelerating pace.

IMPLEMENTATION AND MONITORING

The WTO employs various councils and committees to administer and monitor the application of the WTO's rules for trade in goods, services and intellectual property rights. For example, the WTO may examine trade policies to ensure that trade agreements are clear and well documented. All WTO members must conduct regular reviews of their trade policies and practices. Countries must also submit reports to the WTO as part of the monitoring process.

SETTLING TRADE DISPUTES

Trade disputes between members are not uncommon. The WTO's procedure for resolving trade disputes is vital for enforcing the rules and making sure that trade flows smoothly. Countries bring disputes to the WTO if they think their rights under their agreements have not been preserved. This is what Brazil was doing in the case outlined in 'Getting started'. The WTO appoints independent experts to make judgements relating to a dispute after the arguments from both sides have been presented.

BUILDING MEMBERSHIP

There are around 20 countries that are yet to join. The WTO helps and encourages new members to join up.

SUBJECT VOCABULARY

trade liberalisation move towards greater free trade through the removal of trade barriers

---

DID YOU KNOW?

- One of the activities of the WTO is to gather and publish trade and other economic data in support of its other main activities.
- Another of its activities is to educate the public about what it does.

ACTIVITY 1

CASE STUDY: TRADE DISPUTE BETWEEN PAKISTAN AND SOUTH AFRICA

In 2015, Pakistan decided to challenge South Africa's decision to impose anti-dumping duties (see Chapter 39, pages 319–324) on manufactured cement that Pakistan was selling in South Africa. Pakistani authorities claimed that South Africa had imposed anti-dumping duties of between 15 per cent and 68 per cent on Pakistan's cement. The South African government claimed that the cement imports were damaging the domestic cement industry.

The Pakistani Minister for Commerce requested WTO intervention to protect its trade interests. Prior to this, South Africa was given 4 years to investigate Pakistan's claims. During this time, Pakistani officials said that South Africa:

■ failed to consider the effects of the breakdown in cartels running the South African cement industry

■ failed to examine the entire product range under investigation and just focused on the market for bagged cement

■ denied Pakistani cement exporters access to trade statistics and therefore did not allow them to defend their case.

As a result of South Africa's anti-dumping duties, Pakistan's exports of cement to South Africa have fallen continuously.

▲ Pakistani cement plant

1 What is meant by a trade dispute? Use the example in this case to support your answer.

2 How will South African consumers be affected by the imposition of anti-dumping duties?

3 Describe the role that the WTO will play in settling this dispute.

CRITICISMS OF THE WTO

Despite what seems to be the good intentions of the WTO, it does face criticism. This comes mainly from anti-globalisation bodies and environmental groups. For example, Global Exchange, a body that promotes people-centred globalisation, makes the following claims about the WTO.

■ **It is undemocratic** because the WTO rules are written by and for corporations. The views of consumers, environmentalists, human rights and labour organisations are often ignored.

- **It favours the 'rights' of corporations over those of workers**. For example, the WTO has ruled that it is illegal for a government to ban a product based on the way it is produced, such as with child labour. It has also ruled that governments cannot take into account 'non-commercial values', such as human rights when making purchasing decisions.

- **It is destroying the environment**. For example, the very first WTO panel ruled that a provision of the US Clean Air Act, requiring both domestic and foreign producers to produce cleaner gasoline, was illegal.

- **It favours wealthy nations over poorer ones**. For example, negotiators from poor countries are not even invited to meetings – and then 'agreements' are announced that poor countries did not even know were being discussed. Many poor countries do not have enough qualified staff to take part in all the negotiations. Some do not have a permanent representative at the WTO. This prevents poor countries from representing their interests.

- **It is causing hardship for poorer nations**. Farmers produce enough food in the world to feed everyone. However, it is argued that the corporate control of food distribution means millions of people worldwide suffer from lack of food. In developing countries, as many as four out of every five people make their living from the land. But the WTO insists that market forces should control agricultural policies rather than a commitment to food security and adequate incomes for farmers.

WORLD TRADE PATTERNS

INCREASE IN WORLD TRADE

World trade has increased enormously in the last 55 years. Figure 40.1 shows that total world exports have been accelerating rapidly, particularly since 1985. Here are some reasons why this has happened.

- **Better transport and communications:** More efficient transport systems mean that goods can be shipped more quickly and cheaply. This reduces the cost of selling goods abroad and therefore makes them more attractive to buy. Developments in ICT, such as the internet, means that buyers and sellers can communicate more easily. For example, consumers can buy goods online from sellers all over the world.

- **Relaxing of trade barriers:** Since the 1930s, countries have realised that protectionism does not help economic growth. As a result, nations have discussed ways of increasing free trade. There have been 'rounds' of negotiations in Tokyo (1979), Uruguay (between 1986 and 1994) and more recently Doha (launched in 1999). At these meetings, national leaders discuss trade matters and sign agreements to reduce tariffs and quotas.

- **Development of multinationals:** A lot of world trade has been driven by large MNCs. Their aim is to increase sales around the world and produce goods in locations that allow them to minimise their costs. As a result, they have sold an increasing range of goods and services to an increasing number of countries.

- **Travel and consumer awareness:** Owing to an increase in travel, consumers are more prepared to buy goods from other countries. They welcome greater choice and recognise that imports can satisfy a growing number of needs and wants.

- **Trade agreements:** Most countries in the world have trade agreements with their neighbours that are designed to encourage free trade. One important feature of these agreements is the formation of a trading bloc (see Chapter 39, pages 319–324).

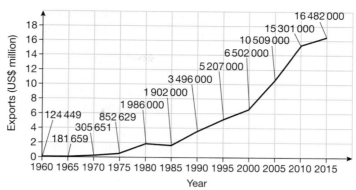

▲ **Figure 40.1** Value of global exports, 1960–2015

TRADE IN DEVELOPED COUNTRIES

Although developing nations are contributing an increasing amount to world trade, it is the developed nations that continue to dominate. Figure 40.2 shows that China, the USA, Germany and Japan were the world's leading exporters and importers of merchandise in 2014.

Exporters			Importers		
	US$ million	%		US$ million	%
China	2 343 000	12.4	USA	2 409 000	12.7
USA	1 623 000	8.6	China	1 960 000	10.3
Germany	1 511 000	8	Germany	1 217 000	6.4
Japan	684 000	3.6	Japan	822 000	4.3
Netherlands	672 000	3.6	UK	683 000	3.6
France	583 000	3.1	France	679 000	3.6
Korea	573 000	3	Hong Kong	601 000	3.2
Italy	529 000	2.8	Netherlands	587 000	0.8
Hong Kong	524 000	2.8	Korea	526 000	3.1
UK	507 000	2.7	Canada	475 000	2.8
Australia	240 000	1.3	Australia	238 000	1.2

▲ **Figure 40.2** World's leading merchandising traders, 2014

- **Loss of trade in manufacturing:** Over the last 30 years, there has been a gradual movement of manufacturing from many Western developed countries to Far Eastern countries such as China and South Korea. For example, the USA now has a rising trade deficit in manufactured goods.

- **More air travel:** People continue to travel the world in growing numbers. Figure 40.3 shows the scale of the increase. Most of this increase results from developed countries. This may be because of the development of 'budget airlines' offering cheap flights to many new destinations. However, countries such as India are also developing their aviation industries.

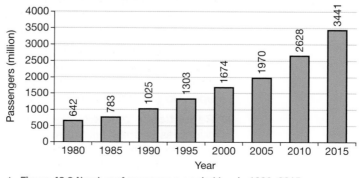

▲ **Figure 40.3** Number of passengers carried by air, 1980–2015

■ **Widening of the development gap:** Although international trade is rising in developing countries and an increasing number of people are being removed from poverty, trade in the developed countries is also growing. As a result, the gap between the rich and poor nations is widening. For example, 30 per cent of Indians, over 200 million people, still live in absolute poverty (Chapter 30, pages 240–249) even though the country has seen a great deal of development in recent years.

TRADE IN DEVELOPING COUNTRIES

Figure 40.4 shows clearly that developing countries have increased their share of world trade between 1995 and 2014. Some examples of recent trends in international trade in developing countries are outlined below.

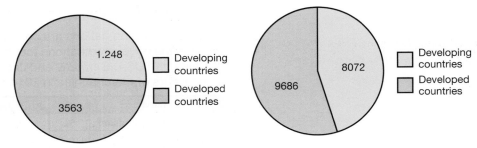

▲ **Figure 40.4** Share of world trade, 1995 and 2014 (US$ million)

■ **An increase in net migration:** An increasing number of people are leaving developing countries to find work in developed countries. For example, the numbers moving between 1990 and 2013 rose from 82.3 million people to 135.6 million.

■ **Increased FDI in Africa:** Many African nations have benefited from an increasing amount of FDI from China. This has helped to increase international trade in these nations. China is Africa's third largest trade partner, following the USA and France. Total FDI in Africa has risen sharply in the last 20 years. In 1995, FDI to Sub-Saharan Africa was US$4583 million. This had grown to US$42 000 million in 2015. FDI is very important for developing countries. This is because the exports of foreign businesses located inside a developed country counts as exports for that country. FDI also creates jobs and raises living standards.

■ **Rise in commodity dependence.** Many developing countries rely heavily on **commodities** for international trade. For example, China's interest in Africa is largely down to its large quantities of natural resources. In 2012/13, two-thirds of developing countries were said to be commodity dependent with about one in every two of these located in Africa. Between 1995 and 2013, commodity dependence has increased by 50 per cent. (A country is described as commodity dependent if revenue from the sale of commodities represents at least 60 per cent of total exports.)

■ **Debt cancellation:** Developing countries will benefit from the cancellation of the entire US$40 000 million debt owed by 18 highly indebted poor countries. The money saved may be invested to help these poor nations open up their economies and grow.

■ **Reduction in barriers:** The majority of WTO members are from developing countries so they will probably welcome trade liberalisation. The potential gains from removing trade barriers are considerable. Developing countries are likely to enjoy improving current balances if more trade barriers can be removed in the future.

MULTIPLE-CHOICE QUESTIONS

▶ 1 Which of the following is an activity of the WTO?
  A Helping multinationals to develop their businesses overseas
  B Settling trade disputes between members
  C Raising money for developing countries
  D Creating new types of trade barrier
Look at Figure 40.5.

▶ 2 Which of the following statements is true of the information shown by the graph?
  A Agricultural imports have fallen over the period
  B Before 1980, agricultural exports exceeded agricultural imports
  C Agricultural exports have fallen over the period
  D Developing countries export more agricultural goods than developed countries

ECONOMICS IN PRACTICE

CASE STUDY: COMMODITY DEPENDENCY

Many developing countries rely heavily on the sale of commodities such as oil, minerals and some agricultural products for the majority of their exports. This reliance is called commodity dependency and is likely to result in difficulties for some countries. For example, when commodity prices fall, revenues from the sale of commodities will also fall, and the balance on the current account will worsen. There may also be a negative impact on employment, growth, fiscal balances and exchange rates.

Some countries have made a special effort to reduce commodity dependency by planning for the future. For example, Uganda has proceeded carefully in developing its oil reserves. The government passed legislation that requires oil revenues to be invested in infrastructure or agriculture. Similarly, Mozambique and Tanzania have resisted the temptation to spend oil revenues quickly. They have spent years drawing up 'master plans', which ensures that a measured approach is taken when developing business interests in the extraction of resources. These countries understand the need for ensuring that the right infrastructure, policy and legal structure are in place before exploiting resources. This is necessary to ensure that the revenues benefit everybody.

Around 75 per cent of WTO members are developing countries. Consequently, developing nations will benefit considerably from the efforts of the WTO in liberalising trade. However, it could be argued that countries that are dependent on commodity revenue need to think about diversifying very soon. The business world is dynamic and factors such as the development of 'green' energy in the near future, for example, will have an impact on the trading patterns of these countries.

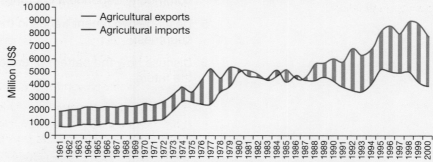

▲ **Figure 40.5** Pattern of agricultural trade for developing countries, 1961–2000

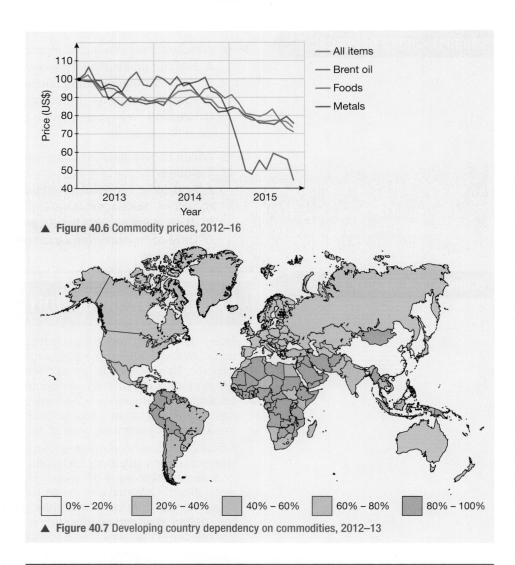

▲ Figure 40.6 Commodity prices, 2012–16

| 0% – 20% | 20% – 40% | 40% – 60% | 60% – 80% | 80% – 100% |

▲ Figure 40.7 Developing country dependency on commodities, 2012–13

CHAPTER QUESTIONS

1 Describe two functions of the WTO.

Look at Figure 40.7.

2 Which continent is most dependent on commodities?

3 Suggest one possible reason for your answer to question (2).

4 Discuss how the price changes shown in Figure 40.6 might impact on commodity dependent countries.

5 Describe two recent trends in the pattern of international trade in developing countries.

6 Discuss how the pattern of trade in developing countries might change in the future.

41 EXCHANGE RATES AND THEIR DETERMINATION

LEARNING OBJECTIVES

- Understand how to define exchange rates
- Understand the factors that affect the supply and demand of currencies: interest rates, currency speculators, imports and exports of goods and services
- Understand how to use supply and demand diagrams to show the determination of exchange rates

GETTING STARTED

Most countries in the world do not use the same currency. For example, the UEA has the dirham, the USA has the dollar, some European countries use the euro and India has the rupee. When countries use different currencies, transactions between individuals and firms in different countries are affected. Look at the examples below.

CASE STUDY: RUHR METAL PRODUCTS

Ruhr Metal Products makes components for car manufacturers in Germany. However, in 2017, the firm received an order from a Japanese carmaker for €2 500 000 of components. The cost in yen to the Japanese car maker was JPY 30 000 000. This was because €1 = JPY 120 (2 500 000 × 120).

CASE STUDY: SALLY WONG AND HANS KROOS

Sally and Hans were going on a 3-month backpack tour of India before they start university. They planned to use credit cards to pay for most of their accommodation and other large expenses. However, they still needed some rupees for smaller payments. They had €2000 for such expenses which they exchanged for Rs140 000. At the currency exchange at Frankfurt Airport where the exchange was made, €1 = Rs70.

Note: These transactions all exclude commission charges.

▲ Most countries in the world do not use the same currency

1 Which currencies are used in (a) Germany, (b) India and (c) Japan?

2 Why do we need exchange rates? Use an example to support your answer.

3 What was the exchange rate in the case of Ruhr Metal Products?

WHAT IS AN EXCHANGE RATE?

SUBJECT VOCABULARY

exchange rate price of one currency in terms of another

Exchange rates are needed because different countries use different currencies. When trading with other countries, payments must usually be made in another currency. In 'Getting started', we learn that €1 = JPY 120. This is the **exchange rate** between the euro and the yen. It shows the price of euros in terms of yen. Similarly, when Sally and Hans converted their €2000 into rupees, the exchange rate was €1 = Rs70. They got Rs140 000 for their €2000.

EXAMPLES OF TRANSACTIONS INVOLVING TWO DIFFERENT CURRENCIES

Example 1: How much will it cost a French firm in euros to buy goods from a British firm that cost £400 000 if £1 = €1.10? The cost to the French firm in euros is given by:

£400 000 × 1.1 = €440 000

Example 2: How much will it cost a British firm in pounds to buy US$300 000 of goods from a US firm if £1 = US$1.50? The cost in pounds is given by:

US$300 000 ÷ US$1.50 = £200 000

Example 3: How many US dollars will be needed by a British firm buying £55 000 of goods from an US firm if £1 = US$1.50? The cost to the British firm in US dollars is given by:

£55 000 × US$1.50 = US$82 500

Example 4: How many pounds can a Japanese business person buy with JPY 100 000 when visiting London if £1 = JPY 150? The quantity of pounds that can be bought is given by:

JPY 100 000 ÷ JPY 150 = £666.67

ACTIVITY 1

CASE STUDY: TORRES MACHINE TOOLS (TMT)

Luis Torres owns Torres Machine Tools (TMT), a Mexican company. It manufactures tools, machines and other equipment for production lines in the food processing industry. About 70 per cent of its output is sold to American producers. However, TMT also buys materials and components from Germany and Spain. At the beginning of 2017, there were three important international transactions.

■ A US firm bought machines from TMT costing MXN 3.6 million.

■ TMT bought components from a German firm for €2.5 million.

■ TMT bought materials from a Spanish firm for MXN 20 million.

1 Calculate the price in US dollars of the machines sold by TMT to the US firm (assume MXN 1 = US$0.05).

2 Calculate the amount paid in MXN by TMT for the €2.5 million components bought from Germany (assume MXN 1 = €0.45).

3 Calculate the amount in euros received by the Spanish supplier for the MXN 20 million of materials sold to TMT (assume MXN 1 = €0.45).

▲ Toolmaking at Torres Machine Tools in Mexico

FACTORS AFFECTING THE DEMAND FOR A CURRENCY

The demand for a particular currency on foreign exchange markets is affected by a number of factors.

INTEREST RATES

Interest rates can affect the flows of money around the world. For example, if interest rates are higher in the UK than in other countries, foreign savers may choose to put their savings in a UK bank. However, before doing this, they will have to buy pounds with their domestic currency. This is because they can only deposit pounds in UK banks. Therefore an increase in interest rates will increase the demand for pounds and cause the exchange rate to rise. A fall in the UK interest rate will have the opposite effect.

CURRENCY SPECULATORS

Speculators are firms, individuals or financial institutions that buy and sell currencies in the hope of making a capital gain (profit). Foreign exchange markets attract speculators because prices of currencies sometimes vary dramatically. This means they buy a particular currency and hope to sell it for a higher price later. For example, if speculators think the value of the pound is going to rise in the future, they will buy pounds. This will increase the demand for pounds and therefore help to drive up the exchange rate.

THE DEMAND FOR EXPORTS

Firms that sell goods and services to foreigners expect to be paid in their own currency. For example, firms in the UK selling goods to Australian firms do not want to be paid in Australian dollars, they want to be paid in pounds. This is because Australian dollars have little use in the UK. Therefore, Australian firms have to obtain pounds and they are likely to get them from a bank. Therefore, demand for UK exports also results in a demand for pounds. If demand for UK exports rises, there will also be an increase in the demand for pounds. In Figure 41.4, this will shift the demand for pounds to the right from D_1 to D_2 and increase the exchange rate (or price of the pound) from ER_1 to ER_2. A fall in the demand for exports will have the opposite effect.

Movements of investment capital can also affect the demand for a currency. For example, if a foreign multinational wants to build a factory in the UK, it will need pounds to pay for the materials, labour and other resources required for the construction. An increase in inward FDI will increase the demand for pounds and, along with it, the exchange rate. A decrease in inward FDI will have the opposite effect.

FACTORS AFFECTING THE SUPPLY OF A CURRENCY

The factors that affect the supply of a currency on foreign exchange markets are similar to those that affect the demand.

INTEREST RATES IN OTHER COUNTRIES

If interest rates are higher in other countries, savers in the UK may decide to place their money in foreign banks. To do this, they must buy foreign currency. This will increase the flow of pounds into the foreign exchange markets, which will increase supply and reduce the exchange rate. The opposite will happen if overseas interest rates are lower than the UK.

CURRENCY SPECULATORS

Speculators can affect both the supply and demand of a currency. For example, if speculators believe that the price of the pound is going to fall, they will sell pounds in exchange for another currency. This will increase the supply of pounds in foreign exchange markets and lower the exchange rate.

THE DEMAND FOR IMPORTS

Imported goods and services have to be bought with foreign currency. Therefore, if UK importers buy more foreign goods and services, they will have to buy foreign currency with pounds. The flow of pounds onto the foreign exchange markets provided by importers increases supply.

Outward foreign direct investment (FDI) can also affect the supply of currency. For example, if UK MNCs develop business interests abroad, such as building a new supermarket, there will be an increase in the supply of pounds in the foreign exchange markets. This is because the multinationals will have to pay for the investment in foreign currency. They buy this with pounds and therefore more pounds flow into the market.

HOW ARE EXCHANGE RATES DETERMINED?

SUBJECT VOCABULARY

foreign exchange market market where foreign currencies can be bought and sold

On 16 February 2017, £1 cost American tourists US$1.25. Will the price be the same a year later in February 2018? The answer is probably no. Like all prices, market forces determine the price of a currency and if those forces change, the price is also likely to change. Currencies are bought and sold like commodities on a **foreign exchange market**. Banks and other financial institutions trade in these markets to obtain foreign currencies for their customers. The forces of supply and demand, as outlined above, determine the price of any currency. For example, if there is increasing demand for sterling, the price of the pound will rise.

Figure 41.1 shows the supply and demand for sterling. The price of sterling in this example is given in terms of the US dollar. The equilibrium exchange rate is where supply and demand for pounds is equal. At this point in the diagram, the price of £1 in US dollars is US$1.50, therefore the exchange rate is £1 = US$1.50. At this exchange rate, Q_1 pounds are traded on the market.

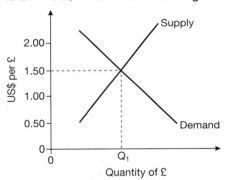

▲ **Figure 41.1** Equilibrium exchange rate

ACTIVITY 2

CASE STUDY: EXCHANGE RATE DETERMINATION

Figure 41.2 shows the market for US dollars. S_1 represents the supply of dollars and D_1 is the demand. The price of dollars in this example is given in terms of the euro.

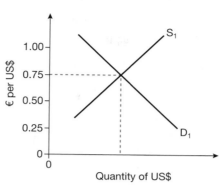

▲ **Figure 41.2** Market for US dollars

1 What is the equilibrium exchange rate between the US dollar and the euro?

2 An Italian tourist plans to spend €3000 on a shopping trip to New York. How many dollars will this buy at the equilibrium exchange rate shown in the diagram?

THE EFFECT OF CHANGES IN SUPPLY AND DEMAND ON EXCHANGE RATES

CHANGE IN SUPPLY

If there is a change in the supply or demand for a currency, there is likely to be a change in the exchange rate. The market for currency is no different from any other market. For example, what will happen if there is an increase in the supply of pounds? Figure 41.3 shows this. In the diagram, an increase in the supply of pounds resulting from importers buying foreign currency with pounds is shown by a shift from S_1 to S_2. This reduces the exchange rate from ER_1 to ER_2, that is, the value of the pound falls. A fall in demand for imports would have the opposite effect.

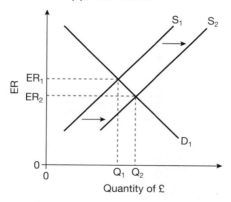

▲ **Figure 41.3** Increase in the supply of pounds in the foreign exchange market

CHANGE IN DEMAND

If demand for UK exports rises, there will also be an increase in the demand for pounds. In Figure 41.4, this will shift the demand for pounds to the right from D_1 to D_2. This will increase the exchange rate (or price of the pound) from ER_1 to ER_2. A fall in the demand for exports will have the opposite effect.

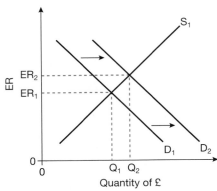

▲ **Figure 41.4** Increase in the demand for pounds in the foreign exchange market

▶ **1** Which of the following factors would affect the demand for a currency?

   A Levels of unemployment

   B The price of imports

   C The demand for imports

   D The demand for exports

▶ **2** Speculators can have an effect on the exchange rate. Which of the following statements about speculators is true?

   A Speculators will only sell foreign currency

   B Speculators help to stabilise currencies

   C Speculation in foreign currency is illegal in most countries

   D If speculators believe that the price of a currency is going to fall, they will sell that currency

CASE STUDY: THE EXCHANGE RATE BETWEEN THE INDIAN RUPEE AND THE US DOLLAR

India and the USA have been trading partners for many years. For example, India is a popular tourist destination for US travellers. In 2015, more than 1.2 million US residents visited India. In 2016, the US sold US$21 689 million of goods to India. In return, India sold US$45 988 million of goods to the USA. Examples of goods sold by the USA to India include precious stones (diamonds and gold), aircraft, machinery, optical and medical instruments and a range of agricultural goods, such as nuts, beans, cotton and fresh fruit. The USA also sold commercial services to India such as military and government services, education and technical services.

The exchange rate between the US dollar and the Indian rupee has improved for the USA in the last 10 years. Figure 41.5 shows the exchange rate between the two currencies from 2007 to 2017. Figure 41.6 shows the market for rupees where ER_1 is currently the equilibrium exchange rate between the rupee and the US dollar.

▲ The Golden Temple in Amritsar – a popular tourist destination in India

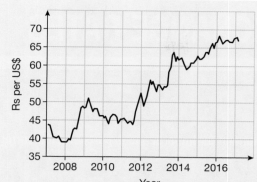

▲ **Figure 41.5** Exchange rate between the US dollar and the Indian rupee, 2007–17

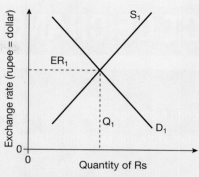

▲ Figure 41.6 Market for rupees

CHAPTER QUESTIONS

1 Calculate India's current balance resulting from trade with the USA in 2016.

2 Describe what an exchange rate is. Use an example from this case to support your explanation.

3 How are exchange rates determined?

4 Show, using a diagram, the likely effect on the exchange rate (in the market for rupees) of an increase in demand for Indian goods from the USA.

5 Show, using a diagram, the likely effect of a fall in the Indian interest rate on the exchange rate (in the market for rupees).

6 Discuss the role played by speculators in the determination of exchange rates.

42 IMPACT OF CHANGING EXCHANGE RATES

LEARNING OBJECTIVES

- Understand how to define exchange appreciation and revaluation
- Understand the impact of exchange rate appreciation on the price and demand for imports and exports and the current account
- Understand how to define exchange depreciation and devaluation
- Understand the impact of exchange rate depreciation on the price and demand for imports and exports and the current account

GETTING STARTED

Exchange rates are not likely to stay the same over a period of time. Exchange rates change or vary when supply and demand conditions for currencies change. For example, if there is an increase in demand for US exports, there will be an increase in demand for dollars and the price of the dollar (or the exchange rate) will rise. Look at the exchange rates below.

CASE STUDY: POUND–EURO EXCHANGE RATE

Sixteen European countries use the euro, including some of the UK's key trading partners such as France, Germany and Spain. In June 2016, the British people voted to leave the EU. This had an immediate impact on the value of the pound. Figure 42.1 shows the exchange rate between the euro and the pound between 2013 and 2017.

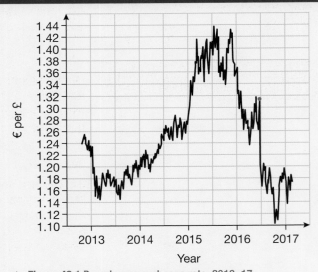

▲ Figure 42.1 Pound–euro exchange rate, 2013–17

Look at Figure 42.1.

1 What was the exchange rate at the end of the period shown?

2 What happened to the value of the pound when the UK voted to leave the EU?

3 Do you think variable exchange rates are good or bad for a firm involved in international trade?

4 Identify the price of three items that you buy regularly. Look up the exchange rates (online or in the newspaper) between your country's currency and that of three other countries. Calculate the cost of these three items in the three other currencies.

WHY DO EXCHANGE RATES CHANGE?

The exchange rate is the price of one currency in terms of another. Like all prices, they can change. This is because market forces determine prices and at any time supply and demand conditions can change. For example, if the UK government raises interest rates, there is likely to be an increase in the demand for pounds as foreign savers take advantage by placing their savings in UK banks. To do this, they have to buy pounds. This increases demand and therefore raises the exchange rate. Figure 42.1 shows how the exchange rate between the pound and the euro has changed in the last few years.

APPRECIATION AND REVALUATION

SUBJECT VOCABULARY

appreciate (of a currency) where the value of a currency rises owing to market forces – the exchange rate increases as a result

revalued (of a currency) when a government fixes a new higher exchange rate

When a nation's currency gets stronger it is said to **appreciate.** This means that a unit of one currency can buy more of another currency. For example, Figure 42.1 shows that the value of the pound against the euro appreciated between the beginning and the middle of 2015. It rose from £1 = €1.28 to £1 = €1.44. This is an appreciation of 12.5 per cent.

In a minority of countries, the exchange rate is fixed, for example Bulgaria, Denmark and Egypt. This means it does not vary – it stays the same all of the time. However, a government might wish to change the exchange so that it reflects current valuations. If the government raises the exchange rate so that it is stronger, the currency is said to have been **revalued**.

DEPRECIATION AND DEVALUATION

SUBJECT VOCABULARY

depreciate (of a currency) where the value of a currency falls owing to market forces – the exchange rate falls as a result

devalued (of a currency) when a government fixes a new lower exchange rate

When a nation's currency gets weaker, it is said to **depreciate**. This means that a unit of one currency buys less of another. For example, Figure 42.1 shows that the value of the pound depreciated sharply against the euro after the UK's vote to leave the EU in June 2016. It fell from £1 = €1.31 to £1 = €1.10 in just a couple of months. This is a depreciation of 16 per cent.

When the exchange rate is fixed, a government might choose to change the exchange rate so that it is weaker. If this happens, the exchange rate will fall and the currency will be **devalued**.

IMPACT OF EXCHANGE RATE APPRECIATION

Changes in the exchange rate can have an impact on the demand for exports and imports. This is because when the exchange rate changes, the prices of exports and imports also change. Look at what happens when the exchange rate rises from £1 = US$1.50 to £1 = US$2.

IMPACT ON EXPORTS

If a UK firm *sells* goods worth £2 million to a US customer, the dollar price at the original exchange rate is US$3 million (£2 million × US$1.50). When the exchange rises, the dollar price of the goods also rises to US$4 million (£2 million × US$2). This means that demand for UK exports is likely to fall because they are now more expensive.

IMPACT ON IMPORTS

If another UK firm *buys* goods worth US$600 000 from a US supplier, the price in pounds at the original exchange rate is £400 000 (US$600 000 × US$1.50). When the exchange rate rises, the sterling price to the importer falls to £300 000 (US$600 000 × US$2). This means that demand for imports is likely to rise because they are cheaper.

IMPACT ON THE CURRENT ACCOUNT

When the exchange rate appreciates, the impact on the current account is likely to be negative. This is because demand for exports is likely to fall (because they are more expensive) and the demand for imports is likely to rise (because they are cheaper). This means that a current account deficit would worsen, for example.

▲ A plane refuelling

ACTIVITY 1

CASE STUDY: IMPACT OF EXCHANGE RATE CHANGES

An airline carrier operating in the UK buys aviation fuel in US dollars. In June 2016, the carrier paid US$900 000 for a fuel order. The same carrier also sells seats to overseas travellers in Spain. In June 2016, the price of a return flight from Madrid to London was £220. Some information relating to exchange rates is given in Table 42.1.

	2016	2017*
£1 =	$1.25	$1.40
£1 =	€ 1.10	€ 1.25

* Estimated for June 2017

▲ **Table 42.1** Exchange rate information

1 Calculate the cost in pounds of the aviation fuel in 2016.

2 Calculate the price in euros of the return flight in 2016.

3 Recalculate the cost in pounds of the aviation fuel at the estimated 2017 exchange rate.

4 Recalculate the price in euros of the return flight at the estimated 2017 exchange rate.

5 How might the demand for aviation fuel and flights be affected by the changes in the exchange rates?

IMPACT OF EXCHANGE RATE DEPRECIATION

A fall in the exchange rate will have the opposite effect on the demand for exports and imports. Look at what happens when the exchange rate falls from £1 = US$1.50 to £1 = US$1.20.

IMPACT ON EXPORTS

If a UK firm *sells* goods worth £2 million to a US customer, the dollar price at the original exchange rate is US$3 million (£2 million × US$1.50). When the exchange rate falls, the dollar price of the goods also falls to US$2.4 million (£2 million × US$1.20). This means that demand for UK exports is likely to rise because they are now cheaper.

IMPACT ON IMPORTS

If another UK firm *buys* goods worth US$600 000 from a US supplier, the price in pounds at the original exchange rate is £400 000 (US$600 000 × US$1.50). When the exchange rate falls, the sterling price to the importer rises to £500 000 (US$600 000 × US$1.20). This means that demand for imports is likely to fall because they are more expensive.

IMPACT ON THE CURRENT ACCOUNT

When the exchange rate depreciates, the impact on the current account is likely to be positive. This is because demand for exports is likely to rise (because they are cheaper) and the demand for imports is likely to fall (because they are more expensive). This means that a current account deficit would fall, for example.

The effects of changes in the exchange rate on the demand for exports and imports are summarised in Table 42.2.

EXCHANGE RATE	PRICE OF EXPORTS	DEMAND FOR EXPORTS	PRICE OF IMPORTS	DEMAND FOR IMPORTS
Rises (appreciation)	Rises	Falls	Falls	Rises
Falls (depreciation)	Falls	Rises	Rises	Falls

▲ **Table 42.2** Summary of the effects of changing exchange rates

ACTIVITY 2

CASE STUDY: NG MOTOR PARTS

Ng Motor Parts, a Chinese automobile parts manufacturer, exports braking systems to a Japanese automobile manufacturer. Each system sells for CNY 500. Ng also imports steel cable from a Japanese supplier. A regular delivery costs JPY 440 000. In May 2016, the exchange rate between the Chinese yuan and the Japanese yen was CNY 1 = JPY 15.

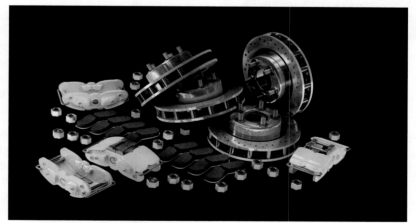

▲ Components for a car braking system

1 Calculate the amount in Japanese yen paid by the Japanese customer for a braking system.

2 Calculate the amount in Chinese yuan paid by Ng for the steel cable.

Ng Motor Parts expects the exchange rate to fall in 12 months' time to CNY 1 = JPY 12. Calculate the effect of this change on the prices of:

3 the export of a breaking system

4 the import of steel cable for Ng Motor Parts.

5 How might the price changes affect demand?

EXCHANGE RATES AND GOVERNMENT POLICY

Over a period of time, a country must pay its way when trading with others. A government should therefore aim to balance the current account. But what can the government do if, for example, there is a large and persistent current account deficit? One approach is to let the currency depreciate. If the exchange rate falls, the price of exports falls and the price of imports rises. Therefore, a deficit on the current account should be reduced because demand for exports would rise and the demand for imports would fall.

How can the government help a currency to depreciate? It can influence the exchange rate by changing interest rates in the economy. Chapter 41 (pages 333–339) showed that if interest rates are reduced, the exchange rate is likely to fall. For example, if UK interest rates were reduced, the value of the pound would fall. This is because the supply of pounds increases on foreign exchange markets as savers withdraw their sterling savings and swap them for another currency. However, there are problems with this policy.

■ The government might not have complete control over the interest rate. For example, in the UK, the Monetary Policy Committee of the Bank of England sets the interest rate.

■ Reducing interest rates to devalue a currency may conflict with other policies. For example, reducing interest rates when a government is also trying to control inflation is likely to cause more inflation.

■ Devaluation will only work if the demand for exports and imports is responsive to price changes. This is discussed below.

EXCHANGE RATE CHANGES AND PRICE ELASTICITY

The effectiveness of government exchange rate policy will depend on the price elasticity of demand for imports and exports. For example, if interest rates in the UK are reduced and the value of the pound falls, a current account balance deficit will only be reduced if the demand for imports and the demand for exports are both elastic. If demand were price inelastic, a fall in the price of exports, for example, would have very little effect on demand and therefore, a current balance deficit would not be significantly reduced.

A country that imports mainly primary goods, such as essential foodstuffs, fuel and minerals, may find it difficult to reduce demand. This is because demand for such goods is likely to be price inelastic and higher prices resulting from a depreciation are not likely to reduce demand significantly. A country that wants to boost exports will be more successful if demand for those exports is price elastic. A depreciation in this case might work if exports are non-essentials such as tourism or consumer durables.

MULTIPLE-CHOICE QUESTIONS

▶ 1 If US\$1 = €1.2, the cost in euros to a German business buying US\$6 700 000 of goods from the USA will be:

A €6 700 000

B €5 583 333

C €8 040 000

D €1 200 000

▶ **2** Which of the following will improve the international competitiveness of a country?

    A An appreciation in the exchange rate

    B A fall in interest rates

    C Higher rates of inflation in that country

    D A depreciation in the exchange rate

ECONOMICS IN PRACTICE

CASE STUDY: THE EFFECTS OF CHANGING EXCHANGE RATES IN THE UEA

Dubai International Airport is the largest and busiest airport in the world. The number of passengers passing through the airport has risen spectacularly since 2010. Figure 42.2 shows that passengers using the airport will more than double by 2020. The airport serves more than 90 different airlines flying to more than 240 different destinations across six continents. The airport complex has experienced significant investment in recent years and this investment is continuing. The number of stands for the very large Airbus A380 passenger jets at the airport is set to increase by 2018 with more coming in the future. The next phase of expansion aims to increase the airport's capacity to 118 million passengers per year by 2023.

Dubai International Airport has a huge shopping complex. In 2014, US$1900 million was spent in the airport – a 7 per cent increase on the previous year. Shops are located in all three of the terminals, however, the largest and most modern is located in Terminal 3. All the stores are open 24 hours a day 7 days a week.

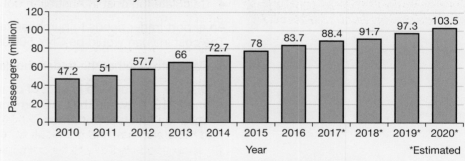

▲ **Figure 42.2** Dubai International airports – passenger traffic, 2010–20

	2017	*2018
AED 1 =	JPY 1.6	JPY 1.8
AED 1 =	CNY 1.9	CNY 1.6
AED 1 =	AUD 0.35	AUD 0.40

*Estimated

▲ Table 42.3 Exchange rate information

▲ Shopping at Dubai International Airport

CHAPTER QUESTIONS

1 Table 42.3 shows that the predictions for the exchange rate in 2018 are different from the actual exchange rates in 2017. Why do exchange rates change?

2 What is the difference between the depreciation of an exchange rate and a devaluation?

In 2017, an airport trader sold goods worth AED 250 to a Japanese traveller.

3 Calculate the cost in yen to the Japanese customer.

In 2017, an Australian traveller purchased some refreshments in an airport café at a cost of AED 65.

4 Calculate the cost in Australian dollars to the passenger.

An airport trader needs to purchase ten new tills from a Chinese manufacturer. The cost in yuan would be CNY 500 000.

5 Calculate whether the trader should buy the tills now or wait until 2018.

6 Discuss the possible impact of changes in the exchange rate (between 2017 and 2018) between the UAE dirham and the Japanese yen and Australian dollar on future airport trade.

EXAM PRACTICE: 2.2 THE GLOBAL ECONOMY

A01   **1**   What is a restriction on the physical quantity of imports coming into a country called? **(1)**

A   Tariff

B   VAT

C   Subsidy

D   Quota

A01   **2**   Sometimes a business will sell goods below cost in a foreign market. What is this practice called? **(1)**

A   Restrictive trade practice

B   Dumping

C   Collusion

D   Price fixing

A02   **3**   Explain **one** reason for the emergence of multinational corporations. **(3)**

The Association of Southeast Asia Nations (ASEAN) is one of the largest trading blocs in the world. It has ten members from the Southeast Asia region. Some of the largest members include Thailand, Vietnam, Malaysia, Indonesia, Philippines and Singapore.

SKILLS ANALYSIS INTERPRETATION

A02 **A03**   **4**   Analyse the impact of this trading bloc on a member country. **(6)**

Like many countries around the world Vietnam has embraced globalisation. In a survey, 95 per cent of Vietnamese respondents agreed that 'trade was good'. The survey also revealed that Vietnamese people thought that trade resulting from globalisation brought jobs and raised wages. The US is one of Vietnam's main trading partners. In 2015, Vietnam sold US$30 000 million of goods to the USA, making it the top market for Vietnamese exports.

SKILLS CRITICAL THINKING REASONING ADAPTIVE INTERPRETATION LEARNING CREATIVITY

A02 **A03** **A04**   **5**   Assess the likely impact of globalisation on a country such as Vietnam. **(9)**

(Total = 20 marks)

PREPARING FOR YOUR INTERNATIONAL GCSE ECONOMICS EXAMINATION (PAPER 1)

PAPER 1 MICROECONOMICS AND BUSINESS ECONOMICS

This complete practice paper will help you prepare for your International GCSE Paper 1 examination.

QUESTION 1

A01

(a) Which of the following will cause the supply curve for motor cars to shift to the left? **(1)**
    A A rise in incomes
    B A fall in indirect taxes on cars
    C A rise in the cost of wages paid to car workers
    D A fall in the cost of raw materials in car manufacturing

A02

(b) Which of the following goods or services are most likely to be provided by the private sector? **(1)**
    A Public transport
    B Policing
    C Environmental services
    D Hotels

A01

(c) What is meant by opportunity cost? **(2)**

A01

(d) Define the term collusion. **(1)**

(e) Define the term supply. **(1)**

A01

A hotel in Sri Lanka incurred fixed costs of LKR 400 000 in January 2017. The variable cost per room let in January was LKR 1000. The hotel charges LKR 2000 per night for a room.

SKILLS PROBLEM SOLVING   **A02**

(f) Calculate the profit made by the hotel in January 2017 if a total of 430 rooms were let. You are advised to show your working. **(2)**

Figure 1 below shows a market in disequilibrium. The current price is £20.

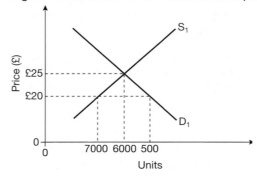

Figure 1

A02

(g) Calculate the revenue that producers would generate at this price. You are advised to show your working. **(3)**

SKILLS ▸ CRITICAL THINKING   **A02**

(h) Explain what might happen in the above market if production costs fell.   (3)

In 2016, the UK voted to leave the EU. One of the implications of this decision is that eventually there will be a restriction in the numbers of migrants entering the country. Some businesses have said that this could cause them difficulties in the future when recruiting staff. Around 6 million migrants are currently working in the UK – many in health care, agriculture, hotels and restaurants.

SKILLS ▸ CRITICAL THINKING ANALYSIS   **A02** **A03**

(i) With reference to the data above and your knowledge of economics, analyse the impact of this decision on labour markets in the UK.   (6)

(Total for Question 1 = 20 marks)

QUESTION 2

A01

(a) If price elasticity of demand for a firm's product is – 2, a 10 per cent increase in price will result in which of the following?   (1)
   A 10 per cent increase in revenue
   B 10 per cent decrease in demand
   C 20 per cent increase in revenue
   D 20 per cent decrease in demand

A02

(b) Which of the following is an activity in the primary sector?   (1)
   A Software development
   B Fishing
   C Road construction
   D Insurance

A01

(c) (i) State the formula for price elasticity of supply.   (1)

A02

   (ii) Calculate the price elasticity of supply for a product when price increases by 12 per cent and the quantity supplied increases by 18 per cent. You are advised to show your working.   (2)

A01

(d) State **one** factor of production.   (1)

A proportion of government expenditure is often allocated to policing. This money may be spent on the wages paid to police officers and the equipment that might be needed by officers when carrying out their duties. Such expenditure is required because of market failure.

A01

(e) What is meant by market failure?   (2)

SKILLS ▸ CRITICAL THINKING   **A02**

(f) Explain the role of the public sector in the production of goods and services.   (3)

Victor Akenga runs a small tour company based in Nairobi, Kenya. He takes groups of up to eight people on 3-day tours of the Masai Mara National Reserve. The business is profitable and in the last 9 years Victor has made a net profit of around KES 200 000 p.a. This is about twice as big as Kenya's GDP per capita. Several of Victor's business friends often ask him why he does not grow his successful business. He says that he is very content running his small enterprise employing just two other people. He can offer a very personal service that some of the big tour operators cannot match.

SKILLS ▸ CRITICAL THINKING REASONING ADAPTIVE LEARNING CREATIVITY   **A02** **A03** **A04**

(g) With reference to the data above and your knowledge of economics, assess the advantages and disadvantages of remaining a small company.   (9)

(Total for Question 2 = 20 marks)

QUESTION 3

Table 1 below shows the income elasticities of demand for four different products: A, B, C and D.

PRODUCT	INCOME ELASTICITY OF DEMAND
A	1.9
B	−2.1
C	0.4
D	−0.6

Table 1

A01

(a) Which of these products is a normal good and is income elastic? **(1)**

    A

    B

    C

    D

A business has fixed costs of US$100 000 and variable costs of US$5 per unit. Units of output are sold for US$25.

A01

(b) What is total variable cost if 50 000 units are produced? **(1)**

    A US$100 000

    B US$250 000

    C US$350 000

    D US$1 250 000

Figure 2 shows a labour market. The equilibrium wage is US$15 per hour. At this wage rate 300 000 workers are employed.

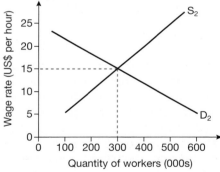

Figure 2

A02

(c) Show on the diagram the impact of a government imposing a minimum wage of US$20 per hour. Show clearly the number of workers that would be employed in the market. **(3)**

Jushna Patel loves football and her favourite team is Aston Villa. Once a month during the season she is taken to Villa Park by her uncle to watch the team play. However, one weekend when she was due to attend a match, she telephoned her uncle to cancel the trip. Four of Jushna's friends had persuaded her to go to the cinema to see a newly released film. Jushna really wanted to go to the match but peer pressure had made her change her mind.

SKILLS ANALYSIS INTERPRETATION

A02

A03

(d) With reference to the data above and your knowledge of economics, analyse the reasons why consumers may not maximise their benefit. **(6)**

In 2014, the Swaziland authorities announced that it wanted to increase competition in the mobile telephone market. At the time, MTN, a South African telecoms company, operated as a monopoly. Around 800 000 of the 1.2 million population were using their services. The authorities said they would give new operators in Swaziland a 10-year, non-exclusive license. In return, they would have to pay the government a 5 per cent royalty. However, in 2016, MTN still had a monopoly and was used by 57 per cent of the population. A report also said MTN was charging high prices. The cost of 300 megabytes of data in Swaziland was ZAR 149. In South Africa, the same amount of data cost ZAR 79.

SKILLS ▶ CRITICAL THINKING
REASONING
INTERPRETATION
ADAPTIVE LEARNING
CREATIVITY

A02
A03
A04

(e) With reference to the data above and your knowledge of economics, assess the impact of monopolies in markets such as telecoms. **(9)**

(Total for Question 3 = 20 marks)

QUESTION 4

In 2015, the working population (those aged between 16 and 59) in China was 911 million. This was 4.87 million lower than 2014. Figure 3 shows the proportion of China's working population employed in each economic sector.

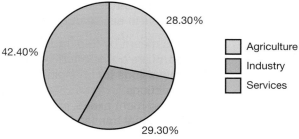

Figure 3

SKILLS ▶ PROBLEM SOLVING

A02

(a) Calculate the number of people employed in the tertiary sector in China in 2015. You are advised to show your workings. **(2)**

In 2016, VTech, the world's largest producer of electronic learning toys, was given permission by the Competition and Markets Authority (CMA) in the UK to buy US rival LeapFrog Enterprises. The deal, worth US$72 million, was investigated by the CMA since it was felt that the merging of the world's two largest suppliers of learning toys would reduce competition in the market. However, after the investigation, the CMA said that competition in the evolving and innovative toy industry would not be threatened. The CMA was confident that choice in the market for learning toys and child tablets would not be reduced, nor would the takeover lead to higher prices. During the investigation the CMA consulted consumers, retailers and a range of toy manufacturers.

The chairman of VTech said, 'We have always believed that the combination of VTech and LeapFrog will give consumers greater choice and ensure ongoing innovation of electronic learning toys.' In the last financial year, VTech's revenue was US$982.9 million.

SKILLS ▶ CRITICAL THINKING
ANALYSIS
INTERPRETATION

A02
A03

(b) With reference to the data above and your knowledge of economics, analyse the factors which might influence the growth of firms. **(6)**

SKILLS ▶ CRITICAL THINKING
REASONING
INTERPRETATION
DECISION MAKING
ADAPTIVE LEARNING
CREATIVITY

A02
A03
A04

(c) With reference to the data above and your knowledge of economics, evaluate the advantages of large firms to consumers. **(12)**

(Total for Question 4 = 20 marks)
(Total for Paper = 80 marks)

PREPARING FOR YOUR INTERNATIONAL GCSE ECONOMICS EXAMINATION (PAPER 2)

PAPER 2 MACROECONOMICS AND THE GLOBAL ECONOMY

This complete practice paper will help you prepare for your International GCSE Paper 2 examination.

QUESTION 1

A01

(a) Which of the following tax changes is most likely to help protect the environment? (1)
   A Decrease in income tax
   B Increase in income tax
   C Increase in landfill tax
   D Decrease in excise duty on petrol

A02

(b) What is meant by free trade? (1)
   A Exports are transported free of charge
   B Commissions for changing currency are waived for international trade transactions
   C A government allows open access to all markets in its country
   D International transactions are free of indirect taxes such as VAT

A01

(c) What is meant by absolute poverty? (2)

A01

(d) Describe **one** reason for reducing poverty. (2)

In 2015, a sample of goods and services cost US$304 in 2015. In 2016, the same goods and services cost US$316.

SKILLS PROBLEM SOLVING

A02

(e) Calculate the rate of inflation in this example. You are advised to show your working. (2)

A02

(f) Using the diagram below, draw the effects of an increase in the interest rate on the equilibrium exchange rate and the quantity of currency. Label the new curve, the new equilibrium exchange rate and quantity. (3)

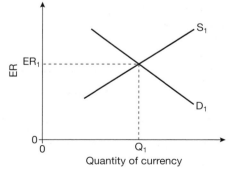

Figure 1

In January 2017, the level of unemployment in Portugal was 10.5 per cent.

SKILLS CRITICAL THINKING

A02

(g) Explain one impact of unemployment on tax revenue. (3)

SKILLS CRITICAL THINKING   **A02**
                             A03

(h) Analyse how a government might use fiscal policy to reduce
    unemployment.   (6)

(Total for Question 1 = 20 marks)

QUESTION 2

A01

(a) Which of the following is used to measure economic growth?   (1)
    A RPI
    B CPI
    C GDP
    D PPC

In 2016, the Chinese government placed a tariff on 'grain-oriented electrical
steel' imported from the European Union, South Korea and Japan. It said this
was necessary because imports from abroad were damaging the Chinese steel
industry.

A02

(b) Which one of the following diagrams shows the market for grain-orientated
    electrical steel following the imposition of the tariff?   (1)

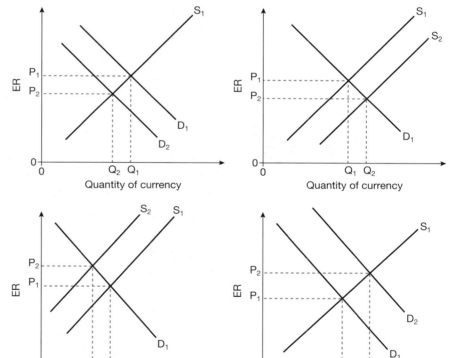

A01 (c) State **one** possible reason for a surplus on the current account.   (1)

A02 (d) What is meant by globalisation?   (2)

A number of reports by the Vietnamese press claim that 'bumbling'
infrastructure projects have resulted in areas of natural beauty becoming
littered with rubbish.

A02 (e) Explain **one** method a government might use to protect the environment. (3)

GDP per capita in Sweden was US$55 186 in 2015.

SKILLS CRITICAL THINKING   **A02** (f) Explain **one** limitation of using GDP as a measure of economic growth.   (3)

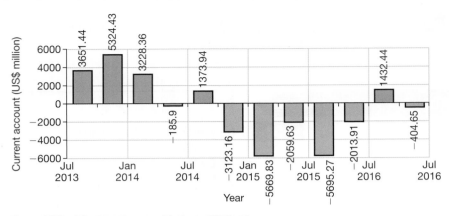

Figure 3 Nigeria's current account balance 2013–16

Nigeria's economy has been struggling since 2014 after the global price of oil fell sharply. Nigeria's economy relies heavily on oil production for employment, income and export revenue. The exchange rate has depreciated significantly and as a result the rate of inflation in Nigeria has risen to around 18 per cent in January 2017. Also, earnings from oil sales will fall since the price of oil is set in US dollars. This is because when the exchange rate falls, Nigeria gets fewer dollars for its currency. The balance on the current account has therefore taken a turn for the worse and the country is running out of foreign reserves.

SKILLS ▸ CRITICAL THINKING
REASONING
ADAPTIVE LEARNING
CREATIVITY

A02
A03
A04

(g) Assess the impact on Nigeria's economy of a depreciating exchange rate.

(9)

(Total for Question 2 = 20 marks)

QUESTION 3

A01

(a) Which type of unemployment occurs when people are temporarily unemployed as they move from one job to another? (1)
   A Voluntary unemployment
   B Structural unemployment
   C Cyclical unemployment
   D Frictional unemployment

A01

(b) What is the main purpose of supply side policies? (1)
   A To increase aggregate demand in the economy
   B To increase the productive potential of the economy
   C To reduce inflation
   D To reduce unemployment

A02

(c) Explain **one** reason for the use of protectionism by a government. (3)

In some countries, governments have had to accept higher levels of unemployment when trying to reduce inflation.

SKILLS ▸ ANALYSIS
INTERPRETATION

A02
A03

(d) Explain how the use of monetary policy to reduce inflation might result in such a trade-off. (6)

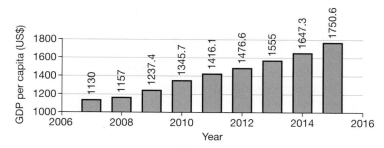

Figure 4 GDP per capita in India, 2006–16

In recent years, India has enjoyed relatively high levels of economic growth. For example, since 2006, growth has been over 7 per cent in most years. This has increased GDP per capita and reduced poverty levels in the country. However, concerns have been raised about damage to the environment resulting from increased economic activity. For example, a report by the World Bank reckoned that environmental degradation cost India about US$80 billion a year.

SKILLS ▶ CRITICAL THINKING **A02**
REASONING
INTERPRETATION **A03**
ADAPTIVE LEARNING
CREATIVITY **A04**

(e) Assess the impact of economic growth in India.   **(9)**

(Total for Question 3 = 20 marks)

QUESTION 4

Table 1 shows the government expenditure forecasts for 2016 and 2017 for New Zealand.

	2016	2017
Forecast government expenditure (NZD million)	74 935	77 110

Table 1

SKILLS ▶ PROBLEM SOLVING **A02**

(a) Calculate to one decimal place the percentage change in forecast government expenditure in New Zealand between 2016 and 2017. You are advised to show your working.   **(2)**

In 2015, global financial direct investment (FDI) amounted to US$713 000 million. The money supported 11 930 projects and created around 1.9 million jobs. India replaced China as the top recipient of FDI while the USA was the top source.

SKILLS ▶ CRITICAL THINKING **A02**
ANALYSIS
INTERPRETATIVE **A03**

(b) Analyse the impact on the USA of outward FDI.   **(6)**

Unemployment in Turkey was around 12 per cent at the beginning of January 2017. This was almost double the rate of 2012. However, according to the Organisation for Economic Co-operation and Development (OECD), unemployment rates for Turkish youths are worse. About 28 per cent of the 15–29 age group in Turkey are classified as NEET — youths 'not in employment, education or training'. The OECD said that the NEET group costs Turkey about US$25 000 million per year. This is around 3.4 per cent of GDP.

SKILLS ▶ CRITICAL THINKING **A02**
REASONING
INTERPRETATION **A03**
DECISION MAKING
ADAPTIVE LEARNING **A04**
CREATIVITY

(c) Evaluate the impact of unemployment in country such as Turkey.   **(12)**

(Total for Question 4 = 20 marks)

(Total for Paper = 80 marks)

COMMAND WORDS

The table below lists the command words that may be used in question papers for the Pearson Edexcel International GCSE in Economics and an outline of what each type of question requires students to do.

COMMAND WORD	THIS TYPE OF QUESTION WILL REQUIRE STUDENTS TO:
(MULTIPLE-CHOICE QUESTION)	Select one or more correct answer from a choice of answers. These questions test recall of knowledge from the specification content or require a calculation to reach the correct answer.
DEFINE	Define a term from the specification content.
STATE	Give an answer, no longer than a sentence, referring to a piece of information from the specification content.
WHAT IS MEANT BY	Define the term x where x is a term from the specification content. There must be two separate parts to the definition.
CALCULATE	Use mathematical skills to reach the answer, based on given data. Calculators may be used and workings should be given.
DRAW	Draw a diagram containing two/three separate awardable points.
EXPLAIN	Give a statement of fact, with two further expansion points. These may expand on each other, or both from the same fact. The answer will be placed in context by the question.
ANALYSE	Write an extended answer, requiring the expansion and exploration of a economic concept or issue. The answer will be placed in context by the question.
ASSESS	Write an extended answer, using given information to weigh up factors and compare them in an economics context.
EVALUATE	Write an extended answer, applying knowledge of specification content, to reach a supported conclusion about an economic situation.

Examples of how these command words are used in Paper 1 and Paper 2 can be found in the *Pearson Edexcel International GCSE in Economics Sample Assessment Materials* for this qualification.

GLOSSARY

absolute poverty where people do not have enough resources to meet all of their basic human needs

administration activities involved with managing and organising the work of a company or organisation

aggregate demand total demand in the economy including consumption, investment, government expenditure and exports minus imports

aggregate supply total amount of goods and services produced in a country at a given price level in a given time period

anti-competitive practices (or restrictive trade practices) attempts by firms to prevent or restrict competition

appreciate (of a currency) where the value of a currency rises due to market forces – the exchange rate increases as a result

assembly plants factory where parts are put together to make a final product

assets things or resources belonging to an individual or a business that has value or the power to earn money

austerity official action taken by a government in order to reduce the amount of money that it spends or the amount that people spend

balance of payments record of all transactions relating to international trade

balance of trade or visible balance difference between visible exports and visible imports

barriers to entry obstacles that might discourage a firm from entering a market

base rate rate of interest set by government or regional central banks for lending to other banks, which in turn influences all other rates in the economy

basic economic problem allocation of a nation's scarce resources between competing uses that represent infinite wants

bi-lateral trade agreement trade deal between only two countries

boom peak of the economic cycle where GDP is growing at its fastest; time when business activity increases rapidly, so that the demand for goods increases, prices and wages go up, and unemployment falls

boom and bust when an economy regularly becomes more active and successful and then suddenly fails

budget government's spending and revenue plans for the next year

budget deficit amount by which government spending is greater than government revenue

bulk buying buying goods in large quantities, which is usually cheaper than buying in small quantities

capital and financial account that part of the balance of payments where flows of savings, investment and currencies are recorded

capital goods those purchased by firms and used to produce other goods such as factories machinery, tools and equipment

capital intensive production that relies more heavily on machinery relative to labour

cartel where a group of firms or countries join together and agree on pricing or output levels in the market

closed shop company or factory where all the workers must belong to a particular trade union

commodities product that can be sold to make a profit, especially one in its basic form before it has been used or changed in an industrial process; examples of commodities are farm products and metals

competition rivalry that exists between firms when trying to sell goods to the same group of customers

complementary goods goods purchased together because they are consumed together

consumer goods those purchased by households such as food, confectionery, cars, tablets and furniture

consumer price index (CPI) measure of the general price level (excluding housing costs)

consumption amount of goods, services, energy or natural materials used in a particular period of time

contractionary fiscal policy fiscal measures designed to reduce demand in the economy

cost-push inflation inflation caused by rising business costs

costs expenses that must be met when setting up and running a business

current account part of the balance of payments where all exports and imports are recorded

current account deficit when value of imports exceeds the value of exports

current account surplus when value of exports exceeds the value of imports

current balance difference between total exports and total imports (visible and invisible)

cyclical or **demand deficient unemployment** unemployment caused by falling demand as a result of a downturn in the economic cycle

de-industrialisation decline in manufacturing

deflation period where the level of aggregate demand is falling

demand curve line drawn on a graph that shows how much of a good will be bought at different prices

demand schedule table of the quantity demanded of a good at different price levels – can be used to calculate the expected quantity demanded

demand-pull inflation inflation caused by too much demand in the economy relative to supply

depreciate (of a currency) where the value of a currency falls due to market forces – the exchange rate falls as a result

depression or **slump** bottom of the economic cycle where GDP starts to fall with significant increases in unemployment

derived demand demand that arises because there is demand for another good

devalued (of a currency) when a government fixes a new lower exchange rate

direct taxes taxes levied on the income earned by firms and individuals

discretionary expenditure non-essential spending or spending that is not automatic

diseconomies of scale rising average costs when a firm becomes too big

disposable income income that is available to someone over a period of time to spend; it includes state benefits but excludes direct taxes

diversified if a company or economy diversifies, it increases the range of goods or services it produces

dividend part of a company's profit that is divided among the people with shares in the company

division of labour breaking down of the production process into small parts with each worker allocated to a specific task

downturn period in the economic cycle where GDP grows, but more slowly

dumping where an overseas firm sells large quantities of a product below cost in the domestic market

economic growth increase in the level output by a nation

economies of scale falling average costs due to expansion

economy system that attempts to solve the basic economic problem

effective demand amount of a good people are willing to buy at given prices over a given period of time supported by the ability to pay

elastic demand change in price results in a greater change in the quantity demanded (alternative term: price elastic)

elastic supply change in price results in a proportionately greater change in the quantity supplied (alternative term: price elastic)

embargo official order to stop trade with another country

enterprises companies, organisations or businesses

entrepreneurs individuals who organise the other factors of production and risk their own money in a business venture

equilibrium price price at which supply and demand are equal

excess demand where demand is greater than supply and there are shortages in the market

excess supply where supply is greater than demand and there are unsold goods in the market

exchange rate price of one currency in terms of another

excise duty government tax on certain goods, such as cigarettes, alcoholic drinks and petrol that are sold in the country

expansionary fiscal policy fiscal measures designed to stimulate demand in the economy

expenditure spending by a government, usually a national government

exports goods and services sold overseas

external benefits positive spillover effects of consumption or production – they bring benefits to third parties

external costs negative spillover effects of consumption or production – they affect third parties in a negative way

external economies of scale cost benefits that all firms in an industry can enjoy when the industry expands

factors of production resources used to produce goods and services, which include land, labour, capital and enterprise

fast-moving consumer good (FMCG) goods, especially food, that sell very quickly and in large amounts

finite having an end or a limit

fiscal deficit amount by which government spending exceeds government revenue

fiscal policy decisions about government spending, taxation and levels of borrowing that affect aggregate demand in the economy

fiscal surplus amount by which government revenue exceeds government spending

fit for purpose usable (by a consumer) for the purpose for which it was intended

fixed capital stock of 'man-made' resources, such as machines and tools, used to help make goods and services

fixed costs (also known as overheads) costs that do not vary with the level of output

foreign exchange market market where foreign currencies can be bought and sold

free rider individual who enjoys the benefit of a good but allows others to pay for it

free trade situation in which the goods coming into or going out of a country are not controlled or taxed

frictional unemployment when workers are unemployed for a short period of time as they move from one job to another

globalisation growing interconnection of the world's economies

goods things that are produced in order to be sold

gross domestic product (GDP) market value of all final goods and services produced in a period (usually yearly), an internationally recognised measure of national income

hostile takeover takeover that the company being taken over does not want or agree to

human capital value of the workforce or an individual worker

hyperinflation very high levels of inflation; rising prices get out of control

imports goods and services bought from overseas

income elasticity of demand responsiveness of demand to a change in income

income inequality differences in income that exist between the different groups of earners in society, that is, the gap between the rich and the poor

indirect taxes taxes levied on spending, such as VAT

inelastic demand change in price results in a proportionately smaller change in the quantity demanded (alternative term: price inelastic)

inelastic supply change in price results in a proportionately smaller change in the quantity supplied (alternative term: price inelastic)

infant industries new industries yet to establish themselves

inferior goods goods for which demand will fall if income rises or rise if income falls

infinite without limits

inflation rate at which prices rise, a general and continuing rise in prices

innovative commercial exploitation of a new invention

interdependence where the actions of one country or large firm will have a direct effect on others

interest rates price paid to lenders for borrowed money; it is the price of money

internal economies of scale cost benefits that an individual firm can enjoy when it expands

inverse relationship (between price and quantity demanded) when price goes up, the quantity demanded falls and when the price goes down the quantity demanded rises

invisible trade trade in services

job rotation practice of regularly changing the person who does a particular job

labour intensive production that relies more heavily on labour relative to machinery

labour mobility ease with which workers can move geographically and occupationally between different jobs

labour people used on production

laying off to stop employing someone because there is no work for them to do

liabilities amount of debt that is owed or must be paid

Lorenz curve graphical representation of the degree of income or wealth inequality in a country

macroeconomics study of large economic systems such as those of a whole country or area of the world

market clearing price price at which the amount supplied in a market matches exactly the amount demanded

market failure where markets lead to inefficiency

market niche smaller market, usually within a large market or industry

market segments groups of customers that share similar characteristics, such as age, income, interests and social class

maximise to increase something such as profit, satisfaction or income as much as possible

menu costs costs to firms of having to make repeated price changes

merit goods goods that are under-provided by the private sector

microeconomics study of small economic systems that are part of national or international systems

minimum wage minimum amount per hour which most workers are legally entitled to be paid

mixed economy economy where goods and services are provided by both the private and the public sectors

monetarists economists who believe there is a strong link between growth in the money supply and inflation

monetary policy use of interest rates and the money supply to control aggregate demand in the economy

money supply amount of money circulating in the economy

monopoly situation where there is one dominant seller in a market

monopolies situation where a business activity is controlled by only one company or by the government, and other companies do not compete with it

mortgage legal arrangement where you borrow money from a financial institution in order to buy land or a house, and you pay back the money over a period of years; if you do not make your regular payments, the lender normally has the right to take the property and sell it in order to get back their money

multinational corporations (MNCs) companies that operate in many different countries

national debt total amount of money owed by a country

national income value of income, output or expenditure over a period of time

nationalised industries public corporations previously part of the private sector that were taken into state ownership

natural monopoly situation that occurs when one firm in an industry can serve the entire market at a lower cost than would be possible if the industry were composed of many smaller firms

new entrant company that starts to sell goods or services in a market where they have not sold them before, or one of these goods or services

niche market market for a product or service, perhaps an expensive or unusual one, that does not have many buyers, but that may make good profits for companies that sell it

normal goods goods for which demand will increase if income increases or fall if income falls

offset if something, such as a cost or sum of money, offsets another cost it has the effect of reducing or balancing it, so that the situation remains the same

offshoring practice of getting work done in another country in order to save money

oligopoly market dominated by a few large firms

opportunity cost cost of the next best alternative given up (when making a choice)

overheat if an economy overheats, demand rises too fast, causing prices and imports to rise, a situation that governments may try to correct by raising taxes and interest rates

patent licence that grants permission to operate as a sole producer of a newly designed product

perfectly elastic (demand) where PED = ∞ (an increase in price will result in zero demand)

perfectly elastic (supply) where PES = ∞ (producers will supply an infinite amount at the given price)

perfectly inelastic (demand) where PED = 0 (a change in price will result in no change in the quantity demanded)

perfectly inelastic (supply) where PES = 0 (the quantity supplied is fixed and cannot be adjusted whatever the price)

piece rate amount of money that is paid for each item a worker produces, rather than for the time taken to make it

policy instruments tools governments use to implement their policies, such as interest rates, rates of taxation, levels of government spending

price elasticity of demand responsiveness of demand to a change in price

price elasticity of supply responsiveness of supply to a change in price

price maker where a dominant business is able to set the price charged in the whole market

price war where one firm in the industry reduces price causing others to do the same

primary income money received from the loan of production factors abroad

primary sector/industry production involving the extraction of raw materials from the earth

private benefits rewards to third parties of an economic activity, such as consumption or production

private costs costs of an economic activity to individuals and firms

private sector provision of goods and services by businesses that are owned by individuals or groups of individuals

privatisation act of selling a company or activity controlled by the government to private investors

product differentiation attempt by a firm to distinguish its product from that of rival

production possibility curve (PPC) line that shows the different combinations of two goods an economy can produce if all resources are used up

production process that involves converting resources into goods or services

productivity rate at which goods are produced, and the amount produced in relation to the work, time and money needed to produce them

progressive taxation where the proportion of income paid in tax rises as the income of the taxpayer rises

proportionate relationship (between price and the quantity supplied) when the price goes up, the quantity supplied also goes up and when the price goes down the quantity supplied goes down

protectionism approach used by governments to protect domestic producers

public goods goods that are not likely to be provided by the private sector

public sector government organisations that provide goods and services in the economy

purchasing power of money amount of goods and services that can be bought with a fixed sum of money

quantitative easing buying of financial assets, such as government bonds from commercial banks, which results in a flow of money from the central bank to commercial banks

quota physical limit on the quantity of imports allowed into a country

rate of interest price of borrowing money

raw materials substances used to make a product

real economy part of the economy that is concerned with actually producing goods and services, as opposed to the part of the economy that is concerned with buying and selling on the financial markets

recession period of temporary economic decline during which trade and industrial activity are reduced, generally identified by a fall in GDP in two successive quarters

regressive taxation tax system that places the burden of the tax more heavily on the poor

relative poverty poverty that is defined relative to existing living standards for the average individual

repatriation (of profit) where a multinational returns the profits from an overseas venture to the country where it is based, typically from a developing country to a developed country (not often the other way around)

reserves amount of something valuable, such as oil, gas or metal ore

retail price index (RPI) measure of the general price level which includes house prices and council tax

revalued (of a currency) when a government fixes a new higher exchange rate

revenue money that a business receives over a period of time, especially from selling goods or services

saturated market in which there is more of a product for sale than people want to buy

scale size of a business

scarce resources amount of resources available when supply is limited

seasonal unemployment unemployment caused when seasonal workers, such as those in the holiday industry, are laid off because the season has ended

secondary income government transfers to and from overseas agencies such as the EU

secondary picketing workers in one workplace or company strike in a group at a particular location in order to support the striking workers in a different workplace or company

secondary sector/industry production involving the processing of raw materials into finished and semi-finished goods

shareholders people or organisations that owns shares in a company

shift in the demand curve movement to the left or right of the entire demand curve when there is a change in any factor affecting demand except the price

shift in the supply curve movement to the left or right of the entire supply curve when there is any change in the conditions of supply except the price

shoe leather costs costs to firms and consumers of searching for new suppliers when inflation is high

social benefits benefits of an economic activity to society as well as to the individual or firm

social costs costs of an economic activity to society as well as the individual or firm

specialisation production of a limited range of goods by individuals, firms, regions or countries

spillover effects effect that one situation or problem has on another situation

structural unemployment unemployment caused by changes in the structure of the economy such as the decline in an industry

subsidiaries companies that are at least half-owned by another company

subsidy money that is paid by a government or organisation to make prices lower, reduce the cost of producing goods or providing a service, usually to encourage production of a certain good

substitute goods goods bought as an alternative to another but perform the same function

supply amount that producers are willing to offer for sale at different prices in a given period of time

supply curve line drawn on a graph which shows how much of a good sellers are willing to supply at different prices

supply side policies government measures designed to increase aggregate supply in the economy

takeover act of getting control of a company by buying over 50 per cent of its shares

tariffs or customs duties tax on imports to make them more expensive

tax avoidance practice of trying to pay less tax in legal ways

taxes amount of money that you must pay to the government according to your income/profit, property or goods, which is used to pay for public services

tertiary sector/industry production of services in the economy

total cost fixed costs and variable costs added together

total revenue amount of money generated from the sale of goods calculated by multiplying price by quantity

trade barriers measures designed to restrict imports

trade liberalisation move towards greater free trade through the removal of trade barriers

trading blocs groups of countries situated in the same region that join together and enjoy trade free of tariffs, quotas and other forms of trade barrier

transactions payment, or the process of making one

unemployment when those actively seeking work are unable to find a job

unitary elasticity (with regard to supply) where PES = 1 (a change in price will be matched by an identical change in the quantity supplied)

unitary elasticity where PED = −1 (the responsiveness of demand is proportionately equal to the change in price)

unsustainable growth economic growth that it is not possible to sustain without causing environmental problems

value-added products or services have an increased value because work has been done on them, they have been combined with other products and so on; this increase in value to the buyer is what the buyer pays for

valued-added tax (VAT) tax on some goods and services – businesses pay value-added tax on most goods and services they buy and if they are VAT registered, charge value-added tax on the goods and services they sell

variable costs costs that change when output levels change

variables something that affects a situation in a way that means you cannot be sure what will happen

ventures new business activities or projects that involve taking risks

visible trade trade in physical goods

voluntary unemployment unemployment resulting from people choosing not to work

wage rate the amount of money paid to workers for their services over a period of time (that is, the price of labour)

wholesalers person or company that sells goods in large quantities to businesses, rather than to the general public

working capital or circulating capital resources used up in production such as raw materials and components

World Trade Organization international organisation that promotes free trade by persuading countries to abolish tariffs and other barriers; it polices free trade agreements, settles trade disputes between governments and organises trade negotiations

INDEX